KT-573-602

Maximum Accessibility

Making Your Web Site More Usable for Everyone

PARK LEARNING CENTRE
UNIVERSITY OF GLOUCESTERSHIRE
PO Box 220, The Park, Cheltenham, GL50 2QF
Tel: (01242) 532721

John M. Slatin, Ph.D.
Sharron Rush

✦Addison-Wesley

Boston ▪ San Francisco ▪ New York ▪ Toronto ▪ Montreal
London ▪ Munich ▪ Paris ▪ Madrid
Capetown ▪ Sydney ▪ Tokyo ▪ Singapore ▪ Mexico City

Many of the designations used by manufacturers and sellers to distinguish their products are claimed as trademarks. Where those designations appear in this book, and Addison-Wesley was aware of a trademark claim, the designations have been printed with initial capital letters or in all capitals.

The authors and publisher have taken care in the preparation of this book, but make no expressed or implied warranty of any kind and assume no responsibility for errors or omissions. No liability is assumed for incidental or consequential damages in connection with or arising out of the use of the information or programs contained herein.

The publisher offers discounts on this book when ordered in quantity for bulk purchases and special sales. For more information, please contact:

U.S. Corporate and Government Sales
(800) 382-3419
corpsales@pearsontechgroup.com

For sales outside of the U.S., please contact:

International Sales
(317) 581-3793
international@pearsontechgroup.com

Visit Addison-Wesley on the Web: www.awprofessional.com

Library of Congress Cataloging-in-Publication Data

Slatin, John M.
     Maximum accessibility : Making Your Web Site More Usable for Everyone /
John M. Slatin, Sharron Rush.
          p. cm.
     Includes bibliographical references and index.
     ISBN 0-201-77422-4 (Paperback : alk. paper)
     1. Web sites—Design.   2. Computers and people with disabilities.
I. Rush, Sharron.   II. Title.

TK5105.888 .S593 2003
005.7'2—dc21   2002006548

Copyright © 2003 by Pearson Education, Inc.

All rights reserved. No part of this publication may be reproduced, stored in a retrieval system, or transmitted, in any form, or by any means, electronic, mechanical, photocopying, recording, or otherwise, without the prior consent of the publisher. Printed in the United States of America. Published simultaneously in Canada.

For information on obtaining permission for use of material from this work, please submit a written request to:

Pearson Education, Inc.
Rights and Contracts Department
75 Arlington Street, Suite 300
Boston, MA 02116
Fax: (617) 848-7047

ISBN 0-201-77422-4
Text printed on recycled paper
1 2 3 4 5 6 7 8 9 10—CRS—0605040302
First printing, September 2002

3703526551

Maximum Accessibility

PARK LEARNING CENTRE
The Park Cheltenham
Gloucestershire GL50 2RH
Telephone: 01242 714333

UNIVERSITY OF
GLOUCESTERSHIRE
at Cheltenham and Gloucester

NORMAL LOAN

2 2 NOV 2007

- 2 DEC 2004
- 4 FEB 2005
2 4 FEB 2005
- 6 JUN 2005
- 3 OCT 2005
- 8 MAR 2006
1 9 JAN 2007
1 9 FEB 2007
2 9 OCT 2007

WITHDRAWN

This book is dedicated,
with love and gratitude and respect,
to Anna Carroll and Ron Hicks.

Contents

Foreword

Accessibility and usability are two tightly intertwined concepts. The first important relationship is that increased accessibility for users with disabilities almost always leads directly to improved usability for *all* users. Guideline number one for all user interface design has always been simplicity. This is true whether designing for blind users, old users, children, international users, mobile users, soldiers on the battlefield, or even the average business executive accessing a Web site or the company intranet on a laptop over a slow modem line from a hotel room during a business trip. Simplicity helps everybody.

Going beyond simplicity, the primary goal of the specific accessibility guidelines discussed in this book may be to help users with disabilities, but most of the guidelines will also improve usability for many other groups of users.

The second significant connection between accessibility and usability is the importance of focusing on the performance, ease of use, and ease of learning for actual users when designing Web sites to accommodate users with disabilities. It is not enough that users are *capable* of accessing a Web site or intranet. It must also be *easy, fast,* and *pleasant* to do so, and the interaction must minimize the probability for user error. If you can get in but it's a pain to be there, then users will not feel welcome. It's better to be allowed in than to be kept out, but it's even better when the user experience during the visit is pleasant and productive.

In a study my group conducted recently, we found that current Web sites are three times harder to use for people with disabilities than for our control group of users without disabilities. (Details are at *http://www.nngroup.com/reports,* from which you can download the full report.)

A second study of senior citizens had a less dramatic but still remarkable outcome: current Web sites are twice as difficult for people older than 65 years to use than for younger users. (You can find details at the Web page mentioned above.) The seniors in our study were not disabled in the traditional sense of the word, and they certainly were able to access the Web sites in the sense that they could get the pages to display, yet the complexity of the designs created major obstacles for them.

If we could get Web designers to consider accessibility as a design goal from the beginning, we could help users in many categories become much more productive in their use of Web sites and intranets without adding to the expense of constructing the design. In fact, simpler designs are often cheaper to build, though they may take more up-front thinking and creativity to plan.

I particularly like the user experience case studies in this book. Reading through these chapters gives great insight into the frustrations users feel when they come across designs that are difficult—or impossible—to use. I encourage you to read the case studies, but I encourage you even more to conduct similar tests of your own designs.

User testing is quite simple to do and always reveals a long list of changes that will improve a design and increase its business value dramatically. Conducting a usability evaluation with users with disabilities is slightly more complex than running a traditional user-testing session because of the need to allow each user to employ the assistive technology to which he or she is accustomed. But it's not that hard: you can go to the users' offices or homes and use their existing setups. The key elements of user testing remain the same. First, get hold of real users—your customers for a Web site or your employees for an intranet. Second, have them sit by the computer and access your design while they perform representative tasks. Ask the users to think out loud so you can find out how they react to each design element and why they take certain paths through the user interface. The third point may be the hardest: you have to shut up and let the users do the talking. Even when they *really* don't like your site. It's better that you learn this in a study rather than after you have released a design that will hurt your reputation and cost you lost business. Ultimately, the lessons of this book should increase your understanding of the importance of the user experience and provide you with practical resources to improve that experience for everyone who visits the sites you create.

—Jakob Nielsen, Ph.D.
Nielsen Norman Group
Mountain View, CA
April 2002

Preface

Maximum Accessibility tells you how to make the World Wide Web more accessible and more usable for everyone, including over 600 million people around the world who have disabilities. That includes 54 million Americans (almost 6 million of whom are children) and 37 million people in Europe [Bureau of the Census 1997; United Nations 2000]. We've written *Maximum Accessibility* for Web designers, developers, and programmers who create complex, data-driven Web applications; full-time Web masters; folks who manage their departmental Web sites with one hand and do full-time jobs with the other; production managers; people who commission the creation of Web resources for their organizations; people who provide community services in community technology centers, nonprofit agencies, and health care facilities; teachers who want to help students learn and get parents involved in their children's education; and, finally, anyone who's interested in creating Web sites that can reach lots of people, showing others how to do it, and helping them understand why.

We assume that you're involved in some way in creating Web pages. This involvement can take many forms, from creating a personal Web site to building huge sites for Fortune 500 companies to posting occasional updates to a small site for your department or a community organization you belong to. Perhaps you train Web developers or include a unit on Web authoring in a course you teach. If you know something about HTML, the underlying language of the Web, you'll appreciate our discussions of the way some pages work (or where they break down). But if HTML isn't your cup of tea, you'll still find plenty to interest you in the examples we've selected and in our explanations of how different aspects of Web design affect people who have disabilities. If you're familiar with disability issues and have been searching for ways to persuade colleagues, managers, or service providers to address the accessibility concerns you've raised, we think you'll find helpful material in this book. If disability is a new topic for you, *Maximum Accessibility* is a good place to start.

Maximum Accessibility is divided into two sections. In Section 1 we answer the question, "What is accessibility and why does it matter?" Here you'll find four chapters that provide a good working definition of accessibility and discuss relevant issues of law and policy, such as the Americans with Disabilities Act. You'll learn about the World Wide Web Consortium's Web Content Accessibility Guidelines 1.0 and the Section 508 federal standards and how they apply. You'll also learn how accessibility awareness can have a positive impact in your community. And you'll get the information you need to make a strong business case for accessibility to members in your own organization and to your customers.

Interspersed among these chapters are four "user experience" chapters that offer detailed case studies, in readable narrative form, to demonstrate how inadvertent accessibility barriers on major Web sites affect the ability of people with disabilities to successfully locate information, explore our rich cultural heritage, and participate in e-commerce. You'll learn how specific features make access harder—and how other features can help. You'll see the accessibility guidelines and standards as they apply to real people using real Web sites.

In Section 2 of *Maximum Accessibility,* we show you how to use those same guidelines and standards to anticipate accessibility challenges and turn them into good design solutions—solutions that work for *all* your users. You'll learn about combining multiple approaches (and multiple media!) to create rich, equivalent alternatives for the content on your Web site. We'll show you how to write effective text equivalents for audio files and images and how to caption the soundtracks and describe the action of videos and animations so that people who aren't in a position to hear or see what's happening on the screen can still follow the important points of what's being said and done. You'll learn how to set up data and layout tables that make sense to the ear *and* the eye, so people listening to your Web site or looking at it on a text-only display will be able to find the information they need and understand what it means. You'll learn how to design Web forms that people can interact with via the keyboard (or any assistive technology device that translates user input into keystrokes—including voice recognition), and you'll learn how to label your forms so that people who use talking browsers know what information they need to give you. You'll learn what you need to do to make scripts accessible to people who don't use a mouse, and how to decide which multimedia player is best for your purposes and your audience. You'll learn how you can create simple PDF files that are accessible to people with disabilities. And you'll learn how to use Cascading Style Sheets to make your pages look great *and* be accessible!

If you're new to accessibility, we suggest that you start with Section 1 to learn about what accessibility is and why it's important. If you're a Web developer, you may want to read the user experience chapters before moving on to the how-to chapters in Section 2. (We've even provided a handy chart to show you which accessibility guidelines and standards are covered in each chapter, so if you're interested in specific issues, use the chart to follow up.) Managers and others who commission Web sites may want to pay special attention to the chapters on accessibility in law and policy and on the business case for accessibility. Those who teach Web authoring will find the detailed examples and explanations throughout the book especially useful.

Maximum Accessibility has many features to help you learn what you need to know. It offers

- In-depth coverage of the Web Content Accessibility Guidelines 1.0 and the Section 508 federal accessibility standards for the Internet.
- Information on building a strong business case for accessibility.
- Detailed user experience narratives that bring accessibility barriers to life.
- Best practices in accessible design.
- Screen shots, screen-reader transcripts, and code examples that provide in-depth understanding.
- How-to chapters that demonstrate the process of thinking through design problems with accessibility in mind.
- Up-to-date information about assistive technologies and design techniques.

After reading this book, you'll become a more valuable resource to colleagues in your organization and to your community. You'll have up-to-date knowledge of accessibility guidelines and standards and how they apply to your situation. You'll be able to solve accessibility problems—*before* users with disabilities point them out! You'll know how to write accessibility into requirements documents, requests for quotes, and contracts. Your Web sites will provide more satisfying experiences for more people. And you'll gain insight into one of the most interesting and challenging issues of our time: how to enable people with disabilities to participate fully in and contribute to society.

ACCESSIBILITY GUIDELINES AND STANDARDS, BY CHAPTER

This table provides a quick reference to WCAG 1.0 and Section 508, each of which is generally referenced throughout the book. References to specific guidelines, checkpoints, and standards appear in the indicated chapters. Guidelines and standards text used with permission.

	Priority	Chapter Reference
Overview of Guidelines and Standards		1, 3, 4, 6
WCAG 1.0 **Guideline 1. Provide equivalent alternatives to auditory and visual content.**		7, 9
1.1. Provide a text equivalent for every non-text element.	P1	2, 7, 9, 12, 13
1.2. Provide redundant text links for each active region of a server-side image map.	P1	7

	Priority	Chapter Reference
1.3. Until user agents can automatically read aloud the text equivalent of a visual track, provide an auditory description of the important information of the visual track of a multimedia presentation.	P1	7, 9, 13
1.4. For any time-based multimedia presentation synchronize equivalent alternatives with the presentation.	P1	7, 9, 13
1.5. Until user agents render text equivalents for client-side image map links, provide redundant text links for each active region of a client-side image map.	P3	7
Guideline 2. Don't rely on color alone.		15
2.1. Ensure that all information conveyed with color is also available without color, for example from context or markup.		15
2.2. Ensure that foreground and background color combinations provide sufficient contrast when viewed by someone having color deficits or when viewed on a black and white screen. [Priority 2 for images, Priority 3 for text]	P2— images P3— text	15
Guideline 3. Use markup and style sheets and do so properly.		5, 15
3.1. When an appropriate markup language exists, use markup rather than images to convey information.	P2	
3.2. Create documents that validate to published formal grammars.	P2	
3.3. Use style sheets to control layout and presentation.	P2	11, 15
3.4. Use relative rather than absolute units in markup language attribute values and style sheet property values.	P2	15
3.5. Use header elements to convey document structure and use them according to specification.	P2	8, 15
3.6. Mark up lists and list items properly.	P2	8

	Priority	Chapter Reference
3.7. Mark up quotations. Do not use quotation markup for formatting effects such as indentation.	P2	
Guideline 4. Clarify natural language usage.		
4.1. Clearly identify changes in the natural language of a document's text and any text equivalents (e.g., captions).	P1	
4.2. Specify the expansion of each abbreviation or acronym in a document where it first occurs.	P3	
4.3. Identify the primary natural language of a document.	P3	11
Guideline 5. Create tables that transform gracefully.		
5.1. For data tables, identify row and column headers.	P1	5, 11, 12
5.2. For data tables that have two or more logical levels of row or column headers, use markup to associate data cells and header cells.	P2	5, 11
5.3. Do not use tables for layout unless the table makes sense when linearized. Otherwise, if the table does not make sense, provide an alternative equivalent (which may be a linearized version).	P2	11
5.4. If a table is used for layout, do not use any structural markup for the purpose of visual formatting.	P2	11
5.5. Provide summaries for tables.	P3	5, 11
5.6. Provide abbreviations for header labels.	P3	5, 11
Guideline 6. Ensure that pages featuring new technologies transform gracefully.	P3	12, 14
6.1. Organize documents so they may be read without style sheets.	P1	15
6.2. Ensure that equivalents for dynamic content are updated when the dynamic content changes.	P3	8

	Priority	Chapter Reference
6.3. Ensure that pages are usable when scripts, applets, or other programmatic objects are turned off or not supported. If this is not possible, provide equivalent information on an alternative accessible page.	P1	14
6.4. For scripts and applets, ensure that event handlers are input device-independent.	P2	14
6.5. Ensure that dynamic content is accessible or provide an alternative presentation or page.	P2	
Guideline 7. Ensure user control of time-sensitive content changes.		
7.1. Until user agents allow users to control flickering, avoid causing the screen to flicker.	P1	13
7.2. Until user agents allow users to control blinking, avoid causing content to blink.	P2	
7.3. Until user agents allow users to freeze moving content, avoid movement in pages.	P2	
7.4. Until user agents provide the ability to stop the refresh, do not create periodically auto-refreshing pages.	P2	7
7.5. Until user agents provide the ability to stop auto-redirect, do not use markup to redirect pages automatically. Instead, configure the server to perform redirects.	P2	
Guideline 8. Ensure direct accessibility of embedded user interfaces.		
8.1. Make programmatic elements such as scripts and applets directly accessible or compatible with assistive technologies.	P1/P2	13, 14
Guideline 9. Design for device-independence.		7
9.1. Provide client-side image maps instead of server-side image maps except where the regions cannot be defined with an available geometric shape.	P1	2, 7, 9

	Priority	Chapter Reference
9.2. Ensure that any element that has its own interface can be operated in a device-independent manner.	P2	7
9.3. For scripts, specify logical event handlers rather than device-dependent event handlers.	P2	10, 13, 14
9.4. Create a logical tab order through links, form controls, and objects.	P3	14
9.5. Provide keyboard shortcuts to important links (including those in client-side image maps), form controls, and groups of form controls.	P3	

Guideline 10. Use interim solutions.

	Priority	Chapter Reference
10.1. Until user agents allow users to turn off spawned windows, do not cause pop-ups or other windows to appear and do not change the current window without informing the user.	P2	7
10.2. Until user agents support explicit associations between labels and form controls, for all form controls with implicitly associated labels, ensure that the label is properly positioned.	P2	7, 10
10.3. Until user agents (including assistive technologies) render side-by-side text correctly, provide a linear text alternative (on the current page or some other) for all tables that lay out text in parallel, word-wrapped columns.	P3	7
10.4. Until user agents handle empty controls correctly, include default, place-holding characters in edit boxes and text areas.	P3	
10.5. Until user agents (including assistive technologies) render adjacent links distinctly, include non-link, printable characters (surrounded by spaces) between adjacent links.		

	Priority	Chapter Reference
Guideline 11. Use W3C technologies and guidelines.		
11.1. Use W3C technologies when they are available and appropriate for a task and use the latest versions when supported.	P2	
11.2. Avoid deprecated features of W3C technologies.	P2	5, 11
11.3. Provide information so that users may receive documents according to their preferences (e.g., language, content type, etc.).	P3	
11.4. If, after best efforts, you cannot create an accessible page, provide a link to an alternative page that uses W3C technologies, is accessible, has equivalent information (or functionality), and is updated as often as the inaccessible (original) page.	P1	7, 8
Guideline 12. Provide context and orientation information.		5
12.1. Title each frame to facilitate frame identification and navigation.	P1	5, 7, 14
12.2. Describe the purpose of frames and how frames relate to each other if it is not obvious by frame titles alone.	P2	7
12.3. Divide large blocks of information into more manageable groups where natural and appropriate.	P2	10
12.4. Associate labels explicitly with their controls.	P2	7, 10
Guideline 13. Provide clear navigation mechanisms.		5, 11
13.1. Clearly identify the target of each link.	P2	
13.2. Provide metadata to add semantic information to pages and sites.	P2	
13.3. Provide information about the general layout of a site (e.g., a site map or table of contents).	P2	
13.4. Use navigation mechanisms in a consistent manner.	P2	5, 7, 11

	Priority	Chapter Reference
13.5. Provide navigation bars to highlight and give access to the navigation mechanism.	P3	
13.6. Group related links, identify the group (for user agents), and, until user agents do so, provide a way to by-pass the group.	P3	7, 15
13.7. If search functions are provided, enable different types of searches for different skill levels and preferences.	P3	
13.8. Place distinguishing information at the beginning of headings, paragraphs, lists, etc.	P3	8
13.9. Provide information about document collections (i.e., documents comprising multiple pages).	P3	
13.10. Provide a means to skip over multi-line ASCII art.	P3	
Guideline 14. Ensure that documents are clear and simple.		
14.1. Use the clearest and simplest language appropriate for a site's content.	P1	
14.2. Supplement text with graphic or auditory presentations where they will facilitate comprehension of the page.	P3	9, 13
14.3. Create a style of presentation that is consistent across pages.	P3	

Section 508 Amendments

Subpart B—Technical Standards
§1194.22 Web-based intranet and Internet information and applications.

(a) A text equivalent for every non-text element shall be provided (e.g., via "alt", "longdesc", or in element content).	2, 7, 9
(b) Equivalent alternatives for any multimedia presentation shall be synchronized with the presentation.	9, 13

	Priority	Chapter Reference
(c) Web pages shall be designed so that all information conveyed with color is also available without color, for example, from context or markup.		15
(d) Documents shall be organized so they are readable without requiring an associated style sheet.		15
(e) Redundant text links shall be provided for each active region of a server-side image map.		7
(f) Client-side image maps shall be provided instead of server-side image maps except where the regions cannot be defined with an available geometric shape.		2, 7, 9
(g) Row and column headers shall be identified for data tables.		5, 11, 12
(h) Markup shall be used to associate data cells and header cells for data tables that have two or more logical levels of row or column headers.		5, 11
(i) Frames shall be titled with text that facilitates frame identification and navigation.		5, 7, 14
(j) Pages shall be designed to avoid causing the screen to flicker with a frequency greater than 2 Hz and lower than 55 Hz.		13
(k) A text-only page, with equivalent information or functionality, shall be provided to make a web site comply with the provisions of this part, when compliance cannot be accomplished in any other way. The content of the text-only page shall be updated whenever the primary page changes.		8
(l) When pages utilize scripting languages to display content, or to create interface elements, the information provided by the script shall be identified with functional text that can be read by assistive technology.		14

	Priority	Chapter Reference
(m) When a web page requires that an applet, plug-in or other application be present on the client system to interpret page content, the page must provide a link to a plug-in or applet that complies with §1194.21 (a) through (l).		13, 14
(n) When electronic forms are designed to be completed online, the form shall allow people using assistive technology to access the information, field elements, and functionality required for completion and submission of the form, including all directions and cues.		7, 10
(o) A method shall be provided that permits users to skip repetitive navigation links.		7, 15
(p) When a timed response is required, the user shall be alerted and given sufficient time to indicate more time is required.		10

Acknowledgments

Accessibility is an immensely rich and complex topic, and we've had lots of help from lots of generous and talented people who've been willing to share their knowledge, their time, their energy, and their passion for making the Web a better place for all of us.

One of those people is Jim Caldwell, whom John met in a windowless office somewhere in what is now the McCombs School of Business at the University of Texas at Austin (UT) in about 1985. Jim showed him something called PC-SAID and suggested calling someone named Jim Thatcher to find out more. Jim Thatcher moved to Austin a couple of years ago and has become a good friend, sharing his enormous knowledge of the Section 508 federal standards and his understanding of how his extraordinary invention, the screen reader for the graphical user interface, has gone on making a difference in the lives of thousands of computer users who are blind. Pat Pound set up the monthly TechLunch meetings that have become a forum for bringing together people from the government, industry, academia, and nonprofit worlds to meet and talk informally about shared interests without having to worry about what's on the agenda; the TechLunch mailing list helps us keep each other informed.

Simon Shostak remembered an American literature class that John taught at UT Austin years ago and recruited him as a judge for the first Accessibility Internet Rally for Austin (AIR-Austin) competition in 1998. Judging AIR for the past four years has provided an extraordinary opportunity to learn about accessibility and to explore ways of helping others learn—and it has been an opportunity to work with wonderful people and organizations. It has been an honor to share judges robes with Phill Jenkins and Guido Corona of IBM, and Jim Thatcher; and more recently with Rashmi Bhat and Caroline Mattei of Prodigy/SBC and former graduate students Bill Wolff, Aimee Kendall, and Olin Bjork. Special thanks to another "judge brother," Jim Allan of the Texas School for the Blind and Visually Impaired, for his extraordinary commitment to accessibility and his eagerness to share what he knows—and his willingness to thrash out code over the phone (or anywhere else, for that matter).

Glenda Sims, Mark McFarland, Morgan Watkins, and others who served on UT's Task Force on Accessible Electronic Information in 1999 have made a difference to the accessibility of Web resources at UT, as have Susanna Wong Herndon and Suzanne Rhodes. Randolph Bias and Jamie Rhodes made the resources of Austin Usability available at an important moment in the history of the Institute for Technology and Learning. Kay Lewis and Matt Bronstad have helped open up some really interesting questions. Annie So, Jay Overfield, David Wynn, and Ross Speir explored accessible design techniques. Peg Syverson has been a great colleague and friend.

Howard Kramer's excellent yearly conference, Accessing Higher Ground, has provided an opportunity to explore some of the institutional aspects of accessibility; the CSUN Conference on Technology and Persons with Disabilities has been a revelation.

We'd also like to thank Tracy LaQuey Parker for arranging the conversation that led to this book, and Steve Guengerich, whose great leap of faith and leadership got AIR (and then the nonprofit advocacy and education organization Knowbility) off the ground. The one and only Jayne Cravens has been an AIR advisor, booster, and staunch advocate for accessibility from the beginning and was crucial in getting the Austin nonprofit community behind the idea; from her post at the United Nations in Bonn, Germany, Jayne continues to provide ideas, encouragement, and information. Rayna Aylward and Colleen Maher of the Mitsubishi Electric America Foundation (MEAF) embody the highest ideals of engaged philanthropy. MEAF has provided crucial support for AIR since 1999. We truly could not have done it without them. And as we roll out AIR across the country, we want to recognize Jon Carmain for driving Rocky Mountain AIR to completion and for his continued passion for developing the business model that will sustain accessibility efforts. We want to thank all the businesses that sponsor AIR and especially IBM and Dell, who sustain the effort through sponsorship, participants, and volunteers. Knowbility's board of directors and staff, including Suzanne Hershey and Steve Hunt, have done remarkable work under trying circumstances in a very short time, and we thank you. We owe an especially big debt of gratitude to Kirk Walker for all his help with bits of code and multimedia scripts and players and for his consistent efforts to improve the lives of people with disabilities—as an engineer, as an occupational therapist, and now as Director of Technology for Knowbility. We are also grateful that the Peter F. Drucker Foundation has recognized the value and innovation of this effort . Kristi Willis and her boss, Lloyd Doggett, U.S.

Congressman for the 10th District in Texas, can always be counted on to support the independence of people with disabilities, and we are proud to work with them. In community technology, we are very fortunate to work with Ana Sisnett, who has worked for many years to open technology opportunities to everyone and who inspires us all. Another amazing, inspiring community leader is Jan McSorley, and we are grateful to have worked with her on the ATSTAR project. We look forward to the changes this project will bring to the capacity of schools to provide assistive technology where it is needed. We offer our thanks and salute the efforts of all the Web developers, nonprofit leaders, and community volunteers who successfully launched AIR—and more than 100 accessible Web sites!—in three cities. Your participation makes the difference, and we are honored to have worked and learned with all of you.

We want to thank the reviewers who read this book in manuscript, sent detailed and careful comments and suggestions, and said we could contact them if we had questions. Liz Fuller, Randolph Bias, Charles McCathie-Neville, and John Gunderson each brought a unique and informed judgment to bear on what we'd written, and this is a far better book than it would have been without their care. Of course the mistakes are all ours!

Karen Gettman and Emily Frey of Addison-Wesley offered encouragement and the gentle prodding we needed to make this book happen. Elizabeth Ryan has facilitated an enormous amount of e-mail and telephone traffic to keep the whole process on schedule. Our thanks to them, and to the other members of the Addison-Wesley team who made this book happen—and made the book itself as accessible as possible. Chrysta Meadowbrooke has done a beautiful job of copyediting, teasing order out of chaos, suggesting small refinements that made big differences, and spending many additional hours writing out her suggestions and queries in a format that worked far better with John's screen reader than the revision-tracking tools did. Katie Noyes and Kim Arney Mulcahy have applied accessibility principles to the material book. Katie's cover design features a compelling image and text that contrast strongly with a background color that's distinctive yet easy on the eyes. Kim's interior design for the book uses a larger-than-usual serif font and opens up the space between lines of text to improve readability. When we discovered that John's scanner simply ignored any text printed against a shaded background, no matter how light, Kim found a different visual marker for top-level section headings and kept creating new sample pages until she had one that worked.

Thanks to Ledia and Mason Carroll for being interested in this project and believing it could be done. Thanks to Ethan Murphy for his sweet nature and encouraging words and to Joe and Addie Rush for their intrepid example. And, finally, thanks, thanks, and thanks again to our spouses, Anna Carroll and Ron Hicks, for love and support and wonderful conversation—and for letting us disappear into the abyss for hours on end. We dedicate this book to them.

—John M. Slatin and Sharron Rush
Austin, TX
April 2002

A Word about Screen Readers

To access the Web, we used a PC running Microsoft Windows 98 and Internet Explorer 5.5 together with a screen reader called JAWS for Windows (version 3.70.87, the most recent version available when we started working on this manuscript in July 2001; later we upgraded to JAWS 4.0 and then 4.01 as these new versions became available). Other popular screen readers include Window-Eyes, HAL, and out-SPOKEN, by GW-Micro, Dolphin, and Alva AG, respectively.

Like other screen readers, JAWS is "transparent" to most applications: it converts material on the computer screen to synthetic speech and reads it aloud, going from left to right and top to bottom. When reading Web content, screen readers and talking browsers (such as IBM's Home Page Reader) signal the presence of links either by speaking the word "link" or by speaking the link text in a different synthetic voice. JAWS distinguishes several types of link. When it encounters a text link, it says the word "link." "This page link" identifies a link to a named anchor on the current page, "link graphic" identifies a link attached to a graphic (for example, an arrow or photograph that serves as a button), and "image map link" prefaces a selectable region of a client-side image map. JAWS reads the ALT text (alternative text that effectively replaces the image for people who cannot see it) associated with graphical links and image map hot spots if ALT text is present; otherwise it speaks the path and filename. Missing or inadequate ALT text can have a devastating impact on the quality of the user experience and thus on the Web site's effectiveness in accomplishing its purpose. (Please see Chapters 2, 7, and 9 for more information about ALT text.)

SECTION 1

Accessibility and Why It Matters

1

Introduction

WHAT IS WEB ACCESSIBILITY?

Maximum Accessibility is a book about how to make the World Wide Web accessible to everyone, including people with disabilities, and why it's important to do that. Let's begin with an operational definition of *accessibility*. Web sites are accessible when individuals with disabilities can access and use them as effectively as people who don't have disabilities.

That's the definition used in Section 508 of the Rehabilitation Act of 1973, as amended by Congress in 1998.[1] This law, usually referred to simply as Section 508, mandates that, as of June 21, 2001, all electronic and information technology used, procured, developed, or maintained by agencies and departments of the U.S. government must be accessible to people with disabilities. This includes approximately

---

1. See *http://www.section508.gov/index.cfm?FuseAction=Content&ID=14*, accessed May 8, 2002.

120,000 federal employees who have disabilities. That's a lot of people, but it's just a tiny fraction of the more than 54 million Americans with disabilities who might one day want or need access to those technologies and the information they produce. Included among the 54 million Americans with disabilities are nearly 6 million children—children who can learn and grow to make significant contributions to the vitality of our society [Bureau of the Census 1997].

Accessibility Guidelines and Standards

The Web Content Accessibility Guidelines 1.0

When we talk about accessibility guidelines and standards, we're referring primarily to the Web Content Accessibility Guidelines 1.0, or WCAG (pronounced *WuhKAG*), and to the federal government's Section 508 Internet and Intranet Accessibility Standards.

The World Wide Web Consortium (W3C) published WCAG 1.0 as a formal Recommendation on May 5, 1999, just over two years after launching the Web Accessibility Initiative (WAI) in April 1997. WCAG 1.0 is one element in a comprehensive accessibility strategy; other WAI recommendations address the authoring tools used to create Web content and the user agents that display that material. In fact, the WAI's first product was a major revision of Hypertext Markup Language (HTML) itself (the W3C is responsible for HTML and related specifications). Replacing HTML 3.2 in December 1997, HTML 4.0 introduced many important changes designed specifically to enhance accessibility for people with disabilities. With the publication of WCAG 1.0 five months later, the WAI had for the first time produced a set of accessibility guidelines for the Web that represented a broad, international consensus among industry representatives, academic researchers, and members of the disability community. This impressive accomplishment was a result of the W3C's rigorous consensus-building process, which we'll describe in Chapter 3.

Section 508

As we'll also explain in more detail in Chapter 3, WCAG 1.0 has become the basis for accessibility standards adopted by the international community. In the United States, a 1998 law called the Workforce Investment Act, which included a major overhaul of Section 508 of the Rehabilitation Act (originally passed in 1973), charged the U.S. Access Board with the task of producing accessibility standards for all electronic and information technologies used, produced, purchased, or maintained by the federal government. WCAG 1.0 provided a solid foundation for the work of the panels set up by the Access Board: the Section 508 Internet and Intranet Accessibility Standards that went into effect on June 21, 2001, exactly six months after being published by the Access Board, are very close to WCAG 1.0's Priority 1 checkpoints.

In our view, WCAG 1.0 is both broader and deeper than the Section 508 standards for Web accessibility. WCAG 1.0 includes a total of 65 checkpoints. These are arranged under 14 separate guidelines and then further organized into 3 priority levels. By contrast, Section 508 includes 16 standards for Web accessibility; there are no separate checkpoints, and there is just one priority level: required. That is, Section 508 compliance requires that all the standards that apply to a given Web resource must be met.

We'll be discussing WCAG 1.0 and Section 508 in detail throughout this book. The complete text of WCAG 1.0 is available from the WAI at *http://www.w3.org/tr/wcag10/*. Also available on this site are checkpoints and an extensive techniques document. The WAI Web site at *http://www.w3.org/wai* also offers links to training materials and a great deal of other information related to Web accessibility. Information about Section 508, including the Internet and Intranet Accessibility Standards and a wealth of other information about Section 508 and how it applies, is available at *http://www.section508.gov*.

Beyond Compliance

The WCAG Working Group produced a checklist to accompany WCAG 1.0 when it was published in May 1999. A number of other organizations have produced comparable checklists for the Section 508 standards as well. These checklists are extremely convenient, but it would be a serious mistake to conclude that accessibility is just a matter of checking off items on a list. It's much more than that—and a lot more *interesting,* too. Accessibility goes beyond compliance with the requirements of Section 508 or WCAG 1.0. It's possible to produce Web resources that conform to WCAG 1.0's Priority 1 checkpoints and comply with Section 508's standards for Web accessibility but *still* don't make sense to people with disabilities—or anyone else, for that matter. Which raises a question: If accessibility isn't compliance with the guidelines and standards, what is it?

Answers to this question can have different starting points, depending on whether you're talking about the way individuals with disabilities use the Web or about the way designers and developers set up Web sites. We'll begin with the user's perspective because that's where it all comes to a head.

Accessibility Is an Aspect of the User Experience

An important thing to notice about the definition of accessibility with which we began is that it's user-centered, not document-centered. In other words, it defines accessibility as an aspect or quality of the individual user's *experience* of the Web site, not a property of the document itself. This has important implications for Web designers and developers: it means that the job is to produce the *experience* of accessibility. That makes it important to have a better understanding of how people with disabilities experience the Web now. Then we'll be in a better position to think of ways to use accessibility guidelines and standards as resources for improving the Web experience, not just a bunch of rules we have to follow.

An analogy with going to see a play or a movie might be helpful here. The experience of going to the theater isn't just about the script (the text of the play). It's not just about the stage set, either, nor about the actors, the director, the producer, the stagehands. The play lives in the way audience members experience the *interplay* of all these things and more (the theater building, the crowd in the lobby, the memories of previous experiences).

Accessibility Is Environmental

In other words, experience doesn't happen in a vacuum. The Web experience isn't just about the particular site you happen to be visiting at the moment. The Web experience, too, lives in the interplay of many elements. There's the Web site, the browser (such as Internet Explorer or Netscape Navigator), the computer hardware, the operating system, and more—including, of course, *you*: your memories and expectations, the mood you're in, the room where you're working, what's going on around you, the other sites you've been to before you reached the one you're looking at now, your body.

For people with disabilities, assistive technologies such as screen readers, talking browsers, refreshable Braille displays, voice recognition, and other alternative input devices are often a key part of the mix. And so is frustration and the memory of having been frustrated before, as site after site turned out to be inaccessible and unusable, in whole or in part.

THE SCALE OF THE PROBLEM

How big a problem is accessibility on the Web? A report called *Beyond ALT Text,* published late in 2001 by Kara Pernice Coyne and her colleague, usability expert Jakob Nielsen, gives us a way to begin measuring the dimensions of the accessibility barrier.

The purpose of the Section 508 accessibility standards and the WCAG 1.0 is to establish parity between the experiences that people with and without disabilities have when they use Web-based resources. *Beyond ALT Text* gives us, for the first time, a measure of how great the *dis*parity between these two groups is.

According to Coyne and Nielsen [2001, p. 3], users with disabilities were about *three times less likely to succeed* than users without disabilities in carrying out such routine Web tasks as searching for information and making purchases.

That's a *huge* discrepancy—and it's not as though the control group of users without disabilities did all that well, either. The control group succeeded 78.2 percent of the time, as against about 26 percent for the users with disabilities [p. 4]. Twenty-six percent is just plain embarrassing. But the figures for people using screen readers and screen magnifiers are even worse: 12.5 percent and 21.4 percent, respectively [p. 4]. Coyne and Nielsen are careful to point out that these figures do not reflect incompetence or inexperience on the users' part: test participants who were blind had been using computers and assistive technology for more than three years [p. 127], and many of them were employed as knowledge workers [p. 124]. But even 78 percent is only a C+! Nothing to write home happily about. And 78 percent is high, say Coyne and Nielsen—typically, usability studies find that the success rate is between 40 and 60 percent. That's an F. The good news is that there's really no place to go but up.

No one *means* for it to be like that—we've never met anyone who deliberately set out to make a Web site that would be inaccessible to 50 million people (except for training purposes). But it happens just the same, not just once or twice but many times. Great Web experiences don't happen often enough for anyone, but for people with disabilities, great Web experiences are downright rare.

ACCESSIBILITY FROM THE DEVELOPER'S POINT OF VIEW: YOU CAN MAKE A DIFFERENCE

You *can* make a real difference in the way people with disabilities experience the Web by designing and building *your* sites so that people with disabilities can access and use them as effectively as people without disabilities. And if you're someone who has responsibility for seeing to it that Web sites get built for your organization, you can make sure the people who will be building the sites for you understand that accessibility—not just compliance—is a high-priority requirement.

Accessibility Guidelines and Standards Are Resources for Design

When we said that accessibility goes beyond compliance we didn't mean that the standards don't matter or that it isn't important to follow the guidelines. But we *did* mean to say that compliance in and of itself isn't the point. The point is maximum accessibility. Accessibility is defined in terms of the user's experience, that is, his or her ability to access and use the site and its resources as effectively as someone without a disability.

That's where the guidelines and standards come in. WCAG 1.0 and the Section 508 standards are means to achieving that end. They're tools you can use to do your part in creating a significantly better Web experience for people with disabilities—and *all* the people who visit your site or use the resources you provide. With that in mind, we'll be talking extensively about guidelines and standards throughout this book to help you add them to your creative repertoire.

Good Design Is Accessible Design

Whether you're a Web developer or someone who manages Web developers, we want to persuade you that *good design is accessible design.* No responsible Web designer, in 2002, would create a Web site knowing that African-Americans, Mexican-Americans, Asian-Americans, or members of any other ethnic or racial group would be unable to use it simply because of their racial or ethnic heritage. It should be equally unthinkable to create Web sites that people with disabilities can't use simply because of their disabilities. It's not enough for a site to be visually appealing. The visual should work in concert with other senses, too. The site should appeal to the ear *and* the eye and allow for economy and ease of movement.

Accessibility doesn't just happen. On the contrary: what you get when accessibility isn't factored into the design equation is a site that's at least partly or maybe completely inaccessible. That's why so many existing sites will have to be retrofitted, often at considerable expense.

This book will show you that there are lots of things you can do to retrofit an existing Web site for accessibility, just as there are lots of things architects and engineers can do to retrofit a building with wheelchair ramps and wider doorways. Thousands of sites will be retrofitted over the next few years. That will make a big difference in the way many people with disabilities experience the Web. But the best experiences will happen as developers who share our belief that *good design is accessible design* make maximum accessibility a design goal from the beginning of every project.

OVERVIEW OF MAXIMUM ACCESSIBILITY

Why Are So Many Sites Inaccessible?

We believe there are two main reasons why so many Web sites are inaccessible. First, most Web developers don't have disabilities themselves, and they may not know anyone who has a disability (or maybe they do but don't realize it). So they may not fully understand how their design decisions and implementation techniques affect people with disabilities. Second, even if Web developers are aware of the problem and committed to fixing it, they may not know how to go about it. We hear the same questions again and again: *Where should we start? What do we do?*

We've written this book to answer those questions. We'll try to tackle both sides of the accessibility challenge, to help readers understand why accessibility is so important and what to do about it. We've divided the book into two sections.

Section 1: Accessibility and Why It Matters

Section 1 lays out the multiple dimensions of accessibility. We'll talk about accessibility and disability in law and international policy. We'll talk about the role of community organizations in raising awareness and providing efficient, cost-effective training to prepare people with disabilities for meaningful participation in the life and work of our society, and we'll talk about the contributions that people with disabilities have made. We'll provide the information you need to build the business case for integrating accessibility into your organization's Web development policies and practices.

USER EXPERIENCE NARRATIVES. Our user experience chapters (Chapters 2, 5, 7, and 8) offer a unique perspective on accessibility. We've provided detailed narratives about the accessibility barriers we encountered when we visited actual Web sites. You can do more than look at screen shots in these chapters—you can read verbatim transcripts of what people who use screen readers hear on these same pages. We'll also go "behind the scenes" to look at the source code, in order to learn about the HTML that produced the experiences we're describing. This will be new to some readers. The powerful Web-authoring tools now on the market allow Web developers to create visually rich, highly interactive sites without writing a single line of HTML code. But because most authoring tools don't automatically support accessible content—as they would if they conformed to the Authoring Tool Accessibility Guidelines 1.0 (ATAG), published by the WAI in February 2000—there will be times when it's necessary to edit HTML source code in order to meet your accessibility goals. In the user experience chapters, you'll have a chance to see what incorrect code looks like. In these chapters, we'll also talk about how the accessibility guidelines and standards apply to the sites we visit, so you'll be able to understand more clearly what to do in your own work—and what to avoid.

Another unique feature of our user experience narratives: they're written to be accessible to people who can't see the screen shots. We've tried to provide enough descriptive detail so that readers who are blind or visually impaired still get a good sense of what's happening on the Web pages we discuss.

The sites we visit aren't obscure ones. They're large sites for the most part, representing large, well-known organizations that have devoted substantial resources to their Web presence—organizations with the means to make their sites accessible if they choose to do so. The problems we describe are typical of the problems people with disabilities encounter on the Web every day. The problems are typical in two ways: (1) they cause real frustration, and (2) most of them could easily have been avoided if the developers had known what to do. That brings us to Section 2.

Section 2: Strategies and Techniques for Maximum Accessibility

In Section 2 we'll tell you about things you can do to create a more accessible Web experience for your users. We'll tell you about the tools and resources that are available to you, and we'll show you specific techniques that enhance accessibility. You'll learn how to write effective text equivalents for everything from small images to complex image maps, charts, and graphs—even works of art. You'll learn how to create Web-based forms that are as accessible to people using screen readers and talking browsers as they are to people who can point and click, and how to design tables so that the data make sense whether you're looking at the page or listening to it. We'll explain how to use Microsoft Word and Adobe Acrobat to create simple PDF documents that are accessible to people using screen readers. You'll learn how multimedia can be an important tool for enhancing accessibility. You'll also learn what to do about scripts, applets, and plug-ins to ensure that all your users can take advantage of your site's interactivity. We'll provide advice for developers of sites that depend heavily on scripting languages to generate complex pages on demand. And we'll show you how to use Cascading Style Sheets to bring out the structural elements of your designs while enhancing their readability and visual appeal.

In each case, you'll learn how accessibility guidelines and standards apply to different situations—and how you can turn those guidelines and standards into resources for creative problem solving.

Beyond the Standards, Beyond the Tools: The Human Element

Something to remember as you use the resources in this book is that, while we will introduce you to some great tools and techniques that will help you make your work more accessible, and even the means to check the accessibility of that work, in the end it all comes down to *people,* the human element that can't be overlooked. People with disabilities who use the Web can be your best source of accessibility testing—as well as loyal customers and great employees. We hope you will learn to incorporate their experiences as you test the usability of your work.

Human review can help ensure clarity of language and ease of navigation. Invite people with disabilities to review your documents. Expert and novice users with disabilities can provide valuable feedback about the barriers they encounter and the things that work well for them. That feedback will help you improve your site for all users. Hearing and seeing and feeling your Web site through the ears and eyes and hands of people with disabilities can be a surprising and sobering experience—it gives new meaning to the tired old cliché that you can't judge a book by looking at the cover, as we'll see in Chapter 2 when we visit a well-known e-commerce site. But the fact that it can be so difficult to predict what a site will *sound* like from the way it looks is exactly why it's so important to get input from people who have disabilities.

2

User Experience: Born to Shop

Accessibility barriers are not created because Web developers want to keep people away from online information. Rather, they most often occur as the result of ignorance. The creators of most inaccessible sites have simply never thought about the fact that people with disabilities use the Internet in the same way as anyone else: for fun, for learning, for community information—and for commerce. This is the first of several chapters in which we illustrate particular design features by inviting you to experience the Web along with us as we browse using assistive technology. In this chapter, we are trying to make a purchase online. Most of the barriers we encounter here are caused by missing ALT text—that is, image maps and buttons that lack the equivalent text alternatives that would make them accessible to people using assistive technologies such as screen readers and talking Web browsers. We demonstrate the experience of missing ALT text in this chapter and provide the means to improve the situation in Chapter 9, Equivalent Alternatives.

HTML Elements and Attributes Addressed in This Chapter

Elements

`<img>, <area>`

Attributes

`alt, longdesc`

Accessibility Checkpoints and Standards Addressed in This Chapter

Web Content Accessibility Guidelines 1.0 Checkpoints

1.1. Provide a text equivalent for every non-text element (e.g., via "alt", "longdesc", or in element content). [Priority 1]

9.1. Provide client-side image maps instead of server-side image maps except where the regions cannot be defined with an available geometric shape. [Priority 1]

Section 508 Standards, §1194.22

(a) A text equivalent for every non-text element shall be provided (for example, via "alt", "longdesc", or in element content).

(f) Client-side image maps shall be provided instead of server-side image maps except where the regions cannot be defined with an available geometric shape.

USER EXPERIENCE NARRATIVE:
LISTENING TO AMAZON.COM

Let's begin our examination with something simple—let's visit a well-known e-commerce site and try to buy something. Experience the first in a series of visits that I (John) made to Amazon.com's Web site as we developed the material for this book. Figure 2–1 shows Amazon's "recommendations," which are based on powerful software that correlates previous purchases with those of other shoppers who've bought the same or similar items.

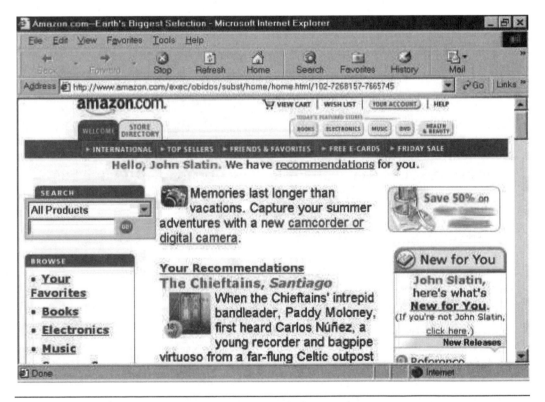

FIGURE 2–1 Screen shot of the home page of the Amazon.com Web site. Accessed July 9, 2001, at *http://www.amazon.com/exec/obidos/subst/home/home.html/ 102-7268157-7665745.* Used with permission.

A recommendation for a new CD by an Irish band, the Chieftains, appears in the center of the screen. The recommendation is surrounded by links to other items and other sections of the massive Amazon.com site. On the left side of the screen, for example, we are invited to search among all products or browse for our favorite books and other items. On the right side, we are offered the opportunity to save 50 percent on food processors or to take a look at something new.

But shoppers who use screen readers and talking browsers have a different experience. What I hear from my screen reader, JAWS, sounds like this:

> Amazon.com dash dash Earth's biggest selection
>
> Image map link href=nsb underline gateway slash one hundred two dash seven million two hundred sixty eight thousand one hundred fifty seven dash seven million six hundred sixty five thousand seven hundred forty five
>
> Image map link href equals nwl underline gateway slash one hundred two dash seven million two hundred sixty eight thousand one hundred fifty seven dash seven million six hundred sixty five thousand seven hundred forty five
>
> Image map link href equals nia underline gateway slash one hundred two dash seven million two hundred sixty eight thousand one hundred fifty seven dash seven million six hundred sixty five thousand seven hundred forty five
>
> Image map link href equals nfd underline gateway slash one hundred two dash seven million two hundred sixty eight thousand one hundred fifty seven dash seven million six hundred sixty five thousand seven hundred forty five

Image map link href equals nh underline gateway slash one hundred two dash seven million two hundred sixty eight thousand one hundred fifty seven dash seven million six hundred sixty five thousand seven hundred forty five

Image map link href equals nh underline gateway slash one hundred two dash seven million two hundred sixty eight thousand one hundred fifty seven dash seven million six hundred sixty five thousand seven hundred forty five

Image map link href equals nw underline gateway. . . .

And so on, through seven more image map links that sound numbingly similar to the ones transcribed above, until we come to something that's a little more intelligible—but still frustratingly hard to understand:

Link graphic mini dash tab slash top navbar dash button dash books

Link graphic mini dash tab slash top navbar dash button dash electronics

Link graphic mini dash tab slash top navbar dash button dash music

Link graphic mini dash tab slash top navbar dash button dash dvd

Link graphic mini dash tab slash top navbar dash button dash drugstore

Then, at last, after 14 image map links and five navigation-bar buttons that link to other sections of the giant online store, a greeting of sorts:

Hello, John Slatin. We have link recommendations for you.

Let's stop here for a few moments. What you have just read (or listened to) is what the JAWS screen reader reports *in the absence of ALT text*. And I never *will* hear the link to that Chieftains album: not only is it link number 60 of 163 links on the page (!), there's no ALT text for it, either. JAWS says only this:

> P slash B zero zero zero zero zero three G five Oh dot zero one point one eight TLZZZZ

Catchy, isn't it? Figure 2–2 shows the Links List that appears in JAWS when I browse the Amazon.com home page.

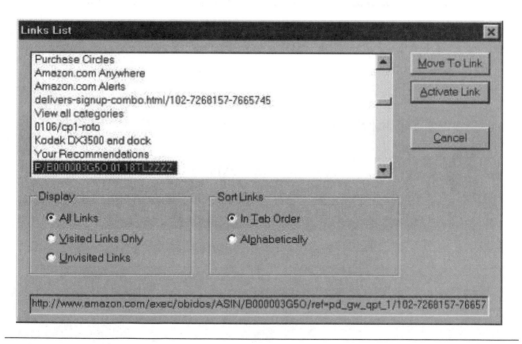

FIGURE 2–2 JAWS Links List. A link identified as P/B000003G . . . is highlighted. This link corresponds to an image of the cover for the new CD by the Chieftains. Accessed July 9, 2001, at *http://www.amazon.com/exec/obidos/ASIN/B000003G5O/ref=pd_gw_qpt_1/ 102-7268157-7665745.* Used with permission.

Closing the Sale

Let's suppose, for the sake of argument if nothing else, that I've actually decided I want to learn more about this new album. I've followed the link (P slash B and so on) to the Buying Info page for the album, *Santiago* (Figure 2–3).

Some of the options are different than those shown in Figure 2–1, yet the screen layout is very similar. Information about the CD in question appears in the middle of the screen surrounded by navigation options and advertisements. The all-important purchasing tools

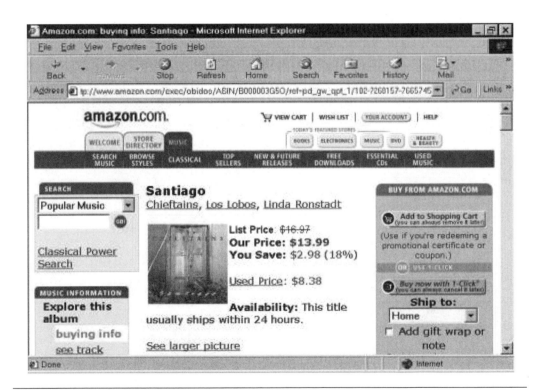

FIGURE 2–3 Amazon.com's Buying Info page for the Chieftains' *Santiago* CD. Accessed July 9, 2001, at *http://www.amazon.com/exec/obidos/ASIN/B000003G5O/ ref=pd_gw_qpt_1/102-7268157-7665745*. Used with permission.

are on the right-hand side, set off in a rectangular box whose background is a different color than the plain white of the page itself.

What I really want to do is to buy this album now and get on with my life—I want to use the 1-Click options I set so painstakingly some time ago to make my purchase, and I'll be on my way.

There's just one hitch. The Buy now with 1-Click button doesn't have any ALT text! This means that there is no way my screen reader can identify it. I could go to 1-Click Settings and make my purchase from there, as some of my friends who are blind have reported they do—but that's not "one-click" shopping, is it? But I have no choice. There's a link called Buy, but as far as I can tell it seems to be about buying gift certificates for my family and friends—a nice thought, but not what I had in mind tonight. There is also a correctly labeled button called Add to Shopping Cart, but using this option to make purchases requires several steps, not just the one click that's available to sighted users. Using the Add to Shopping Cart button also means *listening* to all those graphical links and image map links without ALT text—not just once but twice (at least if I want to review my shopping cart). Making any changes to the shopping cart requires listening carefully to hear the Delete option when it's spoken.

The barriers encountered in this experience are by no means rare. Usually they arise because companies are unaware that alternatives exist that increase the numbers of people who can use their services. We have the stick of government mandates (see Chapter 3) driving the move to accessibility, but we also have two juicy carrots to use: it is the right thing to do and, increasingly, it is the smart business thing to do, as we will see in Chapter 6, The Business Case for Accessibility.

3

Accessibility in Law
and Policy

ACCESSIBILITY: IT'S THE LAW!

This chapter presents an overview of the public policy and legal issues that contribute to the development of Web accessibility standards. You will find pertinent information about:

- The disability rights movement in the United States.
- The Rehabilitation Act of 1973.
- Educational mandates.
- The evolution of laws related to disability rights.
- The Americans with Disabilities Act of 1990.
- The Telecommunications Act of 1996.
- Section 508 of the Rehabilitation Act, amended 1998.
- The U.S. Access Board.
- The Web Content Accessibility Guidelines 1.0.

- The development of policies in Australia, the European Union, Canada, and the United Kingdom.
- Legal challenges over access to Internet resources.
- Other methods for ensuring access to information technology.

THE DISABILITY RIGHTS MOVEMENT IN THE UNITED STATES

On July 6, 2000, the National Museum of American History of the Smithsonian Institute opened an exhibit called "The Disability Rights Movement." Launched in conjunction with other national events commemorating the tenth anniversary of the passage of the Americans with Disabilities Act (ADA), "the disability rights movement exhibition examined the history of activism by people with disabilities, and by their friends and families, to secure the civil rights guaranteed to all Americans," said exhibition curator Katherine Ott [press release].

Of particular note was the fact that the exhibit was symbolically located next to the Greensboro lunch-counter exhibit, which signifies a major milestone of the African-American civil rights movement. As they strive for equality, inclusion in public affairs, and sometimes the right simply to live, members of both groups have experienced the results of stereotyping by society. As we examine the legal history of disability legislation in this chapter, we will do so in the context of the social guarantees of full participation inherent in a democratic system.

Until the last several decades, discrimination and confinement within institutions have been routine for people with a variety of disabilities and medical conditions, including epilepsy, mental retardation, and various physical impairments. Efforts to secure equal treatment, regardless of disability, have been isolated and largely unsuccessful in the United States and throughout the world until relatively recently.

In the United States after World War II, large numbers of veterans who were disabled in the war joined the efforts of parents seeking education and independent-living options for their children with disabilities. Their union formed a strong, articulate coalition of citizens seeking equal rights to societal benefits. Groups mounted organized protests and demanded equal opportunity. The Smithsonian exhibit documented how access to information and communication systems through technologies—such as telecaptioners, teletypewriter devices for telephones, voice-recognition systems, voice synthesizers, screen readers, and computers—is crucial to the success of this important civil rights movement. In addition, these technologies have created unprecedented opportunities for people with disabilities to participate in mainstream activities that support their ability to live independent, productive lives. Educational and professional employment options are greater now than they have ever been.

In order to better understand the ways in which technology enables skill and talent, regardless of disability, consider the following circumstances. In 1964, a young man named James Caldwell mustered out of the United States Navy, where he had served as an officer on submarine duty. Shortly after leaving the service, he received injuries that blinded him and required him to use a wheelchair. He was admitted to the state hospital, informed that he had virtually no rehabilitation options, and advised to reconcile himself to institutional life. Fortunately, Caldwell had a rehabilitation counselor who was informed about emerging technologies to a far greater extent than were the state medical staff. His counselor introduced Caldwell to computer technology, and Caldwell learned to program using punch cards. He went on to earn a Ph.D. from the University of Texas and is leading a very independent and successful life. He married, had children, raised a family, and recently retired from an accomplished career with IBM. He serves as Chair of the Texas Governor's Committee for People with Disabilities and was recognized in Washington, DC, with the Handicapped American Presidential Trophy, 1984–1985, for outstanding service to America in improving the lives of disabled people.

This is but one of millions of examples that demonstrate how advances in technology can greatly enhance society's capacity to provide access to education, employment, and other basic rights of citizenship to people with disabilities. It should not be surprising, therefore, that people of all ages with disabilities consider such access to be a right of citizenship their right and that major legislation has helped shape how our nation uses technology to ensure such rights.

THE REHABILITATION ACT

The Rehabilitation Act is recognized as the first federal civil rights law protecting the rights of persons with disabilities. Signed October 1, 1973, this law prohibits discrimination on the basis of disability under any program or activity receiving federal financial assistance. Section 504 of the legislation provides that "No qualified person with a disability shall, solely by reason of his disability, be excluded from the participation in, be denied the benefits of, or be subject to discrimination under any program or activity receiving federal financial assistance."[1]

---

1. From the text of Section 504, accessed July 12, 2001, at *http://american history.si.edu/disabilityrights/.*

The Evolution of Section 504

Originally, Section 504 was intended to prevent discrimination in employment. By the time the Section 504 rules and regulations went into effect on April 28, 1977; however, a series of amendments extended their coverage to all areas of civil rights, including education, employment, health, welfare, and other social service programs.

Section 504 is currently applied to all entities that receive federal government funds, including states, counties, cities, towns, villages, and their political subdivisions; instrumentalities of states and their political subdivisions; public and private institutions; other health service providers; public and private colleges; public and private agencies; and any other entities that receive federal money.

Each federal agency has its own set of Section 504 regulations that apply to its own programs. Those for the Department of Education (DOE) require that entities that operate public elementary and secondary education programs must provide a "Free Appropriate Public Education" to each qualified person with a disability who is in the agency's jurisdiction, regardless of the nature or severity of the person's disability. Provisions for educational equity were further strengthened in 1975 with the passage of the Individuals with Disabilities Education Act (IDEA).

EDUCATIONAL MANDATES

An IDEA Whose Time Has Come

IDEA requires public school systems to develop appropriate Individualized Education Programs (IEPs) for each child. The specific special education and related services outlined in each IEP are meant to reflect the individualized needs of each student. The IEP must be developed by a team of experts and must be reviewed at least annually. This profound change empowered parents to demand quality education for their children with disabilities.

Interpretation and full implementation of the Rehabilitation Act and subsequent legislation have nevertheless been a challenge to disability advocates. The Commission on Civil Rights has defined discrimination, as it affects people with disabilities, somewhat differently than in other cases. Clearly, to treat those with disabilities as if they were not disabled is not analogous to being color blind to racial differences. To treat people with a disability exactly the "same" as peers without a disability is usually to exclude them from participation in a specific program or activity. The concept of appropriate "accommodation" has therefore become incorporated into policy implementation of the Rehabilitation Act mandates.

Recipients of federal funds therefore may not[2]

1. Deny the opportunity to participate in or benefit from an aid, benefit, or service.
2. Afford an aid, benefit, or service that is not equal to that afforded others.
3. Provide a less effective aid, benefit, or service.
4. Provide a different or separate aid, benefit, or service, unless such action is necessary to provide one that is as effective as those provided to others.
5. Otherwise limit the enjoyment of any right, privilege, advantage, or opportunity enjoyed by others.

---

2. Accessed July 12, 2001, at *http://www.dot.gov/ost/docr/regulations/library/ REHABACT.HTM.*

Expanding Rights to Public Education

A school must therefore afford equal opportunity for learning to students with disabilities, but the learning experience for those students does not have to be *identical* to the experience of students without disabilities. IDEA mandates that such equal opportunity be provided in the most integrated setting possible. Advances in educational assistive technology (AT) have greatly increased our potential ability to deliver on the promise of inclusion. Barriers still remain, however, including ignorance about how to identify and deploy appropriate technologies to meet individual needs.

For example, Ann Moore (not her real name) is a bright 11-year-old girl who has a motor skills impairment that prevents her from writing or using a conventional computer keyboard. It is difficult for her to handle books, so the Internet is a tremendous resource for her. Voice-input software is available, but much of it does not respond to a child's voice. Her parents are committed to keeping her at grade level in her standard classroom, but her teachers do not have the expertise to identify or use appropriate AT to meet her specific needs. In her school district, over 12,000 students are eligible for educational AT, but there are only three AT specialists to assess, diagnose, and test the effectiveness of the solutions. You don't have to do much math to realize the problem here. Although we have made progress in *identifying* the need to include people with disabilities, there is still much to be done to actually *meet* that need.

THE EVOLUTION OF LAW IN CHANGING SOCIETY

The Rehabilitation Act was landmark legislation in which, for the first time, Congress declared that it is of critical importance to the nation that the equality of opportunity and equal rights guaranteed by the U.S. Constitution are provided to all individuals, including those with disabilities. This was a commitment to the essential fact that the complete integration of all individuals with disabilities into normal community living, working, and service patterns was to be held as a final objective, and in making that commitment the federal government established principles of access that have been adopted by society as a whole.

The Rehabilitation Act has been amended several times over the years to address the experiences of implementation and the enormous changes in society and technology. The amendments most relevant to the subject of this book are those made to Section 508. The 1998 amendments to Section 508 mandate that information technology, like other public facilities, must be made accessible to everyone, regardless of disability. We will examine Section 508 in greater detail later in the chapter. First, let's become familiar with the laws that preceded and informed the amendments to Section 508.

THE AMERICANS WITH DISABILITIES ACT

On July 26, 1990, Congress passed the landmark Americans with Disabilities Act "to establish a clear and comprehensive prohibition of discrimination on the basis of disability."[3] This comprehensive legislation extended the promise of equal treatment for people with disabilities into the private arena. Whereas the Rehabilitation Act applies to federal government agencies and those that receive federal funds,

---

3. From the text of the ADA legislation, accessed May 17, 2002, at *http://www.usdoj.gov/crt/ada/pubs/ada.txt*.

the ADA applies to all places of public accommodation, to most employers, and to all Title II entities that deliver government services.

Among the findings that Congress cited in passing the ADA were the historical isolation and segregation of people with disabilities and the fact that, unlike other victims of discrimination, they "have often had no legal recourse to redress such discrimination."[4] The ADA was intended and has become the basis for such legal recourse. It has had profound results in promoting the concepts of greater equality of opportunity, full participation, independent living, and economic self-sufficiency for people with disabilities. We will see that once again, however, the promise of equality contained in this historic Act is still in the process of being fully realized.

Discrimination Defined and Prohibited

The ADA defines a person with a disability as someone who has a physical or mental impairment that substantially limits one or more major life activities, a person who has a record of such impairment, or a person who is regarded as having such impairment. For detailed information about the history and impact of this historic Act, access the ADA home page at *http://www.usdoj.gov/crt/ada/adahom1.htm*. But for now, let's consider the four major sections of the ADA and how they might apply to the Internet.

ADA Title I, Employment

Title I of the ADA prohibits employers of more than 15 workers from discriminating against people with disabilities. It requires that

---

4. From the text of the ADA legislation, accessed May 17, 2002, at *http://www.usdoj.gov/crt/ada/pubs/ada.txt*.

employers provide equal access to all employment privileges, including hiring, promotion, training, compensation, social activities, and others. It requires that employers provide "reasonable accommodation," a concept that has been subject to interpretation by the courts ever since.

For example, suppose a software company employs a computer engineer who is blind. The employee has been a productive member of a team that performs programming functions in a mainframe environment. As the company begins to move more of their staff communications and project management to their internal Web site, what degree of accommodation does the law require them to make for the blind employee?

Theoretically, and within the letter of the law, the company could make intranet-based employee communications available by other means, including documents accessible to screen readers and/or Braille printouts. But what an unnecessary and inefficient duplication of effort! Why not design the employee interface in an accessible fashion that serves everyone equally? In this way, no separate accommodation is needed. Throughout this book, you will see demonstrations that accessible design is inclusive by its nature and precludes the necessity for cumbersome alternative "accommodations."

ADA Title II, State and Local Government Activities

This section of the ADA requires that all government services be made available to people with disabilities regardless of the size of the entity or the receipt of federal funding.

As more government information and services are provided via the Internet, this provision has become a driving force in the development of regulations that affect Web design. Government jobs as well as public meetings and regulatory hearings are often posted to the Internet. In order to fully participate as citizens, it is clear that people with disabilities must be provided with full access to this critical information.

ADA Title III, Public Accommodation

Title III applies to public accommodation and requires that all public spaces be designed, constructed, and altered in compliance with accessibility standards established by the U.S. Access Board. City buses and other public transit are included in the legislative definition of public spaces and were therefore required to be made accessible to people with disabilities.

Among the displays of the Smithsonian exhibit on the history of the disability rights movement was a photograph taken during public protests that led to passage of the ADA. The picture showed that one of the protestors had affixed a sign to his wheelchair stating, "I can't even get to the BACK of the bus." Title III set accessibility standards for purchasing new equipment and timelines for retrofitting older vehicles. Physical access to transportation has been much improved as a result. The fact that we find curbcuts and access ramps in most public buildings is a direct result of this legislation. As we will learn in Chapter 5, however, access to information about transportation services has also become an issue as the Internet becomes a forum for posting updates and schedule changes. Public transit authorities usually rely on federal funding to some degree, so they are becoming more aware of their obligation to provide *all* services in accessible formats. For someone who is blind, public transportation is more than a convenience—it is often the only way to travel to and from a job. Rather than referring blind passengers to a phone line, where they may be put on hold for an operator or may be able to get information only during limited office hours, it makes the most sense to assure that on-line information, including schedule and fee tables, is fully accessible.

The National Federation of the Blind (NFB) also cited the mandates of Title III when it sued for improved Internet access in 1999. The NFB based its case on the assumption that the Internet is public space and therefore subject to the requirement, under Title III, to accommodate the needs of people with disabilities. We will examine the NFB's lawsuit against America Online (AOL) in greater detail later in the chapter.

ADA Title IV, Telecommunications

Title IV addresses telephone and television access for people with hearing and speech disabilities. It requires that common carriers (such as telephone companies) maintain interstate and intrastate telecommunications relay service (TRS) 24 hours a day, 7 days a week. TRS enables callers with hearing and speech disabilities who use telecommunications devices for the deaf (TDDs), which are also known as teletypewriters (TTYs), and callers who use voice telephones to communicate with each other through a third-party communications assistant.

Such services can make a huge difference in the lives of people who are deaf or hard of hearing and the hearing people with whom they communicate. According to Ed Bosson, Relay Administrator for the Texas Public Utilities Commission:

> It is heartening to know that telecommunications relay service (TRS) continues to evolve into [a] better and innovative service. It is as it should be. I take pride in the fact that Texas [offers] Texas Video Interpreting Service (TVIS). Relay Texas

offers wonderful services such as Voice Over (VCO), Speech to Speech (STS), Caller ID, and . . . [a] horde of new upcoming ideas. . . . We all are equal in human terms[;] thus we should also be entitled to all new and innovative ideas. [Bosson 2002]

THE TELECOMMUNICATIONS ACT

In 1996, Congress amended Section 255 and Section 251(a)(2) of the Communications Act of 1934 with the passage of the Telecommunications Act of 1996. This legislation requires manufacturers of telecommunications equipment and providers of telecommunications services to ensure that such equipment and services are accessible to and usable by persons with disabilities. These amendments ensure that people with disabilities will have access to a broad range of products and services such as telephones, cell phones, pagers, call-waiting, and operator services that were often inaccessible to many users with disabilities.

The law provides exceptions for situations that cause "undue burden" or where businesses or other entities can document that compliance is not "readily achievable." Section 255 defines "readily achievable" as "easily accomplishable and able to be carried out without much difficulty or expense."[5] Even within the exceptions granted by the legislation, however, telecommunications services and equipment must nevertheless be compatible with existing peripheral devices

---

5. From the text of Section 255, Subpart A, Section 1193.1, printed in the *Federal Register*, February 3, 1998. Accessed May 20, 2002, at *http://www.access-board.gov/telecomm/html/telfinal.htm*.

or specialized customer premises equipment. Section 255 therefore encourages manufacturers and service providers to consider access needs during the design and development of their products and services, so that expensive and burdensome retrofitting for access will not be necessary.

SECTION 508 OF THE REHABILITATION ACT

We promised a further look at Section 508, which has had such an impact on Web design practice in the United States. More than three years after its passage, we find an increase in awareness of accessibility but a high level of confusion about how the standards apply to various sectors of society. As part of the Workforce Investment Act of 1998, Congress revised Section 508, which was originally an amendment to the Rehabilitation Act of 1973. Signed into law on August 7, 1998, the Section 508 amendment mandates that when "Federal departments or agencies develop, procure, maintain, or use Electronic and Information Technology (EIT), they shall ensure that the EIT allows Federal employees with disabilities to have access to and use of information and data that is comparable to the access to and use of information and data by other Federal employees."[6]

The 1998 amendment therefore requires federal EIT to be accessible to people with disabilities, including federal employees and members of the public who may be seeking information from the Web sites of federal agencies. Section 508 standards are referenced

---

6. From the text of Section 508, accessed May 17, 2002, at *http://www.usdoj.gov/ crt/508/508law.html.*

throughout the book as we provide techniques to meet federal mandates that apply to Web-based applications. The chart at the front of the book provides an index to which book chapters contain information relevant to specific standards and other guidelines.

THE U.S. ACCESS BOARD

The U.S. Access Board is the agency charged with defining the means by which access mandates are measured and enforced. The Access Board has developed standards for access to public buildings, transportation, and other physical spaces. In passing Section 508, Congress required the U.S. Access Board to publish standards to define EIT and to establish the technical and functional performance criteria necessary for access to such technology. The Board had first to determine the intent of the law, create a mechanism for public input, and then develop implementation standards. The Board accepted public comments for several months. Input by individuals and organizations, as well as guidelines developed by consensus over many years, informed the standards ultimately issued by the Access Board. Most notable among the work that formed the basis for Section 508 is that of the Web Accessibility Initiative (WAI) of the World Wide Web Consortium (W3C). Section 508 Web accessibility standards were largely based on the Web Content Accessibility Guidelines of the W3C, which we examine in the next section of this chapter.

The final standards for implementation of Section 508 were issued on December 21, 2000. According to the law, federal agencies were permitted a six-month grace period after the standards were issued to demonstrate that information technology systems met the standard. Federal agencies became subject to civil rights litigation for noncompliance under Section 508 after June 21, 2001. While the pur-chasing regulations in the Federal Acquisition Rule provide the real teeth, the courts are the final enforcement mechanism for Section 508 provisions regarding information technology.

WEB CONTENT ACCESSIBILITY GUIDELINES

Setting Global Standards

We mentioned that the provisions of Section 508 were based on the work of the W3C. Specifically, Section 508 evolved from the Web Content Accessibility Guidelines 1.0 (WCAG), which themselves are the result of years of consensus building with input from numerous individuals, educational institutions, and businesses.

Founded in 1994, the W3C is a consortium of over 500 member organizations, originally organized by the Centre Européen de Re-cherche Nucléaire (CERN [European Center for Nuclear Research]) and by the Massachusetts Institute of Technology (MIT). Currently, the W3C is led by Tim Berners-Lee, the inventor of the World Wide Web (who was employed at CERN when he wrote the initial propos-als for what is now the Web). The W3C has nearly 60 staff and is jointly hosted by the MIT Laboratory for Computer Science in the United States, the Institut National de Recherche en Informatique et en Automatique (INRIA) in Europe, and the Keio University Shonan Fujisawa Campus in Japan. The W3C Web site, *http://www.w3.org/*, contains a wealth of well-organized materials about the Consortium's research, guidelines, and progress in creating a World Wide Web that allows for the highest degree of cooperation and information ex-change. The ongoing goal of the W3C is to "develop interoperable technologies (specifications, guidelines, software, and tools) to lead the Web to its full potential as a forum for information, commerce, communication, and collective understanding."[7]

So, how does this happen? Well, some would say too slowly because of the consensus-building process that is used, but we'll let you decide as you explore the process of developing policy recommendations. There are many areas of work in the W3C, addressing a full range of topics that affect the evolution of the Web. Consensus building is an important part of the process since the W3C has no real enforcement mechanism and must depend on the willingness of its partners to adopt and promote the specifications that it develops. Several hundred dedicated researchers and engineers working for W3C member organizations contribute their time and skills to developing protocols and technologies that will allow the Web to fulfill its full potential to become a truly universal and democratic communication medium. Every effort is made to ensure that developments are global in scope and as inclusive as possible.

The W3C's Process for Producing Recommendations

In order to build consensus among its diverse membership, the W3C follows a rigorous and systematic process. Documents that become formal W3C Recommendations must go through several distinct stages. During the first stage of development, the documents are called Working Drafts. Each document goes through many Working Drafts (as many as one per month); these are produced and discussed by members of the relevant WAI Working Group and made available for public comment as well. When the group agrees that the draft is

---

7. From the W3C site, accessed May 17, 2002, at *http://www.w3.org*.

stable, the W3C director publishes it as a Candidate Recommenda-tion. At this point, the goal is to gather information about actual im-plementations of each checkpoint: the document can advance only when at least two successful implementations of each checkpoint have been identified. The document then becomes a Proposed Rec-ommendation awaiting approval by the W3C's member organiza-tions. Only when that approval has been received is the document published as a formal Recommendation. (If you're interested in learning more about this and other aspects of the W3C process, you can find the full W3C process described in the World Wide Web Con-sortium Process Document at *http://www.w3.org/Consortium/Process/ Process-19991111/process.html.*)

The W3C launched the WAI in April 1997 specifically to address the question of how to expand access to the Web for people with dis-abilities. The WAI's activities are only a part of the W3C's tremendous overall effort, but they are the most relevant to our purposes. We refer most often to the WCAG and occasionally to the Authoring Tool Acces-sibility Guidelines 1.0 (ATAG), published in February 2000, and the User Agent Accessibility Guidelines 1.0 (UAAG), currently in Candi-date Recommendation status. (Version 2.0 of the WCAG is a Working Draft as of May 2002, but discussion of WCAG 2.0 would be premature at this point. You may view the most recent public Working Draft on the W3C's Technical Reports site at *http://www.w3.org/TR/WCAG20/.*)

WAI recommendations are the result of years of research—gath-ering data, forming Working Groups in several related areas, report-ing, developing preliminary recommendations, taking comment, making final recommendations—leading to the Guidelines. The WCAG 1.0 Recommendations are organized into three levels of pri-ority. The WCAG Working Group provides a self-identifying rating system—from A to triple A—to indicate the level of conformance to the three priority levels. Table 3–1 explains the WCAG 1.0 priority levels and correlates them to the rating system.

There can be no doubt that the influence and result of the WAI work has been profound. We have seen that government policy as defined in Section 508 is driving U.S. accessibility efforts. Section 508 standards are largely based on the Recommendations of the WAI. And, as we shall see in the next section, most other nations have established WCAG 1.0 itself as the standard.

TABLE 3–1 WCAG 1.0 Priority Levels and Rating System

Priority	Rating	Conformance Standard
1	A	Developers MUST satisfy Priority 1 (P1) checkpoints in order to attain a minimum degree of accessibility. Otherwise, one or more groups will find it impossible to access information in the document. Satisfying P1 checkpoints is a necessary component of allowing many people access to Web documents.
2	AA (Double A)	Developers SHOULD satisfy P2 checkpoints for a higher degree of accessibility. The Canadian federal government has mandated compliance to the P2 level.
3	AAA (Triple A)	Developers MAY address P3 checkpoints for maximum accessibility and usability. Some P3 provisions have been mandated in public policy. For example, the Section 508 standards require a means to skip over navigation elements and proceed to the main content of a Web page, even though this is a P3 guideline.

Source: Adapted from information accessed on May 17, 2002, at *http://www.w3.org/TR/WAI-WEBCONTENT/#priorities.*

ACCESSIBILITY IS A GLOBAL CONCERN

Although Section 508 has received wide attention in the global community of people concerned with Internet policy and common standards, strategies outside of the United States have been just as powerful and, in some cases, more effectively implemented. As more government services came online, nations throughout the world developed accessibility policies. The WAI indexes information about these global efforts on its page titled "Policies Relating to Web Accessibility" (see *http://www.w3.org/WAI/Policy*).

Governments from Japan to Portugal have endorsed the concept and principle of universal access and have implemented policies to support their endorsement. Let's look at a few of them. Australian government initiatives, for example, provide a good example of proactive measures to assure access to the Internet for all citizens.

Accessibility Is Good Business in Australia

Although Australia passed the Disabilities Discrimination Act (DDA) in 1992, there was debate about whether the provisions of the DDA were sufficient to ensure equal access to online information and opportunities and whether the Act could be extended to apply to the Internet. Under the jurisdiction of the Australian Human Rights and Equal Opportunity Commission (HREOC), DDA provisions were explicitly extended to online information. In a report issued in 1999, HREOC confirmed that:

> Provision of information and other material through the Web is a service covered by the DDA. Equal access for people with a disability in this area is required by the DDA where it

can reasonably be provided. This requirement applies to any individual or organization developing a World Wide Web page in Australia, or placing or maintaining a Web page on an Australian server.

So, while Section 508 in the United States applies to federal Web sites and has been unevenly adopted by state and local governments, the Australian government has extended the standards beyond government services to include all commercial sites as well. It is well worth noting that this has not had a debilitating effect on the development of e-commerce or other Australian business activity on the Web.

European Union Incorporates Accessibility into eEurope Action Plan

In June 1999, the Portuguese parliament became the first European nation to pass a resolution specifically mandating Web accessibility. Also in 1999, as part of its eEurope initiative, the European Union European Commission issued a proposal titled "eEurope—An Information Society for All," which proposed that the European Commission and Member States would commit themselves to making the design and content of all public Web sites accessible to people with disabilities. The eEurope Action Plan 2002, adopted by the Feira European Council in June 2000, is a wide-ranging initiative designed to speed up and extend the use of the Internet to all sectors of European society. The action plan includes five targets for promoting "participation for all in the knowledge-based society." One specific target area is the accessibility of Web sites for people with disabilities. The plan emphasizes that "public sector Web sites and their content in Member States and in the European institutions must be designed to be accessible to ensure that citizens with disabilities can access information and take full advantage of the potential for e-government."[8]

An array of European institutions, including universities and the 15 European Union Member States, are executing the Action Plan. The Commission's goal of integrating Web accessibility within national and institutional policies for public information services and standards began with the adoption of the WCAG 1.0 and the recommendation for policy alignment among Member States. A High Level Group on Employment and the Social Dimension of the Information Society, which is composed of representatives from all the Member States, was mandated to monitor these developments. An eAccessibility Expert Group was established to support the work of the High Level Group. The eAccessibility Expert Group provides written and oral input to a review of progress of the Member States' adoption and implementation of WCAG 1.0. This review describes a variety of approaches, plans, and methods for using the Guidelines. The eAccessibility Expert Group has also agreed to organize monitoring exercises among the 15 Member States.

Canada Raises the Bar

The Canadian government has adopted WCAG 1.0 checkpoints through the Priority 2 level—a very impressive commitment. With the passage of the Access to Information Act of 1985, the Canadian government established an explicit intention to provide information

---

8. From the eEurope Action Plan 2002, accessed May 17, 2002, at *http:// europa.eu.int/information_society/eeurope/action_plan/pdf/actionplan_en.pdf.*

in accessible formats to all citizens. Since 1995, when the deputy ministers of the Treasury Board's Information Management Subcommittee approved the government-wide Internet strategy, Canada has been progressive in extending this commitment to include Web-based information. The original Canadian government Internet strategy initiative recognized the importance of including everyone. As a result, accessibility was a feature incorporated in original guidelines and templates for early government information sites as they were being developed. Therefore, when accessibility became a legislatively mandated feature of government sites in 1998, the established habits and precedents of accessible design supported a very effective accessibility policy implementation process.

Launched in spring 2002, the new Canadian government site (*http://canada.gc.ca/main_e.html*) has done an excellent job of implementing the accessibility principles proposed in 1998. Although we have only begun to explore the site as this book goes to press, we are pleased with the overall consistency of the site design. In addition, policy makers have provided a system to ensure that those responsible for putting government information on the Web have access to a high degree of support and guidance to ensure accessibility, usability, and timeliness.

Policy Implementation in the United Kingdom

The British Disability Discrimination Act (British DDA) of 1995 formed the basis for a campaign by the Royal National Institute for the Blind (RNIB) to ensure equal access to government services by users who are blind or have other disabilities. Even though the British DDA does not directly address the Internet, the RNIB successfully persuaded government ministries of the vital importance of inclusion. In December 1999, when Minister of State at the Cabinet Office Ian McCartney announced UK Online—a major initiative to ensure that everyone in the United Kingdom who wants it will have access to the Internet—the needs of people with disabilities were recognized and addressed. With the announcement, the government established departmental e-Ministers, an overall governmental e-Minister, and an e-Envoy. This New Media Team has the responsibility of realizing the UK Online initiative. The e-Ministers report monthly to the overall governmental e-Minister, who reports to the Prime Minister. In cooperation with efforts of the EU, the British New Media Team developed recommendations and an Action Plan for delivery of the UK Online strategy. Reports that have been presented to the Prime Minister to date are available from the Web site of the e-Envoy at *http://www.iagchampions.gov.uk/index.htm*.

IS THE INTERNET PUBLIC SPACE?

Now that we have seen some of the efforts that public institutions have made to establish commitment and develop policy, let's examine how policy is monitored and enforced.

Olympics Case Has International Consequences

As we saw above, Australia has a strong commitment to accessible information technology. In a 1999 lawsuit, Bruce Lindsay Maguire sued the Sydney Organizing Committee for the Olympic Games. On June 7, Maguire—who is blind—complained to the Commission that he was unlawfully discriminated against in three respects: the failure to provide Braille copies of the information required to place orders for Olympic Games tickets, the failure to provide Braille copies of the Olympic Games souvenir program, and the failure to provide a Web site that was accessible to the complainant.[9] Maguire sued under the provisions of the Australian DDA and in August 1999 the HREOC found in his favor. Although the designers of the site argued in court that it would take months and millions of dollars to remedy, once the ruling was handed down they managed it in days for an estimated cost of less than $30,000.[10]

Maguire's victory established that Australia's DDA covers Web sites, and the precedent set by the decision has had consequences throughout the world. Unfortunately, as we will learn in Chapter 14, the Olympic Committee did not learn from its own experience, so it failed to create accessible online information in 2002. In the meantime, however, many public institutions and governments *did* respond favorably to the message delivered in this case and adopted useful measures to meet the needs of people with disabilities.

National Federation of the Blind Sues America Online for Access

While Australia considered the case of the Olympics, another landmark court case occurred in the United States. On November 4, 1999, the NFB sued AOL, asking that the courts declare that the Internet is a

9. Accessed January 12, 2002, at *http://scaleplus.law.gov.au/html/ddadec/0/2000/ 0/DD000120.htm.*
10. Accessed January 12, 2002, at Ten.20.net Magazine, *http://www.ten-20.com/ 2olympicWebsite.html.*

public space and therefore subject to the public accommodations rule of the ADA. Although the case was settled out of court, it raised questions that have yet to be fully addressed. Many people, including some within the community of people with disabilities, believed the lawsuit to be ill considered and feared that it might create backlash rather than solutions. Marc Maurer, President of the NFB, responded thus:

> AOL has something in the neighborhood of twenty million subscribers. It has decided to become the company that will create the standard for providing information to the public. That standard excludes the blind. We have repeatedly asked in the past that this standard be modified to include blind participants. Sympathetic responses have been made, but modifications have not come.
>
> How long should we wait?
>
> How much patience should we have?
>
> How much tolerance should the blind be expected to possess?
>
> Why should other people have what the blind can never get?
>
> We are not prepared to be shut out or ignored or intimidated or forgotten. If the information age is important (and we are repeatedly told that it is), we who are blind intend to be as much a part of it as anybody else. This is the message we sent through the filing of the lawsuit." [Maurer 2000, p. 4]

On July 26, 2000—the tenth anniversary of the passage of the ADA—the NFB announced it would drop its suit against AOL in return for specific accommodations. AOL agreed to publish a policy on accessibility and make it an integral part of its service to consumers.

This included the intent to create the means for screen readers and other technologies to interface with AOL's portal. The agreement provided one year to review the progress made and allows the federation to file suit again if problems remain.

Although there were no definitive court rulings, AOL's settlement included accessibility improvements to its system, and the NFB case generated increased interest in the applicability of nondiscrimination law to the Internet.

A Congressional hearing held on February 9, 2000, considered whether the ADA should apply to the Internet. After lengthy testimony, the subcommittee, chaired by Congressman Charles Canady (R–FL), concurred with the Justice Department. The conclusion stated that "the ADA does apply to the Internet, and . . . [due to] the substantial First Amendment implications of an application of the ADA to the Internet, the development of a legislative record on these issues now would likely prove valuable to all interested parties."[11]

By early 2001, Maurer was able to say in a progress report, "the currently distributed version of the AOL access system is, in many respects, usable by the blind. In other words, progress is being made. A great deal of work remains, but much has been accomplished."

Who Needs Accommodation?

According to census data, more than 750 million people worldwide have disabilities, and those numbers are increasing as the population

11. House Subcommittee Hearing Committee Transcript, February 9, 2000. Accessed May 17, 2002, at *http://commdocs.house.gov/committees/judiciary/hju65010.000/hju65010_0f.htm.*

ages. These data also show that people with disabilities, as a group, continue to occupy an inferior status in society and are severely disadvantaged socially, vocationally, economically, and educationally. The ADA, the DDA in Britain and Australia, and other initiatives throughout the world have completely redefined society's responsibility to this population. The potential now exists—and is supported by advances in technology—to fully include people with disabilities in societal opportunities and to finally change that status.

What Is Accessible Information Technology?

As defined by both the WAI and the Section 508 standards, an accessible information technology system is one that can be operated in a variety of ways and does not rely on a single sense or ability of the user. For example, a system that provides output only in visual format will not be accessible to people with visual impairments, and a system that provides output only in audio format will not be accessible to people who are deaf or hard of hearing.

Some individuals with disabilities may need accessibility-related software or peripheral devices (commonly referred to as assistive technology or AT) in order to use Web pages and systems that comply with standards. These may include text-to-speech mechanisms, alternative navigation systems such as joysticks, magnification tools, or any of a host of software and hardware devices. It is important to note, however, that not all accessibility issues involve the use of AT. Navigation systems, color choices, and flashing content are among the elements that can cause access barriers to users who do not employ AT at all.

REMEDIES OUTSIDE OF THE COURTS

The Power of the Purse

One of the most effective tools for ensuring that accessible information technology becomes more widely adopted and employed is the ability to make purchasing decisions. We saw how Australian mandates support a healthy e-commerce environment that is fully accessible. Governments are increasingly requiring compliance to accessibility standards as they issue request for proposals to technology vendors. Companies, particularly W3C members like IBM, are developing and enforcing internal standards that they pass along to vendor companies. University systems and school districts can support accessible design by including these techniques in curriculum requirements and internal Web standards and templates.

Applying Standards to Federal Purchases in the United States

The statute that amended Section 508 also required the Federal Acquisition Regulatory Council to revise the Federal Acquisition Rules (FARs) to incorporate the Access Board's standard within six months after it was final. Published in the *Federal Register* on April 25, 2001, the FARs were amended to define how businesses that contract with the federal government, regardless of their size, are required to comply with the standard set by Section 508. Included in the FAR ruling was the observation that "since the statute imposes private enforcement, where individuals with disabilities can file civil rights lawsuits, the Government has little flexibility for alternatives in writing this regulation. To meet the requirements of the law, we cannot exempt small businesses from any part of the rule" [Federal Acquisition Rules 2001, p. 20894].

Government agencies are huge technology customers. The U.S. federal government alone is the largest buyer of information technology in the world, so it is not surprising that the need for compliance with the standards established by Section 508 and conformance with WCAG 1.0 is currently driving much of the interest in Web accessibility. This has both beneficial and unfortunate aspects.

The Good News . . .

It is, of course, beneficial for attention and resources to be dedicated to ensuring that the Internet is accessible. In fact, it is our purpose to demonstrate in these pages that benefits accrue throughout the online community when sites are designed with access in mind. We believe that the federal government is demonstrating appropriate leadership in ensuring that everyone can participate as producers and consumers in the information marketplace. The benefits of accessible design, as we will see throughout this book, often extend beyond those afforded to people with disabilities and create favorable experiences for a wider group of users.

Throughout history, attempts to accommodate the needs of people with disabilities have led to technological advances. For example, the telephone and the transistor were both the result of inventors who were trying to help the deaf. Similarly, it turns out that accessible Web sites are more usable not only by people with disabilities but also by anyone who uses wireless or text-based browsing devices. Consider this scenario: Many businesses use graphic images of text—particularly on headers and logos—in order to maintain a certain look and feel. A prospective customer is on the way to your office and has misplaced the address and phone number. The customer accesses a wireless browsing device to find contact information. If you have wisely included alternative text along with the graphic image that contains the office address, your customer arrives on time and happy. If, however, you have failed to do this, your customer cannot get the needed information and may be unnecessarily frustrated. Perhaps the information is embedded in that graphic file but is also listed further along as text. Accessible design allows your customer to search, to skip redundant navigation, and to make choices about how to get the information in the way that is most personally usable. And, as appliances become more interactive, the adoption of common standards and protocols will foster a much higher degree of successful interactivity.

. . . And the Challenge

The unfortunate aspect of reliance on government mandates comes from the sense that compliance—rather than maximum accessibility and usability—is the goal. As we will see, an information technology system, such as a Web site, can be made strictly adherent to guidelines, standards, or rules and still not be usable by a significant portion of the population. Accessibility lies not in the document but in the experience of the user. Achieving maximum accessibility therefore requires input and feedback from actual users in order to be accurately assessed. So, although the regulations have spurred interest in accessible design, we will see that to meet the spirit of the law, we must go beyond both the regulations and the law.

There are also conflicting views about the roles that must be performed in order to achieve maximum accessibility. One point of view depends heavily on the tools—the assistive devices—to mediate and decode the technology for the user with disabilities. This attitude is willing to tolerate the lag time that assistive technology development will impose on users. Others, including us, believe that principles of universal design can be successfully applied to emerging technologies. Governments and other institutions throughout the world are finding that it is the will to invent new solutions that keeps society moving progressively forward. We urge you to use the principles, techniques, and tools presented within this book not only as you broaden the accessibility of existing applications but also as you develop new ones.

NOW THINGS GET REALLY INTERESTING

Technology has extended our society's capacity to enable people with disabilities to fully participate in educational and employment opportunities. The legislation we have considered is a noble accomplishment and is the result of the efforts of a growing community of people who are determined to be included in the progress of society. Legislation alone, however, is not enough. Subsequent chapters will present some innovative grassroots strategies and provide you with tools you can use to complete the process of inclusion.

The 2000 "Disability Rights Movement" exhibit at the Smithsonian, where we began this chapter, clearly illustrated how people with disabilities have struggled for basic human rights and dignity throughout the nation's history. An interesting aspect of the Smithsonian exhibit was its interactivity, illustrating the fact that technological advances enable information to be rendered in varied formats that allow for broader access and more user choices. Web-based kiosks were designed for visitors to use, regardless of ability or disability. They operated with an easy-to-use, three-button interface. They easily accommodated users sitting in a wheelchair or standing. The kiosk display duplicated the exhibition by using visual and audio descriptions, graphic images, and captioned video clips, allowing several alternative means of accessing the same information. Within the exhibit, accessible design—of both the physical and virtual aspects of the exhibit—was the standard. We wrote this book to help you incorporate that standard into your own work.

4

Grassroots Efforts Support Maximum Accessibility

BUILDING COMMUNITY THROUGH TECHNOLOGY

This chapter includes examples from different local communities that illustrate how Web accessibility contributes to community development. You will find information about:

- Grassroots efforts to increase accessibility.
- E-government implications and community technology centers.
- Accessibility, community relations, and the Accessibility Internet Rally (AIR).
- The importance of community efforts for the future of the accessibility movement.

ROOTS ROCK! THE POWER OF GRASSROOTS EFFORTS

In July 1995, the U.S. Department of Commerce published a study it had conducted to examine personal computer and Internet use. Called *Falling through the Net*, the report was the first formal recognition by the federal government of the disparities in access to technology that existed for entire groups of people. This is the report that coined the phrase "digital divide." Although many people have found reason to object to that term since then, due in part to a basic misunderstanding of what it meant, there can be no doubt that the phrase served as an early "heads up" to those who care about democracy and equity as they are affected by technology.

Falling through the Net raised public awareness of access issues that educators and community leaders had long been struggling with. The report, for the first time, called attention to a serious societal challenge: If our society has in fact chosen to become an information marketplace, do we not have the responsibility to ensure that everyone has equal opportunity to participate as producers and consumers?

Communities throughout the country have been seeking ways to include the greatest numbers of citizens in the benefits of technology, including access to the Internet. As city services go online and public technology access programs are organized, people with disabilities remain the most consistently underserved. In this chapter, we will look at various communities and examine some successful ways in which they have increased awareness of the need for maximum accessibility and strengthened their communities at the same time.

GOVERNMENT SERVICES ONLINE

The development of e-government initiatives has raised the ante on accessibility. The obligation of government agencies to provide equal services to all citizens is unquestioned. Many state, county, and municipal government agencies are following the lead of the federal government in making information and services available via the Internet. Web sites that provide a high degree of interactivity are increasingly employed to offer government services and to allow citizens to fulfill civic responsibilities, including licensing, tax payments, and communication with elected officials. This is a tremendous way to encourage citizen engagement with government, and clearly it is a case in which the attainment of the highest level of accessibility cannot be compromised.

Federal mandates for accessibility, the Section 508 provisions examined in Chapter 3, have been followed by state legislative mandates and, in many cases, municipal or other local government policy statements of commitment to accessibility. Savvy commercial software developers will keep this in mind as they market their services to state and local government entities that may need a high level of accessibility compliance to be able to purchase software and implement e-government initiatives.

Accessibility Efforts by the City of San Jose and Others

Among the most progressive cities in the United States in this regard is the City of San Jose, California. The San Jose home page displays a link called "Access Instructions for Users with Disabilities." Following the link takes you to the page shown in Figure 4–1.

A few things are worth noting here. First is the clarity of the design. This site must be usable by the broadest imaginable range of users—the entire multilingual, multigenerational, multicultural, and variously abled citizenry of the region. The designers have employed a consistent navigation scheme that seems straightforward and fairly intuitive—at least to some. And therein lies another noteworthy feature. There are several different paths to the information a user may

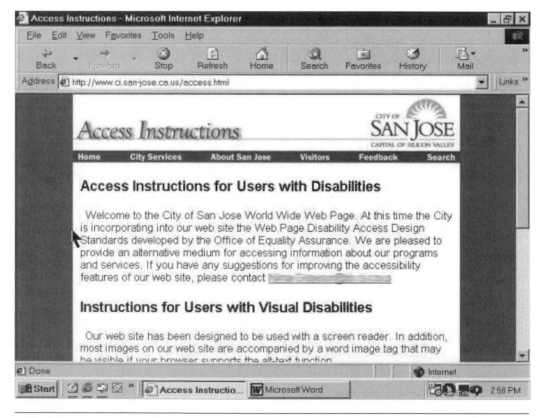

FIGURE 4–1 Screen shot of a page explaining the accessibility features of the City of San Jose Web site. Accessed January 2, 2002, at *http://www.ci.san-jose.ca.us/access.html*.

be seeking. Rather than depending on what might seem intuitive, the developers supplied various options so each user can decide how to navigate the site. Providing options is good design and is also very helpful for users who may employ assistive technology to browse. What is "intuitive" to people using assistive technology may be affected by the logic of the particular assistive devices they use. For example, someone who uses a mouse or joystick may believe it to be intuitive to point and click, but for someone who has never used a pointing device, the idea may be far from intuitive.

The accessibility options on the San Jose site are direct and clear. The page of instructions for users with disabilities, illustrated in Figure 4–1, is very helpful. The user learns what standards are being used and what considerations have been made, and—just as importantly—the page explains about unsolved access barriers. For example, when we accessed this site, the city had begun Web casting city council and other public meetings but had not yet solved the challenge of closed captioning for a live event. Not only does the disclaimer communicate the basic awareness and respect for the city's responsibility, but the public relations value of the explanation cannot be overestimated. In light of the accessibility features that *are* built into this site, we can be confident that the city is not just paying lip service, as some organizations do, but has a serious commitment to accessibility. In such a case, we are likely to accept their explanation and offer feedback.

So in that spirit, we offer this critique. There are a couple of significant improvements needed to complete the accessibility of the City of San Jose site. It would be helpful if the link to the accessibility features were higher in the listed link order than 37 among 54. But, most important, a critical feature has been left entirely out of the navigation scheme—the option to skip the navigation and proceed directly to the main content of the page. Figure 4–2 shows how this works.

Designed by a team of developers from Catapult Systems during the fourth annual Accessibility Internet Rally (more about that program follows), the site for Volunteer Legal Services includes many features that make the site as widely accessible as possible. Key among these is the Skip to Main Content link provided from an invisible image at the top of each page. Users of screen readers (or mobile browsing devices) are given the option to skip navigation elements entirely

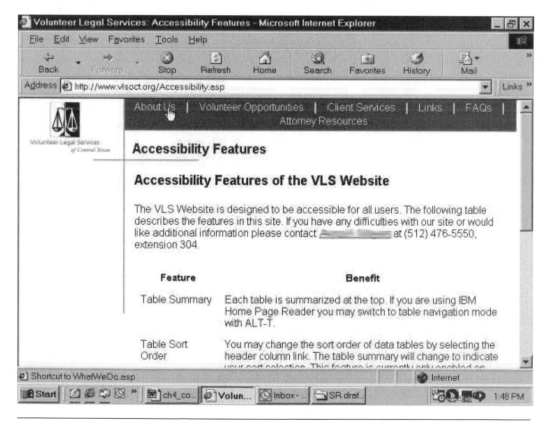

FIGURE 4–2 Screen shot of the Volunteer Legal Services Accessibility page. Accessed January 3, 2002, at *http://www.vlsoct.org/Accessibility.asp.*

and to immediately enter the main content of the page. This is an accommodation that saves untold time for the user and costs almost nothing for the developer. It somewhat approximates the ability of the sighted user to scan past content that is repetitive and of no interest. Meanwhile, people who do not use assistive devices are completely unaware that the accommodation has even been made since it is invisible.

Public Responsibility

Government agencies and other providers of public services are increasingly aware of their responsibility to provide equitable access to information and services. Efforts to ensure inclusive services may be motivated by a sense of civic responsibility and may also come from the desire to avoid legal action. The final enforcement mechanism for government accessibility mandates is, after all, the dreaded lawsuit. Despite popular myth, most people do not scour their environments looking for reasons to sue the government, the business community, or each other. Lawsuits are expensive and time consuming regardless of the outcome, and most people would just as soon avoid them. People with disabilities are no different, and as they live daily with the challenges of accommodation, they are likely to be understanding and appreciative of sincere efforts in that direction. If the solution is less than perfect, a brief explanation of status and intent goes a long way toward creating goodwill and extending the patience of the user, especially if continuous progress toward maximum accessibility is demonstrated. The two sites featured above are exemplars of attempts to achieve accessible solutions for government and nonprofit entities as they increase their online services.

Community Technology Centers

The idea of providing access to technology in community settings evolved during the late 1970s and especially in the 1980s. Educators, parents, and community organizers throughout the country sought effective ways to provide socially or economically disadvantaged individuals with access to a range of emerging technologies, including personal computers and eventually the Internet. Many of these projects were delivered within community settings, such as libraries, neighborhood recreation halls, and senior activity centers.

One of the most successful of these projects was Playing to Win, founded by Antonia Stone, a former public school teacher who started a computer technology center in the basement of a housing development in Harlem in 1983.[1] The Harlem Community Computing Center provided the neighborhood with public access to personal computers as well as basic support for learning how to use the technology. By 1990, Playing to Win was a network that included six technology access programs in Harlem, the Boston area, Washington, DC, and Pittsburgh. Through a series of grant-funded programs and strategic alliances, the group has grown into a national nonprofit organization, the Community Technology Center Network, or CTC Net, with a membership of more than 500 community technology programs nationwide. CTC Net supports affiliate organizations by providing resource materials, conference opportunities, and evaluation methodologies. In addition, there are thousands of unaffiliated community technology centers that make huge differences in the lives of people of all ages, genders, ethnicities, and races.

---

1. For more history information, see *http://www.ctcnet.org/history.html.*

The excesses of the dot-com world have been documented and endlessly analyzed. Largely unnoticed, however, is the fact that the atmosphere of inevitability that sprang up around the dot-com craze led to the perception that technology growth was all-pervasive and accelerating. This perception had implications for community technology. There came to be an increased acceptance of the need to begin to address access for those who had been left out. This led to greater government and foundation support for initiatives to bridge the digital divide. Even though the bloom has faded somewhat from the dot-com rose, we still feel the effects in terms of a growing need for improved basic skills, consistent technology training, and community commitment to ensuring technology access.

One of the basic misunderstandings of the term "digital divide" occurred because people believed it to be referring to the lack of access to hardware. This type of perception led Federal Communications Commission Chairman Michael Powell to compare the digital divide to the "Mercedes divide"—want one, can't afford one.[2] Efforts to address the digital divide may have seemed to some as not much more than a desire to put laptops in the unemployment line. But in fact it did not take long for advocates within most community development initiatives to realize that the true division in access to technology opportunities went far beyond the ability to access hardware. As computers became more available in public technology settings—such as libraries and community centers—training and outreach became a clear necessity. In some neighborhoods, computer use was seen as "women's work" because an aunt or sister used one at her job.

---

2. As quoted in Clewley [2001], Powell stated on February 6, 2001, "I think there is a Mercedes divide. I would like to have one, but I can't afford one."

Classroom technology might sit idle because teachers were not trained and could not integrate technology use into their classroom goals. Seniors and adults from low-income segments of society often had no exposure and therefore no idea of how to even begin to use computers and the Internet. If surveyed, they would simply state that they had no interest in technology.

As the results of corporate excess and hubris ripple through the economy, this is a good time to examine the enormous accomplishments achieved by groups of local nonprofit visionaries whose creative energy and dedication to equity of access to technology continue to overcome woefully inadequate financial resources. Despite decades of shoestring budgets and dependence on volunteer labor, the numbers continue to grow of people who are gaining confidence, job skills, literacy, and independence due to community technology efforts. It is our belief that the business world could learn quite a bit about maximizing resources from this effort—but that is the topic of another book.

Access to technology, delivered through various locally determined methods within community settings, has improved since the Department of Commerce issued the first *Falling through the Net* report in 1995. Subsequent follow-up reports show increased access to technology and knowledge of basic computer and Internet skills by previously disenfranchised groups. "Nonetheless," the executive summary of the 2000 study reports, "a digital divide remains or has expanded slightly in some cases, even while Internet access and computer ownership are rising rapidly for almost all groups."[3] The

---

3. From the 2000 *Falling through the Net* report, accessed May 28, 2002, at *http://www.ntia.doc.gov/ntiahome/digitaldivide/execsumfttn00.htm.*

August 2000 data show that persons with disabilities are only half as likely to have access to the Internet as those without a disability: 21.6 percent compared with 42.1 percent. And while just under 25 percent of those without a disability have never used a personal computer, close to 60 percent of those with a disability fall into that category. Within this group, people who have impaired vision and problems with manual dexterity have even lower rates of Internet access and are less likely to use a computer regularly than people with hearing and mobility impairments. This difference holds in the aggregate, as well as across age groups.

Serious barriers to access for people with disabilities remain and are central to current digital divide challenges. In February 2001, President George W. Bush announced his administration's New Freedom Initiative, in which he recognized that this nation must do more to fulfill its obligation to citizens with disabilities. He emphasized the important role that communities had to play in meeting that obligation. "The United States," he said, "is committed to community-based alternatives for individuals with disabilities and recognizes that such services advance the best interests of Americans."[4]

ADDRESSING ACCESS BARRIERS IN COMMUNITY TECHNOLOGY CENTERS

Many community technology centers—in true grassroots fashion—are cobbled together from a few hardware and software donations and the vision of local people to improve the lives of their children

---

4. As quoted in U.S. Department of Health and Human Services [2002].

and neighbors. Founded with little or no actual funding, staffed by volunteers, the large majority of community technology centers began as improvised local projects and may still contain formidable barriers to full participation for users with disabilities. Obstacles may include physical barriers, such as entryways that are difficult to navigate, inaccessible computer workstations, and rows that are too narrow for wheelchairs to pass among stations. In many cases, community technology labs are tucked away in unused corridors or storage areas of public buildings with other purposes, such as recreation halls or senior centers. The physical access needs of people with disabilities were most often not even considered as neighborhood groups scrambled for unused space in which to provide public computers and training.

Physical barriers are often compounded by the fact that assistive technology devices are seldom provided at community technology centers. In the rare cases where such devices *are* present, assistive technology services may not be marketed to the community, or the staff may not know how to support the use of assistive technology. With limited resources, community technology centers are seriously challenged to understand how to accommodate the needs of users with disabilities.

The Alliance for Technology Access

When it is successfully implemented, technology can radically change the life of someone with a disability—providing unprecedented opportunities for participation in the daily education, employment, and routine tasks that most people take for granted. The Alliance for Technology Access (ATA) is another national affiliate group that has done outstanding work. Based in San Rafael, California, the ATA pursues its mission of connecting children and adults with disabilities to technology tools through an array of services that began in 1978 with the establishment of a network of Technology Resource Centers. The Centers provide resources at no cost to children, their parents, and people of all ages with all disabilities to help them learn about assistive technology and identify the right solution for them at different stages in their development. By raising awareness and providing the tools that can lead to increased technology access for people with disabilities, the ATA improves the quality of life and supports the greater independence of millions of children and adults with disabilities.

As people with disabilities become more adept at using technology tools in general and at using technology specifically to make connections to the world that support their independence, it is critical for a democratic society to meet those needs. This must include ensuring that Internet-based information is designed to be accessible. Fortunately, the tools to achieve that are readily available. The key is to raise public awareness of the need and of the overall societal benefit. An illustration of one method that is having good results is found in Austin, Texas.

The Accessibility Internet Rally

Austin is a city that benefited from the tech boom in ways that created local disparities in income and in access to those benefits. While per capita income soared during the 1990s, low-income wages stagnated or actually decreased. The numbers of people living below the federal poverty line increased by over 11,000 in Austin in the years between 1990 and 1999, while the city was experiencing its greatest economic growth in decades [Community Action Network 2001]. There was an influx of technology workers from regions where housing costs had been much greater. The result was that it became increasingly difficult for those who were not directly participating in the tech boom to rent or buy adequate housing.

Because of these and other economic factors, a strong perception of "us and them" developed in Austin. "Us" were seen to be the poor schmucks who lived in pre-tech Austin, and "them" were seen as those tech folks who came from elsewhere to ruin "our" city. Never mind that Michael Dell was a Texas native and a student at the University of Texas (UT) at Austin when he created the little engine that became the Dell Computer Corporation—the perception was strong and it held. A look beneath the surface reveals how that perception was developed and why it has so much power.

Neighborhood schools, for example, were startling demonstrations of inequity, and the tech community was largely inactive in addressing the issue, despite the long-range repercussions for the industry. Although there were token gifts to isolated schools, the technology community failed to provide systematic leadership on how to address and minimize inequity. The nonprofit sector was suddenly expected to meet the growing needs of people who were being increasingly squeezed by economic forces. The percentage of homeless persons, of medically uninsured families and children, and of people lacking the basic resources they needed to sustain a normal life was increasing faster than the general population. Churches, homeless shelters, and soup kitchens were extending their limited resources to meet unexpected needs and not always succeeding.

Access to technology and training was seen as essential, but it was very difficult to engage the tech community in a meaningful, sustained effort to deliver that training. In short, while technology businesses were entirely remaking the community and benefiting from incentives funded by local government and UT, they were not perceived to be returning value to the community at large. The high-tech sector was perceived to be in but not of the community.

This was the situation in 1998 when a small group of people came together and made a real difference by creating bonds across the region's various sectors in unexpected ways. Fortunately for the community, there were significant exceptions to the general lack of tech-sector engagement. Steve Guengerich, the CEO of a nonprofit organization that served people with disabilities, was not your typical nonprofit CEO. Steve came from a high-tech background and had helped create a startup company that succeeded. Guengerich chose to take advantage of his good fortune in an exceptional way—he explored a number of innovative ways to contribute to his community. His tenure as a nonprofit CEO led him to wonder why it was that, in a town filled with bright, entrepreneurial, high-tech executives, none were on his organization's board of directors, nor were they significantly involved with most of the community organizations he dealt with daily. In brainstorming with staff, associates, and other community leaders about ways to engage the technology sector in community life in a more meaningful way, the Accessibility Internet Rally for Austin (AIR-Austin) was born.

Steve met with the chair of the Austin Mayor's Committee for People with Disabilities, another high-tech executive named Rachel Sartin. They invited input from organizations that served the technology needs of underserved populations and the nonprofit community and attracted the enthusiastic cooperation of some remarkable people and groups. Goodwill Industries of Central Texas, under the direction of CEO Jerry Davis, became a partner in the effort to engage the high-tech community in addressing the barriers faced by people with disabilities. Sue Beckwith, an employee of the City of Austin and the founder of Austin FreeNet, was an early supporter as well. The AIR coalition brought together the coauthors of this book. Sharron Rush was a development officer at Easter Seals Central Texas and took the lead in organizing and producing the first AIR-Austin. In canvassing the community for others who were working on technology access issues, she met Dr. John Slatin, founder of the Institute for Technology and Learning (ITAL) at UT. John provided expert guidance in Web accessibility issues and recruited Jim Allan, Web master for the Texas School for the Blind and Visually Impaired and a member of the WAI of the W3C, to help develop program standards.

The number of dedicated community leaders who were willing to contribute to improving technology access continued to grow. Sue Soy worked for the City of Austin History Center, and she and her husband Jack Jordan were instrumental in the founding of the Metropolitan Austin Interactive Network, known as MAIN. Jayne Cravens, founder of the Virtual Volunteering Project and the current director of online volunteer programs for the United Nations, was at UT during that time. She had done pioneering community technology work and was sensitive to the technology access needs of both people with disabilities and the nonprofit sector. It is impossible to overstate the importance of their spirited support.

Brainstorming sessions were built on the idea of community Web raisings held periodically by MAIN. These sessions were day-long tutorials to help nonprofit groups design and build Web sites, which were then hosted for free by MAIN. Since many of the organizers were from organizations that served people with disabilities, they knew how important it was to make accessibility the key element of Web development activities. Elements of the plan came together as Guengerich insisted that, although raising accessibility awareness was the ultimate purpose, a competitive component should be included to appeal to the high-tech mentality. A clearly defined, limited time commitment was essential, as was the inclusion of a broad spectrum of the community. The program that we envisioned would serve a diversity of missions, constituencies, and primary languages to demonstrate that community programs that meet the needs of people with disabilities also serve the greater community, often in unanticipated ways.

As the momentum grew, the community responded. Rudy Rodriquez and Jerry Ollier of Infotec donated their professional training facility to the effort. Goodwill Industries of Central Texas provided logistical and staff support each year. The Goodwill team, led first by Jamie Fraser and recently by Malcomb Gardner and Debbie Danziger, continues to be a full partner in the annual effort to produce AIR in Austin. Phill Jenkins of IBM's Accessibility Center showed up to participate in 1998 and has since become a keystone of the group, serving as a lead trainer and advisor in the activities.

After a couple of months of brainstorming, the group issued a challenge to the high-tech community: "Come join the race to accessibility! Enter the Accessibility Internet Rally for Austin and you can win awards, help your community, gain new skills, and have a great time!"

We recruited teams of three to five Web developers, usually from the same company, and asked them to make several commitments. They would attend a training session in which they would learn about accessible Web design—what it meant, why it mattered, and how to do it. We also taught them what to expect from their nonprofit partners. Teams agreed to attend a high-tech happy hour where they would meet the nonprofit group they were paired with. Finally, they made the commitment to attend the eight-hour AIR at the Infotec technology training center.

Nonprofit organizations that served a variety of missions applied for the opportunity to receive professionally designed Web sites. Representatives from these organizations were required to attend training as well, though of a slightly different type. Nonprofit executives were made aware of the fact that accessible Web sites are particularly important for mission-driven organizations. Many of those executives, such as Ana Sisnett of Austin FreeNet, understood the need and were now gratified to find the means to begin to meet the challenges faced by FreeNet clients with disabilities. Nonprofit groups learned to prepare their information for the competition, how to market a nonprofit mission via the Web, and what to expect from their teams. When we brought them together, the results amazed the community.

AIR-Austin has become a highly anticipated annual event. Convincing people to pay a fee to donate services and skills that were in such high demand was not as difficult as might be imagined. We found that many technology workers were eager to engage with the community but lacked the time and opportunity to explore their options. Even in the midst of an economic downturn, we have found that members of the high-tech sector respond generously and enthusiastically when given an opportunity that they understand, in which their time commitments are clearly defined, and in which they can use the skills and tools they value. The competitive element makes it just that much more fun.

The results of AIR went far beyond what we anticipated. An increased awareness of disability issues led many organizations and individuals to want to continue to work for improved access to technology opportunities. AIR created relationships between the technology and the nonprofit sectors that continue to develop and to return community benefits for years.

Hundreds of Web developers have now learned about Web accessibility in a context that is lively and fun and that returns social rewards as well. Most professional developers had simply never thought about accessibility before. Many of them had never considered the possibility that someone who was blind or who had other disabilities might be trying to access information online. Most of them responded with eagerness to master the techniques and to learn to incorporate them into their daily design work. Some took it even further. Encouraged by federal mandates and anticipating the changing requirements of so many Web sites, some companies developed their accessible design skills as a means to distinguish themselves from their competitors and to win business.

We recruited students with disabilities to participate as volunteers and, in cases where they had acquired the necessary level of skills, to join teams. The resulting camaraderie was invaluable, as Web professionals observed that these students were sharp, skilled, and very capable and that their disabilities were irrelevant to their ability to do good work. AIR produced unexpected longer-term results as well. Because of relationships developed during the Rally and the changing perceptions on the part of developers, we were able to subsequently place students with disabilities within some of these companies as summer interns. Without participation in Rally activities, these companies indicated they would not seriously have considered hiring students with disabilities.

The AIR program for raising public awareness of the need for accessibility on the Web has been successfully replicated by local community leaders such as Diane Musha of Productivity Point in Dallas, Texas, and Jon Carmain and Kathy Morris of CCTI in Denver, Colorado. Compumentor is making similar efforts in San Francisco, California. If you are considering this program for your community, be advised that funding the replication effort is a challenge because AIR is entirely unconventional. Although corporate and private foundations often claim they are looking for innovation, it takes an active imagination indeed to envision a grassroots, community development program that looks like a contest. The Mitsubishi Electric America Foundation (MEAF) has that imagination and has supported the Rally since 1999.

Support from MEAF Lays the Foundation

Just a word here about the exceptional vision that MEAF demonstrates. It is not a large foundation, and yet it is focused in its giving and clear about its goals. Its purpose is to empower youth with disabilities through technology. MEAF program officers offer not just funding but also connections to their national volunteer network as well as their experience in measuring results and assessing future potential. Innumerable other groups and individuals have contributed to the success of the AIR program; we invite you to visit *http:// www.knowbility.org* to learn more about them.

By 1999, the success of AIR had created a substantial group of Web professionals who had a better understanding of the issues and the opportunities of including people with disabilities in the information marketplace. Now that they were awake to the challenges, many AIR participants were ready to address them on an ongoing basis. Community leaders perceived the need for a year-round, national effort to promote and facilitate barrier-free information technology, so they founded Knowbility in February 1999. Knowbility produced all subsequent AIR activities and is responsible for bringing the program to other cities throughout the country.

Adapting AIR to Other Settings

The central concept of AIR is to train developers in the basics of accessible design and allow them to demonstrate their skills in a contest. The original model, which included nonprofit organizations as the demonstration sites, had beneficial community development results as well. The model can be easily modified, however, for different purposes. At UT Austin, for example, Dean Robert May of the Red McCombs School of Business listened to our urging to bring the benefits of AIR to the UT campus. Dean May recognized the critical importance of access in a university setting. He recognized that, as more services are delivered online, universities have a particular responsibility to lead by assuring that all services are available to all students. In 2000, Dean May led the other deans in issuing a University Challenge.

The first AIR-UT changed the model from a one-day competition to a three-month contest. College staff developers were provided with accessibility training and resources and were then given several months to incorporate accessible design into their sites. Judges made awards and provided feedback to help ensure that online university resources are accessible to students, faculty, and staff with disabilities. St. Edward's University of Austin, Texas, joined the University Challenge in 2001 after purchasing the Infotec training site. Because the tradition of hosting the AIR program annually is so strong in Austin and St. Edward's is responsive to community needs, that school is now an AIR partner as well.

In October 2000, after just two years of organizing communities around the powerful idea of information technology inclusion, the AIR program was one of two "Recognized Programs" of the prestigious Peter F. Drucker Foundation, which annually recognizes effective nonprofit innovation. AIR has been featured at the National Labor Skills Summit in Washington, DC, as a best practice and praised in a White House press release as an exceptional means to address the digital divide. This community-based effort to maximize the accessibility of the Internet has been recognized as being globally effective and important. The next challenge is to take local success and replicate it throughout the country.

WHERE DO WE GO FROM HERE? BUILDING NATIONAL CONSENSUS

In 2002, world-renowned usability expert Jakob Nielsen served as the National Chair of the AIR replication effort. In speaking about his commitment to the program, Nielsen noted:

> Regulations alone won't solve the problem. The public and Web designers need to develop awareness of the problems facing users with disabilities. The sad thing is that most of these issues, such as text size and clear pictures, are fairly simple to fix once you realize you're designing for this audience. The AIR program has been shown to be a very effective means of raising awareness at the grassroots level in a competitive context that is enjoyable and that produces good results.[5]

---

5. As quoted in Knowbility [2001]. Reprinted with permission.

AIR replication in Dallas (AIR-DFW) and Denver (Rocky Mountain AIR) in 2000 produced those good results in terms of a number of accessible Web sites for nonprofit organizations, a feeling of camaraderie and community connection, and an increased understanding of the need for access by people with disabilities. The second annual AIR programs in those cities, scheduled for October and November 2001, respectively, were postponed following the attacks on the World Trade Center and the Pentagon on September 11. Roots for AIR activities in those communities had not had time to fully set, so the uncertainty and distraction of world events disrupted organizational efforts. AIR-Austin, by contrast, had become so much a part of the community life that it was a comfort and a touchstone.

The week of the Rally is an active time. We hold a lively, music-filled "kickoff" in which we announce the pairing of nonprofit groups with development teams. In Austin, in 2001, the kickoff for the September 15 Rally was scheduled for the evening of September 11. As the day's events unfolded, we tried to determine what to do. We thought about canceling but reluctantly decided that there was no way to cancel that evening's activity unless we postponed the entire Rally, so we pushed on. We canceled the music, took a much lower-key tone and expected that not more than a few of the 150 registrants would come by.

And an utterly amazing thing happened. More than 120 people showed up, in various states of shock and grief. Every nonprofit and all but one tech team was represented. Adam Weinroth, the local Rally Chair, thanked everyone for coming. Adam spoke about the day's events and had the group observe a few minutes of silent contemplation of the tragedy and where we might be headed.

Several people remarked that they were glad they had somewhere to go and how good it was to be with people engaged in hopeful activities.

Dr. John Houghton of St. Edward's University spoke from the stage to say that on this day when we had seen the worst that humans could do, it was fitting to end it by dedicating ourselves to work that was needed in our community and to demonstrating the best that is in us. We then matched everyone up, and an aura of joyful service to the community seemed to envelop us all. Throughout the week, we continued to hear messages of gratitude for creating a forum where people felt they were actively engaged in improving their community.

It was a strong reminder of how important this effort is in creating bonds within the community, of bringing people together around an array of good causes, and of how much people want to dedicate themselves to things beyond the scope of their own interests. It was inspiring to see that sense of service demonstrated.

Once integrated into a community, the AIR model is a powerful force for building consensus. Knowbility is currently creating an AIR replication process that fosters greater local ownership and that can be customized for the needs of various communities and purposes. As we offer this experience nationally, we are looking for ways to bring communities together on many levels.

Key elements to successful replication and sustainability include

- A strong local nonprofit partner with connections to funders and the nonprofit community.
- A strong high-tech industry lead in the region, able to convincingly communicate the benefits to business and to mobilize the technology sector around the issue.
- The support of local government entities.
- An active advisory board, willing to provide advocacy and leadership.

- An effective public relations effort, able to get the word out in a clear and focused manner.
- Realistic timelines and funding goals.

In order to promote maximum accessibility as the Internet continues to evolve, there is certainly the need for state and federal mandates. The role of local, community-based initiatives is just as important to this effort, however. The September 11, 2001, attacks on New York and Washington and the effects of recession have resulted in an understandable reordering of priorities for programs that receive government and foundation support. Funding for community technology efforts has been cut, and local efforts struggle to maintain the ground they gained during the last decade. Despite the bust of the dot-com boom, the numbers of educational, employment, and consumer resources available online continue to grow. Therefore, the need for equal access has never been greater for millions of children and adults with disabilities. Increasingly, the opportunity to achieve equal access to learning, to work, and to the ability to lead an independent life requires access to basic information technologies. Although economic and world conditions have changed dramatically since 1998, this basic human need has not diminished, and it remains a challenge to our society to provide equitable access. We urge readers to support community technology efforts in your region and to advocate for the full accommodation of children and adults with disabilities within those efforts.

It is in the local communities that we can build understanding, acceptance, and ownership of the concept of accessibility. This understanding is essential to ensuring that the development of accessible technology is not confined to the narrow idea of compliance to a static standard. Rather, we must broaden our ideas of inclusion so that accessibility is a key feature in all considerations of new technology. We have the opportunity to include people with disabilities in mainstream society as consumers and producers to an unprecedented extent. E-government initiatives, community technology efforts, and grassroots development activities like AIR all contribute to our ability to succeed in realizing this opportunity.

5

User Experience: On the Bus

GETTING THERE IS HALF THE FUN

This is the second of our user experience chapters, in which we illustrate the impact of particular design features by inviting you to experience the Web along with us as we browse using assistive technology. In this chapter, we are trying to locate and understand the schedule for a specific bus route in Austin, Texas. You will see that most of the barriers we encounter have to do with the lack of table organization and labeling that could, in fact, make this a fairly straightforward and relatively easy task.

HTML Elements and Attributes Addressed in This Chapter

Elements

<pre>, <table>, <caption>, <thead>, <tbody>, <tr>, <th>, <td>, <form>, <abbr>, <acronym>

Attributes

`headers, summary`

Accessibility Checkpoints and Standards Addressed in This Chapter

Web Content Accessibility Guidelines 1.0 Checkpoints

3.0. Use markup and style sheets and do so properly.

5.1. For data tables, identify row and column headers. [Priority 1]

5.2. For data tables that have two or more logical levels of row or column headers, use markup to associate data cells and header cells. [Priority 2]

5.5. Provide summaries for tables. [Priority 3]

5.6. Provide abbreviations for header labels. [Priority 3]

11.2. Avoid deprecated features of W3C technologies. [Priority 2]

12.0. Provide context and orientation information.

12.1. Title each frame to facilitate frame identification and navigation. [Priority 1]

13.0. Provide clear navigation mechanisms.

13.4. Use navigation mechanisms in a consistent manner. [Priority 2]

Section 508 Standards, §1194.22

(g) Row and column headers shall be identified for data tables.

(h) Markup shall be used to associate data cells and header cells for data tables that have two or more logical levels of row or column headers.

(**i**) Frames shall be titled with text that facilitates frame identification and navigation.

GETTING INFORMATION
ABOUT GETTING AROUND TOWN

Millions of Americans spend huge amounts of time in their cars every day, driving to and from work, school, shopping centers, doctors' offices, and the homes of friends and relatives. Many people don't think twice about jumping in the car and driving to the store to pick up an extra quart of milk or a bottle of detergent. Some people climb into their cars when they get angry or upset and just drive around until they calm down. Our entertainers sing about riding around in their automobiles—Chuck Berry, Jan and Dean, the Beach Boys, and Lyle Lovett. Our novelists celebrate it—think of Jack Kerouac's Beat classic, *On the Road*. And then of course there are the movies—*Thelma and Louise, Scent of a Woman, Breathless*.

But there are people in the United States who don't drive—not because they don't want to, for the most part, but because they can't. Some can't drive because the nature of their disabilities is such that it makes driving impossible. Others can't drive for economic reasons. Seventy percent of people with disabilities who are willing and able to work are unemployed; over a third of Americans with disabilities have incomes below $15,000 a year.[1] The poverty that so often accompanies

---

1. Bush Administration. Executive Summary: Fulfilling America's Promise to Americans with Disabilities. Accessed May 22, 2002, at *http://www.dol.gov/_sec/ programs/ptfead/freedom_init.htm#2*.

disability prevents them from owning cars and makes it difficult for them to access the jobs that might allow them to do so.

Twenty-five million Americans with disabilities depend on public transit to get where they need to go—to schools, doctors' offices, stores, friends' houses, places of worship, job interviews, and all the other places that Americans go. The ADA mandates that public transportation be accessible to people with disabilities, and there has been considerable progress since the ADA took effect in 1992. But the situation is still a problem. According to the present Bush Administration:

> Transportation can be a particularly difficult barrier to work for Americans with disabilities. In 1997, the Director of Project Action stated that "access to transportation is often the critical factor in obtaining employment for the nation's 25 million transit dependent people with disabilities." Today the lack of adequate transportation remains a primary barrier to work for people with disabilities: one-third of people with disabilities report that inadequate transportation is a significant problem.[2]

Which brings us to the topic of this chapter. Part of the challenge of access to public transportation is access to information about public transportation, especially to information about routes and schedules.

---

2. Bush Administration. Executive Summary: Fulfilling America's Promise to Americans with Disabilities. Accessed May 22, 2002, at *http://www.dol.gov/_sec/ programs/ptfead/freedom_init.htm#2.*

Many public transportation systems publish their route and schedule information on the Web. These schedules are usually—though not always, as we'll see—in the form of HTML *data tables*. The WCAG 1.0 defines data tables as those used to "represent logical relationships among data," in this case the relationships among *times* and *locations*. Most of this chapter is concerned with specific examples of the way various public transportation systems use HTML tables to make their schedules available and suggested features that can be incorporated to improve accessibility for users with disabilities.

We'll examine schedules published by Capital Metro in Austin, Texas; by the Long Island Rail Road and New York's Metropolitan Transportation Authority; and by the Santa Clara Valley Transportation Authority in California, along with passing references to other systems. In each case, we'll be interested not just in the tables themselves but also in the larger context in which these tables are used to present information about bus routes and schedules. Ultimately, however, we're not concerned about the tables at all: we're concerned about the *quality of the rider's experience on the Web*.

Our only concern as Web developers might be to publish schedule information; by the same token, our riders may be interested in nothing more (or less) than finding out what time a specific bus will reach one specific intersection. We have to remember, though, that each rider is going to have an *experience* of some sort when she or he comes to our site. Riders will succeed in finding the information they're looking for or they'll fail. If we do our job well, most riders won't even notice what we've done—they'll merely come to the site, get what they need, and go on about their business. In this chapter, then, our aim is to think about the kinds of experiences riders might have as they try to use the bus schedules published on the Web.

THE TROUBLE WITH TABLES

The trouble with tables is that they're meant for the eye, not the ear. They also make significant cognitive demands. To understand a table, you have to be able to read in two dimensions (horizontal and vertical, x and y) simultaneously, matching up the contents of individual data cells with row and column names that often provide only slender clues about the relationships the data embody.

Web designers aiming for maximum accessibility have to understand and address these challenges. People who rely on screen readers and talking browsers—including both people who are blind or visually impaired and people with cognitive difficulties such as dyslexia—have to hold row and column headers in their minds as the screen reader reads from cell to cell across each row. As the screen reader moves down from one row to the next, it becomes harder and harder to remember those row and column headers; the table sounds more and more like a list of meaningless numbers.

People with disabilities aren't the only ones who have trouble understanding tables. Design guru Edward Tufte has spent much of his career demonstrating how hard it is to understand the visual display of quantitative information—and how devastating the consequences of poorly designed information displays can be. The explosion of the space shuttle *Challenger* in 1986 is his case in point. Tufte argues that poorly structured charts made it difficult for NASA decision makers to grasp the strong correlation between low temperature and O-ring failures like the one that caused the fatal fuel leak aboard the *Challenger*. The following examples aren't quite so dramatic, but it is worth keeping in mind that many people rely on the information presented in tables to make routine decisions that affect their day-to-day lives—looking up bus schedules, for example.

USER EXPERIENCE NARRATIVE: AUSTIN'S CAPITAL METRO

Like most other people who are legally blind, I (John) do not drive, depending instead on rides from my spouse, colleagues, and friends, as well as taxis and the city's bus system. I needed to get downtown for a meeting, so I thought I'd visit the Capital Metro Web site and look up the schedule for Route 7 Duval, which passes near my home and continues downtown past the University.

When I reached *http://www.capmetro.org* I thought I had struck paydirt. The Capital Metro site actually had a link on its Routes and Schedules page labeled Schedules for the Visually Impaired! Delighted by this evidence of a commitment to accessibility, I pressed the enter key on my keyboard to follow the link.

Dazed and Confused

I was bewildered by what happened next. The page I came to was a simple, unformatted list of all the files in the directory (folder) on the Capital Metro Web server where the schedules are stored. We're usually not meant to see these listings—they appear only when the browser points to a directory that doesn't include a file called *index.htm* or *index.html*, which most Web servers are programmed to display by default if no other filename is specified in the URL. Some servers are set up to use other default filenames (*default.asp*, for example). In any case, these occurrences are relatively rare; most directory listings are protected against unauthorized viewing.

Capital Metro's directory listing page of routes and schedules files was headed *www.capmetro.org /VIEW/_Routes/*—the name of the directory/folder that contained the schedule files, and this was what the

JAWS screen reader read to me. The rest of the page listed those files as links. The files were listed in alphabetical order, but most of the filenames began with the words *dillo* (a free trolley service for commuters and shoppers) or *route* (the Capital Metro standard bus system). The first word in the filename was followed by an underscore, a number sign (#), another underscore, and *then* the actual route number, so I had to go through quite a few filenames before I found what I was looking for. Figure 5–1 shows a screen shot of the directory list-

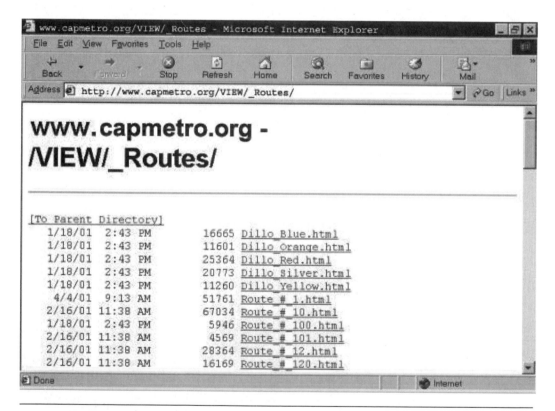

FIGURE 5–1 Screen shot of the Web page returned by following a link labeled Schedules for the Visually Impaired on the official site of Austin's Capital Metro public transit system. Accessed June 9, 2001, at *http://www.capmetro.org/VIEW/_Routes/*. Used with permission.

ing. If you look closely, you'll see that I had to scroll even farther than you might think because the filenames are not sorted in what most ordinary people would think of as alphabetical and numerical order. An ordinary person might assume that *route_#_6* would be followed immediately by *route_#_7*. But in this sorting scheme (which is conventional for computer directories), *route_#_6* is followed by *route_#_61*, then *route_#_62*, and so on.

Scrolling through the links shown on the screen, I eventually found the schedule for Route 7. I pressed the enter key to follow the link. The next thing I heard was something like this:

Route number colon 7

Route name colon 7 dash Duval 27 dash Dove Springs

Saturday

Northbound

I then heard the words "Aberdeen slash Rundberg," followed by a stream of numbers read without pause or punctuation:

Seven twenty six seven thirty seven fifty seven fifty-seven . . . and so on.

After several lines of this, I heard something I recognized as the name of an intersection, followed by another stream of numbers. As shown in Figure 5–2, the numbers were evidently times when the bus was due to cross the intersection—but there were two problems.

The first problem had to do with my own geographical orientation to Austin, where I've lived for over 20 years. What I now recognized as the first intersection listed on the page (Aberdeen Way at

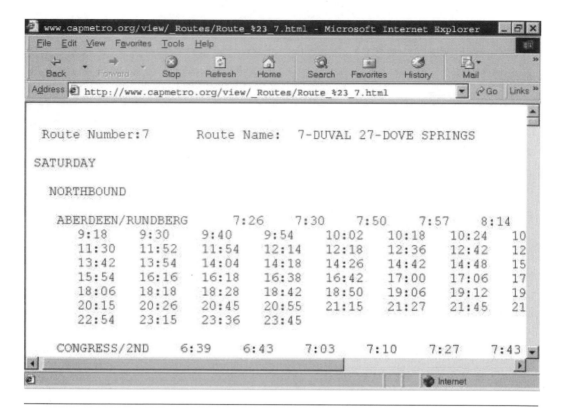

FIGURE 5–2 Screen shot of the schedule designed for visually impaired riders of Austin Capital Metro's Route 7. Accessed May 28, 2001, at *http://www.capmetro.org/view/ _Routes/Route_%23_7.html*. Used with permission.

Rundberg Lane) is in North Austin. The next intersection listed, at Second and Congress, is in downtown Austin, more than eight miles to the south of Rundberg Lane. But the schedule was for the northbound run. So I felt geographically disoriented.

The second problem was that there was no way to tell what the numbers represented, no way to use the format to identify the association of the timepoints with any intersection whatsoever. Pressing the keystroke (Alt+Ctrl+NumKeypad5) that allows JAWS users to identify the current location in a data table, together with associated column and row headers, if any, produced only the report "row zero column zero" (the coordinates for the upper-left corner of the screen). Since I was clearly *not* at that screen location, this meant that I wasn't in a table at all.

Viewing the Source: The Route 7 Schedule for People with Visual Impairments

I next decided to look at the source code for the page in order to learn why I was having so much trouble with it. The first thing I found was that instead of putting the schedule information into an HTML table, the site designers had used an old and now mostly outmoded tag, <pre>, which allowed Web developers in the early days (before 1994) to preserve layouts (including tables) that were too complex for HTML to manage at that time. The screen shot in Figure 5–3 shows part of the source code, including the <pre> tag.

Visually, the source code is actually more legible than the Web page shown in Figure 5–2. But that is hardly the point, and in any case the source code is just as difficult to understand for someone using a screen reader or talking browser.

A Deliberate Arrangement

The Web pages we've been discussing were published in a genuine effort to make information about bus routes and schedules accessible to riders who are blind and visually impaired. It's worth noting that the <pre> tag is *not* what differentiates the schedule for visually impaired passengers from the one designed for Capital Metro's sighted

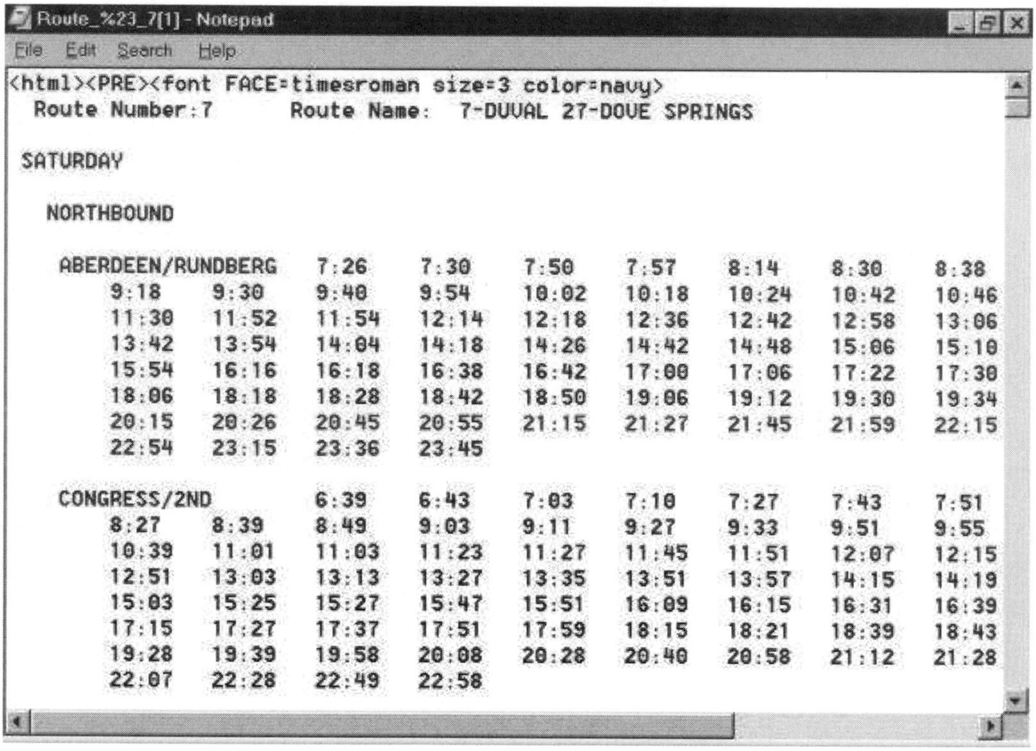

FIGURE 5–3 HTML source code for Capital Metro's Route 7. Accessed May 28, 2001, at *http://www.capmetro.org/VIEW/_Routes/Route_%23_7.html*. Used with permission.

riders; the <pre> tag was used in both situations, as you'll see later in Figure 5–6.

A Table Listing Routes and Schedules

The main link to the Current Schedules and Maps page from the Capital Metro Routes and Schedules page led to a route listing that was formatted quite differently, using an HTML table (Figure 5–4).

This table was not as easy to follow as it could have been, but it was far easier to locate the link to the schedule for Route 7 than it was

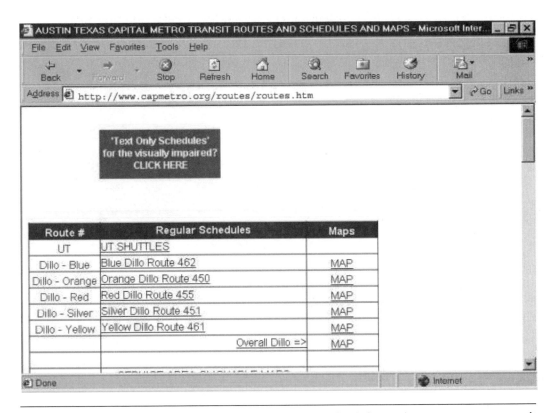

FIGURE 5–4 Screen shot of Capital Metro's Current Schedules and Maps page. Accessed June 3, 2001, at *http://www.capmetro.org/routes/routes.htm*. Used with permission.

on the page specifically intended for visually impaired riders (see Figure 5–2)—and it really was a table. The route numbers functioned as links to the page that displayed the corresponding schedule information. Therefore, people using screen readers could locate a chosen route. Using the Links List feature in JAWS, for example, allowed me to get there quickly, as shown in Figure 5–5.

So far, so good. However, the schedule attached to this link (as shown in Figure 5–6) was no harder for someone using a screen reader to manage than the one we discussed a moment ago—but it

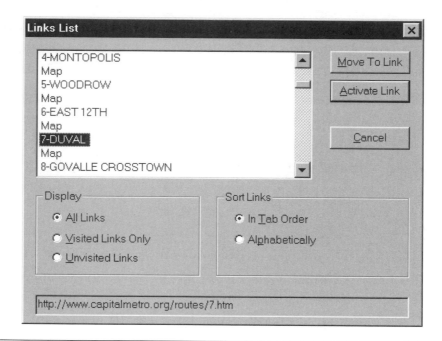

FIGURE 5–5 Screen shot of the JAWS Links List dialog, with "7-DUVAL" highlighted. Pressing the enter key activates the link to the appropriate schedule.

was actually *different* from the schedule that visually impaired riders saw or heard.

Differences Between the Current Schedule and the Schedule for Visually Impaired Riders

The schedules for sighted and visually impaired riders were different in three important ways.

1. The schedule for sighted riders displayed the weekday schedule first, whereas the schedule for visually impaired riders showed the Saturday schedule first.

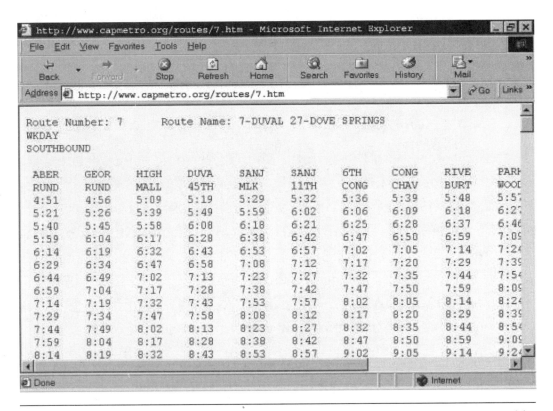

FIGURE 5–6 Screen shot of the schedule for Capital Metro's Route 7. Users access this schedule intended for sighted riders via a link from the table of current schedules and maps shown in Figure 5–4. Accessed June 3, 2001, at *http://www.capmetro.org/routes/7.htm*. Used with permission.

2. The schedule for sighted riders displayed information about the southbound route first, whereas the schedule for visually impaired riders showed the northbound route first.

3. The schedule for sighted riders appeared to list more time-points than the schedule for visually impaired riders.

These differences added up to a violation of an important principle of accessibility. The Capital Metro site did *not* provide equivalent access to the information necessary to make decisions about bus travel across the city.

We Have to Stop Meeting Like This

Our encounters with the Capital Metro site took place in late May and early June 2001. In early July, however, Capital Metro officials and Web developers met on two different occasions with us, with other representatives of Knowbility, Inc., and with a group of passengers who are blind. The meetings explored the challenges we have described and discussed a range of short- and long-term solutions. The short-term results are promising: in August 2001, Capital Metro revised both its timetables *and* their presentation on the Web site. The new version is a distinct improvement. The schedule shown in Figure 5–7 is for Route 7—the same route we examined earlier. The schedule has now been formatted as an HTML table, with the abbreviated names of intersections defined as column headers that can be recognized by assistive technologies. (We'll discuss the techniques below and explore them more thoroughly in Chapter 11, where you'll learn to create accessible tables.)

As gratifying as were the meetings with Capital Metro staff and the results they achieved, one of the purposes of this book is to make Web accessibility more widely accepted. While we sincerely appreciate the effort made by Capital Metro's staff members once they understood the issues, it should not be necessary for local advocates to meet with every public service company in order to gain access to information. More professionals are coming to understand the need, the benefits, the tools, and the techniques of accessible design, and as

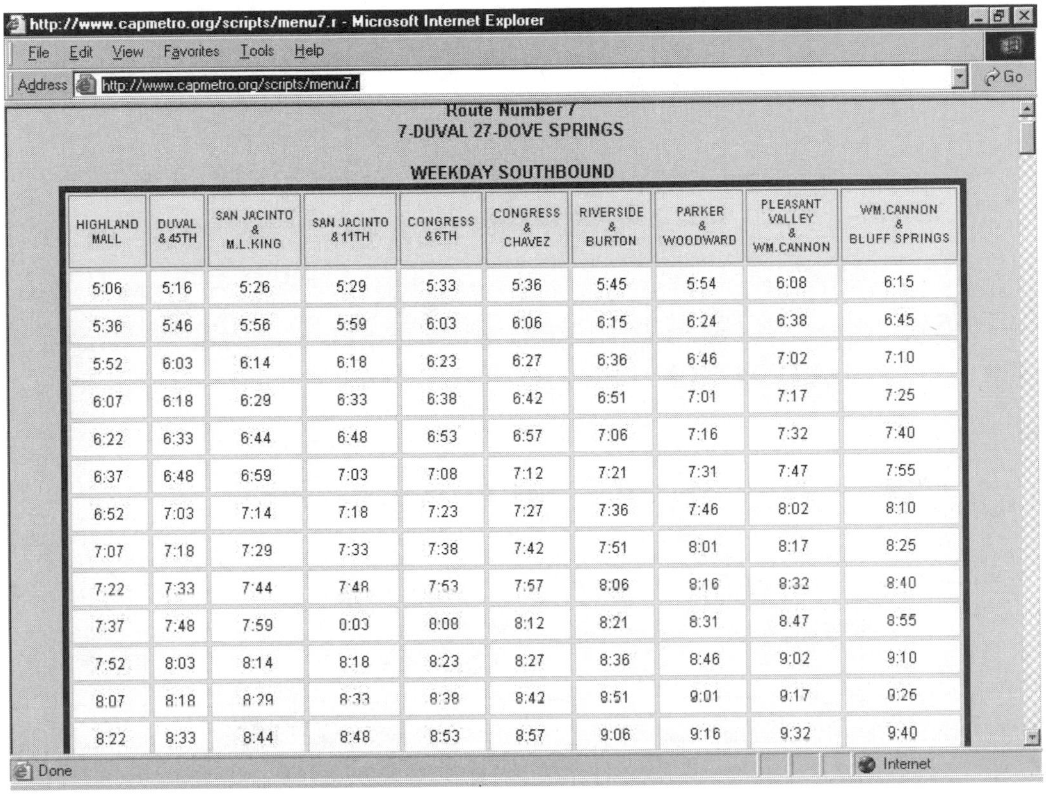

Route Number 7
7-DUVAL 27-DOVE SPRINGS

WEEKDAY SOUTHBOUND

HIGHLAND MALL	DUVAL & 45TH	SAN JACINTO & M.L.KING	SAN JACINTO & 11TH	CONGRESS & 6TH	CONGRESS & CHAVEZ	RIVERSIDE & BURTON	PARKER & WOODWARD	PLEASANT VALLEY & WM.CANNON	WM.CANNON & BLUFF SPRINGS
5:06	5:16	5:26	5:29	5:33	5:36	5:45	5:54	6:08	6:15
5:36	5:46	5:56	5:59	6:03	6:06	6:15	6:24	6:38	6:45
5:52	6:03	6:14	6:18	6:23	6:27	6:36	6:46	7:02	7:10
6:07	6:18	6:29	6:33	6:38	6:42	6:51	7:01	7:17	7:25
6:22	6:33	6:44	6:48	6:53	6:57	7:06	7:16	7:32	7:40
6:37	6:48	6:59	7:03	7:08	7:12	7:21	7:31	7:47	7:55
6:52	7:03	7:14	7:18	7:23	7:27	7:36	7:46	8:02	8:10
7:07	7:18	7:29	7:33	7:38	7:42	7:51	8:01	8:17	8:25
7:22	7:33	7:44	7:48	7:53	7:57	8:06	8:16	8:32	8:40
7:37	7:48	7:59	0:03	0:08	8:12	8:21	8:31	8:47	8:55
7:52	8:03	8:14	8:18	8:23	8:27	8:36	8:46	9:02	9:10
8:07	8:18	8:29	8:33	8:38	8:42	8:51	9:01	9:17	0:26
8:22	8:33	8:44	8:48	8:53	8:57	9:06	9:16	9:32	9:40

FIGURE 5–7 The new schedule for Capital Metro's Route 7, now formatted as an HTML table. Accessed May 22, 2002, at *http://www.capmetro.org/scripts/menu7.r.* Used with permission.

this information is more effectively shared, we can all stop meeting like this.

More improvements are expected in future updates to the Capital Metro site. Perhaps most importantly, these meetings opened up a new line of communications between the transportation system and an important customer group that will lead to continuing improvements in the way riders experience the quality of the city's public transportation system.

OTHER EXAMPLES

You'd Have to Be an Acrobat: Bus Schedules in New York City

New York City bus schedules are equally if not more problematic than the ones for Capital Metro. New York's Metropolitan Transportation Authority posts its bus schedules in Adobe's Portable Document Format (PDF), as in the screen shot shown in Figure 5–8.

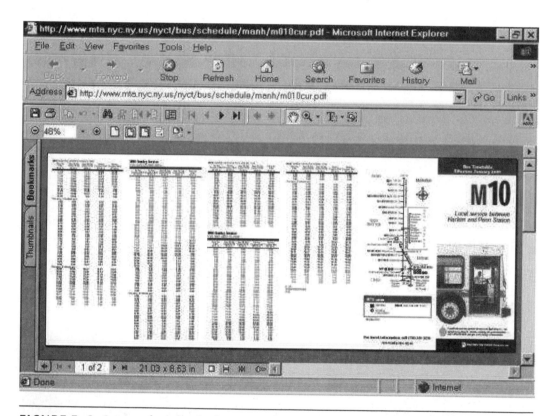

FIGURE 5–8 Screen shot displaying part of the Long Island Rail Road page for Babylon Village. The page shows part of a table listing times for selected stops on the route from Babylon Village to Penn Station in Manhattan. Accessed June 9, 2001, at *http://www.babylonvillage.com/long_island_railroad/*. Used with permission.

It's hard to believe that this schedule is any more accessible to people who can see it than it is for those who can't: the font is *tiny*, perhaps only three or four points. And even though Adobe Acrobat provides a magnification tool, a screen reader may be everyone's best bet! Even so, it would be a hard task. Used in tandem with Adobe's Acrobat 5 Reader, the JAWS screen reader is able to read some, but not all, of the information in this dense, complexly formatted schedule. For example, JAWS reads the abbreviated names of bus stops listed across the top row of the schedule, then reads the times listed on the next row, and so on. But, as with the Capital Metro schedules, it is impossible to tell what times are associated with the individual stops. Moreover, the Acrobat 5 Reader—the first version of Acrobat to work with JAWS and other assistive technologies, representing a major victory for accessibility advocates—has been available for less than a year as of this writing, and it will be some time before it's safe to assume that most people will have this version. (Usability expert Jakob Nielsen suggests that it may take as long as two years for new software versions to become widely disseminated.) We'll talk more about PDF documents and accessibility in Chapter 12.

On Board: The Long Island Rail Road Schedule

It doesn't have to be quite so hard. The Long Island Rail Road, which is also part of the New York Metropolitan Transportation Authority, does a considerably better job with the schedules for its commuter trains. The screen shot in Figure 5–9 shows a portion of the page with part of the schedule for trains from Penn Station in downtown Manhattan to Babylon Village on Long Island. This schedule shows only a few of the many stops the train makes on its homeward journey—Penn station,

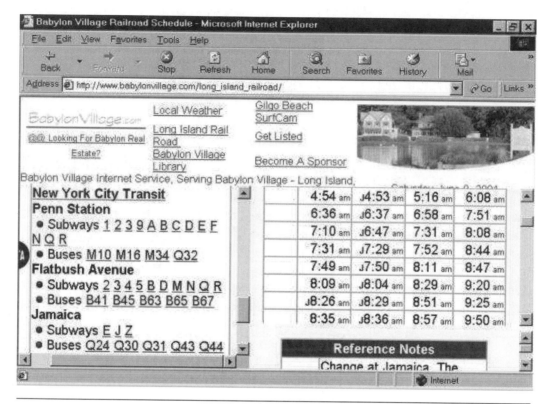

FIGURE 5–9 Screen shot displaying part of the Long Island Rail Road page for Babylon Village. The page shows part of a table listing times for selected stops on the route from Babylon Village to Penn Station in Manhattan. Accessed June 9, 2001, at *http://www.babylonvillage.com/long_island_railroad/*. Used with permission.

then Flatbush Avenue in Brooklyn, Jamaica in Queens, and lastly Babylon Village. There are links to a more complete train schedule and to the schedules for connecting bus service (including the PDF schedule we discussed in the previous section). On the same page (but not shown in this screen shot) there is another table providing links to the timetables for weekday and weekend rail service to Long Island and to New York City.

The schedule from Penn Station to Babylon Village—unlike those for Capital Metro—is formatted as an HTML table. This means that people using screen readers and talking browsers can get some basic information about this schedule. Instead of hearing just a list of stations followed by a stream of numbers, they can determine which station is associated with a specific time listed in the table. This is very important because of the extremely complex page layout, which includes several frames, one of which is borderless. As Figure 5–9 shows, the table headings actually scroll up off the screen into a borderless top frame as the passenger moves deeper into the schedule.

Even if the column headings are out of sight when the screen reader says, "Seven thirty one A M," JAWS users can press Alt+Ctrl+ NumKeypad5 to hear the following information: "Row 11. Column 4. Jamaica. Seven thirty one A M."

This is a small thing; nonetheless, it is quite helpful. This JAWS feature would be even more useful, however, if we could get directional as well as positional information—are we going *toward* Babylon Village or *away* from it?

But this is the best JAWS can do with the information that the table markup gives it to work with. The code fragment below shows the markup for the column heading Flatbush Avenue. Note the `<th>` element.

```
<th><fontsize="-1">Flatbush<br>Avenue</font></th>
```

JAWS relies on `<th>` elements like these to create a simple association between the column headings that identify train stops and the data cells (`<td>` elements) that show times. Figure 5–10 shows the HTML source code for the data cells.

The markup makes each data cell (`<td>` element) show the time for a scheduled stop in the user's default font, followed by the notation "am" or "pm" in a smaller font. But that's as far as it goes.

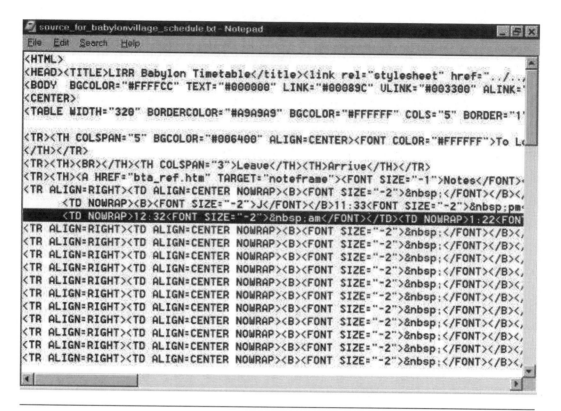

FIGURE 5–10 Source code for the Long Island Rail Road's weekday schedule of commuter trains from Penn Station to Babylon Village, Long Island. A line is highlighted to show the complex formatting of a typical data cell. Accessed June 10, 2001, at *http:// www.babylonvillage.com/long_island_railroad/*. Used with permission.

PROBLEM SOLVING: DESIGNING A NEW BUS SCHEDULE

OK. You get the point, and now you're ready to move on to a solution. What are you supposed to *do*?

This is where Web accessibility guidelines and standards come in. Throughout this book, you will find references to both Section 508 and WCAG 1.0. These guidelines and standards aren't just "rules" that you have to follow in order to avoid getting into trouble. They can offer valuable insight into some ways of addressing the problems we've been discussing, in order to make these online schedules more usable and accessible, not just for people with disabilities, but for *everyone,* without the trouble and expense of creating and maintaining two (or more) versions of the same site.

Applicable Section 508 Standards

For example, Section 508, Chapter 1194.22 (g), makes a succinct statement about tables, as follows: "(g) Row and column headers shall be identified for data tables."

This is the technique we saw in the code fragment for the Babylon Village train schedule above. But we also saw that the <th> element by itself may not be enough to help readers grasp complex schedule information. This is why paragraph (h) adds a further requirement: "Markup shall be used to associate data cells and header cells for data tables that have two or more logical levels of row or column headers."

WCAG 1.0 Checkpoints 5.1 and 5.2, upon which these standards are based, provide essentially the same requirements for marking up a table correctly.

If the developers of the Babylon Village train schedule had used the type of markup specified in paragraph (h), screen readers would be able to tell Long Island Rail Road passengers not only *where* the train would be at 7:31 but also whether it was headed for Babylon Village or Penn Station—information that is no longer *visually* available on the screen.

Screen readers and talking browsers "transform" tables into synthetic speech, and the accessibility guidelines urge us to create pages that "transform gracefully," an admonition that is, no doubt, subject to debate. But at the very least it means that it has to be possible to listen to the table and understand it, without having to strain any harder for that understanding than is absolutely necessary. At best, it ought to mean that people with disabilities are able to draw upon contextual and circumstantial information in their efforts to read the table, much as people without disabilities do; someone with a disability should not have to experience him- or herself as *making an effort* to figure out what time the bus is coming—or at least no more of an effort than someone without a disability. In Section 2, you will learn coding techniques for creating tables that allow such ease of use.

Other Applicable WCAG 1.0 Checkpoints

WCAG 1.0 goes beyond the two points mentioned above. Two other checkpoints under Guideline 5 come into play here as well. While you will learn about these in some detail in Section 2, it is worth mentioning here other attributes that can make tables much easier to use.

Checkpoint 5.5: Provide Summaries for Tables

Checkpoint 5.5 suggests providing a summary for the table itself. The `<table>` element's `summary` attribute is designed for this purpose. You might think of the `summary` attribute as an `alt` attribute for a table. It serves as a description for the entire table. The `summary` *attribute* should not be confused with the `<caption>` *element*: the `summary` attribute does not appear on the screen, but the `<caption>` element does. Since the `<caption>` element *does* appear on the screen, you can use it to identify the table and its purpose, while the `summary` attribute helps people using screen readers, talking browsers, or refreshable Braille displays understand how the table is organized. (See Chapter 11 for further discussion of table summaries and captions.)

Checkpoint 5.6: Provide Abbreviations for Headers

Checkpoint 5.6 suggests using the abbreviation element (<abbr>) to help people using screen readers and talking browsers make sense of the terse abbreviations that are sometimes imposed on designers by the visual constraints of the screen. This would clearly be very helpful for riders trying to determine which intersections the bus crosses.

Unfortunately, current browsers and screen readers do not appear to support the automatic expansion of the <abbr> and <acronym> elements. (*Expansion,* in this context, means that the screen reader or talking browser speaks the full name instead of the abbreviation.) But that doesn't mean you have to give up on this point. Designers of the bus schedules on the Santa Clara Valley Transportation Authority site, which we will examine next, used a separate table of abbreviations to identify intersections whose names are abbreviated in the schedule itself.

Checkpoint 11.2: Avoid Obsolete Features of HTML

But of course none of this would work at all on the schedule pages on the Capital Metro site (as it appeared when we visited it in June 2001). As noted earlier, these schedules are not constructed as HTML tables at all but are instead set up as preformatted text using the <pre> element, which does not support *any* of the features discussed above. This use of the <pre> element might have been appropriate prior to the introduction of the <table> element in early drafts of the HTML 2.0 specification. Use of the <pre> element on the Capital Metro site in 2001, however, would fall under WCAG 1.0 Guideline 11, and especially Checkpoint 11.2: "Avoid deprecated features of W3C technologies [including older versions of the HTML specifications]." The <pre> element would be considered a "deprecated" or obsolete feature for the purposes of presenting a bus schedule because it has been superseded by the <table> element.

Guideline 3: Distinguish Content and Structure from Presentation and Layout

In fact, the editors of WCAG 1.0 make exactly this point in explaining the recommendation (Guideline 3) that designers separate content and structure on the one hand from presentation and layout on the other. Elements like <pre> and <font> are *presentation* elements, while elements like <ol> (ordered list) and <table> identify *structural* components of the document or their place in its *logical* organization. The editors write that "using presentation markup rather than structural markup to convey structure (for example, constructing what looks like a table of data with an HTML <pre> element) makes it difficult to render a page intelligibly to other devices" such as screen readers and other assistive technologies.

Guideline 12: Provide Context and Orientation Information

Both versions of the Capital Metro bus schedule we saw in May and June 2001 (for sighted and for visually impaired riders) suffer from other problems as well. Neither page has a TITLE element, for example, so the browser window simply displays the URL, which is harder to understand than a title such as "Schedule for Route 7 Duval." This comes under WCAG 1.0 Guideline 12, "Provide context and orientation information." Checkpoint 12.1, which is roughly equivalent to

Section 508's paragraph (i), applies specifically to frames (it reads, "Title each frame to facilitate frame identification and navigation"), but it is equally important to provide accurate, meaningful titles for *all* pages on the site. The Babylon Village schedule page, for example, is clearly titled, "Babylon Village Railroad Schedule" (see Figure 5–9).

Guideline 13: Provide Clear, Consistent Navigation

WAI Guideline 13, which has no real counterpart in the Section 508 Web standards, stipulates that designers should "Provide clear navigation mechanisms," and goes on to explain that devices such as navigation bars, site maps, and orientation information are not only important for users who are blind or visually impaired but also helpful for all users. Consistency, the WAI adds, is especially vital for people who have cognitive difficulties (Checkpoint 13.4). This is one of those things that seems almost self-evident now: of course there should be navigation bars! But there are no navigation mechanisms at all, and no embedded links, on the Capital Metro schedule pages we examined earlier in this chapter (see Figures 5–2 and 5–6); riders are entirely dependent on their browser's Back button or History functions.

We can see that transportation sites are particularly challenging. Let's wrap up the chapter by looking at one site that successfully incorporates many of the features we have mentioned and one that tries an unconventional approach with limited success.

Partway Home: The Santa Clara Valley Transportation Authority

The Santa Clara Valley Transportation Authority offers riders a choice among multiple versions of its bus schedules. The site indicates that, besides the schedule that most people use, schedules are available in "ADA accessible" and PDF versions, and there is even a map in Firepad format that enables a graphic interface for the Palm Pilot! (See Figure 5–11.)

This interesting approach was somewhat compromised by the fact that the navigation bar on this and all pages on the Santa Clara Valley Transportation Authority site was coded in such a way that people using Internet Explorer and JAWS were forced to listen to a rapid-fire reading of a Javascript Routes menu in the left navigation bar that lists the numbers for every route in the transportation system—including regular buses, express buses, shuttle buses, and light

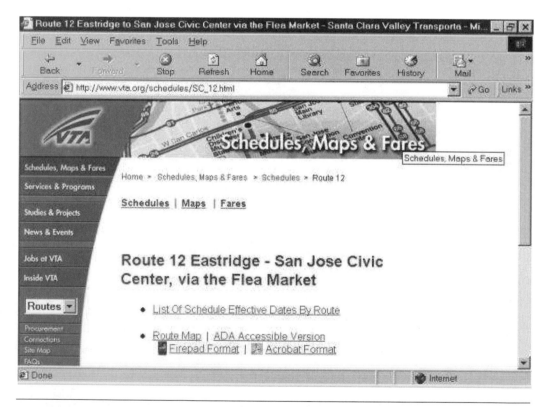

FIGURE 5–11 Screen shot of Santa Clara Valley Transportation Authority (VTA) page listing available schedules for bus route 12. Accessed June 9, 2001, at *http://www.vta.org/schedules/SC_12.html*. Used with permission.

rail!—unless they caught the Bypass Navigation link right at the beginning of the page and thought fast enough to use it. You had to miss that link only once to understand how important it was. And although the Santa Clara Valley Transportation site has now corrected the problem we've just described, you have to encounter only a few pages like this one to understand how fragile such accessibility workarounds can be. That is, Skip Navigation links are workarounds almost by definition—they're usually add-ons like wheelchair ramps attached to older buildings, not integral to the original design.

Looking at a Typical Schedule: Route 12, Eastbound, Saturdays

TABLE OF ABBREVIATIONS. The Saturday schedule for eastbound Route 12 is typical of the thoughtful way this site presents route and schedule information. The screen shot in Figure 5–12 shows a page with two tables. The first spells out the full names of the intersections whose abbreviated names are listed at the top of the schedule; this strategy compensates effectively for the lack of browser support for the <abbr> element.

THE BUS SCHEDULE. The bus schedule, which is contained in the second table, appears below the table of abbreviations. The abbreviated names of the intersections are on the top row. The next line says that "PM times are shown in bold." (These afternoon and evening times are not distinguished in any other way, however, so this important information is lost on people using screen readers and talking browsers. By contrast, the Babylon Village train schedule includes the "am" and "pm" designations as part of the schedule data.) The third line repeats

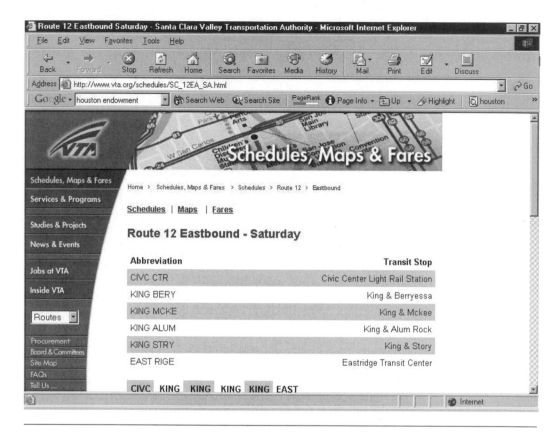

FIGURE 5–12 Screen shot of the Saturday schedule for the Santa Clara Valley Transportation Authority's eastbound Route 12. Accessed June 9, 2001, at *http://www.vta.org/schedules/SC_12EA_SA.html.* Used with permission.

the identifying information for the route. The next row is the first line of the actual schedule and shows the time when the bus will reach each intersection.

VIEWING THE SOURCE. The second table, which presents the schedule, is formatted as a complex table, using the <thead> and <tbody> elements as well as the <tr>, <th>, and <td> elements found in HTML's simple table model. This allows people using screen readers and talking browsers to stop on any timepoint and determine what intersection is associated with it. If you access this schedule with JAWS, you might get to a timepoint and find yourself unable to figure out where the bus would be at that moment. You might hear something like the following:

Ten oh two ten seventeen ten twenty four ten twenty seven ten thirty two ten forty four ten thirty two ten forty seven . . .

The designers have made it easier for sighted riders to run their eyes up and down the columns by shading every other one. Without an equivalent way for riders with visual or cognitive impairments to identify a relationship between a given number and a specific intersection, the schedule would be meaningless garbage. But there *is* a way this time, as there was not on the Capital Metro site the first time we tried to use it. The designers have used HTML features that make it possible to get auditory information about the association between a timepoint and an intersection. You can stop when JAWS says, "ten forty seven," for example, and ask JAWS to tell you where you are. It will respond, "Row 5. Column 2. King Berry. Ten thirty two. Ten forty seven."

First JAWS tells you where you are in the table—at *row 5, column 2.* Then it reads the abbreviation for the intersection: *King Berry,* which the table of abbreviations expands to *King and Berryessa.* Then JAWS reads the first timepoint on this row, *ten thirty two*—the time at which this particular bus sets out from the Civic Center—and finally repeats the timepoint where you had stopped reading through the schedule. Of course it takes far less time to do all this than to read about it here.

What we have just described appears to be the default for the way the JAWS screen reader responds to the combination of the <thead> and <tbody> elements with the more common <tr>, <th>, and <td> elements. Specifically, it reads the contents of the <th> element at the head of the current column, then the contents of the first cell (<td> or <th>) in the current row.

The screen shot in Figure 5–13 shows a portion of the source code for this table, including the <thead> element and several rows of <th> elements within the <thead> element.

LOOSE ENDS. But there's a little fly in the ointment. We went back to the page that lists all the different schedules available for this route and selected the ADA Accessible Version link. The schedule wasn't there! Instead, as shown in Figure 5–14, we got a message that said,

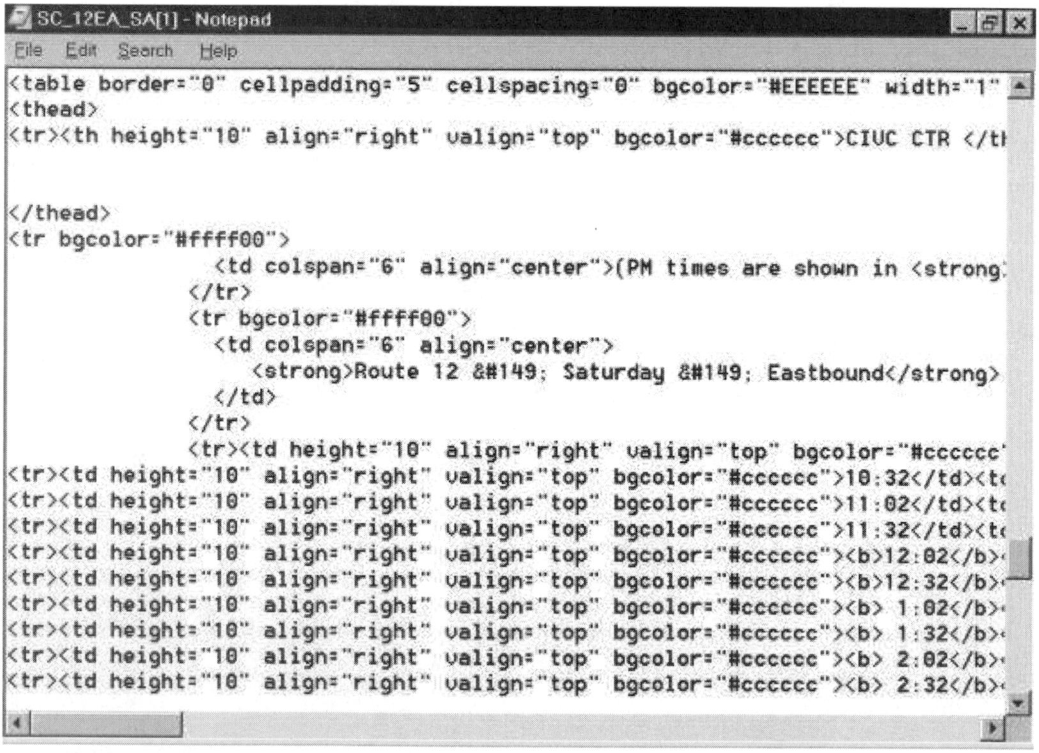

FIGURE 5–13 Source code showing the use of the <thead> element in the Route 12 bus schedule. Accessed June 9, 2001, at *http://www.vta.org/schedules/SC_12EA_SA. html*. Used with permission.

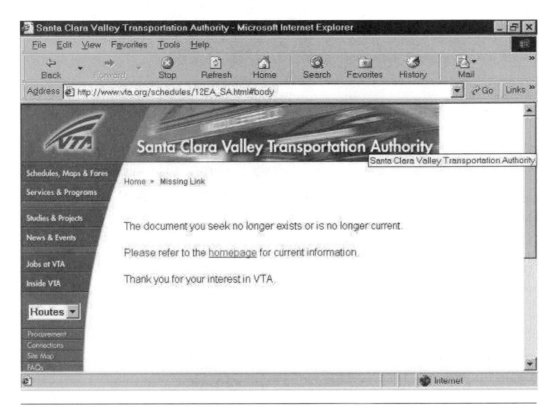

FIGURE 5–14 Screen shot of the page announcing that the ADA accessible version of the Route 12 bus schedule "no longer exists or is no longer current." Accessed June 9, 2001, at *http://www.vta.org/schedules/12EA_SA.html#body*. Used with permission.

"The document you seek no longer exists or is no longer current. Please refer to the link homepage for current information." (*Screen reader note*: JAWS automatically inserts the identifier, *link,* whenever it encounters a link. When "home page" is run together as one word, JAWS pronounces it as *hahhmipage.*)

This was very disappointing. What happened, we assumed, was that a recent redesign had made a separate, ADA accessible version redundant. We thought this was a good thing, of course—exactly the practice we advocate in this book! We assumed that someone had forgotten to update the page that listed the available schedules to reflect the change. This last step is essential: a blind person or someone with a cognitive impairment who really needed this schedule in order to plan his or her day would probably have selected the ADA accessible schedule *first* and might well have given up when he or she heard that the page no longer existed. After all, he or she would have assumed that the other schedules listed would *not* be accessible.

But our assumption was wrong. On a subsequent visit to this site, the ADA Accessible Version link led to a page that provided information in a "narrative" format: "From terminal on First—Right onto Taylor—Right onto Miller—Right onto Mission," and so forth.[3] It's extremely helpful to have this little narrative about the route. However, this is *not* actually an alternative version of the *schedule*: in order to find out the actual times when the bus should reach a given intersection, you have to return to the schedule we've been discussing. As we'll explain further in Chapter 8, this sort of problem occurs frequently as a result of well-meaning attempts to address accessibility concerns by providing multiple, variant versions of the "same" information: all too often, the information *isn't* the same, and the discrepancies can lead to confusion and frustration both for site designers doing their best to do the right thing and for people seeking information they need.

An Unusual Approach: Tri-Met Public Transportation for Portland, Oregon

The Tri-Met site, available at *http://www.tri-met.org/home.htm*, is an unconventional design that aims for compatibility with all browsers,

---

3. Accessed May 24, 2002, at *http://www.vta.org/schedules/SCA_12_DIRECT.html#*.

including text-only browsers such as Lynx. Route information includes narrative route descriptions as well as links to connecting routes. The schedule format avoids tables in favor of a simpler format that lists the names of intersections (fully spelled out) down the left-hand side of the page; the times for each intersection are listed on the line that begins with the name of the intersection. This makes it very easy to determine the schedule for any given intersection, but it is more difficult to understand the complete schedule for an individual run. However, using the site's trip-planning form may solve this problem (Figure 5–15).

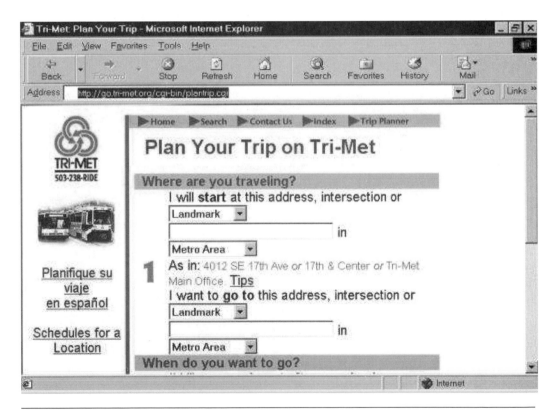

FIGURE 5–15 Screen shot of the trip planner on the Tri-Met public transportation system for Portland, Oregon. Accessed June 16, 2001, at *http://go.tri-met.org/cgi-bin/ plantrip.cgi*. Used with permission.

Unfortunately, the form's fields are not properly labeled—but that's a topic for another chapter. We'll discuss some of the challenges associated with forms in Chapter 8, and we'll show you some solutions in Chapter 10. In the next chapter, we'll explain the business case for accessibility.

6

The Business Case for Accessibility

IMPROVE ACCESS AND IMPROVE RETURN ON INVESTMENT

In this chapter, we look at the issue of Internet accessibility within the context of the business and corporate environment. We present information of value to human resources departments and company management, including the following:

- Reasons why making Web sites accessible to everyone makes good business sense.
- How to sell accessibility to clients and colleagues.
- How to test and deliver accessible online systems.
- How to create an accessibility team and plan for accessibility.
- How improving Web access for everyone affects the bottom line.

ACCESSIBILITY IS GOOD BUSINESS

The Internet has become a central business tool and, despite the excesses and recent gloomy reports from the dot-com sector, its use continues to grow. As online business models mature, smart businesses are realizing that the prosperous baby-boomer generation is aging and that, like every other generation before them, they have an increased likelihood of experiencing disability. When these numbers are added to the numbers of children born with disabilities and people who acquire a disability as the result of an injury or disease, they reflect a large and growing market. Accommodation for the needs of this substantial population is therefore a good business strategy as well as a civil rights issue. The facts are given below.

- More than one in five people experience a long-term disabling condition at some point in their lifetime [LaPlante and Carlson 1996].
- These numbers are increasing as the population ages [Desai et al. 2001].
- More than 750 million people worldwide have a disability, including more than 55 million Americans [McNeil 2001].
- In the United States, the percentage of those who are self-employed is 12 percent higher among people with disabilities [Singer 2000].
- The aggregate income in the United States of people with disabilities exceeds $1 trillion [Gingold 2001].

A market of this size is of great interest to any business. This chapter examines the growing market of computer users with disabilities and offers some insights into effective means to reach them via the Internet.

With over 750 million people in the world experiencing a disability, this is a substantial market. Figure 6–1 shows estimates of the numbers of people within different categories of disabilities in the United States. To compile this chart for AIR trainings, Phill Jenkins of the IBM Accessibility Center used statistics from the U.S. Census Bureau [McNeil 2001].

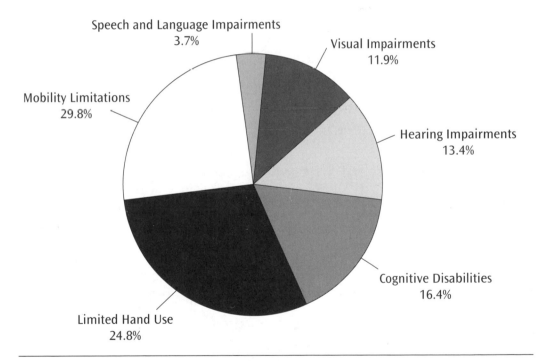

FIGURE 6–1 This pie chart depicts the following percentages of people with different types of disabilities in the United States: mobility limitations, 29.8%; limited hand use, 24.8%; cognitive disabilities, 16.4%; hearing impairments, 13.4%; visual impairments, 11.9%; speech and language impairments, 3.7%. Created by Phill Jenkins, based on statistics from the U.S. Census Bureau [McNeil 2001]. Chart used with permission.

As we learn to accommodate this significant population, we also learn that the accommodations made for this group will nearly always provide unexpected benefits to the broader population. It has become the standard since the passage of the ADA in 1990 for architects and builders to incorporate physical access into building design. Public buildings now are designed to facilitate access by people with various disabilities through halls, doorways, staircases, and elevators. Our society is now coming to understand the importance of similar access standards for public places that happen to be online. We are agreeing on standards and developing techniques that will facilitate access for a greater number of users of Web-based information, goods, and services. If you construct a building, it's easier and cheaper to put in access for people with disabilities during the initial design and construction than to add it on later. The same is true of Internet and other software accommodations.

Tools Created for One Group Can Serve Everyone

Consider some physical accommodations. The entry ramps that are now routinely provided in public buildings or the curbcuts that allow navigation on city streets are examples of accommodations that were created for people who use wheelchairs and walkers or who cannot otherwise use steps easily because of impairment. Take a moment to think about who uses these accommodations most often. Parents pushing strollers, young children, the elderly, and mail carriers pushing bins of mail use them. Bicyclists and skateboarders use them, and you can bet that the delivery driver who unloads the soda truck is very happy that curbcuts are available.

The telephone and the transistor were both the result of inventors trying to improve conditions for people with hearing impairments. Closed captioning on TV was created so that this group of people could have equivalent access to television programming. However, closed captions turn out to be very helpful for those who are learning English or who are learning to read. And by far the most common use of closed captioning is found in airports and restaurants with television displays that allow all customers to follow a television broadcast despite the noise of the crowd.

The lesson here is clear: the computer tools that you develop with accessibility in mind will ultimately serve a much broader audience. Throughout history, the need to accommodate people with disabilities has spurred technological invention. You will find that many of the suggestions we make throughout the book provide Web authors greater control over pages. Accessibility techniques often shorten download times for all users. Many accessible design practices have the additional benefit of allowing improved access by those who use wireless devices and cell phones to browse the Web.

Some designers initially think that making a Web site accessible is going to mean curbing creativity and fun in designs. Not so! These techniques absolutely do not discourage the use of any particular design element. Rather, we emphasize flexibility. We encourage you to learn to provide alternative ways to achieve the desired effect, thereby allowing greater numbers of people to have access to your work.

Making an accessible site does not limit your creativity; in fact, many Web sites that have won awards for their designs are also fully accessible. In an accessibility training that we conducted, one designer objected to the curtailment of his creativity. "No one ever told

Michelangelo what to paint," he claimed. Never mind the leap he made to equate himself with one of the world's great geniuses—clearly this developer had never heard of Pope Leo! Our trainee was therefore unaware of the fact that Michelangelo created breathtakingly imaginative and creative works under the strict oversight of the Catholic Church. Considering that, he might have taken this lesson instead: inspired achievements can be attained within defined limits. Not surprisingly, this lesson holds when it comes to Web site design.

Growing Markets

U.S. census data indicate that one in every five Americans has a disability at some point in life. Statistics also show that the tendency to experience a disability increases with age. Our society is growing proportionately older, and the chart in Figure 6–2 demonstrates that this is happening at an accelerating rate. We can easily see that the need for disability access will increase along with the numbers. As the technology evolves, we must ensure that disability access is a prime consideration in the delivery of the technology to everyone in society.

People with disabilities want the same things as anyone else in society—the opportunity to learn, to work, to contribute to society, and to earn a higher standard of living. Dr. James Caldwell, Chair of the Texas Governor's Committee on People with Disabilities, whose story we related in Chapter 3, asserts that "the current potential for using technology to level the playing field for people with disabilities is unprecedented. We must create systematic ways for communities to realize that potential" [Caldwell 1998].

The need for accessible information technology is predicated on an implicit logic of resource management. Despite the economic down-

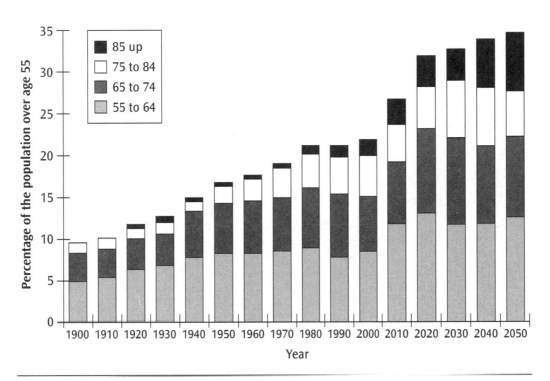

FIGURE 6–2 The bar chart pictured here was developed for AIR accessibility trainings by volunteer Phill Jenkins of the IBM Accessibility Center. It shows that the percentage of the U.S. population over 55 has increased dramatically since 1900. Based on U.S. Census data [McNeil 2001], population growth is depicted by a series of segmented bars, with a different colored segment to indicate ages 55–64, 65–74, 75–84, and 85 and over. In 1900, less than 10% of the reported census population was over 55. By 1960 the number of people in this age group had nearly doubled to 17% of the population. The percentage continued to increase throughout the 20th century. As the baby-boomer generation ages, more than 30% of the population is projected to be 55 or older by 2030. Chart used with permission.

turn in 2001, the number of people accessing online business services is increasing. While we can recognize that many Internet business models were unrealistic, the fact remains that people are eager to use the Web for educational, recreational, and employment purposes. Thousands of jobs remain unfilled, even after company layoffs, because of the lack of qualified, trained technology personnel. Since the passage of the ADA in 1990, the number of patents for assistive technology devices has exceeded 40,000. Technological devices, including many that are used to provide access to the Web, are being introduced, improved, and used at an accelerating rate. The *New York Times* estimates that the market for assistive technology devices, software solutions, and services will exceed $4.3 billion by the end of 2002.

There are sound reasons to make every effort to ensure that our high-tech workplaces as well as the public spaces on the Internet are fully accessible to people with disabilities. The value of increased public awareness will be measured by a growth in the economic independence of people with disabilities who are given access to employment and educational opportunities. These are practical reasons that will contribute to the bottom line and justify the costs involved in making them so. We have the technology to engage the skills and talents of millions of people who are eager to participate. And we must not overlook the human costs involved if we neglect this responsibility.

Accessibility as a Component of Usability

Usability is a quality of Web design that is widely studied. Usability engineering has become central to the process of virtually all commercial Web development. Coyne and Nielsen [2001a] indicated that the Web's current usability is about *three times* better for users without disabilities than it is for users with disabilities. Users with disabilities were able to complete assigned tasks less than 25 percent of the time!

A more general study of user challenges by usability guru Randolph Bias and Deborah Mayhew [1994] demonstrated that usability barriers result in lost efficiency, decreased sales, and fewer return visits for sites that contain barriers. Features that slow visitors down, confuse them, or otherwise impede their ability to accomplish their tasks actually cost a company in lost business. Here are some common findings of these and other usability studies.

- The Bias and Mayhew study showed that incorporating usability features into the design process can improve brand image, customer satisfaction, and customer retention.
- According to researcher Elizabeth Millard, "The best sites we've found are usable only 42 percent of the time, and none that we have studied are usable a majority of the time. . . ."[1]
- Studies by Forrester Research [Souza et al. 2000] estimate that sites can lose up to 50 percent of potential sales and return visitors if customers can't find merchandise or become frustrated with the process.
- A study by Zona Research [Mackenzie 2000] found that 62 percent of Web shoppers have given up looking for the item they wanted to buy online.

SELLING ACCESSIBILITY

As accessibility awareness percolates through the business community, your customers may need your help in understanding how your

---

1. Quoted in "How Can I Encourage People in My Organization to Conduct Usability Engineering and Testing?" Accessed June 12, 2002, at *http://usability.gov/basics/#encourage.*

commitment to accessible design is an advantage to them *and to their customers as well.* A discussion with a group of Web developers at the University of Texas at Austin revealed that many of them are committed to Internet accessibility, despite initial skepticism when first exposed to the idea of incorporating design techniques to accommodate the needs of users with disabilities. The reasons they cited for why they eventually bought into the idea of accessibility provide us with useful insights as we make the case for accessibility within our communities and to business and educational organizations.

In some cases, the developers had a close friend or relative with a disability or had observed someone with a disability trying to use the Internet. Several cited a workshop or accessibility training that had given them a broader perspective, such as the trainings we offer as part of the AIR activities mentioned in Chapter 4 and as continuing education classes (called Accessibility 101) on the University of Texas campus. Some developers worked for employers actively committed to inclusion, who promoted internal policies in support of that commitment.

As we will see with a later example from Prodigy Communications, mid-level management and development support is necessary for implementation purposes, but leadership from upper-level management is just as necessary so that accessibility is integrated throughout the company culture.

Phill Jenkins, Accessibility Program Manager in IBM's Accessibility Center and a member of the W3C, offers another persuasive argument. When he trains professional designers in preparation for our annual AIR, he reminds them that new, smaller, more portable wireless devices are becoming an increasingly convenient way for many people to browse the Web. For this group as well, the most useful sites are those that are most universally, and therefore most accessibly, designed.

The point is that once you understand the need for accessibility, there are several approaches that will help your colleagues and customers understand not only the need but the benefits as well. It cannot be denied that federal government mandates, developed as a result of Section 508 of the Rehabilitation Act as we discussed in Chapter 3, are also key drivers in selling accessibility. It helps to be able to tell potential customers that, in fact, this is the law. The problem with relying solely on that technique is that the law is ambiguous, it is untested, and its precise application is currently somewhat in dispute. So we recommend that, while they should certainly be part of your sales tool kit, government mandates are not the only argument for accessibility. There are clear business benefits, too, as we continue to explain below.

The Business Benefits of Accessibility

The numbers are growing of businesses and business associations that recognize the benefits of accessibility. The WAI of the W3C drafted business plans and implementation strategies for a variety of settings, including government, educational, and corporate institutions, and made those strategies available online (see Figure 6–3).

In listing the business benefits of accessible Web design, the WAI's Education and Outreach Working Group provides links to topics including market share, improved efficiency, social responsibility, legal liability, and benefits matrices. A notice that the information contained is in draft form heads the page along with an e-mail address for providing input to the working group.

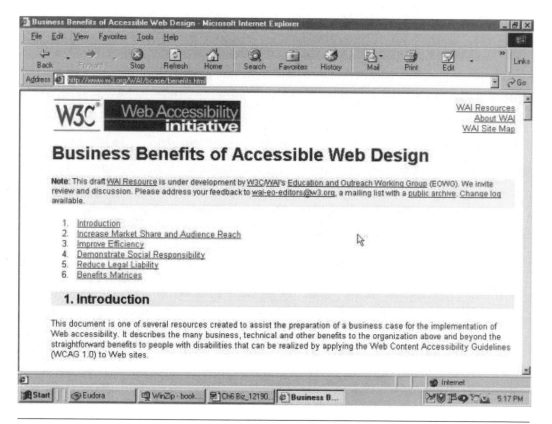

FIGURE 6–3 Screen shot from the W3C site explaining the business benefits of accessible design. Accessed January 3, 2002, at *http://www.w3c.org/WAI/bcase/benefits.html*. Used with permission.

Making the Case

There are essentially three categories of customers that require different sales approaches.

Federal Departments and Agencies

The first category includes all federal government agencies. If your potential customer is in this category, your sales task is essentially done. For such entities, accessibility is a requirement. There is no question of the need for compliance, although there may be significant confusion about how to get there. In this case, you will not have to sell the client on the idea of accessibility. Rather, you will simply need to demonstrate your understanding of the issue and your competence. For prospective clients who are other than federal government agencies, however, the issue is not so clear.

Corporations, Nonprofit Groups, and Local Government Agencies

Companies, nonprofit groups, and local government agencies who do significant business with federal agencies, or who are funded by them, comprise a second category. These potential clients have good reason to pay attention to accessibility issues. Most are aware of the mandates but confused about what they mean. In these cases, your familiarity with accessibility questions will provide your client with a source of expert guidance. An effective sales technique will incorporate your ability to deliver accessible design with little or no increase in costs to your client. The Weinschenk Consulting Group provides tools to help you measure the return on investment in usability/accessibility design practices; see *http://www.weinschenk.com/tools/roi.asp.*

For example, Navidec is a software development company that participated in the Rocky Mountain Accessibility Internet Rally. Company management quickly understood accessibility tools to be valuable new skills. Navidec redesigned its own site to be more accessible and then aggressively marketed its accessible design skills at a time when the State of Colorado was issuing local accessibility mandates. The company carved out a niche and established itself as the local accessibility expert; as a result, Navidec gained several new clients with whom its employees are working to develop long-term relationships. For clients who have government-related business or who are interested in developing vendor relationships with government agencies, the fact that the Navidec team has clear information and experience in meeting emerging requirements is a strong element that continues to set Navidec apart from other prospective Web development companies.

Other Customers

The final category is the potential client who is not aware of accessibility issues or who views them with indifference or even hostility. This is tricky, but the use of a few simple questions can often get the client to change perspective. "Would you construct your office in a way that people with disabilities could not work there?" you might ask such a client. "Would you hold a product demo or a press conference in a place that excluded entire groups of people?" In most cases, the answer is no. With this opening, you usually have the opportunity to demonstrate that the accessibility features you are advocating will only enhance the user experience for the company's customers or employees and will not limit its ability to be innovative with the delivery of its online message.

Knowbility, the nonprofit organization that grew from the AIR, maintains an online curriculum that addresses many of these issues. When trying to "sell" accessibility within your own agency, consider copying and distributing the "Why Is Accessibility on the Internet Important?" page on Knowbility's site at *http://www.knowbility.org/ curriculum/intro.html*. (We've reproduced the text in the appendix of this book.) The list offers various Internet user scenarios for consideration. It provides practical examples of how accessibility improves the experience for all users, not just a particular group. It also demonstrates that universal design neither curbs creativity nor adds significantly to the cost of building or maintaining a Web site. Finally, the list suggests that accessible design greatly increases the number of people who can become users of your client's site.

Using the statistics and logic we covered earlier in this chapter, you can convince many prospective clients of the fact that they can increase both their customer market and their potential employee pool. Here is an example of ways in which accessible design can help companies retain skilled technology workers.

Accessibility Increases Employee Productivity

Don Mauck is a computer programmer in Denver, Colorado, who is blind. He has worked for many years for a software development company as a productive and valued member of various teams. As the communications tools for his internal team moved online, they increasingly left behind the text-based information-sharing systems Don was accustomed to using. The company replaced these systems with tools that depended on nested Java scripts. There were techniques to make this system accessible, but no one in the company was aware of them. The company did not realize how this new system was curtailing Don's ability to participate with his team, and he was being inadvertently left out.

Following a half-day accessibility training, the team was much more aware of the problems. Just as important, the company now had access to a variety of excellent solutions that could satisfy the needs of all users. In a subsequent follow-up, Don told us that the classes had made

> differences on both our dot-com site and our internal site that were truly rewarding for me to see. The fact that my colleagues were able to see the issues and find immediate ways to resolve them is a testament to both their understanding about what was the right thing to do and the tools you provided to help make that happen. We are constantly making more changes and improving all of our sites [personal communication, used with permission].

Experiences like this tend to convince even the most skeptical people of the value and importance of accessible design.

DELIVERING ACCESSIBILITY

Now let's assume that you've sold the client on the fact that yours is the best team to create an accessible achievement of their online goals. What next? You must ensure that your staff has the understanding and the resources to deliver the product you promise. They must believe in it and they must know how to achieve accessibility in an efficient and stylish way that will meet your company's standard for excellence. Let's look at some methods you might use to get everyone on the same accessible page.

Catapult Systems: Building Accessibility into Your Corporate Culture

The winner of the 2000 AIR for Austin was a team of four enthusiastic designers from the consulting, design, and development company

Catapult Systems Corporation. Figure 6–4 shows the home page for this award-winning e-business firm. This dynamically generated corporate site provides clear navigation, textual information for all images, and the ability for visitors using screen readers to skip navigation and go to the main content of any page.

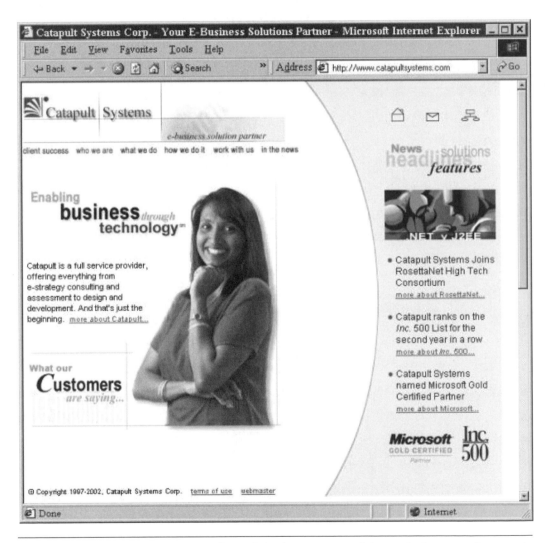

FIGURE 6–4 Figure 6–4. Screen shot of the home page of Catapult Systems. Accessed January 5, 2002, at *http://www.catapultsystems.com*. Used with permission.

For the Rally competition, the team was led by Matthew McDermott, an astute project manager who foresaw the potential for increasing his company's expertise and its ability to attract new clients based on its knowledge of accessibility. Matthew developed internal training sessions for the sales force, the project managers, and the consultants. The courses, based on the training provided to the AIR participants, extended those basic lessons to include training on how to sell and plan for accessibility and how to develop sophisticated applications that fulfill business needs while addressing the issues of accessibility. Catapult's state agency clients were introduced to emerging federal mandates and offered immediate accessibility solutions. Besides attracting new clients with its ability to deliver accessible design, Catapult also increased its contracts with existing clients. For this company, accessible design has become a core deliverable in its skill set, and this is paying off, modestly at first and increasingly as time goes by and the company's portfolio of accessible business solutions continues to grow.

Testing for Accessibility

Now that you have made the commitment and convinced your clients of the value of creating accessible online information, how will you know when you are successful? Testing for accessibility can begin in your own browser. You can turn off the graphics capability to see what information is available when images are eliminated. Specialized browsers can be helpful. Lynx is a text-only browser widely used by people with slow connections to the Internet. Opera is a browser that provides several easy-to-activate (and deactivate) options that will help you test your content under various conditions. Home Page

Reader is a speaking browser that renders text to speech. There are also a number of automated accessibility verification tools—and those numbers are growing. Some of the best work on the development of tools to aid in accessible design has been done by or in conjunction with the Trace Center at the University of Wisconsin. Trace was among the first to develop guidelines for accessible Web design. The Center for Applied Special Technology (CAST) used these guidelines when it developed its first online accessibility-testing tool, Bobby (see Figure 6–5).

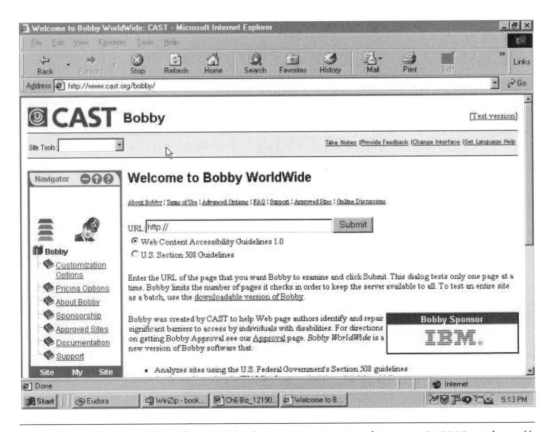

FIGURE 6–5 Screen shot of the Bobby home page. Accessed January 3, 2002, at *http://www.cast.org/bobby*. Used with permission.

Recently Trace collaborated with the University of Toronto's Adaptive Technology Resource Center to develop the A-Prompt Web accessibility-verifying tool. Let's look briefly at Bobby and A-Prompt for an idea of some available resources for testing and maintaining the accessibility of your site. We then offer some suggestions about accessibility verification in general that should help you determine how much of that task can be successfully automated. Some of that process will necessarily require human oversight, but for now, let's look at some of the most useful tools.

Bobby

The Bobby home page contains an input form for submitting a URL for accessibility testing. Links at the top of the page provide use options, and the navigation section at the left of the page provides links to more information, history, pricing, and support. The page is illustrated with the smiling face of a bobby (the familiar term for a British policeman) wearing a helmet that displays the universal wheelchair symbol for disability.

You can submit a URL for online testing of one page at a time, or you can download a stand-alone version of the tool for testing multiple pages (such as large sites), including materials that are not yet posted to the Web. With the release of version 3.3 in December 2001, Bobby can check for compliance with Section 508 federal standards as well as conformance with the WAI's Web Content Accessibility Guidelines 1.0. With this release, use of the online version is still free; the stand-alone version is now available for a nominal fee.

An important caveat: Bobby is a very ingenious product and a very useful place to begin checking your site for accessibility. Like all automated accessibility evaluation tools, however, Bobby requires a significant amount of manual checking to ensure accessibility. Fortunately, the tool produces a line-by-line analysis of the accessibility errors it detects. It refers to violations of specific checkpoints in WCAG 1.0 (the default) or the Section 508 standards. The tool also provides suggestions for how to remove inaccessible features and how to manually check items that Bobby is unsure of. If you have been wondering about the accessibility of a site you frequent, you might just run the URL through Bobby for an introduction to the barriers that the site may contain and the way Bobby presents information about them.

A-Prompt

A consideration in retrofitting existing online materials for accessibility can be the time and cost involved in doing so. When access barriers are encountered in the design of an existing site—such as missing ALT text or data tables without heading attributes—it can seem tedious and time consuming to repair the code for each occurrence of repetitive errors. In making the business case for accessible design, we now can refer developers to automated repair tools that speed the process considerably.

The A-Prompt (Accessibility Prompt) Toolkit is available for download at no cost from the A-Prompt Web site at *http://aprompt.snow.utoronto.ca/*. A joint collaboration between the Adaptive Technology Resource Centre at the University of Toronto and the Trace Center at the University of Wisconsin, A-Prompt is based on WCAG 1.0. Like Bobby, A-Prompt can be configured to check for compliance to different levels of WCAG, depending on user needs. A-Prompt version 1.05 and later can also be configured to check for compliance with Section 508 federal standards.

When it detects an accessibility barrier, A-Prompt displays a dialog box to guide the user to fix the problem. Many repetitive repair tasks, such as the addition of ALT text or the replacement of server-side image maps with client-side image maps, can be automated (see Chapter 9 for an explanation of why server-side image maps cause accessibility barriers). A-Prompt then assigns a Conformance ranking to the repaired file.

Other Automated Tools

Other automated tools and accessibility repair services are commercially available. A partial list appears below.

- AccVerify is an accessibility checker by HiSoftware.
- Lift for Dreamweaver is a product of UsableNet that helps developers accustomed to using Dreamweaver create usable and accessible content without having to learn a new software environment. Lift software is also available for a number of other applications.
- SSB Software makes a pair of automated software tools: InSight for diagnostic purposes and InFocus for repair.
- You can test accessibility features by using a speaking Web browser such as IBM's Home Page Reader or a screen reader such as JAWS.
- ZoomText is a magnifying software program that you can use to test how your site will perform for people who have low vision.

It's important to make one or more of these evaluation and repair tools available to the developers in your organization—or, if you outsource Web development, to make sure that the developers you hire have ready access to good evaluation tools. As with any other software, the tools we've discussed have different strengths and limitations, and in our work at the Institute for Technology and Learning, we've found that it's often best to use several of them in combination. (For information about other evaluation and repair tools, see Resources and Tools for Accessible Design in the appendix.)

Evaluation Tools Cannot Replace Human Judgment

It's important to bear in mind that these automated evaluation and repair tools don't and can't tell you the whole accessibility story; they're able to detect with certainty only a small fraction of the accessibility problems that might occur on your site. This means that the best way to use these automated tools is as a *supplement* to human judgment. National accessibility expert Jim Thatcher presents a very helpful analysis of how this works. On his Web site (*http:// www.jimthatcher.com/*), Thatcher goes step by step through each of Section 508's provisions for Web site accessibility. He instructs readers about what automated verification tools can reasonably be expected to accomplish and what elements require human judgment.

We agree with Thatcher that verification tools are terrific for locating such things as missing ALT text (see Chapters 5, 7, 9, and 12), form elements without labels (see Chapters 7 and 10), and data tables without properly identified row and column headers (see Chapters 2, 5, and 11). And because these tools also point out places where manual checks and user reviews are required, they can help you identify parts of the site where including users with disabilities in usability testing may be most productive. When you come right down to it, there's still no substitute for live users!

With the best automated tools and the best will in the world, you will nevertheless not be able to meet the needs of absolutely everyone under absolutely all conditions. Staying current on universal design standards and gathering information about how people experience your site will ensure that your Web site serves as many customers as possible.

Many developers who attend Knowbility trainings say they struggle with how accessible their sites should be and which audience to use as the priority. To encourage them to broaden the usability of their sites to a larger population, we often remind the developers of the huge number of older Web browsers still in use. "But newer browsers can be downloaded for free!" they exclaim. "Why are people still using the old ones?" Limited hard drive space is one reason; limited budgets are another. Many schools, libraries, and community technology centers, for example, use donated computers that have less memory and less disk space than today's computers—and slower Internet connections as well. The same is true of many home computers. It might be a good idea, then, to keep in mind this rule of thumb. Jakob Nielsen estimates that it takes approximately 18 to 24 months for new technologies to become fully distributed throughout the user population. If Nielsen's estimate holds for free software like Web browsers, the lag time for assistive technology—which is definitely *not* free and is often quite expensive—is likely to be even longer. Unless you're running a "bleeding-edge" technology business, then, where your reputation depends on using the latest and greatest, it's a good idea to avoid using techniques that require your customers to own bleeding-edge tools themselves.

But you don't have to just make assumptions and hope you get it right. You can take some proactive steps to find out what your users want and need.

Soliciting Feedback

Soliciting ongoing feedback from customers about your site and its usefulness is valuable in many ways: it can provide information that you and your developers need to improve your site—and it can build trust among your customers. A blind user that we know found that a redesign of the Merrill Lynch site made it much more difficult for him to get the information he needed on his investments. Fortunately, Merrill Lynch provided an avenue for discussion of the new design and corrected the most significant barriers after receiving his input.

A feedback form on your site or an e-mail address for customer input can provide you with valuable understanding of how people are using your pages. It helps to let people know you are open to hearing about their experiences on your site. A simple line stating that you have thought about accessibility creates a great deal of goodwill that encourages people to provide feedback and useful suggestions. Several of the accessibility checkers we discussed, including Bobby and A-Prompt, will provide you with an accessibility icon to let your users know of your commitment to accessibility. And organizations that consult on accessibility, such as Knowbility, can also provide a statement and seal to certify the process you have incorporated to ensure accessibility.

Including People with Disabilities in User Testing

Of course, if your site has serious access barriers, there may be no way to receive feedback from people with disabilities, since many users will be prevented from accessing that opportunity. It is important to include expert and novice users with disabilities as part of any usability testing you do before you launch your site. These users can provide valuable feedback about the extent of any accessibility or usability problems. Professional usability testing firms, such as Austin Usability, routinely pay representative users to perform prescribed tasks as part of their systematic usability engineering services. Ensure that any usability team you hire incorporates the experiences of *all* users as they test your site.

If you are a small organization with budget constraints, you might consider creating a test group by contacting local agencies that serve people with disabilities and asking them to help you form a volunteer group to visit your Web site and provide feedback regarding the site's accessibility and usability.

There are many online discussion groups that center on human interactions with computer technology and the Internet. Two of those that might help you get in touch with people who use assistive technologies, as well as people who design Web sites and software with users in mind, are listed below. To access either of these groups, log on to *http://groups.google.com* and enter the discussion group name. Post a URL to the newsgroup to invite feedback about members' experiences on the site you are testing.

1. **alt.comp.blind-users** is a very low-traffic discussion group via USENET for people with site impairments using Internet technologies and those studying or creating assistive technologies.
2. **comp.human-factors** is a group for the discussion of human–computer designs and interfaces. The audience is primarily Web designers and graduate students studying human–computer interface (HCI).

Can You Satisfy Everyone?

Many people who have attended our trainings have said they struggle with how accessible their site should be. For instance, solutions that overcome barriers for people who use screen magnifiers may actually create barriers for some people with cognitive disabilities. So, while you should accept the fact you won't be able to completely satisfy everyone all the time, your commitment to universal design standards and accessible design techniques will keep your Web site serving the greatest number of customers possible, including growing numbers of users of mobile browsing devices. Maximum accessibility is, in fact, the wave of a very fast arriving future. The end result will be better Web experiences—not just for people with disabilities but for everyone.

SUSTAINING ACCESSIBILITY

The dynamic nature of online services and information makes maintenance of accessibility a critical issue. Web sites that are designed to be accessible will still need updates and revisions, just as any Web site does. If your site has been built according to accessible design standards, or if your dynamic pages have been logically constructed with accessibility in mind, this will not be difficult. Probably the single most important factor is for company management to commit to accessibility up front. A policy of accessibility "from this point forward" may be chosen following review of employee and customer needs. When businesses look at thousands, then thousands more or even millions of company Web pages, they may feel that the task of retrofitting all of these for accessibility is close to impossible. We suggest creating a special interest group for accessibility with representation from key departments.

Assembling an Accessibility Team

We recommend that your team make an initial assessment of the level of awareness within the company of general accessibility issues—the need, the benefits, and the law. The team members should survey key staff to measure the overall understanding of the opportunities that technology has created for people with disabilities. The accessibility team will then be able to determine the extent to which the company is prepared to fully include people with disabilities as both producers and consumers. It is important, as you develop this working group within your company, to include human resources representatives, information technology professionals, and especially people with disabilities who are employed by the company.

The group members can then determine the means to gather information about internal company awareness of issues that can guide them as they make an information technology accessibility plan. They will probably want to make assessments about key management and staff awareness of the size of the market share of the population of people with disabilities. They should determine to what extent staff is aware of different kinds of disabilities, the impact of an aging population, and the numbers of people with disabilities who are online. Many of the other topics we have covered in this chapter, including knowledge of emerging government accessibility standards and the business benefits of creating information technology that people with disabilities can access, might be included in an initial survey. The team might also want to investigate whether the staff knows about the ways in which assistive technology levels the playing field by enabling people with disabilities to be independent and productive or about available resources for tapping into this underutilized potential work-force. The team must also include technology specialists who stay abreast of emerging technology developments and tools.

Developing a Plan

Once these assessments have been made, the accessibility team can determine what next steps would be appropriate. This may include training designed to increase awareness of identified issues of concern to the company, introduction to resources, successful hiring and re-tention practices, and/or hands-on tools and techniques for accessible Web design. This process will result in the development within your company of a working accessibility team with access to training and employment resources throughout the communities in which the company has facilities.

The team will probably develop a stated commitment and dem-onstration of Web accessibility to include in company materials, em-ployee orientation, and community outreach. As its understanding of the issues grows, the group can create an accessibility policy that clearly articulates design standards and testing procedures for future Web page development. It will be very helpful to develop a procedure that provides to anyone who experiences access barriers on preexist-ing pages an alternative for retrieving needed information. This may be as simple as a disclaimer on key pages stating that if users experi-ence accessibility problems, they can send an e-mail to a specific ad-dress or call a customer help number. Customer support staff must be given appropriate avenues to follow in this contingency in order for it to be most effective. Once again, an indication that your company is aware of the need for alternative means of accessing information creates enormous goodwill.

Let's see how these elements might work together in a product development environment. Prodigy Communications CTO Bill Kirkner and his development team created an excellent model of how company policy can create a strong foundation for accessible products. As they developed the next generation of their online user interface and customer console, for launch at the end of 2001, they followed the general procedure outlined below.

1. *Goals analysis*: Aware of the growing consensus for accessible design, the company made the commitment to accessibility at the outset and incorporated it into the overall business plan for the new products.
2. *Team consensus*: In order to ensure that the development team understood the challenges and opportunities of accessibility, all development staff—*and management*—were trained to accessibility standards. The accessibility team included representatives from all departments.
3. *Early design phase*: Integration of accessibility training and user interface specifications into the early design phase was aided by user testing.
4. *Middle design and early implementation phase*: Prodigy continued to test and improve the accessibility of the user interface and scalable back-end applications.
5. *Beta testing*: At this point, Prodigy invited us to view the developing products prior to launch and to identify any issues or accessibility concerns. We engaged in a useful dialog and, al-

though there were still some issues to be resolved, were impressed with the company's effort. We looked forward to the launch of a public portal that allowed for greater accessibility than either of us had previously encountered.

6. *Launch*: As of this writing, Prodigy has been acquired by SBC, so the fate of the accessible engine that drove this software is unknown. SBC has partnered with Yahoo! to provide portal services to its online customers, and we hope that the accessible technology pioneered by Prodigy will be included as the mergers and partnerships take shape.

Exact outcomes for your own products, of course, will be predicated on your particular circumstances and your staff, customer, and company needs. The point is to examine the opportunity and the need and to make a plan that is consistent with your own business objectives. Businesses throughout the country are realizing the benefits of including people with disabilities in their customer outreach and employee recruitment efforts.

TIME WELL SPENT

It takes time to make sure all images and image maps have meaningful text alternatives. It takes time to perform accessibility testing and respond to the results. It takes time to program your authoring tools to prompt for accessibility. But just as the removal of physical access barriers—by such means as curbcuts, ramps, and automatic door openers—makes physical space easier for everyone to navigate, so it is with electronic curbcuts. As sites are made more accessible, usability is improved for *all* users. Among the findings of usability studies are the following facts [Donahue et al. 1999].

- Each dollar spent on usability returns $10–100 in product benefit.
- It can cost as much as 100 times less to fix usability problems before launching a product rather than after launch.
- Usability improvements increase user productivity by an average of 25 percent, improve user morale, reduce documentation costs, reduce training costs, and reduce customer support costs.
- Usability engineering has demonstrated reductions in product development cost and time of 33–50 percent.

Also, Bias and Mayhew [1994] found that including usability as part of the design process can improve brand image, customer satisfaction, and customer retention.

If revenue and customer satisfaction are among your company's goals, you will agree that the time expended to create usable, accessible Web sites is well spent when you consider these facts; and as the population ages, the issue will become increasingly important. This prosperous, tech-savvy generation will eventually use assistive devices. Many already are. As this occurs, we may come to redefine accessibility as the ability for businesses to access this growing group of customers. In the next chapter we demonstrate this by discussing the growing number of cultural and science museums using the Internet to increase both the numbers of visitors to their facilities and the variety of services they offer via the Web.

7

User Experience: Museums on the Web

ACCESSING CULTURE AND HISTORY

Perhaps the central theme of accessible design is the need for text alternatives to graphic elements. In this chapter, we illustrate the importance of this provision as we examine how museums represent their enormous collections of physical artifacts and information. We address a number of accessibility issues, paying particular attention to the treatment of ALT text and other equivalent text alternatives, as we explore online collections.

HTML Elements and Attributes Addressed in This Chapter

Elements

`<img>`, `<table>`, `<area>`, `<form>`

Attributes
`alt, longdesc, width, align`

Accessibility Checkpoints and Standards Addressed in This Chapter

Web Content Accessibility Guidelines 1.0 Checkpoints

1. Provide equivalent alternatives to auditory and visual content.

1.1. Provide a text equivalent for every non-text element (e.g., via "alt", "longdesc", or in element content). This includes: images, graphical representations of text (including symbols), image map regions, animations (e.g., animated GIFs), applets and programmatic objects, ASCII art, frames, scripts, images used as list bullets, spacers, graphical buttons, sounds (played with or without user interaction), stand-alone audio files, audio tracks of video, and video. [Priority 1]

1.2. Provide redundant text links for each active region of a server-side image map. [Priority 3]

1.3. Until user agents can automatically read aloud the text equivalent of a visual track, provide an auditory description of the important information of the visual track of a multimedia presentation. [Priority 1]

1.4. For any time-based multimedia presentation (e.g., a movie or animation), synchronize equivalent alternatives (e.g., captions or auditory descriptions of the visual track) with the presentation. [Priority 1]

7.4. Until user agents provide the ability to stop the refresh, do not create periodically auto-refreshing pages. [Priority 2]

9. Design for device-independence.

9.1. Provide client-side image maps instead of server-side image maps except where the regions cannot be defined with an available geometric shape. [Priority 1]

10.1. Until user agents allow users to turn off spawned windows, do not cause pop-ups or other windows to appear and do not change the current window without informing the user. [Priority 2]

10.2. Until user agents support explicit associations between labels and form controls, for all form controls with implicitly associated labels, ensure that the label is properly positioned. [Priority 2]

10.3. Until user agents (including assistive technologies) render side-by-side text correctly, provide a linear text alternative (on the current page or some other) for all tables that lay out text in parallel, word-wrapped columns. [Priority 3]

11.4. If, after best efforts, you cannot create an accessible page, provide a link to an alternative page that uses W3C technologies, is accessible, has equivalent information (or functionality), and is updated as often as the inaccessible (original) page. [Priority 1]

12.1. Title each frame to facilitate frame identification and navigation. [Priority 1]

12.2. Describe the purpose of frames and how frames relate to each other if it is not obvious by frame titles alone. [Priority 2]

12.4. Associate labels explicitly with their controls. [Priority 2]

13.4. Use navigation mechanisms in a consistent manner. [Priority 2]

13.6. Group related links, identify the group (for user agents), and, until user agents do so, provide a way to bypass the group. [Priority 3]

Section 508 Standards, §1194.22

(**a**) A text equivalent for every non-text element shall be provided (e.g., via "alt", "longdesc", or in element content).

(**e**) Redundant text links shall be provided for each active region of a server-side image map.

(**f**) Client-side image maps shall be provided instead of server-side image maps except where the regions cannot be defined with an available geometric shape.

(**i**) Frames shall be titled with text that facilitates frame identification and navigation.

(**n**) When electronic forms are designed to be completed online, the form shall allow people using assistive technology to access the information, field elements, and functionality required for completion and submission of the form, including all directions and cues.

(**o**) A method shall be provided that permits users to skip repetitive navigation links.

MUSEUMS IN THE UNITED STATES

Museums are big business in the United States and throughout the world. Hundreds of millions of people visit them each year [Yee 2001], spending millions of dollars to see blockbuster exhibits or stroll through the permanent collections. Tourists to Europe often choose their itinerary based on a desire to visit a particular museum [Goldstein 2000]. The United States International Travel Industry reports that 20 percent of the nearly 50 million people from other countries who visited the United States in 1999 visited museums and art galleries during their stay [U.S. Department of Commerce 2000]. In the state of Pennsylvania alone, over 14 million people were reported as visiting 242 of the nation's museums in 1997 [Shockey 2000]—probably a fraction of the actual count, since another 700 museums were not included in the survey. In this chapter, we visit the Web sites of cultural and scientific museums from around the world. Our explorations particularly focus on the most visited museum in the United States—the Smithsonian Institution in Washington, DC—and on the second-most visited, the Metropolitan Museum of Art in New York City.

Museums and Accessibility, Offline

Meeting accessibility requirements has been a major challenge for many of the world's museums. Many of these museums are housed in buildings constructed decades or even centuries before anyone even dreamed of the ADA, the DDA, or other legislation aimed at ensuring physical access to buildings for people with disabilities. Renovation projects usually trigger legislative requirements that these older buildings must be retrofitted with wheelchair ramps and other accessibility features that were not part of the original design. This can be difficult under the best of circumstances, but it is especially tricky in the case of historic buildings, including historic houses, that form the majority of the 8,000 or so museums in the United States because the "historic" designation carries with it stringent requirements aimed at preserving the historic characteristics that make these buildings museums in the first place.[1] Of course museums in Europe face similar challenges when it comes to making centuries-old museum buildings accessible by contemporary standards.

Curatorial staff have also had to develop new techniques and strategies for mounting exhibitions that are accessible to a diverse audience that includes people with disabilities. The Smithsonian Institution's "Guidelines for Accessible Exhibition Design," for example, include a requirement that artifacts that are essential to understanding the core concepts and themes of an exhibition must be accessible to the touch, either directly or through the use of reproductions and models.

But that's just the beginning. Exhibition designers must also ensure that display cases are accessible to people who are short or seated in wheelchairs as well as to people who are standing. Inside the display cases themselves, designers should use color and light to make sure that the objects are fully visible. Lighting, color, and floor surfaces in the galleries must combine to delineate a clear circulation route into, through, and out of the exhibition. Text on labels and signs must contrast clearly with backgrounds, and exhibitions and information about them should be addressed to a variety of "intellectual levels" and accessible to people who do not read English and cannot see text. Audiovisual materials and interactive kiosks must include closed or open captions and audio descriptions, and kiosks and

---

1. For further information, see the American Association of Museums' Technical Information Service Resource List at *http://www.aam-us.org/infocenter/index.htm* and the United States Access Board at *http://www.access-board.gov.*

their controls must be accessible to people with and without disabilities. In some cases, full transcripts of audio materials (rather than synchronized closed captions) are required. Galleries must include places where tired visitors can stop and sit down to rest their feet and contemplate the artifacts around them; these areas too must make provision for people with disabilities. The same applies to museum auditoriums and theaters, where accessible seating must be available—not just in one part of the room (which would effectively segregate people with disabilities) but throughout the space.

Jan Majewski, author of the Smithsonian's guidelines, argues that attention to accessible design yields significant enhancements in the quality of the museum experience for *all* visitors, not just those with disabilities.[2] We couldn't agree more.

Museums and the Web

Many museums have invested heavily in Web resources, reaching out to attract visitors as well as providing information and resources for people who are unable to visit in person. As the National Museum of Australia planned its Web site, one of the key purposes cited in the action plan was to drive tourist business to the city of Canberra.[3] For many museums, Web-based outreach efforts have had a significant impact. For example, the University of California at Berkeley's Museum of Paleontology reported an average of 15 walk-in visitors per

---

2. From "Guidelines for Accessible Exhibition Design." Accessed June 9, 2002, at *http://www.si.edu/opa/accessibility/exdesign/start.htm.*

3. From the National Museum of Australia Action Plan. Accessed June 8, 2002, at *http://www.nma.gov.au/actionplan/onlineactionplan.pdf.*

day before bringing a Web site online in 1997; the Web site has attracted up to 15,000 hits in a single day—a thousandfold increase in its exposure to the public. The National Museum of American Art averaged 125,000 walk-in visitors per year; its Web site receives many times that number of visits, averaging 10,000 per day. A majority of museums responding to a 1998 survey reported that their Web sites were either "important" (52.2 percent) or "very important" (25.9 percent) to their work [McNabb 1999]. The most important reasons for maintaining a Web site, according to these respondents, were public relations (39 percent), education (27.3 percent), and an obligation to share their resources with the public (17.6 percent).

The number of visits to online museums shows a marked upward trend. Visits to the Virtual Library Museums Page increased from 57,064 in 1994 to 2,810,285 in 1998 [McNabb 1999]. The increase has been even greater since those data were compiled. For example, in December 1999, the Web site of the National Museum of Science and Industry in the United Kingdom recorded over 920,000 hits [Streten 2002]. The Houston Museum of Natural Science [2001] recorded more than 584,000 hits in 1999.

But museum Web sites are still based on inappropriate models, according to Katie Streten of the United Kingdom's National Museum of Science and Industry. The starting point for Streten's keynote address at Museums and the Web 2000, cited above, is a critique familiar to readers of Jakob Nielsen's *Designing Web Usability* [2000]. Nielsen says that designing Web sites to mirror the internal administrative structure of the company or organization is a mistake; in order to find the information they need, users first have to figure out which part of the organization might be responsible for it. Streten says that something similar is true of museum Web sites. She writes that museum sites "have been structured in much the same way as the Museum's own administrative structure," and she goes on to ask, "How can we move [toward] site structure that focuses on visitor needs rather than our own internal structure?" [Streten 2000].

Streten's answer is to practice user-centered design—to identify the needs and interests of the people who use the museum's Web resources and design to meet those needs. The AccessFirst Design concept [Slatin 2001, 2002] extends this principle. Taking the needs of people with disabilities as the starting point for design leads to aesthetically richer, more productive, and more satisfying Web experiences for *everyone,* not just for people with disabilities. It's important to remember, too, that what people with disabilities want—just like everyone else—isn't just *information*: it's a quality *experience.*

For the rest of this chapter, we invite you to come along as we survey a number of the world's most visited museums. We'll start out at the Smithsonian Institution in Washington, DC, with brief visits to the Web sites of three of its component museums. After leaving the Smithsonian, we'll quickly review several other museum sites in the United States and Europe, then conclude the chapter with an extended visit at the elegant site of the Metropolitan Museum of Art in New York City.

A WHIRLWIND TOUR OF MUSEUM WEB SITES

The Smithsonian Institution

The Smithsonian Institution is an important national asset. A vast organization, it comprises 16 separate museums and 8 research centers with combined collections totaling over 240 million artifacts—150 million in the museums themselves, the rest in associated libraries and archives. Fewer than 2 percent of the collection is on display at any one time. The federal appropriation for the Smithsonian in fiscal year 2001 was $454.9 million [Bley 2001].

The developers of the Smithsonian's Web site faced a huge challenge. They had to create a way to access a dauntingly huge and diverse collection representing the digitized holdings of multiple component museums with different missions and different types of collections. At the same time, they had to create an aesthetically and intellectually rich experience for visitors of many different backgrounds and capabilities, including scholars and casual tourists from all over the world and people of all ages and educational backgrounds.

On our first visit to the Smithsonian site in July 2001, we were disappointed to encounter a number of significant accessibility barriers. As a national museum, the Smithsonian receives significant federal funding, as mentioned above, and we assumed that the Smithsonian Web site was required to meet Section 508 accessibility standards. Our assumption was wrong, however: the Smithsonian is not bound by Section 508 because it is actually a National Trust, not an agency of the federal government. Nonetheless, we were aware that the Smithsonian had made significant efforts with regard to accessibility (including the exhibit on the disability rights movement discussed in Chapter 3 as well as the "Guidelines for Accessible Exhibition Design" cited earlier in this chapter), and we assumed that the site design would take the needs of people with disabilities into account. But our hopes were dashed pretty much right off the bat.

The site has undergone a major revision since that initial visit, but in July 2001, the home page at *http://www.si.edu* required that Flash 5 be installed on the user's computer in order to access a continually changing list of links. Flash 5 objects are inaccessible to screen readers, refreshable Braille displays, and text-only browsers, yet the information in the Flash window was not available in any other way. The Smithsonian home page as we found it on that first visit also spawned a confusing pop-up window that presented an advertisement for a current exhibit at one of the Smithsonian museums. That pop-up window included a form where visitors could "register" for the Smithsonian site; we had the mistaken impression that we would have to register in order to use the Smithsonian site from this point on—but the `<input>` elements contained within the `<form>` element had no `<label>` elements to identify them, and the form was inaccessible to people using screen readers, talking browsers, refreshable Braille displays, and text-only browsers. Finally, the page included numerous images (`<img>` elements) without the required `alt` attributes.

We found other serious problems during that first visit as we moved into the "interior" of the Smithsonian Web site. The online collections portion of the site, then available at *http://digilib.si.edu/digilib/main.asp* but taken down sometime around mid-October 2001, used a template including four frames with `name` attributes like `body` and `navbody` that had little meaning for the user. Links to information about the artifacts displayed on these pages were unintelligible, consisting only of database record numbers like the ones on the Amazon.com site discussed in Chapters 2 and 8. Onscreen text identified the artifacts, but it was difficult for someone using a screen reader to determine which label was associated with which object.

The Smithsonian Web site was redesigned in spring 2002; as a result, we cannot show you screen shots of the site as it appeared throughout 2001. The new home page at *http://www.si.edu* solves the problems we encountered on our first visit—the Flash animation and the pop-up window with its unlabeled form have been banished, and all `<img>` elements have the required `alt` attributes. But other problems remain unsolved, and new ones have been introduced. A brief discussion of selected Smithsonian Web sites will show you what we mean.

The Smithsonian's HistoryWired Site

Launched in August 2001, the Smithsonian's site, HistoryWired: A Few of Our Favorite Things (Figure 7–1), offers a promising approach to the challenge of showcasing a vast collection in a way that takes account of visitors' interests as they change over time—for example, in response to current events.

At any given time, HistoryWired offers 450 highlights from the Smithsonian's Museum of American History; the artifacts on display change as visitors express their preferences. To accomplish this, the HistoryWired site uses technology first developed by *Smart Money* magazine to help investors. *Smart Money*'s programmers adapted the technology so that people visiting HistoryWired can affect its development by expressing their preferences. The visitor can rate any artifact; the higher the rating an artifact receives, the more space the category to which it belongs is given on the site. It's a great idea!

But, as it launches, the page immediately spawns a pop-up window—just like the old Smithsonian home page. Anecdotal evidence suggests that most people find such pop-ups annoying. But pop-ups can be bewildering for users who are blind, for users who have cognitive impairments, and for many elderly users as well, and WCAG 1.0 Checkpoint 10.1 makes it a Priority 1 requirement to avoid spawning new windows without first notifying the user.

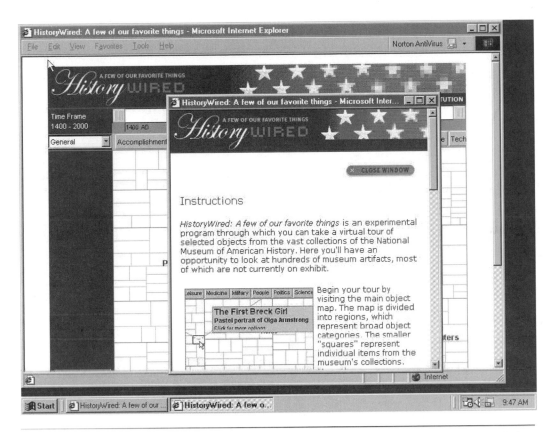

FIGURE 7–1 Screen shot of the introductory page of the HistoryWired section of the new Smithsonian Web site. Accessed June 10, 2002, at *http://historywired.si.edu/ index.html*. Used with permission.

The use of the pop-up technique is especially problematic in the case of HistoryWired because the pop-up window contains instructions on how to use the site's interactive tools, including the Java "map" that provides a visual indication of the strength of visitors' interests. This map is inaccessible to people using screen readers, talking browsers, refreshable Braille displays, and text-only browsers, so perhaps it's fitting (if a bit ironic) that the instructions for using it are presented via a technique that represents an accessibility barrier. The instructions in the pop-up window do refer to a text-only alternative to this map—but the very users who most need that alternative version will miss the instructions. Putting crucial instructions in a pop-up window is a poor design decision for many reasons, not least of which is the fact that pop-ups are usually associated with highly intrusive and unwelcome advertisements, and many people simply close them as soon as they recognize that a pop-up has appeared.

The text-only version of HistoryWired (available at *http://history wired.si.edu/text.cfm*) is used for a legitimate reason: to provide access to functionality that cannot be made accessible in any other way (WCAG 1.0 Checkpoint 11.4). The text-only version isn't really text-only, however. As shown in Figure 7–2, once you choose a topic from the text-only index page and proceed, the pages display images of highlighted artifacts.

We wanted to learn about the ENIAC computer, the machine that launched contemporary digital computing. We were distressed to discover that neither the image of the ENIAC nor the related image has ALT text. (JAWS reports the larger of these two images as "link graphic objects/342a." It reports the other image as "thumbs/342a," which might lead users to the mistaken belief that it is a thumbnail version of the larger image. In fact it is a small picture of ENIAC's principal designer, J. Presper Eckert.)

We might have liked to see more artifacts like this one, but we had trouble expressing our preferences. The page includes a `<form>` element where, as explained on the screen, visitors can "vote" on whether they'd like to see "More" or "Fewer" objects like this one. Visitors then use radio buttons to indicate how strong their preferences are on a scale from 1 to 10. However, there are two problems.

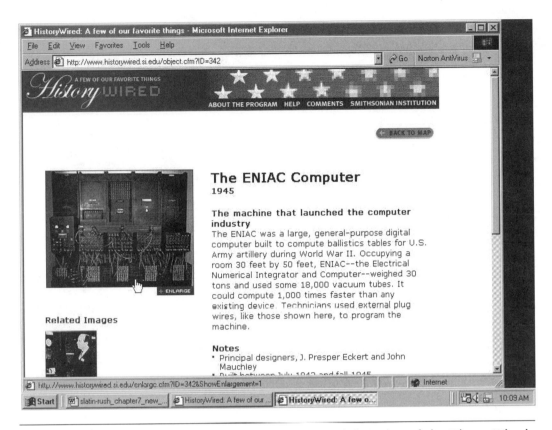

FIGURE 7–2 Screen shot of a page from the "text-only" version of the HistoryWired site. Accessed June 10, 2002, at *http://www.historywired.si.edu/object.cfm?ID=342*. Used with permission.

1. The radio buttons are not associated with the instructions visible on the screen; JAWS reports only the radio button's label and status.

2. JAWS reports only one option, "Fewer," and reports it multiple times as you press the up or down arrow key. As a result, it's impossible to know what you're voting for or what rating you're assigning to it.

Chapter 10 provides information about how to make forms accessible. We will find, as we explore some other museum sites, that inaccessible forms are but one of many barriers encountered by seekers of scientific and cultural information who have disabilities or who use assistive devices to browse the Internet.

The Smithsonian's National Air and Space Museum Site

The National Air and Space Museum site at *http://www.nasm.si.edu/* includes a link (the first on the page) called "text v". This link goes to a so-called "text-only" version of the site at *http://www.nasm.si.edu/ NASMhome_t.html* (which in turn has a link to something called "icon version"). The "text-only" version of the site includes a graphical logo that *apparently* has no ALT text: JAWS reports it as "graphic NASMicon_60.jpg (12271 bytes)." When we checked the source code, however, we found that there was an `alt` attribute for this image after all—but instead of saying something like "National Air and Space Museum logo" or "Home," it repeated the name of the image file. (See Chapter 9 for information about writing effective ALT text and other text equivalents.)

As inappropriate as this ALT text is, however—and it's surely just a mistake overlooked in the haste to bring the site online—it's not the most important issue here. More important is the fact that it isn't really clear why a text-only version is necessary: according to WCAG 1.0 Checkpoint 11.4, such text-only variants are appropriate only for individual *pages* that cannot be made accessible by other means—not for entire sites. We'll discuss the reasons for this in detail in Chapter 8. For now, we'll simply point out that the "Non-JavaScript Tour" of the exhibit "Apollo to the Moon" pictured in Figure 7–3—perhaps provided to enhance accessibility—includes numerous graphical links

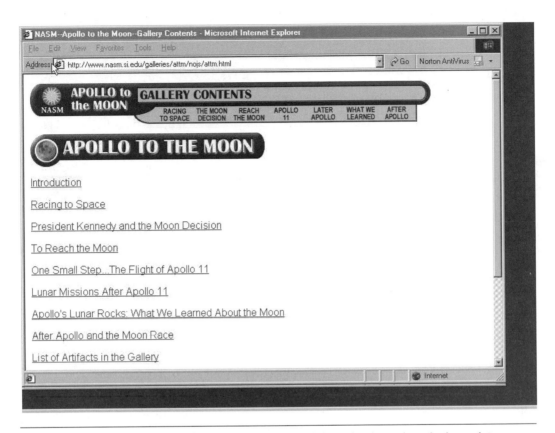

FIGURE 7–3 Screen shot of a page from the Smithsonian's National Air and Space Museum site. The images contain no ALT text. Accessed on June 10, 2002, at *http://www.nasm.si.edu/galleries/attm/nojs/attm.html* in an attempt to take a "Non-JavaScript Tour." Used with permission.

that do not have `alt` attributes. On June 10, 2002, the Bobby accessibility evaluator (see Chapter 6) reported 23 images without `alt` attributes on this page alone.

The Smithsonian's Hirshhorn Museum Site

There is a fascinating section called Art Interactive on the Hirshhorn Museum Web site. Located in Washington, DC, the Hirshhorn is an outstanding museum devoted to twentieth-century art; it is also one of the Smithsonian museums. Visitors can use the Art Interactive section to explore different types of art and learn about the materials artists have used and how the works are created—at least some visitors can do so. But a visitor with a visual impairment who wants to learn about assemblages and found art (such as collages or sculptures made from discarded objects in which the artist recognized interesting possibilities) may be frustrated.

Following the Assemblage/Found Object link takes us to a page that contains content about the subject we chose but that, according to JAWS, is confusingly mistitled "Animals in Art" (Figure 7–4). As we access the content, we realize that we have indeed come to the page we intended, but the title read by JAWS has nothing whatever to do with that content. The page is dominated by a large image of a work by a French artist, Jean Dubuffet (1901–1985). The work is called "The Soul of Morvan"; according to the text on the page, it features grape wood and vines as well as rope, tar, and metal. The text goes on to explain that the artist "used grapevines from the wine-growing region of Morvan, France, to evoke a weatherworn man laboring in a vineyard. By leaving the materials in a rough, earthy state, Dubuffet made the sculpture even more expressive." While this text is useful, even evocative for people who know what grapevines look or feel like, it would be difficult for someone who cannot see the image on the screen to understand how grape wood, vines, rope, tar, and metal come together to create the image of a man—and even more difficult to understand what any of this has to do with the topic Animals in Art.

The Hirshhorn site also includes a page titled Accessibility (at *http://hirshhorn.si.edu/visit/accessibility.html*). The page describes the

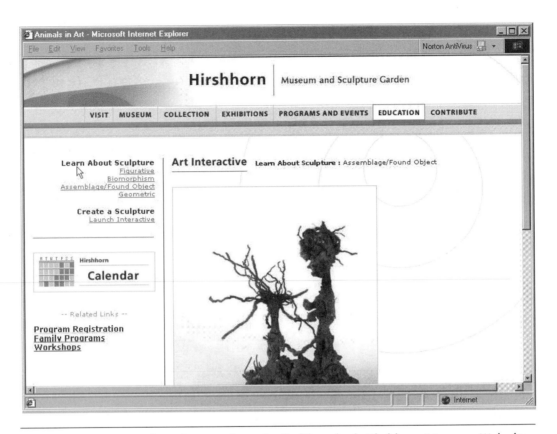

FIGURE 7–4 Screen shot of a page from the Smithsonian's Hirshhorn Museum Web site. Accessed June 10, 2002, at *http://hirshhorn.si.edu/education/interactive/assemblage.html*.

location of parking spaces, restrooms, and other facilities that meet the physical needs of people with disabilities. But there is no reference at all to the accessibility of the Web site itself, and there are several untagged graphical links on the page; there is also a link called, weirdly, Void (0), which actually appears on all pages that we visited on the Hirshhorn site (appropriately enough, the Void link does not seem to work). Like all the other pages we visited on Smithsonian Web sites, the Hirshhorn's Accessibility page has no way to bypass repeated navigation links, as WCAG 1.0 Checkpoint 13.6 recommends. Consequently, people using screen readers, talking browsers, and refreshable Braille displays must plow through all the navigation links before reaching the substance of the page.

World Museums on the Web

Museums around the world face the same challenge as the Smithsonian: they have to find ways to represent their collections and make them available to users from diverse backgrounds and with a wide range of knowledge and skills. Many museum Web sites use graphical links as an interface to various parts of their collections. In many cases, the image of a typical artifact from the collection serves as a link to information about the history and extent of the collection, as well as digitized highlights; in some cases (such as London's Tate Gallery), the entire collection is available online. This can be an effective strategy, but it can also present accessibility barriers. Although both WCAG Checkpoint 1.1 and Section 508 paragraph (a) require text alternatives for images and other non-text elements, this basic requirement is overlooked on many museum sites.

On the Collections page of the Musée du Louvre in Paris (*http://www.louvre.fr/*), for example, a picture of the Venus de Milo is used as a link to a page that provides an overview of the collection of Greek and Roman antiquities and links to more detailed historical information and images. Someone who uses a screen reader, talking browser, refreshable Braille display, or text-only display when visiting the Louvre site has no way of knowing that this option is available, however. When the screen reader encounters the images on the Collections page, it announces that we are reading a table with eight columns and six rows that contains links such as "ao/ao_f," "ae/ae_f," "ager/ager_f," "sculp/scu_f," "oa/oa_f," "peint/peint_f," "ag/ag_f," "palais/pal_f," and "aaoa/aaoa_f." Which of these would you follow to learn more about Venus if by some chance someone had informed you to use the graphic image of that famous statue to get to the antiquities? The correct choice would be "ager/ageréf," an abbreviation for "Les antiquités grecques, étrusques, et romaines" (Greek, Etruscan, and Roman antiquities)—but how could you know? The words "Antiquités grecques, étrusques, et romaines" are right there on the screen—but if you use a screen reader you'll never hear them, because they're actually part of the image that includes the Venus; from a technical standpoint, they're not text at all but are instead part of the graphic. (See Chapter 9 for more about the distinction between text and images of text.) It would be easy for the Louvre's Web team to solve this problem by adding an alt attribute for each <img> element in this graphical menu; in this case, the ALT text might read "Les antiquités grecques, étrusques, et romaines"—exactly the words that appear on the screen.

We ran into similar problems on the home page of the new Guggenheim Museum in Bilbao, Spain. The link to the Bilbao site on the Guggenheim's home page at *http://www.guggenheim.org* opens in a new browser window without notifying the user (WCAG 1.0 Checkpoint 10.1 warns against this). The visually elegant Bilbao site contains only four graphical links, none of which has a text alternative as required by WCAG 1.0 Checkpoint 1.1: JAWS identifies them only as "link graphic idioma 1," "link graphic idioma 2," "link graphic idioma 3," and "link graphic idioma 4."[4]

---

4. Accessed June 10, 2002, at *http://www.guggenheim-bilbao.es/idioma.htm*.

Back in the United States, the Houston Museum of Natural Science Web site (*http://www.hmns.org*) contains a mix of textual and graphical links. Sighted users see a menu of textual links on the left side of the screen; these lead to information about events and programs at the museum, ticket purchases, camps, museum membership, and so on. Sighted users also see a number of prominent graphical links. On this site, both types of links present accessibility problems. The link text displayed on the screen is tiny—and it's not easy to enlarge because the font size is "hard-coded" to 8 points by the attached Cascading Style Sheet (CSS), which makes it impossible for people using some graphical browsers to increase or decrease font sizes to meet their needs (violating WCAG Checkpoint 3.4; see Chapter 15 for a discussion of style sheets). But people using screen readers, talking browsers, or refreshable Braille displays may not get that far anyway: before they have the opportunity to read the text links, they have to sit through a list of 14 graphical links attached to <img> elements. Those graphical links should be associated with ALT text that says exactly what sighted users see on the screen. The ALT text is missing, however, so the screen reader announces, "link graphic c3a," "link graphic c4a," "link graphic c5a," "link graphic c6a," and so forth, all the way to "link graphic c16a." In the absence of ALT text for the graphical links, users without visual access have no way of knowing whether the text links are redundant or not; these users are excluded from important navigation options available to people who can navigate visually.

The Web site for the Boston Museum of Fine Arts (*http://www.mfa.org*) begins with a "splash screen" that displays a single, untagged image before automatically launching the home page (a practice that violates WCAG Checkpoint 7.4). The home page (like other pages on the site) makes heavy use of image elements without `alt` attributes. Searching the collections database for images by Claude Monet turned up 42 records—but the links to those records were unintelligible. Instead of ALT text, they used only the database record numbers ("link graphic fif=zoom/123-34.fpx&obj=iip,1," says JAWS, and then "link graphic fif=zoom/123-18.fpx&obj=iip,1," and so on) alternating with links to additional information about each work.[5] But each of those links is labeled "More," so again it's impossible for people using screen readers, talking browsers, refreshable Braille displays, or text-only displays to keep track of where the links go.

Other problems we encountered on the sites we visited included image map links with missing ALT text for their `<area>` elements (the Louvre, Paris; the Museum of Science and Industry, Chicago; the Museum of Modern Art, New York); text too small to be easily legible and difficult or impossible to resize (the Whitney Museum of American Art, New York; the Tate Gallery, London); multiple pages with the same title but different content (the Louvre, Paris; the Whitney Museum of American Art, New York); use of multiple frames with titles that do not assist orientation and navigation (the Louvre, Paris); and the absence of any way to skip over the many links that are repeated on each page of each site (all sites). Table 7–1 provides a quick overview of the museum sites we visited and the accessibility barriers we encountered.

Table 7–1 has three columns. Column 1 is the name of the museum we visited online. Column 2 is the URL. In Column 3 are some brief and by no means comprehensive comments about barriers

---

5. Accessed June 10, 2002, at *http://www.mfa.org/artemis/results.asp.*

TABLE 7–1 Accessibility Barriers on Selected Museum Web Sites

Museum	URL*	Comments
Chicago Museum of Science and Industry	http://www.msichicago.org	Graphical links have no meaningful information, for example, "link graphic button." Text links have redundant titles, making them difficult to sort and therefore to use by users with screen readers.
Houston Museum of Natural Science	http://www.hmns.org/	No alternatives are provided for graphic information—including important navigation links.
Musée du Louvre	http://www.louvre.fr/	Frames names provide no orientation information. Graphic image links appear without meaningful alt text.
Museum of Fine Arts Boston	http://www.mfa.org/	Splash screen with untagged image automatically redirects to front page with pop-up window containing untagged images. Online collection database search is usable but returns unintelligible links that are database records.
National Museum of Australia	http://www.nma.gov.au/	ALT text could be more meaningful, and there is an inaccessible calendar of events, but by and large, a fairly usable site.
Smithsonian Institution	http://www.si.edu/	Mislabeled forms, use of inaccessible Java elements, pop-up windows, lack of ALT text on image maps, and misleading page titles.

TABLE 7–1 *Continued*

Museum	URL*	Comments
The Guggenheim (Bilbao, Spain)	http://www.guggenheim-bilbao.es/	Pop-up windows are unannounced, graphic links with no ALT text.
The Menil Collection	http://www.menil.org/collections.html	Unlabeled graphic links, unannounced auto-refresh to a home page that contains links labeled Button 6, Button 8, Button 7, Button 3, Button 4—not in numerical order!
Whitney Museum of American Art	http://www.whitney.org/	Site has insufficient user control options (font size is specified in style sheets) and inconsistent use of alt tags for graphics.

* All sites were accessed on June 8, 2002, except for the Smithsonian site, accessed February 16, 2002.

that we encountered. (A linearized version of the table appears in Appendix C.)

While it's clear that developers of some museum Web sites (the National Museum of Australia, for example) are taking the needs of people with disabilities into account, the strongest impression we took away from our whirlwind tour of museums on the Web was that museums have yet to embrace Web accessibility as an important part of their mission to preserve the artistic and cultural heritage of the communities they serve.

USER EXPERIENCE NARRATIVE:
THE METROPOLITAN MUSEUM OF ART

We promised you an extended look at the Metropolitan Museum of Art Web site. We now invite you to experience the extraordinary collection of the Metropolitan Museum of Art in New York City, familiarly known as the Met, as we explore the site using JAWS. Before we begin, however, we want to acknowledge the cooperation and great community spirit demonstrated by the Met staff, and especially librarian Eileen Sullivan. The Met necessarily safeguards the integrity of how its collection is publicly represented and reproduced. Our request to the Museum was outside the norm and yet, once Ms. Sullivan helped us to communicate to the Met about how we would use these images to improve Web use for people with disabilities, the Met staff members fully cooperated by granting us permission to print screen shots of their Web site to illustrate our experiences there. We are grateful to them for their interest in promoting access to these rich materials for all users, including those with disabilities.

Let's get started with our exploration. In comparison to the vast sprawl of the Smithsonian or the enormous holdings of the Louvre, the Metropolitan Museum of Art seems almost petite, with a mere 2,000,000 objects. Yet here, too, we encounter unexpected accessibility barriers that reduce the site's effectiveness and lower the quality of the user experience.

The design of the Met's home page as shown in Figure 7–5 is apparently simple: a rectangular image on the left displays an artifact from the Museum's collections, and accompanying text gives a brief description of the artifact. The page displays a bronze statue of a dancer from the Greek and Roman Art collection; the accompanying

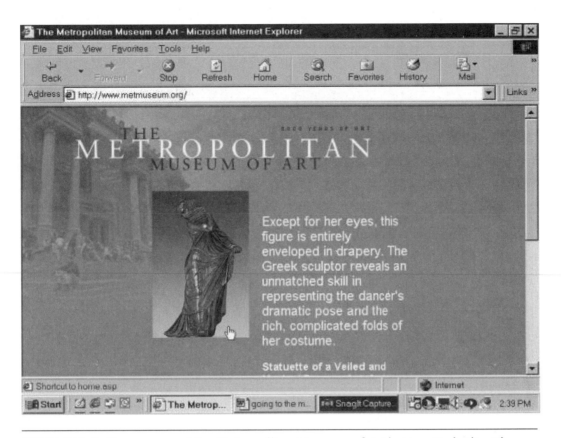

FIGURE 7–5 Home page of the Metropolitan Museum of Art in New York City. View number 1. Accessed July 29, 2001, at *http://www.metmuseum.org*. Used with permission.

text is probably the same as that on the placard that identifies the physical statue in the Greek and Roman gallery. After approximately 30 seconds—just about long enough for JAWS to read the masthead and the descriptive text that accompanies the image of the dancer—the page updates itself, automatically and silently. The ALT text for the image on the original page (Figure 7–5) read simply and unhelpfully, "Image"; the new image (Figure 7–6) is identified as a link to a "Special Exhibition." The exhibition is unnamed, however, so the ALT text is of little value.

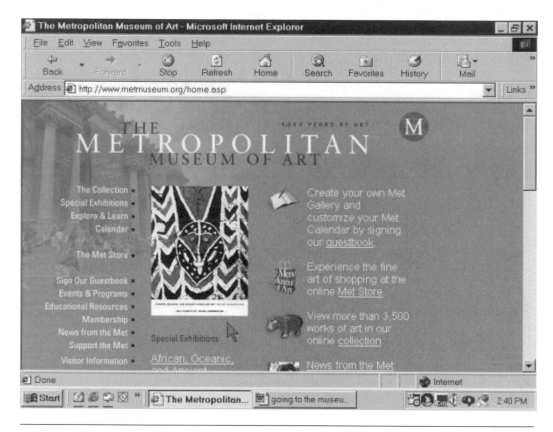

FIGURE 7–6 The Metropolitan Museum of Art's home page after a silent update, with a different image and descriptive text and a much expanded list of links. Accessed July 29, 2001, at *http://www.metmuseum.org/home.asp*. Used with permission.

Automatic Refreshes and Redirects Are Accessibility Barriers

It isn't simply that one image replaces another without notifying us of the impending change: we are actually taken to another page, though the change is so smooth and so subtle that we didn't notice it at first. There are other changes, too. In the space where the home page initially displayed the caption for the image of the dancer, there is now a two-column table whose left-hand column contains several small icons (representing a guest book, for example) and whose right-hand column invites us to do something (such as creating a personalized view of the collection and a personalized calendar of events by "signing" the guest book).

This sort of auto-redirect is fairly common practice on today's Web—but, like the pop-up window on the Smithsonian's History-Wired site, it's a very problematic practice from the standpoint of accessibility. For visitors who use screen readers and talking browsers or have other difficulties with reading or focusing their attention, this unexpected change in screen display may pose an insurmountable obstacle. As Jim Allan of the Texas School for the Blind and Visually Impaired said to us recently, "It's like trying to watch TV when someone else has the remote." Allan was talking about pop-up windows, but his comment applies equally well to automatic refresh.

For now, the answer is to follow WCAG 1.0 Checkpoint 7.4: "Until user agents provide the ability to stop the refresh, do not create periodically auto-refreshing pages."

Visiting the Collection

Like the designers of the Smithsonian's online collections, the Met's Web designers, Icon Nicholson, faced a formidable design challenge: they had to decide how best to represent an immense, diverse, and important collection in the online environment. Of note is the difference in the sheer amount of material represented on the two sites. The Smithsonian's HistoryWired site highlights 450 objects at any given time. By contrast, the Met's online highlights include some 3,500 objects chosen from a total of 2 million—50 items from each curatorial department in the Museum (Arms and Armor, Egyptian

Art, Greek and Roman Art, Medieval, and so forth) plus the entire European painting collection.[6]

The bulk of the screen introducing the collection (Figure 7–7) is taken up with an explanation of the collection and its size and variety. The description of the Met collection's scope is followed by brief descriptions of the individual curatorial departments with links to

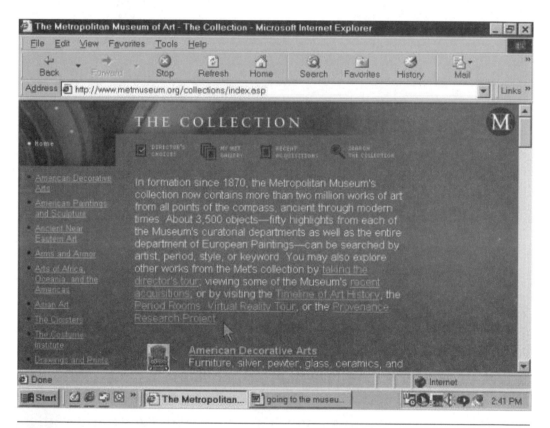

FIGURE 7–7 Screen shot of the Metropolitan Museum of Art's Collections page. Accessed July 22, 2001, at *http://www.metmuseum.org/collections/index.asp*. Used with permission.

6. For more about the Met's curatorial departments, see *http://www.met museum.org/collection/index.asp*.

their respective highlights sections. Perhaps inevitably, these links repeat most of the navigation links that appear on the left-hand side of the page.

Navigation Links Can Be an Accessibility Barrier

This is a trivial thing for sighted users, hardly worth noticing. But it can become a matter of considerable frustration for people using screen readers, talking browsers, or refreshable Braille displays. JAWS reported the Met's first page (Figure 7–5) as having only seven links. This is delightfully simple, but the pleasure is short-lived: there are 40 links on the page that replaces it (Figure 7–6), and *98* on the Collections page (Figure 7–7), many of them links down the left-hand margin. A layout scheme like this, in which 35 navigation links form the first cell of a `<table>` element used just for layout, forces screen readers to read the entire list of navigation links before getting to the "meat" of the page—on *every* page, every time. With JAWS's speech rate set at approximately 220 words per minute, this takes roughly 35 seconds! By contrast, the explanatory text takes only about 26 seconds at the same rate. You do the math—a *lot* of time is lost here. And of course the effect is multiplied many times over as users who are blind encounter the same phenomenon on site after site in the course of a day's work. For example, Jim Thatcher [2001a] reported that he listened to the CNN site with IBM's Home Page Reader "for over five minutes" before he came to what was supposed to be the lead story.

Skip to Main Content Links

The solution is to provide a method that lets users bypass repeated navigation links if they wish to do so. CNN addressed the problem that Thatcher reported, for example, by adding a Skip to Main Content link as the first link on every page. WCAG 1.0 recommends this practice, but the checkpoint (13.6) is buried deep under the heading of Guideline 13, which deals with a host of issues related to the mandate for clear, consistent navigation. It might seem odd that this item gets such low priority, but it reminds us how quickly things have changed on the Web. It's worth noting here that the idea of using navigation bars in the first place is also buried pretty deep within Guideline 13—and it too rates only a Priority 3 recommendation. Section 508, paragraph (o), published two years and many endlessly repeated navigation links later, uses stronger language: it *requires* that developers incorporate a method for skipping over such repeated links and other navigation bars. Even though the Met does not *have* to comply with the Section 508 standards, a Skip to Main Content or Skip Navigation link would indeed be a welcome addition here, as it is on the CNN site.

Setting ALT to Null

Like the navigation links, the descriptions of the curatorial departments and associated links are arranged in a two-column table. Column 1 represents the department with a thumbnail image, which is also a link to that department's page in the Collections site; Column 2 contains the explanatory text, as in the lower portion of Figure 7–7.

With so much onscreen text to see and hear, the developers evidently—and quite appropriately—felt that ALT text for the thumbnails would be superfluous. They tried to force screen readers and talking browsers to skip over the thumbnail images by including empty `alt` attributes in the code—that is, the `alt` attribute is present but no content is assigned to it, as in the code fragment reproduced below from the Collections page shown earlier.

```
!<-- item picture -->
<td width="55" align="right">
   <a href="department.asp?dep=4">img src="art/
      co_img_4.gif" alt
   border="0"></a><br>img src="art/spacer.gif" width="55"
   height="15" border="0"></td>
```

This code creates a table cell whose contents are identified by a comment in the code as the "item picture." There are actually two <img> elements in the cell: the item picture and a transparent spacer image. The code for the item picture includes a kind of placeholder for ALT text, which is apparently intended to force screen readers and talking browsers to ignore the image and go directly to the item description in the next cell. The effort fails, however, because the syntax for the empty alt attribute is incorrect: it should read alt="", not simply alt or alt=" ", with an empty space between the quotation marks). The result: exactly the *opposite* of what the designers evidently intended. Instead of skipping the image, the screen reader falls back on the filename and reads it: "art/co_img_4.gif," it intones robotically.

Exploring the Collection

We now give the floor to John to relate some personal background that guides our choice for the next exploration.

When I was a child I visited The Cloisters, a beautiful museum operated by the Met and devoted to medieval art. The Cloisters page provides a detailed description of the building itself and its relation to the Met's main building on Fifth Avenue. I'd like to explore some illuminated manuscripts, which have fascinated me since I saw my first one on a visit to Toronto with my parents in 1959 or '60.

Let's look closely at a page that contains such an illuminated manuscript (Figure 7–8). There are a number of noteworthy features. First of all, there are several options for viewing the highlights for this segment of the Met's collection.

- The default view, which we'll examine in some detail, shows one image at a time, as in Figure 7–8.
- Choosing to view 10 images at a time produces a page that uses what is by now the familiar two-column table with a reduced-size image in the left-hand column and the caption text (in a reduced font) on the right.
- There is also an option labeled "View 10 Text Only," which displays only the title and accession number (the accession number indicates the date when the object was added to the collection) for each object; the object's title is a link to the single-image or default view.
- And, finally, you can view all 50 highlights at once, as shown in Figure 7–9.

The screen shot in Figure 7–9 shows a set of thumbnail images, five to a row. You can run your eye over them to find the one you want, then click to go straight to the default view of the object you've selected. But you'd better be *able* to run your eye across the screen and pick out what you want to look at: there is no ALT text here. Or rather, the images *do* have `alt` attributes, but in each case the `alt` at-

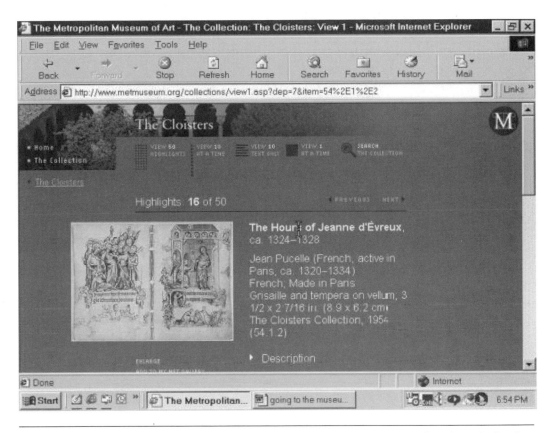

FIGURE 7–8 Screen shot of a page from the Metropolitan Museum of Art's Web site for The Cloisters, a branch museum dedicated to medieval art. Accessed July 22, 2001, at *http://www.metmuseum.org/collections/view1.asp?dep=7&item=54%2E1%2E2*. Used with permission.

tribute has been set to empty using the syntax alt=""—the correct syntax, as opposed to the incorrect example cited above. Through no fault of the Web designers, this results in different behavior, depending on which version of JAWS you're using and on which user settings you've chosen. Versions 3.7.047 and 3.7.087 seem to assume that the coding was a mistake, so instead of skipping over the images these two versions of JAWS report the (unintelligible) pathname for each image. JAWS 4.01 does the same thing. The much earlier JAWS 3.5,

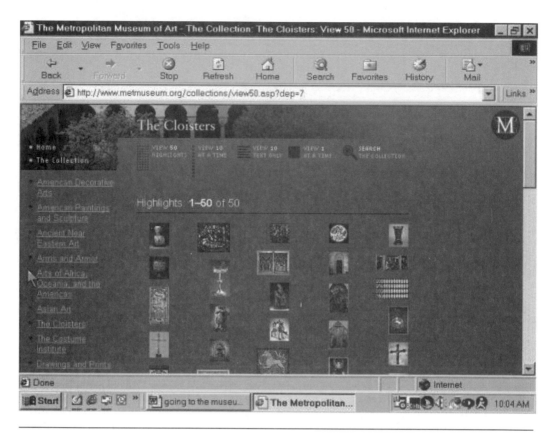

FIGURE 7–9 The Metropolitan Museum of Art's View 50 screen shows all 50 highlights for The Cloisters collection. Each highlight is represented by a thumbnail image. Accessed August 6, 2001, at *http://www.metmuseum.org/collections/view50.asp?dep=7*. Used with permission.

on the other hand, responds correctly to the empty `alt` strings; so does JAWS 4.02, the current version as of this writing. That is, JAWS versions 3.5 and 4.02 ignore the images—all of them. The result? JAWS 3.5 and 4.02 read the navigation links on the left side of the screen, and that's it. Versions 3.7 and 4.1, on the other hand, report the navigation links as well as the filename for each image. It's hard to say which is worse—both are pretty hideous as far as the quality of the user experience is concerned.

There are really two issues here. One has to do with assistive technology; the other has to do with Web design. First there is the inexplicable decision by Freedom Scientific, the maker of the JAWS software, to back away from supporting correct HTML syntax for empty ALT text. As a Web designer, you are of course not responsible for this strange behavior on the company's part, which puts you in an uncomfortable bind from which there seems to be no good way out. But this brings us to the second issue: the original design decision. From a purely *technical* standpoint, the Icon Nicholson team members did the right thing when they used alt="" to create an empty alt attribute for each thumbnail image on the View 50 page (assistive technology vendors should support the accessibility standards!). But in our view, Icon Nicholson made a poor *design* decision when the team members decided against identifying each image so that people using screen readers, talking browsers, refreshable Braille displays, and text-only displays could easily understand what's on the page and make appropriate choices. In other words, the best solution here would be to provide meaningful ALT text for each image. This in turn raises some important issues about the design of the underlying database that stores the images and information about them: each record in the database should include a field for ALT text, so that the script that generates the highlights pages can make that ALT text available to users who need it.

Consistent Design

Let's go back to the default view—one highlight image at a time—as shown in Figure 7–8. The screen layout is similar to that of the first pages we encountered on the Met site. The image of a medieval illuminated manuscript appears on the left side of the screen, with the caption text beside it on the right. Above the image, a legend informs us that we are looking at number 16 of 50 highlights. This consistent use of layout resonates nicely with WCAG 1.0 Checkpoint 14.3: "Create a style of presentation that is consistent across pages." Usability experts recognize consistent page layout as a contributing factor in the successful completion of tasks by all Web site visitors, especially those who have cognitive disabilities or difficulty reading.

Exploring the Image

The illustration has been carefully formatted for the Web: the image size is just 23K, a size that will download easily even on a fairly slow modem connection. The image is also "zoomable"—that is, selecting the image produces an enlargement (Figure 7–10).

Once the image has been enlarged, you can then click on an area of the image to "zoom in" more closely on that area, as in Figure 7–11.

This feature is valuable for fully sighted visitors (for example, art history students who can't travel to New York). It could also be extremely beneficial for visitors with low vision who may be able to appreciate the image if they can zoom in on more detailed views.

Equivalent Text Alternatives

But there's trouble in this art-lover's virtual Paradise. The "zoom" feature would be even more valuable if the site provided an equivalent text alternative for each "view" of the image, as WCAG 1.0 and Section 508 require. Section 508, paragraph (l), puts it very clearly: "When pages utilize scripting languages to display content, or to create interface elements, the information provided by the script shall be identified with functional text that can be read by assistive technology."

The problem is that you can zoom in on a portion of the image that interests you, but you can't "drill down" into the text description

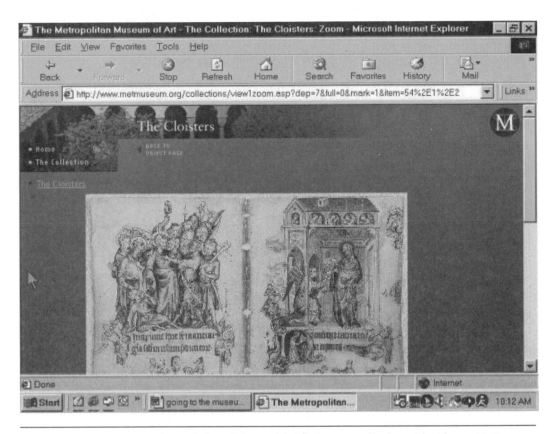

FIGURE 7–10 Screen shot of The Cloisters highlight page displayed in Figure 7–8, now showing an enlarged view of the illuminated manuscript, which fills most of the screen. Used with permission.

for additional detail. This may sound like an outlandish expectation, but it isn't. The same people who might benefit from zooming in on the image—an elderly person with macular degeneration, for example, or an art history student with 20/20 vision who happens to live 1,800 miles from the Met—might well be able to learn a great deal with the help of additional textual detail that corresponds to the visual display. The existing mechanism for zooming in to a more detailed view of the image, with the substitution of client-side image maps for the server-side maps used on the current site as discussed below,

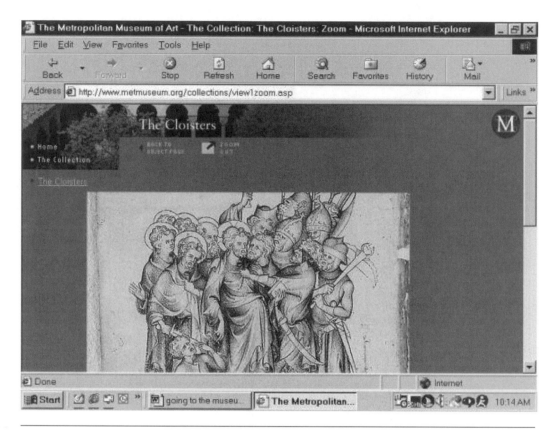

FIGURE 7–11 A detail of the illuminated manuscript, viewed close up. This is produced by clicking on part of the enlarged image shown in Figure 7–10. Used with permission.

would also serve to present additional descriptive detail that would be accessible to people who cannot see the images at all. (See Chapter 9 for a discussion of Adam Alonso's useful guidelines for describing works of art and other complex images.)

There are a few other details to take care of as well. The enlarged image in Figure 7–9 can be accessed via the keyboard—the image in Figure 7–8 is a graphical link to the enlarged view of itself. But people using nonvisual displays would have to guess at that since the ALT text seems to be missing (JAWS reports "images slash cl015v dash 016r period r"). Then, when we move to the next level of detail, the ability to zoom in on details of the enlargement *requires* a mouse: what JAWS reports as "Click on image to zoom button" is apparently a server-side image map overlaid on an `<input>` element of type `button`. And here again is an unnecessary (and surely unintentional) barrier to access.

Server-Side Image Maps Are Accessibility Barriers

WCAG 1.0 Guideline 9 states the general principle that applies here: "Design for device-independence"—that is, allow for a range of input devices, including keyboard, voice, headwand, and other assistive technologies. These assistive technologies generally map to the keyboard (so that interface elements that are keyboard accessible are usually accessible to other assistive technologies as well). Server-side image maps violate the principle of device-independent design because they require the use of a pointing device. This doesn't just affect people who are blind: it affects anyone who can't easily point and click, including people with cerebral palsy, Parkinson's disease, carpal tunnel syndrome, and a wide variety of other conditions such as stroke or hand tremors that are sometimes associated with old age.

Both WCAG 1.0 and the Section 508 standards call for developers to avoid server-side image maps if at all possible and specify compensatory action when avoiding server-side maps isn't an option. WCAG 1.0 Checkpoint 9.1 asks Web authors to "Provide client-side image maps instead of server-side image maps except where the regions cannot be defined with an available geometric shape [Priority 1]," and Checkpoint 1.2 tells us what to do if we have to go server-side: "Provide redundant text links for each active region of a server-side image map." The Section 508 standards, paragraphs (e) and (f), are substantively identical to the WCAG 1.0 checkpoints.

There's nothing on the Metropolitan Museum site to require server-side image maps. The zoomable images on the Met's highlights pages are divided into simple quadrants. Since one of the available geometric shapes for the `<area>` elements that form the selectable regions of client-side image maps is a rectangle (`rect` attribute), there is no need to use server-side maps. This means that eliminating the accessibility barrier created by the use of server-side image maps would be a trivial matter, technically speaking. It would only be necessary to replace the server-side image maps with client-side image maps. The selectable regions of these client-side image maps (`<area>` elements) would then be keyboard accessible, and associating ALT text with each `<area>` element would allow people using screen readers, talking browsers, refreshable Braille displays, and text-only browsers to identify the regions. Once they've made their choices, the server could display the detailed view with appropriate companion text. As with the ALT text for the thumbnail images on the View 50 page discussed above, this would require changes to the underlying database and the scripts that generate the zoomed images.

There are even some tools that make it easy to automate the process of converting server-side image maps to client-side image maps. One such tool is A-Prompt, which we mentioned in Chapter 6.

The Web Page as an Experience in Time: The Problem of Reading Order

But other problems will be more difficult to resolve than the issue of image maps. The placement of some images on the page (the source code shows repeated use of a spacer image including multiple "transparent" spacer images) and the way `<table>` elements are used to control page layout throw the reading order out of whack.

The most important of these disruptions occurs immediately after the screen reader has finished reading the caption text beside the highlight image. The extended description discussed above is what should logically come next, and this is the impression you get when listening to the page: after JAWS finishes the caption, it next says "Graphic arrow description," thereby identifying the small, right-facing triangle next to the word "Description." But the description is *not* what comes next. Here's a transcript of JAWS reading the illuminated manuscript highlight page from the point immediately following the caption text.

Graphic arrow description
Graphic arrow link alternate views
Graphic arrow link provenance slash ownership history
Link graphic the Met store
Link graphic related store items
Link graphic explore and learn more
Link graphic online resources
Link graphic view my Met gallery
Link graphic related
Link graphic support
Link printing instructions

And now, *finally*, here comes the description we've been waiting for. JAWS says:

Description
The two hundred nine folios of. . . .

Visualizing the Problem

The screen shots in Figures 7–12 and 7–13 illustrate the reading-order problem visually. They were created with an accessibility evaluation tool called The WAVE, designed by the late Len Kasday of Temple University. Figure 7–12 shows the part of the page from Figure 7–8 that contains an image from *The Hours of Jeanne d'Évreux*, plus the caption text that appears to the right of the image.

The numerals and directional arrows in Figure 7–12 show the order in which screen readers, talking browsers, refreshable Braille devices, and text-only displays will read the page elements. The cones with slash marks inside indicate graphics with missing ALT text. Most of these are spacer images inside the data cells of a nested table used for layout.

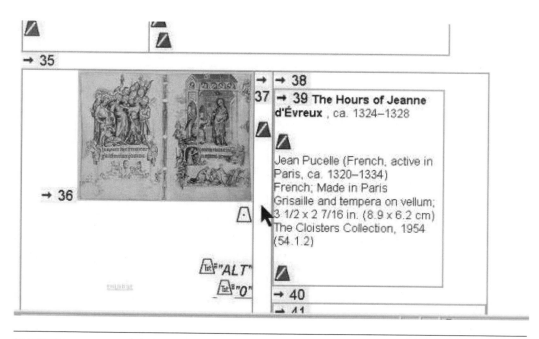

FIGURE 7–12 Partial view of the page generated by The WAVE to evaluate the accessibility of the illuminated manuscript page shown in Figure 7–8. The WAVE was accessed August 5, 2001, at *http://www.temple.edu/inst_disabilities/piat/wave/*. Used with permission.

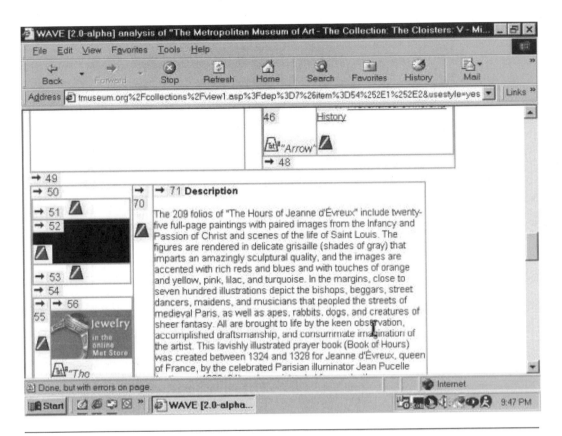

FIGURE 7–13 Second view of the Metropolitan Museum of Art's illuminated manuscript page as analyzed by The WAVE, showing the extended description of *The Hours of Jeanne d'Évreux* as the seventy-first element on the page. The WAVE was accessed August 5, 2001, at *http://www.temple.edu/inst_disabilities/piat/wave/*. Used with permission.

A second screen shot of the same page (Figure 7–13) shows how far apart in reading order are the caption text about the manuscript page and the contextual description of the *The Hours of Jeanne d'Évreux*. The image of the manuscript page in Figure 7–8 is the thirty-fifth element on the page. The description, which had seemed about to follow immediately, is not element 36—it's actually the seventy-first element on the page!

In Figure 7–13, the extended description of *The Hours of Jeanne d'Évreux* appears as the seventy-first element on the page—the contents of a data cell inside a nested table. Beside it, on the left, is another table cell containing elements 51–53—all apparently spacer graphics that either lack ALT text or have empty `alt` attributes with incorrect syntax. Below that is another cell containing elements 55–58, which include spacer images and graphical links to the Met Store and another view of the collection.

Reading Order Matters!

The point of all this is that reading order matters; it matters just as much as, and pretty much the same way as, the order of operations matters in a math problem. And for people whose experience of the Web depends mostly or entirely on *listening to text read aloud by a robot,* reading order may be just about everything. (Please see Chapter 9 for discussion of how graphic placement affects reading order.)

TEXT EQUIVALENTS CAN OPEN THE DOORS OF PERCEPTION

The striking visual elements contained in the Metropolitan Museum's elegantly designed pages would not have to be eliminated to create a rich, accessible experience for the visitor who uses assistive technology. And because the sites we visited, like an increasing number of Web sites, are database-driven, many of the accessibility improvements we've discussed need only be designed and coded once in order to take effect across the entire site. For example, you can use CSS to position the navigation links to satisfy the expectations of sighted users. In the same process, you can make the substance of the page fully accessible to people using screen readers and related assistive devices. This means that changes need only be made once to be both accessible *and* easily propagated throughout the site. (See Chapter 15 for details.) This explains why it's unnecessary to create text-only versions of image- and media-heavy sites, a point we'll take up in detail in the next chapter.

Our goal is to create a context for guidelines and accessibility standards that we will examine in greater depth in subsequent chapters. As we discover the coding examples and techniques that solve the problems we encountered in this chapter, we hope you come to agree that good design is, indeed, accessible design.

8

User Experience: Text-Only Alternatives

It's fairly common practice for complex or media-rich sites to offer text-only versions, and after reading about the problems we've encountered at various sites on the Web, you may be thinking that text-only might be a good way to meet the challenge of making your site accessible. We want to persuade you that text-only *isn't* the way to go most of the time. In this chapter, we'll visit several sites whose text-only versions offer a substantially different—and substantially less satisfying—user experience than their media-rich originals.

HTML Elements and Attributes
Addressed in This Chapter

Elements

`<a>`, `<img>`, `<area>`, `<table>`

Attributes

`alt`

Accessibility Checkpoints and Standards Addressed in This Chapter

Web Content Accessibility Guidelines 1.0 Checkpoints

3.5. Use header elements to convey document structure and use them according to specification. [Priority 2]

3.6. Mark up lists and list items properly. [Priority 2]

6.2. Ensure that equivalents for dynamic content are updated when the dynamic content changes. [Priority 1]

11.4. If, after best efforts, you cannot create an accessible page, provide a link to an alternative page that uses W3C technologies, is accessible, has equivalent information (or functionality), and is updated as often as the inaccessible (original) page. [Priority 1]

13.8. Place distinguishing information at the beginning of headings, paragraphs, lists, etc. [Priority 3]

Section 508 Standards, §1194.22

(k) A text-only page, with equivalent information or functionality, shall be provided to make a Web site comply with the provisions of this part [of Section 508, §1194.22], when compliance cannot be accomplished in any other way. The content of the text-only page shall be updated whenever the primary page changes.

ISN'T TEXT-ONLY A COMMON PRACTICE?

Many sites do offer text-only variants. However, it's ironic that, for example, when we visited the National Science Foundation's Web site in July 2001, the first link on the site was a *graphical* link (!) to a "text version of [the] NSF Web site."[1] The New York State site also has a graphical link to a text-only version, this one labeled "Welcome to New York State homepage click here for text version."[2] The states of Alaska, Colorado, Connecticut, Illinois, Missouri, Montana, Nebraska, Oklahoma, South Dakota, Virginia, Washington, Wisconsin, and Wyoming all offered access to text-only versions of their sites as of late July 2001. The new White House site unveiled in September 2001 had a text-only link (which was still there in early June 2002).[3] So did the U.S. government's main site for disability information when we visited in July 2001 (Figure 8–1).

The text-only link remained in place on the government's disability information site until the next major update in September 2001, when the site was renamed "DisabilityDirect." Besides eliminating the unnecessary text-only link, the redesigned DisabilityDirect site shown in Figure 8–2 includes a number of accessibility and usability enhancements. The most notable are the clearly labeled Main Menu of navigation links on the left side of the screen and a search field, correctly labeled "Search this site," in the upper-right corner. (This

---

1. From the home page of the National Science Foundation Web site, accessed July 21, 2001, at *http://www.nsf.gov.*

2. From the home page of the New York State Web site, accessed July 21, 2001, at *http://www.state.ny.us/.*

3. See the White House Web site at *http://www.whitehouse.gov.*

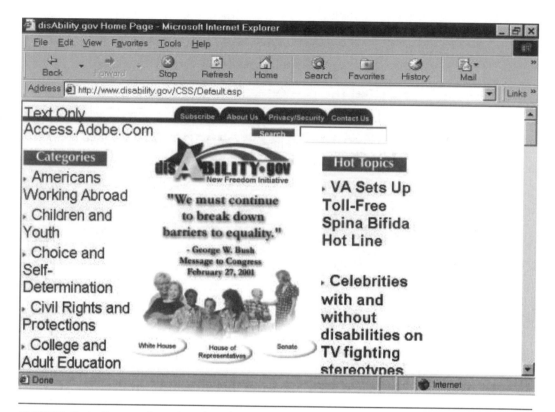

FIGURE 8–1 Screen shot showing the text-only link at the upper left of the U.S. government's Web site for disability information before its redesign. Accessed July 21, 2001, at *http://www.disability.gov*. Used with permission.

prominent placement of the search engine is consistent with the recommendations of Kara Pernice Coyne and Jakob Nielsen in *Beyond ALT Text*, which was published a month or so after the DisabilityDirect site went live in September 2001.)

There's no need to go the text-only route in most cases, and we'll see later that doing so can create problems far worse than those it's supposed to solve.

Many of the people who rely on ALT text when they visit your site are *already experiencing the site as text-only*. Depending on how the

FIGURE 8–2 Screen shot of the redesigned and renamed U.S. government's Web site for disability information. There is no longer a text-only link. Accessed February 22, 2002, at *http://www.disability.gov*. Used with permission.

screen reader or talking browser is configured, an image (<img> element), image map hot spot (<area> element), or other graphical link without ALT text is either an annoying interruption in the stream of synthetic speech or it's not there at all—the screen reader ignores it and the user never even knows it exists. This is one reason why it's inappropriate to create a *separate* text-only version of your site, aside from the fact that WCAG 1.0 Checkpoint 11.4 and Section 508 paragraph (k) both say that you should do so only as a last resort when you've exhausted all other avenues in your quest for accessibility. Under these circumstances, unless you're prepared to make your entire site text-only for everyone (if you're using Cascading Style Sheets to style your text, for example), you're better off concentrating on the quality of the ALT text associated with the images and other elements on your existing site—and, of course, on providing the best possible *onscreen* text as well. (See Chapter 9 for further discussion of the relationship between onscreen and offscreen text.)

USER EXPERIENCE NARRATIVE 1: THE NATIONAL PUBLIC RADIO SITE

Let's look more closely at an example. Like the U.S. government's old disability information site, National Public Radio's site offers a text-only link in the upper-left corner of the page (Figure 8–3).

Listening to NPR's Home Page

Here's how the JAWS screen reader speaks the first 23 items on the main page of NPR's site.

NPR hahmapage

Visit our link text dash only page

Link graphic NPR

Combo box NPR programs A dash Z

Go button

Edit enter keywords

Find button

Link news

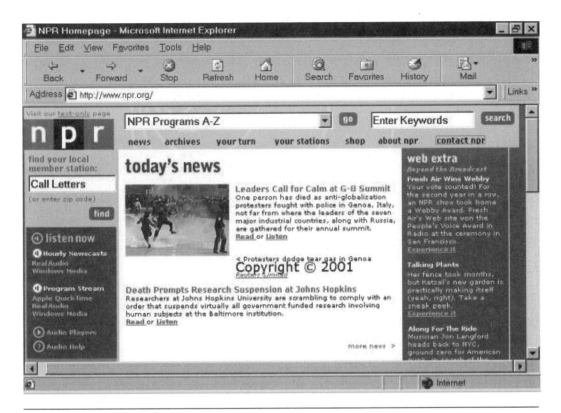

FIGURE 8–3 Screen shot of the home page for National Public Radio. A link to the text-only version of the site appears in tiny letters in the upper-left corner of the screen. Accessed July 21, 2001, at *http://www.npr.org*. Used with permission.

Link archives

Link your turn

Link your stations

Link shop

Link about NPR

Link contact NPR

Find your local member station colon

Edit call letters left paren or enter ZIP code right paren

Find button

Graphic listen now

Hourly newscasts

Link RealAudio

Link Windows Media

Program stream

Link Apple QuickTime

Link RealAudio

Link Windows Media

Link Audio Players

Link Audio Help

Graphic our online partners

Link graphic PBS slash sbanner [pbsbanner] underline enproam
[nprhome]

Link audible dot com for downloadable NPR programming

Link Adaptive Path User Experience Consultants

Link graphic NPR shop

[And so on. . . .][4]

Visiting NPR's Text-Only Page

The text-only link leads to a menu of links that is indeed text-only
(Figure 8–4).

This page doesn't qualify as an "equivalent alternative" to the primary NPR site. The text-only menu is organized quite differently from

---

4. Transcript of JAWS reading the National Public Radio home page, accessed
July 21, 2001, at *http://www.npr.org.*

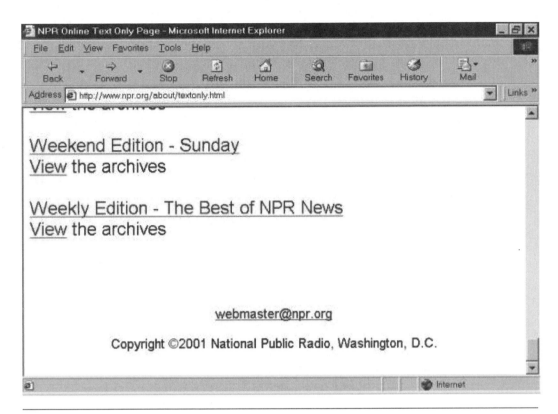

FIGURE 8–4 Screen shot of National Public Radio's text-only menu. Accessed July 21, 2001, at *http://www.npr.org/about/textonly.html*. Used with permission.

the menu on the main home page. By labeling groups of links (Main Navigation, Audio Help, Radio Programs), it provides some contextual information that isn't available on the page we listened to and looked at a moment ago, as suggested by WCAG 1.0 Checkpoint 13.8 ("Place distinguishing information at the beginning of headings, paragraphs, lists, etc."). But the text-only menu does not include the news items that are prominently displayed on what is clearly the *real* home page, nor does it include the links that run down the right side of the screen. Moreover, some of the links (the link to *All Things Considered*, for example) point back to graphically intense pages.

For comparison with the transcript of the main page presented earlier, here's how JAWS reports the first 23 items on the text-only page.

National Public Radio Online

Main navigation

Link news

Link program archives left paren good for searching right paren

Link your turn

Link your stations

Link shop

Link about NPR

Link contact NPR

Audio help

Link audio players

Link audio help

Radio programs

Here's a listing of NPR's produced and distributed programs period. Link all songs considered link listen to the latest show or link view the archives

Link all things considered registered

Link listen to the latest show or link view the archives

Link along for the ride

Link view the archives link American Radio Works At the Opera view the archives beyond 2000 Billy Taylor's Jazz view the archives Car Talk registered the changing face of America

Link view the archives The Connection the Diane Rehm Show Fresh Air registered with Terry Gross listen to the latest show or view the archives Jazz from Lincoln Center

Link Jazz Profiles view the archives Jazz Set with Branford Marsalis Justice Talking Latino USA Living on Earth Lost and Found Sound view the archives Marian

Link McPartland's Piano Jazz The Merrow Report Morning Edition registered listen to the latest show or view the archives National Press Club view the archives NPR Playhouse

NPR World of Opera On the Media registered Only a Game Performance Today registered Public Interest Radio Expeditions view the archives Rewind says you exclaim Selected Shorts Sunday

Link Baroque Symphony Cast Talk of the Nation view the archives

[And so on. . . .][5]

Something has gone seriously wrong here. It isn't just that the information on this page differs from what's available on the main page or that it's in a different order. The page is "broken"— from the point immediately after the link to a show called *Along for the Ride,* links for multiple shows and their archives are run together in an incoherent way. It's impossible to tell where the links will go.

Problems at the Source

This is not a good thing, of course. But when we looked at the source code, we were amazed that the page worked at all. To begin with, the document doesn't start with the obligatory HTML tag (`<html>`)—though it does *end* with the end-HTML tag (`</html>`). It has just a tiny `<head>` section (it contains nothing but a `<title>` element) sitting atop

---

5. Transcript of JAWS reading the text-only version of the National Public Radio site, accessed July 21, 2001, at *http://www.npr.org/about/textonly.html.*

a distorted <body> section consisting of a <table> element that has a beginning <table> tag and not one but *two* closing tags several lines apart (</table> ... </table>). And on the table—chaos. The first line of code inside the <body> element looks like this:

```
<table width=650><td><tr>
```

It's common practice to use tables to lay out lists of links, and presumably that is the intention here. But the code is backwards: it puts the first table row (the <tr> element) inside the first data cell (the <td> element). There is no closing tag for either the data cell or the row, and there are no more rows or cells. Instead, links are presented as items in a list (using the <li> element), but the beginning and end of the list are not identified—a violation of WCAG 1.0 Checkpoint 3.6 ("Mark up lists and list items properly"). And only *some* of the links are organized into a list. Those arranged under Audio Help and Radio Programs are simply separated by line breaks with the <br> element. What appear on the screen to be section headings (Audio Help, Radio Programs, and so on) are actually just phrases formatted as bold text, whereas they would be more appropriately tagged as structural sections of the document (<h1>, <h2>, <h3>, and so on) in accordance with WCAG 1.0 Checkpoint 3.5 ("Use header elements to convey document structure and use them according to specification"). And then the whole thing breaks down, as shown in the source code below from the National Public Radio text-only page.

```
<a href="/programs/theride/index.html"> Along for the
Ride</a> <br><a
href="/ramfiles/theride/lfunderburg/aftr.lfunderburg.01.
rmm"><!-- Listen</a> to the latest show <img
src="bullet.gif">
```

```
--> <a href="http://www.npr.org/programs/
theride/archives.html">View</a> the
archives<br><br>
```

This is the point at which JAWS began running the names of radio programs together. In the code fragment shown above, the first two lines, from the initial <a href . . .> to the first occurrence of </a>, define a link to a radio program called *Along for the Ride*. Then comes trouble. Following a line break (<br>) comes the beginning of a new link. But where the link text should be (it's supposed to read "Listen to the latest show") there is instead a comment tag (<!-- . . . -->), which tells the browser to ignore what it encloses. That comment is clearly meant to enclose (and thus cause not to appear on the screen) an image called bullet.gif, which has evidently been caught red-handed trying to sneak onto this text-only page. Unfortunately, though, the comment tag starts a little early, and it *also* captures what was supposed to be the link text *and* the closing tag of the link. Then comes the beginning of a new link to the archives for this show—but the browser and JAWS are forced to try to treat this new link as the link *text* for the unclosed link to the audio files for the most recent edition of the show. Meltdown.

How did this happen? We can't say for sure, but we'll hazard a guess. The person to whom the job of making a text-only version was assigned did what so many HTML developers do: he or she copied the source from a version of the page that included some graphics and pasted it into a new document. Then he or she realized that there were images in there and went back in to comment them out of the code. This developer clearly was in a hurry and didn't have time to test the page—not even to eyeball it quickly, let alone put it through the W3C's online HTML Validation Service at *http://validator.w3.org/*, which would have caught the error even if no one else did. (So would an authoring tool conforming with the Authoring Tool Accessibility Guidelines 1.0, had there been any such tools.) And that was that.

(We are pleased to note that, as of June 2002, the broken links on this text-only menu have been mended: the source code still contains the <img> element, but the comment tag is correctly placed now so that only the link to the most recent show is commented out. The other errors described above remain, however.)

The text-only version is no doubt well intentioned. But the good intentions matter only if they're carried through to every level of the site, and in this case as in many others that doesn't happen. The links on NPR's text-only menu, for example, point back to the graphical version of the site. And selecting the link for the afternoon news show *All Things Considered* brings up the screen shown in Figure 8–5. The page for *All Things Considered* is dense with text, but there are a number of images and graphical links as well—this is *not* a text-only page. This bouncing back and forth between text-only and graphical pages isn't especially problematic in the case of *All Things Considered*. But in the next section of this chapter, we'll show you how confusing it can be when a user is "slammed" unpredictably from one version to another without warning.

USER EXPERIENCE NARRATIVE 2: A RETURN TO AMAZON.COM

Many developers have told us that text-only variants of their sites wouldn't be prone to the kinds of problems we saw on the site discussed above. These developers argue that their sites are database driven: pages are generated on the fly as the server executes scripts

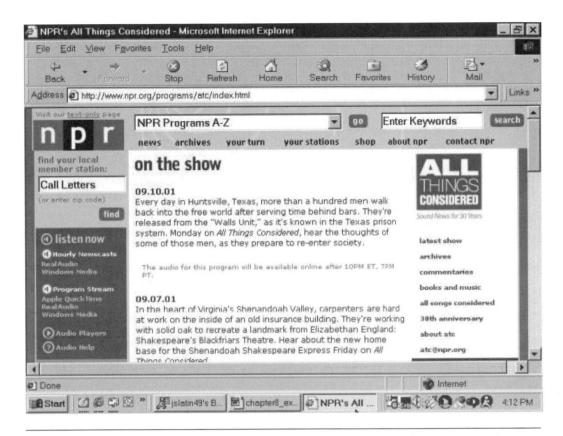

FIGURE 8–5 Screen shot of the graphical version of the *All Things Considered* site at NPR, reached by selecting a link on the text-only menu. Accessed September 8, 2001, at *http://www.npr.org/programs/atc/index.html*. Used with permission.

based on the user's actions, and the kinds of mistakes we've been talking about just wouldn't happen.

This is probably true in some cases. In theory, at least, it's possible to write your scripts in such a way that the server can generate either media-rich or text-only pages on demand, with the content of the text-only version being identical (except for the images) to that of the media-rich pages. But this can be a double-edged sword, as the following example illustrates.

Generating the Text-Only Version Automatically

I (John) decided to go back to Amazon.com, which I first visited in Chapter 2, for another short shopping expedition. Amazon.com, it turns out, does offer a text-only alternative to its main home page, though it's hard to find the link way down at the bottom of the page (Figure 8–6).

The link to the text-only version of the site is link 157 on a page with 175 links. If you have the patience to listen carefully while JAWS

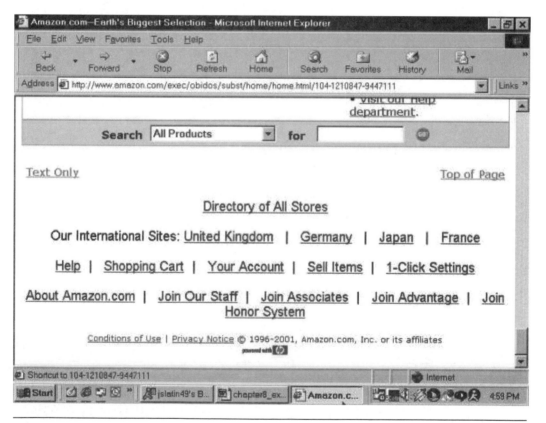

FIGURE 8–6   Screen shot of the bottom of Amazon.com's home page. The text-only link is on the left side of the screen, above links to Amazon.com's "stores" outside the United States. On the same line, on the right, is a link back to the top of the page. Accessed September 8, 2001, at *http://www.amazon.com*. Used with permission.

reads through all those links until the text-only link comes up, you can access the text-only version of Amazon.com's site (Figure 8–7).

As an auditory experience, this is substantially more coherent than the experience of the graphics-heavy home page of the main site. But there are odd moments all the same, as JAWS reports in the transcript shown below.

> Hello, John Slatin. We have recommendations for you. (If you're not John Slatin, click here.)
>
> New Lower Prices!

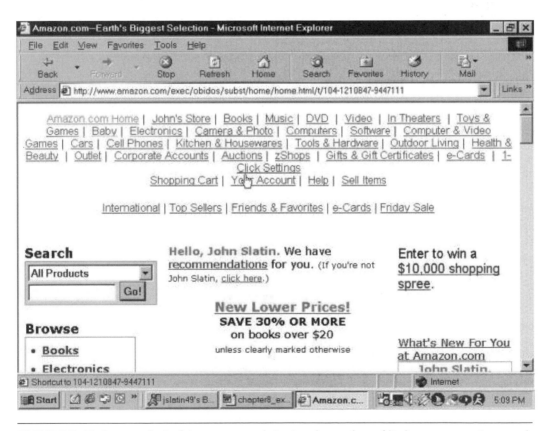

FIGURE 8–7 Screen shot of Amazon.com's text-only version of its home page. Accessed September 8, 2001, at *http://www.amazon.com/exec/obidos/subst/home/home.html/t/ 104-1210847-9447111*. Used with permission.

SAVE 30% OR MORE

on books over $20 unless clearly marked otherwise

t/104-1210847-

9447111&message=197740,gw_lr_dvd_phantom_menace,18

Return to the origins of Darth Vader and the Galactic Empire.
Preorder Star Wars: Episode I, The Phantom Menace on DVD.

104-1210847-

9447111?name=dscm&file=user/promo

[And so on. . . .][6]

As this JAWS transcript shows, there are still several links identified only by stupefying strings of alphanumerics meant for machines,
not humans, and there are other links labeled "Click here" and "Read
more" that don't work out of context (for example, when read as part
of the JAWS Links List).

Worst of all, when I tried to buy the recommended CD by the
great flamenco guitarist, Paco de Lucia, I learned (by using the JAWS
Links List to scroll through all 145 links on the page) that the text-
only version of the Buying Info page (Figure 8–8) still doesn't identify
the button for one-click purchasing!

Amazon Access: Been There, Couldn't Do That

On December 6, 2001, the lead story in *E-Commerce News* announced a new version of the Amazon.com Web site called Amazon

---

6. Transcript of JAWS reading the text-only version of Amazon.com's home
page, accessed September 8, 2001, at *http://www.amazon.com/exec/obidos/subst/
home/home.html/t/104-1210847-9447111.*

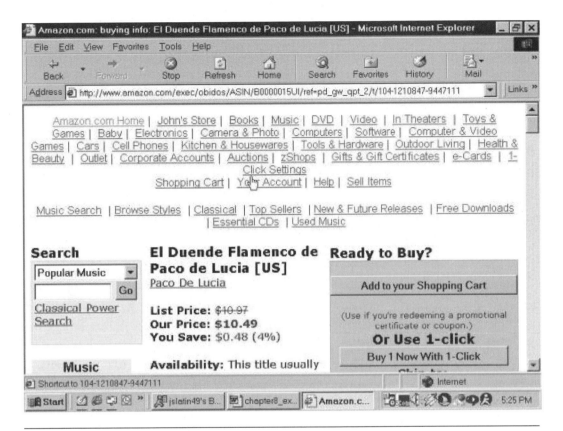

FIGURE 8–8 Screen shot of the text-only version of a Buying Info page on the Amazon.com site. A button for one-click purchasing is visible on the screen but not reported by JAWS. Accessed September 8, 2001, at *http://www.amazon.com/exec/obidos/ASIN/ B0000015UI/ref=pd_gw_qpt_2/t/104-1210847-9447111*. Used with permission.

Access. The article created the impression that the site had been designed specifically to meet the needs of people who are visually impaired. The *E-Commerce News* reporter wrote: "Online retailing behemoth Amazon.com is making it easier for the visually impaired to shop on the Internet by launching an alternative version of its Web site designed for customers who use screen access software" [Cox 2001].

Given the problems I'd encountered with the original and text-only versions of the Amazon.com site, this seemed a really promising development, and I was eager to try the new, accessible version.

The screen shot in Figure 8–9 presents what the news item (and subsequent correspondence with Amazon.com) described as a "streamlined version" of the Amazon.com site. Centered at the top of the page is a simple graphic, which the ALT text identifies as the Amazon.com logo. Beneath the logo is a link to information about secure shopping, and below that is the line, "Welcome John Slatin." Beneath

FIGURE 8–9 Screen shot of Amazon Access, the site supposedly designed for shoppers with visual impairments. Accessed January 4, 2002, at *http://www.amazon.com/access*. Used with permission.

the welcome message is a two-part search form, consisting of a pull-down menu (which JAWS identifies as a combo box) from which the user can select a product category (the default is All Products) and, on the next line, an input field for entering search text. There is a Go button underneath the input field. Then there's a link to information about movies playing in theaters near me, and finally a two-column list of links to Amazon.com's product categories. The Books link appears as the first link in the left-hand column, and the Recommendations link ends the list in the right-hand column.

This is indeed streamlined—this page has only 14 links, compared to 175 on the primary Amazon.com site as we saw it in Chapter 2 and compared to the text-only counterpart discussed earlier in this chapter, which sometimes has even more links than the primary home page on the same day. (On June 5, 2002, for example, JAWS reported 183 links on the primary home page and 186 links on the text-only version of the same page.) Unfortunately, however, Amazon Access is another disappointment. The first bad sign is that the text next to the search form (the word "Find") is not associated via the <label> element with either the pull-down menu of product categories or the search field itself. As a result, when I pressed Ctrl+Home+Ins (the keystroke that directs JAWS to the first form element on any page), I heard "Combo box all products"; pressing the tab key produced only the all-too-familiar word "Edit," indicating that the cursor was inside an input field, but provided no information about what to enter.

Next, I decided to check out what recommendations Amazon.com had in store for me, so I followed the Recommendations link. Much to my surprise, this brought me to a log-in screen (Figure 8–10)—something I hadn't expected, since (a) the site had identified me by name right up front and (b) neither the original Amazon.com site nor the

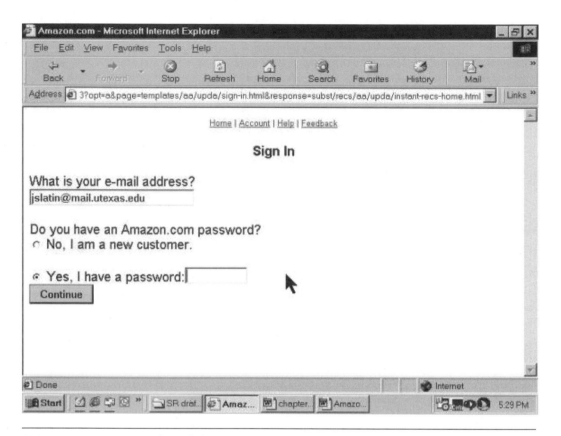

FIGURE 8–10 Screen shot of the Amazon Access sign-in page that appears when the user selects the Recommendations link. Accessed January 4, 2002, at *http://www.amazon.com/ o/dt/upda-1.0-pocketpc/flex-sign-in/102-7504432-1709753?opt=a&page=templates/aa/ upda/sign-in.html&response=subst/recs/aa/upda/instant-recs-home.html*. Used with permission.

text-only version discussed earlier in this chapter requires user sign-in when the user is recognized.

The sign-in page is even simpler than the Amazon Access home page. Centered at the top of the screen are four text links: Home, Account, Help, and Feedback. Beneath them are the words "Sign In". The rest of the page contains a simple form. The question "What is your e-mail address?" appears on a line by itself, directly above an input field in which my e-mail address was entered automatically. On the next line is another question, "Do you have an Amazon.com password?" with the two possible answers (No and Yes) presented as radio buttons. To the right of the Yes option (the default selection) is an input field where the user can enter the password. On the next line is a Continue button.

So now we have two mysteries. Why isn't the search form on the home page labeled correctly? And why do I have to sign in even though the site identified me correctly by name?

It turns out that there's an answer to the second question. Amazon Access is designed to allow for the possibility that someone may be accessing Amazon Access from a public terminal or kiosk. An e-mail message I received from Amazon.com customer service on December 15, 2001, explained: "Please know that this page uses Amazon.com's customer personalization feature. If you are using a public terminal, or if you are greeted by the wrong name, simply click on the 'Recommendations' link to log into your account."

The assumption about public terminals seems reasonable, since many people with disabilities use their local public libraries for Internet access. But I was using my own computer in this case, not a public terminal, and the computer had greeted me with the right name; yet I still had to sign in before I could see my recommendations. I don't have to do that on Amazon.com or the text-only version.

And then there's the fact that, like the search form on the Amazon Access home page, the sign-in form isn't fully accessible. The prompts are associated with the input fields only by proximity, not via the HTML <label> element as they should be. As a result, people using older screen readers (often the case in public-access settings like libraries and community centers, as noted in Chapter 4) may have difficulty identifying the information they need to enter. Such problems can affect anyone using a public terminal, not just people with disabilities.

Or suppose the site had displayed the wrong name when I brought up the Amazon Access site? There's nothing on the screen to tell me to select the Recommendations link if I need to change the sign-in name. In fact, what to do in such a case is far less clear on Amazon Access than it is on the original Amazon.com site, where the following greeting appears in the middle of the screen: "Hello, John Slatin. We have recommendations for you. (If you're not John Slatin, click here.)"

And—it should come as no surprise by now—if I weren't John Slatin, entering another e-mail address on the sign-in form and selecting the radio button to indicate that I don't have a password will bring me to yet another simple but unlabeled form (Figure 8–11).

It's hard to believe that such simple forms on such simple pages—pages ostensibly designed with accessibility in mind—are not labeled.

I really did want to hear those recommendations. So I went ahead and logged in. This brought me to a page that listed recommendations in all product categories; I chose music. Again I encountered problems (some of which would have been detected by the W3C's HTML Validation Service), which I described in the following e-mail to feedback@amazon.com on December 14, 2001.

. . . The following is a transcript of what the JAWS screen reader reported when I visited the www.amazon.com/access [site] for the first time: Specifically, here's a partial transcript of how the JAWS screen reader (version 4.00.103) reported my music recommendations. Note particularly the text that follows AVG REVIEW colon and Track list colon. . . . (This material shows up in the Links List as well as in say-all mode).

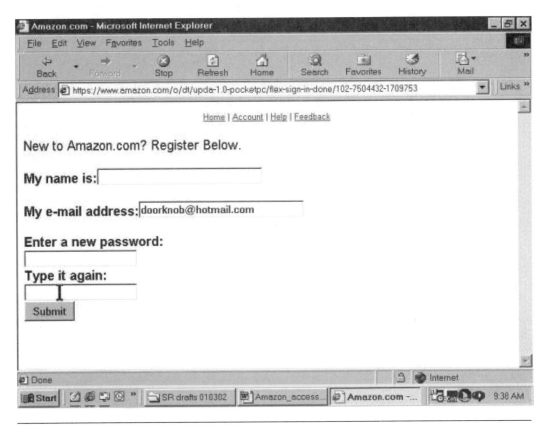

FIGURE 8–11 Screen shot of the new account registration page on the Amazon Access site. Accessed January 5, 2002, at *https://www.amazon.com/o/dt/upda-1.0-pocketpc/flex-sign-in-done/102-7504432-1709753*. Used with permission.

== transcript of JAWS session begins here ==

Amazon.com

Home |

Account |

Help |

Feedback

Amazon.com

Music

Long Black Veil

Artist: The Chieftains

Our Price: $14.99

List Price: $17.97

You Save: $2.98 (17%)

Format: Audio CD

Num. Discs: 1

Availability: Usually ships in 24 hours

Release Date: January 24, 1995

Avg. Review:

B000003FRH/002-8498066-4312835

Track list

B000003

== transcript ends ==

The stars graphic for review rating does not have ALT text. And there's a <P> tag inside the <A> tag for the track list, which is why you get the garbage instead of a meaningful link.

1. The search field on the home page (www.amazon.com/access) is not labeled. JAWS reports simply "Edit:" without telling users what they should enter. It is a trivial matter to associate a LABEL element with an INPUT element.

2. The /access site requires customers to enter their passwords in order to review [t]heir recommendations. This is not true on either www.amazon.com or on the text-only site that you can link to from www.amazon.com (the link is down near the bottom of the page, in case you didn't

know it was there; it's been there for quite a while). This requirement to enter the password is there despite the fact that the site correctly identified and greeted me by name. Why should visually impaired users have to jump through hoops that sighted customers don't have to go through?

3. The recommendations offered to me on /access are different from the ones I get from www.amazon.com (which are the same as the ones I get from the text-only version).

I and many others in the blind community were excited when we heard that Amazon had announced an accessible site. It is a real disappointment to find that it's just hype—the site is not truly accessible, and it does not offer equivalent functionality to the main Amazon site.

Sincerely,
John Slatin

The reply I received the next day did not inspire confidence. The message apologized for the difficulty I had experienced—and then, astonishingly, informed me that "Visually impaired customers with screen-reading or text-to-speech software can access a streamlined version of Amazon.com's regular Web site by visiting the following URL: http://www.amazon.com/access" [e-mail communication from feedback@amazon.com, December 15, 2001].

Progress Report

I returned to the Amazon Access site in January 2002 to verify what I thought I had seen on my previous visit. Déjà vu all over again: the book the site recommended to me was exactly the same one it recommended in December 2001—Richard A. Lanham's *The Electronic Word: Democracy, Technology, and the Arts* (1993), a superb book that I have often used in the graduate courses I teach (see Figure 8–12). This may have been a fluke: the music recommendation, by contrast, was different. More importantly, I'm pleased to report that some of the problems that I and others reported to Amazon.com in December 2001 had been fixed.

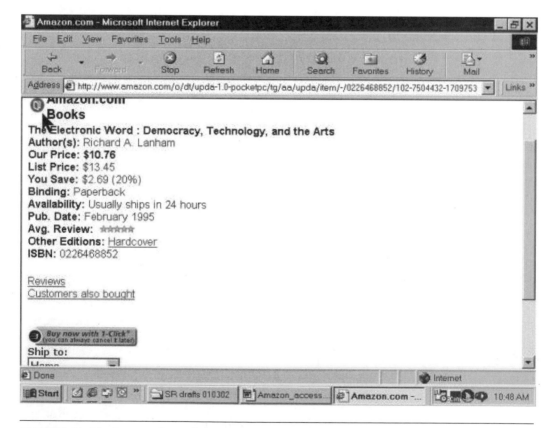

FIGURE 8–12 Screen shot of the Buying Info page for the book recommended by Amazon Access on January 5, 2002, at *http://www.amazon.com/o/dt/upda-1.0-pocketpc/tg/aa/upda/item/-/0226468852/102-7504432-1709753*. Used with permission.

Specifically, JAWS now correctly reported both the average review rating (5.0 stars in this case) and the button marked "Buy now
with 1-Click" (previously JAWS had identified it only as a Submit
button, with no indication of what was actually being submitted).
This was a distinct improvement. But there were—and are—still
unresolved problems as well. For example, JAWS is unable to locate
the links pointing to reviews or (for audio CDs) the track list. Figure 8–13 shows the JAWS Links List for the page on Gillian Welch's
2001 CD, *Time (the Revelator)*.

These are mere technical bugs, and fixing them is—or should
be—a trivial matter of going in and straightening out some botched
code; once fixed, links to reviews and track lists will be available on
Amazon Access as they are on the primary and text-only versions of
the site.

But the bugs aren't only technical. Also missing from the Amazon
Access site is the opportunity to write a review; rate a book, CD, or
other product; or probe a little deeper by choosing the "Explore this
book" link available on the primary site. These are not trivial omissions: such activities, in my judgment, are central to the experience of
shopping on Amazon.com. Despite the improvements to Amazon
Access, I still agree with what I wrote to a friend in December 2001 to
explain my disappointment with Amazon Access:

> I think I disagree with you about their having gotten down
> to the "essence" of Amazon.com. Or rather, they've defined
> the essence as "buying a book" from them. And maybe that's
> true, from *their* standpoint—the only thing they care
> about is selling stuff. Fine. But for me as a book-buyer (or
> music-buyer, or software-buyer, and so on, but especially as

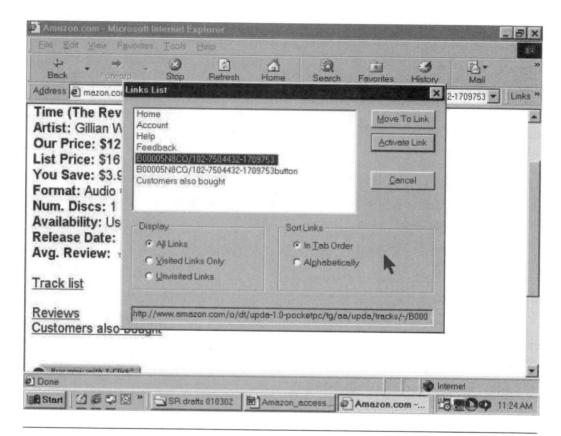

FIGURE 8–13 Screen shot of the Buying Info page for a CD on Amazon Access, with the JAWS Links List superimposed. Links to reviews and track lists are not identified in the JAWS Links List, although they are visible on the screen. Accessed January 5, 2002, at *http://www.amazon.com/exec/obidos/dt/upda-1.0-i/tg/aa/upda/item/-/B00005N8CQ/ 103-6028773-7169400*. Used with permission.

a book-buyer), the "essence" of what I'm doing is browsing—when I could go to bricks-and-mortar bookstores or libraries, the pleasure was in gathering up armsful of books and hunting around in them, looking at the table of contents and the index, dipping into the book to sample the quality of the prose, getting a feel for the author's angle, skill, and so on. What makes the brick-and-mortar Barnes & Noble and Borders so successful is that they emulated the old-fashioned mom-and-pop bookstore, where you could get your books together and go sit down somewhere and read till you'd made up your mind and were ready to go up to the register and plunk down your money for the one(s) you really had to have.

The whole point of Amazon's having invented all that "mass customization" and the NetPerceptions stuff that maps my purchases onto other people's purchases and builds recommendations is to approximate that kind of activity on-line—and the reviews and the rating systems are all part of that, all part of creating the impression that, even sitting in your desk chair at 2:00 A.M. in your underwear, you're still part of a community of readers.

That kind of thing is very important to the blind people I know. And it's what amazon.com/access *doesn't* provide access to. And I think they're making a big mistake if they think that the "essence of Amazon.com" consists in buying things quickly.

No one is required to write reviews, of course. But people who can use the main site can write reviews if they want to, while customers for whom Amazon Access is Amazon.com don't even have the option. This is not a trivial matter: it goes to the heart of what accessibility means.

Amazon Access Was Not Designed for the Visually Impaired

The fact is that Amazon Access was not designed primarily to be accessible to people with disabilities, despite the impression created by stories like the one in *E-Commerce News*, which quotes Robert Frederick, manager of the company's Amazon Anywhere program: "Making online shopping . . . accessible to all people remains one of Amazon's main goals. . . . [W]e hope this new site will greatly improve the shopping experience for our customers who use screen access software" [Cox 2001].

The <meta> tags in source code for the Amazon Access home page[7] tell a different story, as shown in the code below. (<meta> tags are part of the document's <head> element. They are meant to be read primarily by machines—search engines rely on them, for example—not humans.)

```
<head>
<title>Amazon.com</title>
<meta name=Handheldfriendly content="true">
<meta name=PalmComputingPlatform content=true>
</head>
```

That's the entire <head> element. There is nothing here about accessibility. What this says very clearly is that Amazon Access was designed for wireless access on cell phones and handheld devices, and I think the site is probably just fine for that (or will be once the programmers get rid of the actual bugs). But people who are blind don't use Palm Pilots or similar products, which are very graphical. And they don't use cell phones to browse the Internet because cell phones sold in the United States don't yet have the capacity to speak screen content the way screen readers and talking Web browsers do. Neither

---

7. Source code accessed on June 5, 2002, at *http://www.amazon.com/access.*

JAWS, Window-Eyes, nor Home Page Reader supports any Pocket PC or handheld computer—not the iPAQ, not Palm, not Handspring.

You don't have to take my word for it. The December 6, 2001, story in *E-Commerce News* makes the same point: "The new site is powered by the company's mobile commerce platform, Amazon Anywhere, which provides wireless access to Amazon's Web sites. . . ." Then, driving the point home, the article goes on to say that these slimmed-down versions of the primary Amazon site "are designed specifically for wireless phones, PDAs and other non-standard Internet browsers" [Cox 2001].

The Saga Continues

The next day, I went back again to the Amazon Access site; this time, I placed an order for a CD using the Buy now with 1-Click button. The following day, I received an e-mail from Amazon.com saying that the company couldn't ship my order because the credit card number had been declined by the issuing bank. The e-mail message contained a link to a page where, it said, I could "update" the payment method. Interestingly, this link did not point to a page on the Amazon Access site but went instead to the main Amazon.com site. How could I tell? Easy: here's what JAWS reported when the page came up.

> Amazon.com: Help / Using Your Account / Updating Payment Information for Your Order
>
> ref=top_nav_sb_help/102-7504432-1709753
>
> ref=top_nav_wl_help/102-7504432-1709753
>
> ref=top_nav_ya_help/102-7504432-1709753
>
> ref=top_nav_hp_help/102-7504432-1709753

ref=nh_help/102-7504432-1709753

ref=nh_help/102-7504432-1709753

ref=nw_help/102-7504432-1709753

ref=ndi_help/102-7504432-1709753

577394/102-7504432-1709753

577394/102-7504432-1709753

283155/102-7504432-1709753

5174/102-7504432-1709753

130/102-7504432-1709753

404272/102-7504432-1709753

577394/102-7504432-1709753

ref%3Dtab%5Fgw%5Fgw%5F1/102-7504432-1709753

tabs/yourstore-off-sliced._ZCJOHN%27S,0,2,0,0,
verdenab,7,90,90,80_

tabs/books-off-sliced

tabs/electronics-off-sliced

tabs/toys-off-sliced

tabs/garden-off-sliced

tabs/software-off-sliced

tabs/music-off-sliced

ref%3Dtab_gw_storesdirectory/102-7504432-1709753

Help

Help

Using Your Account

Updating Payment Information for Your Order

Updating Payment Information for Your Order

It's easy to review or change the payment information for any order that has not yet entered the shipping process.

Log in to Your Account to update or review payment information
for your recent orders now. Once you've signed in, follow these
simple instructions:

[And so on. . . .][8]

After listening to this point on the page (which took a long time),
I had trouble believing that I'd find the business of updating my account information quite as "easy" as the page suggested (in fact, I had
tried to do so several months earlier and had found it difficult, even
with help from a sighted friend). Then I had an inspiration: I'd go to
Amazon Access—which should be much easier for something like
this—and take care of it there! So off I went.

The first part of the process went smoothly enough. I discovered
that another order I had attempted to cancel the previous day (from
the original Amazon.com site) had not in fact been cancelled. I'm
pleased to say that I was able to cancel it relatively easily on Amazon
Access. That left just the matter of updating the account information.
There was nothing wrong with my credit card. The problem, as I
could tell when I listened to the page, was that somehow the database
had reversed the shipping address for my office and the billing address, with the predictable consequence that the bank rejected the
transaction. (As far as I know, this information was correct the last
time I placed an order through the original Amazon.com site—it had

---

8. Transcript of JAWS reading the first part of the page to which I was directed by
a link from an Amazon.com e-mail in order to update billing information.
Accessed January 6, 2002.

required several e-mail exchanges to make it so, including an ac-knowledgment of a bug in the database scripting and an assurance that the bug had been corrected.) But, OK—I wanted the CD and I was prepared to go in and straighten things out.

The instructions on the page told me to "click the Edit button un-der Payment Method below to specify a new payment method for this order." I noted the device-dependent wording (assuming that I would be clicking the button) and scrolled down the page so I could select the Edit button and get on with it. But wait—something had gone terribly wrong. . . .

I listened to the page (Figure 8–14) several times. There was no Edit button under Payment Method. There was no Edit button any-where on the page. There was only a link at the bottom of the page to cancel an unshipped item. Been there, done that. Not what I needed to do now in any case. I tried refreshing the page to see if somehow that Edit button would turn up. But something else turned up instead.

Instead of reloading the page I was on, my attempt to refresh the page brought up the sign-in screen instead—a not unreasonable pre-caution, I guess—but it wasn't the Amazon Access sign-in page. It was the sign-in page for the original Amazon.com site! (See Figure 8–15.)

I am not making this up. I was in the Twilight Zone. E-commerce quicksand—worse than voicemail. I was trying to give these people my money. But it was just too much work. "Maybe," I thought, "maybe I'll just ask my wife for a ride to my locally owned and oper-ated record store, where I can tell one of the nice and really knowl-edgeable humans who work there what I want, and just take it home with me." At least the sales tax would go back into the Austin econ-omy. Some of it would even go to Capital Metro. Maybe they'd use it to enhance their Web site.

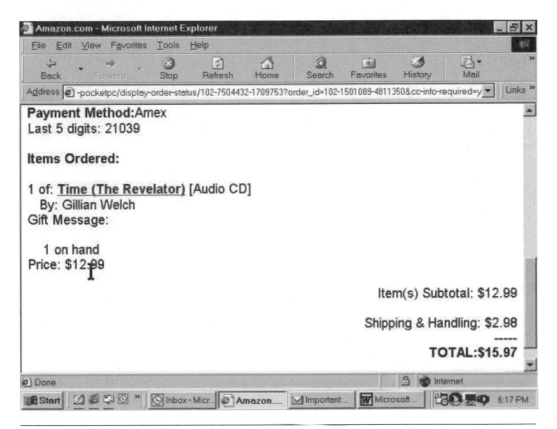

FIGURE 8–14 Screen shot of the Amazon Access page where the instructions say there is an Edit button under Payment Method—but no such button exists. Accessed January 6, 2002, at *https://www.amazon.com/o/dt/upda-1.0-pocketpc/display-order-status/102-7504432-1709753?order_id=102-1501089-4811350&cc-info-required=y*. Used with permission.

FINDING SOLUTIONS: TOWARD MAXIMUM ACCESSIBILITY

What broke down in the cases we've examined here wasn't just HTML code. What broke down was a *process*, and that's one of our key points here. Even with the best intentions in the world, text-only variants are almost inevitably second tier; they're poor cousins to the

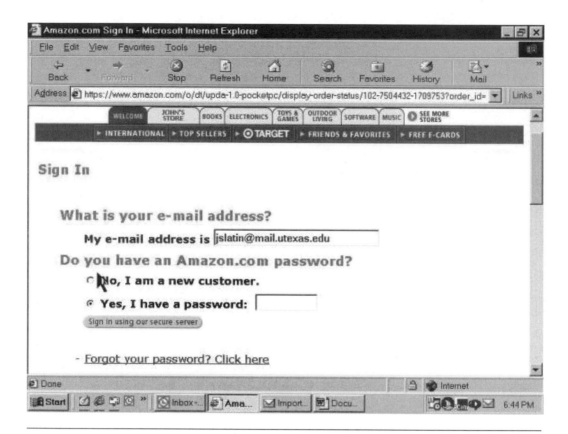

FIGURE 8–15 Screen shot of the sign-in page that appeared when I refreshed the Amazon Access page where I was trying to update my account information. Accessed January 6, 2002, at *https://www.amazon.com/o/dt/upda-1.0-pocketpc/display-order-status/ 102-7504432-1709753?order_id=102-1501089-4811350&cc-info-required=y*. Used with permission.

(media-) rich folks at the fancy-dress ball. They receive far less attention from designers, developers, and managers than the media-rich primary pages do, and it shows. Separate is not equal.

The Amazon Access site raises similar issues. There's no evil there, either. Just a misunderstanding, perhaps even an inevitable one. Those of us in the accessibility community have been "selling" accessibility, in part, by making the point that many of the techniques that support enhanced accessibility for people with disabilities—especially people who are blind or visually impaired—are also essential to support wireless access. Perhaps what we see on Amazon Access, then, is evidence of what happens when these claims are interpreted too literally, when they're understood to mean that designing for wireless access is the same thing as designing for accessibility to people with disabilities. In Section 2 of this book, we'll show that what's really necessary is to turn the telescope around. Maximum accessibility means starting with the needs of users who have disabilities and building from there.

So let's try thinking about this problem from a different standpoint. It's important to approach ALT text and the notion of "equivalent alternatives" as much more than something we need to provide to help out those who are unfortunately unable to see the images or hear the sounds on our Web sites. Instead, we can recognize that equivalent alternatives like ALT text, for example—like other well-written and meaningful text, like well-crafted images—are important resources for excellent design, elements that we can take advantage of as we work to create the best possible experience for everyone who visits our sites. That's maximum accessibility!

SECTION 2

Strategies and Techniques for Maximum Accessibility

9

Equivalent Alternatives

THE PRIME DIRECTIVE: EQUIVALENT ALTERNATIVES FOR MAXIMUM ACCESSIBILITY

The "prime directive" of Web accessibility—the number-one item in both WCAG 1.0 and the Section 508 federal accessibility standards that took effect in June 2001—is the requirement to provide "equivalent alternatives" for visual and auditory elements of the Web site. In this chapter, to explore what that means, we begin at the beginning. We start with ALT text, then move on to other kinds of text equivalents; finally, we briefly discuss uses of other media as alternatives *to* text.

HTML Elements and Attributes Addressed in This Chapter

Elements

`<img>`, `<area>`, `<script>`, `<applet>`

Attributes

`alt`, `src`, `longdesc`, `width`, `height`

Accessibility Checkpoints and Standards Addressed in This Chapter

Web Content Accessibility Guidelines 1.0 Checkpoints

1. Provide equivalent alternatives for auditory and visual content.

1.1. Provide a text equivalent for every non-text element (e.g., via "alt", "longdesc", or in element content). This includes: images, graphical representations of text (including symbols), image map regions, animations (e.g., animated GIFs), applets and programmatic objects, ASCII art, frames, scripts, images used as list bullets, spacers, graphical buttons, sounds (played with or without user interaction), stand-alone audio files, audio tracks of video, and video. [Priority 1]

1.3. Until user agents can automatically read aloud the text equivalent of a visual track, provide an auditory description of the important information of the visual track of a multimedia presentation. [Priority 1]

1.4. For any time-based multimedia presentation synchronize equivalent alternatives with the presentation. [Priority 1]

9.1. Provide client-side image maps instead of server-side image maps except where the regions cannot be identified with an available geometric shape. [Priority 1]

14.2. Supplement text with graphic or auditory presentations where they will facilitate comprehension of the page. [Priority 3]

Section 508 Standards, §1194.22

(**a**) A text equivalent for every non-text element shall be provided (e.g., via "alt", "longdesc", or in element content).

(**b**) Equivalent alternatives for any multimedia presentation shall be synchronized with the presentation.

(**f**) Client-side image maps shall be provided instead of server-side image maps except where the regions cannot be defined with an available geometric shape.

AN ALTERNATIVE TO IMAGES: ALT TEXT

The idea of equivalent alternatives is fundamental to Web accessibility for people with disabilities. We might think of this as a kind of "principled redundancy"—providing multiple paths to key ideas and information to ensure that all roads do in fact lead to Rome.

The most common type of equivalent alternative is *ALT text*, which should be associated with images and selectable regions of image maps. ALT text is a short phrase that succinctly identifies the image and makes its function clear to a person who cannot see the image. For image maps, ALT text is associated with each selectable area to allow people using screen readers, talking browsers, and refreshable Braille displays to access the links and understand where they go.

Technically speaking, the term *ALT* refers to a specific HTML *attribute* that can be attached to a number of HTML *elements*. The most important of these elements are images (<img> elements) and selectable areas of client-side image maps (<area> elements), and we concentrate on these in this chapter.[1]

The ALT text is generally a phrase or short sentence that forms the content of the alt attribute. This apparently simple idea has great power. Missing or inadequate ALT text can make your Web site completely unusable for people with disabilities such as blindness, low vision, and cognitive disabilities caused by traumatic brain injury or learning disabilities. By the same token, writing effective ALT text can provide a significantly better experience not only for people with these disabilities but also for just about everyone who visits your site. This is because the process of *writing* ALT text will lead you to clarify both the purpose of each element on each page and the organization of the elements in relation to one another.

Sample HTML for ALT Text

The HTML code for associating ALT text with an image looks like this:

```
<img src="http://www.somewhere.edu/images/imagefile.jpg"
     height="340" width="160" alt="Photo of Slatin's head">
```

---

1. Other HTML elements require other means for providing alternative content. WCAG 1.0 recommends synchronized audio descriptions and captions for multimedia; Section 508 requires them. Also, scripts, applets, plug-ins, and other embedded or ancillary materials must be accessible as well. When these elements and their functions cannot be made directly accessible to people with disabilities, the site should provide alternative ways to access the same information or interactions through equivalent functionality. See Chapter 13 to learn about alternatives for multimedia objects such as video, audio, and animation. See Chapter 14 for discussion of alternatives for the <script> and <applet> elements.

where

- `img` is the HTML image element.
- `src` is the HTML attribute identifying the name and location of the image file to be displayed.
- `height` is the height of the image, measured in pixels.
- `width` is the width of the image, measured in pixels.
- `alt` is the HTML attribute that contains the text to be associated with the image. This text is read aloud by screen readers and talking browsers, displayed by text-only browsers, and converted to Braille characters by Braille displays. In some browsers, it also appears briefly as a "tool tip" when the mouse passes across an element that has an `alt` attribute (and no `title` attribute, which takes precedence).

Characteristics of Effective ALT Text

In order to be effective, ALT text should

- Be short: 150 characters or fewer, including spaces and punctuation.
- Make sense *out of context,* for example, when read aloud by itself or as an item in a list of links spoken by a screen reader or talking browser, or when rendered as Braille. (Examples of links presented in the JAWS Links List appear in Chapters 2, 5, and 8.)
- Make sense *in context,* for example, when read aloud as part of a larger page that contains other text.
- Contribute to the intelligibility of the page as an *auditory experience.*

We'll discuss these issues as we go along. First, though, let's look at the issue of equivalence itself.

Equivalence

When is an alternative an *equivalent* alternative? Suppose the visual design of your page calls for a red arrow that serves as a graphical link to the next page in a sequence. The ALT text for this image should *not* be "right arrow" or "red arrow": it should say "Next page." It isn't appropriate to use phrases like "Link to next page" or "Go to next page," either, and certainly not "Click here to go to the next page" (we've seen all of these in various places). Why? There are several reasons.

First, it's redundant. Assistive technology devices generally inform their users when they encounter links. The JAWS screen reader, for example, inserts the word "link"; IBM's Home Page Reader speaks link text (including ALT text for graphical links) in a different voice than it uses for other content; Braille displays insert additional Braille characters, such as "lnk". So it's redundant to use such phrases in the ALT text for graphical links. People who use screen readers, talking browsers, and refreshable Braille displays already have to spend more time on typical Web tasks than people who can point and click; redundant phrases just make it take even longer because users have to *listen* to each one (or scan it with their fingers).

Second, beginning the ALT text for every graphical link with a phrase like "Go to . . ." may interfere with an important navigation aid. JAWS, for example, includes a Links List feature (as seen in several of the user experience chapters in the first section of this book). Users can navigate this scrollable list of links *alphabetically*—that is, pressing a letter takes you directly to the next link that begins with that letter. In our current example, pressing the *n* key would let us jump directly to the "Next page" link. If all the links begin with the same letter (*g*, for example), this convenience is lost.

Finally, "Click here" doesn't work for two reasons. First, it's device-dependent, assuming the use of a mouse. You may think that this is silly: surely everyone can translate the word "Click" into the action that's appropriate for whatever input device they're using. But that apparently simple act of translation may be beyond the cognitive grasp of some users—people with traumatic brain injury, for instance, might have trouble; even if they're able to do the translating, the effort required may be tiring. Second, spatial references like the word "here" or the phrase "on the left" might pose similar problems, both for people with cognitive impairments and for people who can't see the screen: where is "here" when you're listening to the page? Where's "left"?

Length and Intelligibility

ALT text should be short, but it still has to contribute to the intelligibility of the page. So how short is too short? It's not unusual to encounter ALT text containing just one or two words. This may not be enough, however, to provide the information people really need. Jared Spool and his colleagues at User Interface Engineering [1997] found, for example, that a link's value for users depends on how well those users are able to predict where the link will take them and on how easy it is to recognize differences among the links on the page. Predictability, in turn, depended heavily on the *descriptiveness* of the link text; longer phrases containing 5–12 words yielded higher predictability than shorter ones.

These findings by Spool et al. have important implications for the length of ALT text, too, especially when it's used as link text or as an important identifier for an entire page or site. The ALT text for the first image on the General Motors site, for example, consists of just two letters: "GM."[2] It's easy to think that this should be fine—after all, there can't be many people in the Web-using world who don't know what GM is! But remember that people using screen readers and talking browsers are *listening* to the Web, not scanning visually for familiar signs and logos. The ALT text for the General Motors logo is extremely short and goes past the ear very quickly; people using screen readers and talking browsers may not be entirely certain of what they've heard. The Fujitsu site says only the single word "Fujitsu,"[3] risking similar disorientation—especially if the user got to the Fujitsu site by following a link from another site that didn't clearly indicate the destination. The Sprint site, only marginally better, announces itself as "Sprint dot com."[4] Even on the site for Jared Spool's firm, User Interface Engineering, the ALT text for the logo is just "U I E logo."[5] This is fine if you already know where you are, but unintelligible if you don't.

The point here is that for people listening to a screen reader or talking browser, ALT text is an experience in *time,* not in space. The ALT text shouldn't take up more time than necessary, but it also shouldn't go by so quickly that the user misses it or has to have it re-

---

2. Accessed July 15, 2001, at *http://www.gm.com.*
3. Accessed July 15, 2001, at *http://www.fujitsu.com.*
4. Accessed July 15, 2001, at *http://www.sprint.com.*
5. Accessed July 15, 2001, at *http://world.std.com/~uieWeb/index.html.*

peated. (An analogy: Talking wristwatches like the one I [John] use play a little chime and the word "It's" before announcing the time, giving the user a better chance to get ready to hear the time when the watch speaks it.)

When ALT Text Should Be "Silent"

The fact that ALT text must contribute to the intelligibility of the page as an *auditory or tactile reading experience* suggests that there are times when ALT text might actually get in the way. For example, many Web developers use transparent "images" in order to achieve specific layouts. People who use screen readers, talking browsers, Braille displays, or other text-only devices will not be helped if they have to *hear* every such image identified! Similarly, when the page already contains a detailed description of an image (such as a chart, graph, or painting), ALT text may be unnecessary. In such cases, however, the image element (<img>) must still have an alt attribute because when there's no alt attribute present at all, screen readers and talking browsers read the contents of the src attribute (the name and location of the image file) instead.

The appropriate technique in these cases is to include an "empty" alt attribute. In Web developers' jargon this is called "setting the alt attribute to null." Setting the alt attribute to null forces screen readers and talking browsers to behave as if the ALT text isn't there.

The HTML for setting a null alt attribute looks like this:

```
<img src="http://www.somewhere.edu/images/spacer.gif"
    alt="">
```

Note: As we saw in Chapter 7, setting the `alt` attribute to null isn't always a straightforward affair. Nonetheless, we strongly encourage you to use this technique *when it's appropriate for the image to be "silent."* This is a judgment call and, as with any other judgment call, you should test it against the responses of actual users.

Sliced Images

Designers sometimes "slice" large, complex images into several smaller images in order to speed up the time it takes for the complete page to appear on the screen. This technique has some important advantages, but there are potential disadvantages from an accessibility standpoint. That's because there's a difference between what users see on their screens and what screen readers, talking browsers, and Braille displays "see" when they process the HTML source code.

What users see on their screens looks like a single image. But screen readers and talking browsers "see" a succession of individual (`<img>`) elements. Each of these `<img>` elements has to have its own ALT attribute—if it doesn't, people using assistive technologies will hear the filename for each of the "slices." What the designer intended as a beautifully coherent visual impression breaks up into a multitude of incoherent auditory fragments. Associating the same alt text with each "slice" isn't the solution either. People listening to the page would hear the same phrase repeated over and over again for no apparent reason.

The solution is to write the ALT text for the *first* slice—the first `<img>` element in the composition—as if you were writing the ALT text for the whole large image. Then, set the `alt` attribute to null (*alt*="") for each of the remaining slices. In this way, someone using a screen reader, talking browser, or refreshable Braille display will hear or read the ALT text that identifies the entire image, and their assistive technologies will ignore the other slices. In other words, these users will experience the page as if it contained just the one image, just as people who look at the page see it.

Sliced Images That Act Like Image Maps

The exception to the procedure we've just described comes when the sliced image is actually intended to serve as an image map. In this case, some of the individual slices will actually become graphical links, while others don't. The ALT text for each of these graphical links should identify the link destination, just as it would for any other graphical link. The remaining slices, the ones that don't act as links, should have empty `alt` attributes so that screen readers and talking browsers will ignore them.

Considerations of Reading Order

The confusion we encountered at the Web site of the Metropolitan Museum of Art in Chapter 7 illustrated that reading order matters: it can make the difference between an informative and successful visit to a Web site and a very frustrating one. We mention this here because the order in which people using screen readers, talking browsers, refreshable Braille devices, and text-only displays encounter ALT text, whether on its own or in relation to other text on the screen, can make a huge difference in the users' ability to use the site effectively and thus in the quality of their experience.

Screen readers, talking browsers, refreshable Braille devices, and text-only displays all work from left to right and top to bottom, just the way most speakers of English and European languages learned to read in school. But whereas part of *our* development as literate citizens involved learning that we don't always have to read in such a linear way (and that sometimes we shouldn't), the technologies we're discussing here aren't smart enough to know that. So they just plow ahead like the robots they are, stupidly reading whatever's in their path "in the order it was received," as the voicemail robots put it so eloquently.

The placement of images and text on a page determines the reading order, so it's up to Web site developers to control the reading order. It's pretty simple, from a purely technical standpoint—just a matter of placing elements on the page in such a way that the reading order makes sense. But this is harder than it sounds: since the ALT text is programmatically tied to the image (that is, `alt` is an *attribute* of the `<img>` *element*), the positions of the images on the page determine the order in which assistive technology devices read the ALT text. This may mean rethinking the way you place those images. (See Chapter 11 for further discussion of reading order in layout tables. See Chapter 15 for ideas about how to use Cascading Style Sheets to control the relationship between the order in which elements are displayed visually and the order in which they're read by screen readers, talking browsers, and Braille displays.) It may also mean thinking much harder about crafting the individual phrases of ALT text so that they make sense both when they're read on their own out of context (for example, by someone using the JAWS Links List) *and* when they're read as part of a whole page or a section of it. This becomes especially important if you've used visual proximity to create groups of related links or other elements because the relationships may get lost in the translation from visual to auditory mode. You've designed those visual relationships to be recognizable in a split-second glance—but people using screen readers, talking browsers, and refreshable Braille displays hear (or manually scan) the items *one at a time;* this can sometimes take a very long time, too.

Since your pages probably contain both text and graphics, you will also have to take into account the interplay of *offscreen* text stored in alt attributes with *onscreen* text, like the text links and captions and extended descriptions on the Metropolitan Museum site discussed in Chapter 7. As we discussed there, tools like The WAVE can be invaluable resources for meeting this challenge. As we said in Chapter 7: reading order matters!

WHEN ALT TEXT ISN'T ENOUGH: EXTENDED DESCRIPTIONS

ALT text works well for simple images, graphical links, and image maps. But there are times when developers must use rich, complex images to convey rich, complex ideas and information. In these cases, ALT text by itself is too short to accomplish this important task. For example, if the page includes a graph or chart representing complex logical or mathematical relationships, or a photograph of a historic event, an extended description should supplement the ALT text.

You may include the extended description in the content of the page itself or on a separate page linked to the page that displays the image. (Which of these is the right solution in a given instance depends on the context and on what will best help your audience understand what you want them to understand.) HTML 4.0 includes a longdesc attribute designed for this purpose, but this technique has not been well supported until quite recently. As of March 2002, however, both IBM's Home Page Reader, versions 3.0 and higher, and JAWS 4.01 support the `longdesc` attribute. The `<img>` element may include both `alt` and `longdesc` attributes, as in the following example.

```
<img src="images/dillonatflavin.jpg"
   alt="John and Dillon in front of a Dan Flavin
       light-sculpture"
   longdesc="johndill_flavin_description.htm">
```

There is an important difference between the `alt` and `longdesc` attributes: the value of the `alt` attribute is the text that will be rendered by user agents that cannot display the image, while the value of the `longdesc` attribute is the name of an HTML file that contains the extended description.

In the absence of support for the `longdesc` attribute, some developers have used a "d-link" (description-link) instead—that is, a lowercase letter "d" that serves as a link to the page that contains the text description. The "d" is positioned close to the image. Some developers, however, are reluctant to use the d-link because it's difficult to integrate into the visual design of the page; others have expressed concern that users who aren't familiar with the convention will regard the d-link as some sort of mistake. Still others worry that multiple d-links on a page with multiple images will confuse people using screen readers, talking browsers, refreshable Braille devices, or text-only displays. If you share those concerns, we recommend that you either use the `longdesc` attribute or integrate the extended description into page content—where it may be welcomed by many of your users!

An Example: The Institute for Technology and Learning

At the top of the home page of the Institute for Technology and Learning (ITAL), with which I (John) am associated, is a heading that reads, "Institute for Technology and Learning at The University of Texas at Austin." An image of the Institute's name as it appears in Grade 2 Braille is displayed above the printed words, and the ITAL logo appears on the right side of the screen (Figure 9–1).

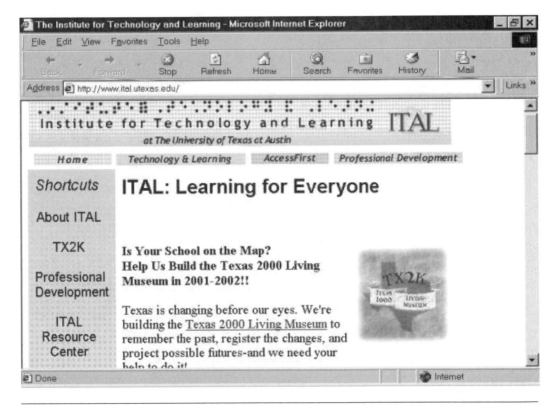

FIGURE 9–1 Screen shot of the home page of the Institute for Technology and Learning. The banner across the top includes graphical text and a logo. Accessed July 14, 2001, at *http://www.ital.utexas.edu*. Used with permission.

Graphical Text, Textual Text, and Prose: What's the Difference?

The whole banner, including the ITAL logo, is a graphic (the ITAL logo is a separate image). This makes no difference to sighted visitors, who simply read the words as they appear on the screen. But from the computer's standpoint, graphical text isn't text at all—it's a *picture* of text, so the words are just part of the banner image. Such graphical text can't be recognized by screen readers, talking browsers, Braille displays, text-only browsers such as Lynx, certain PDAs, and two-way pagers—or by conventional browsers with images turned off to speed up Web access for people with older computers or slow modems. And that means that the banner by itself is unintelligible to the people using these devices.

Since the banner is "invisible" to so many users and user agents, we attached an `alt` attribute containing the words "The Institute for Technology and Learning at the University of Texas at Austin" to the image. Here's the source code.

```
<img src="/images/masthead.gif" width="655" height="72"
    alt="The Institute for Technology and Learning at the
    University of Texas at Austin">
```

The only difference between the ALT text and the graphical text displayed onscreen is the word "The" at the beginning of the ALT text. This creates a short auditory "beat" to help listeners orient their attention—a little trick learned from years of wearing a talking wristwatch that precedes its announcements of the time with a little chime and the word "It's," as in "It's nine thirty-nine A.M." By making the ALT text nearly identical to the graphical text in the banner image, we ensure that people visiting our site are able to tell where they are right away, whether they're using conventional browsers like Internet Explorer and Netscape Navigator or other user agents, with or without assistive technologies.

But this isn't to say that we haven't lost anything along the way. We included Braille characters in the design of the banner graphic because we wanted to do more than announce our name and university affiliation. We wanted to send a message about our commitment to accessibility and elegant design. But the ALT text doesn't capture this at all. This is as it should be: as we've noted, the alt attribute is *supposed* to contain short phrases that stand as *functional* equivalents of the images with which they're associated, not (or not usually) *descriptions* of those images.

ALT Text as Offscreen Text

The ALT text for ITAL's banner graphic contains 13 words and 78 characters, including spaces and punctuation. You're probably thinking that this is awfully long, and certainly it's considerably longer than average ALT text. It *would* be too long—much too long—if it were meant to be *displayed* onscreen in addition to the actual banner graphic. But of course it isn't meant to be displayed that way: ALT text is by definition written for people who can't see or comprehend the images and meant only to be picked up by screen readers, talking browsers, and text-only or Braille displays—though a side benefit is that it's also available to search engines.

ALT Text as Image Replacement

It would be hard to overstate the importance of the fact that ALT text isn't meant to be viewed *alongside* the image. For people using screen readers, talking browsers, refreshable Braille devices, or text-only displays, *the ALT text replaces the image.* These users will never have a chance to decide whether the ALT text is really a satisfactory "equivalent" for the image. The ALT text is all they have to go on, so it has to stand on its own!

The ALT text for the ITAL banner image is well within the 150-character *de facto* limit imposed by the default line-length setting for JAWS, the most widely used screen reader. But the ALT text is still too short to convey the full meaning of a complex image like the ITAL masthead.

Extended Descriptions as Equivalents for Complex Images

All of this helps us understand one reason why the requirement to provide equivalent alternatives goes beyond the `alt` attribute. Since the success of many Web sites depends at least in part on people's ability to grasp the meaning of complex charts, graphs, photographs, and other artwork, including corporate logos, maximum accessibility involves crafting equivalent alternatives for them. These often take the form of prose descriptions like the following description of the ITAL masthead.

> The masthead graphic displayed on each page presents our name in both inkprint and Braille characters. Adjacent to this is the ITAL logo, consisting of the initials ITAL superimposed on a yellow wireframe globe.

This description consists of 34 words and 211 characters, including spaces and punctuation; it's part of an even longer explanation of page layout and navigational design for the ITAL site as a whole. The material resides on a separate page; the link from the home page is attached to a clear image, one pixel high by one pixel wide, which remains transparent to the eye while the screen reader picks up the ALT text. Here's the source code for the ALT text.

```
<a href="/stafftools/access/nav_overview.html">
   <img src="/images/clear.gif" width="1" height="1"
   alt="Please select this link for information about
   accessible navigation" border="0"></a>
```

Using the `alt` attribute of an invisible image as a link to an extended description is a "kludge," a clunky workaround to which ITAL's Web designers resorted because browsers and assistive technologies available when the ITAL site was being developed in summer 2001 did not yet support the `longdesc` attribute—though the attribute had been part of the HTML specification since 1997 as a way to manage such extended descriptions. (As we noted above, assistive technology is now beginning to provide support for this attribute, making it a more valuable resource for design.) Another strategy—in some ways the simplest—is to include the extended description on the same page where the image you're describing is displayed. The Metropolitan Museum of Art site discussed in Chapter 7 employs this technique to excellent effect.

Text Description as a Design Element

Despite the problems we encountered while visiting the Metropolitan Museum site, the use of text as an important element in the site's visual and conceptual design is worth considering here. The Metropolitan Museum used informative text very effectively as a *design element*, rather than hiding it or throwing it away. Let's revisit these pages with that in mind.

A page we discussed at length in Chapter 7 presents a highlight of the Metropolitan Museum's vast collection of illuminated manuscripts. On this page, an onscreen caption provides useful information about the manuscript and its creator; this is presumably catalog copy. But there's more. An extended description is available on the same page, providing a vivid, detailed account of the image and its context. Here's a sample:

The 209 folios of "*The Hours of Jeanne d'Évreux*" include twenty-five full-page paintings with paired images from the Infancy and Passion of Christ and scenes of the life of Saint Louis. The figures are rendered in delicate grisaille (shades of gray) that imparts an amazingly sculptural quality, and the images are accented with rich reds and blues and with touches of orange and yellow, pink, lilac, and turquoise. In the margins, close to seven hundred illustrations depict the bishops, beggars, street dancers, maidens, and musicians that peopled the streets of medieval Paris, as well as apes, rabbits, dogs, and creatures of sheer fantasy.[6]

Making effective use of extended descriptions as elements in the visual design of a site requires more than font and color selection. It requires attention to the art and craft of prose, too. In the following section we examine some useful guidelines for describing complex images.

---

6. From the Metropolitan Museum of Art's online description of "*The Hours of Jeanne d'Évreux*," accessed June 19, 2002, at *http://www.metmuseum.org/ collections/view1.asp?dep=7&item=54%2E1%2E2.*

Alonzo's Guidelines for Describing Works of Art

The practice of describing extremely complex visual images has a long history in fields as diverse as technical communication and art history. Both fields make their contributions to Adam Alonzo's brief but excellent paper, "A Picture Is Worth 300 Words" [2001], which offers useful guidelines for describing works of art.

Alonzo, the Accessible Arts Coordinator at Wright State University in Dayton, Ohio, suggests that extended descriptions of complex images should run 250–300 words. At 202 words, the complete description of the *Hours of Jeanne d'Évreux* is shorter than Alonzo's guidelines suggest, yet it's long enough to convey a lively sense of the illuminated manuscript from which the illustration came and short enough to function successfully as an element in the visual design of the page.

In his paper, Alonzo offers six guidelines for describers.

1. Be objective.
2. Be brief.
3. Be descriptive.
4. Be logical.
5. Be accurate.
6. Miscellaneous.

Alonzo's third guideline, "Be descriptive," gives a good sense of what a skilled writer can accomplish within a short space, offering suggestions for describing shape, size, texture, color, composition, and technique.

Visual descriptions should utilize a broad vocabulary of vivid terminology to describe various features of art objects. Some common terms are categorized below.

Shapes can be described as: square, cubed, rectangular, flat, straight, circular, spherical, cylindrical, curved, rounded, triangular, conical, pyramidal, angular, irregular, jagged, sloped, diagonal, horizontal and vertical. These words can be used not only to identify the overall shape of the object, but also to describe geometric patterns within it. Avoid the use of words that imply action (unless the object actually does move). For instance, use "curved" instead of "curving." Also avoid imprecise colloquial terms such as "squiggle" or "zigzag."

Size can be described as: small, tiny, short, miniature, large, tall, monumental, thick, thin, narrow, wide, life-size, true to size, large scale and small scale. The object's dimensions, provided with the catalogue data, will inform visitors of its actual size.

Texture can be described as: smooth, glossy, coarse, grainy, rough, worn, weathered, scratched, cracked, broken, rippled, grooved, patterned, striped, dotted and perforated.

Color can be described as: intense, vivid, bright, light, dark, dull, pale, faint, solid or blended. Do not avoid references to color on the assumption that they will be meaningless to visitors who are blind. First of all, descriptions will be used by people without visual disabilities. Second, many people who are now blind were able to see in the past and are able to recall colors. Third, colors sometimes have symbolic meaning in works of art. However, avoid interpretive phrases like "warm gold" or "angry red."

Composition (or the arrangement of elements in a work) can be described as: low, high, above, below, parallel, perpendicular, in the foreground (or background), to the left (or right). When referring to relative locations, describe objects from the viewer's perspective, unless referring to the left or right of a character portrayed in the work.

Artistic technique can be described as: realistic, abstract, unnatural, simplified, detailed, precise, imprecise, sharply defined, blurred, splashed, brushed or stroked. [Alonzo 2001]

This is not a license for complete imaginative liberty, of course. The writer is responsible to the objects she or he is describing, and the choices are constrained by the need to meet Alonzo's other guidelines as well as this one. You can't just be descriptive, for example; you have to be logical, too. Alonzo puts it this way:

In order to be easily understood, visual descriptions must describe objects according to a logical sequence. Descriptions should begin with a general overview of what the object is and what it portrays. Depending upon what type of object it is, it may be appropriate at the outset to mention its color and surface texture, and perhaps its construction.

Following the overview, the various portions of the object should be described in detail, in some orderly fashion such as left to right or top to bottom. After one portion of the work has been described, an explicit transition should be used to identify the next area and its spatial relationship to the last. If part of the object is extremely complex, describe each segment separately, perhaps in a numbered sequence.

Depending on their design, sculptures or other three-dimensional works will likely need to be described from more than one angle. Use a logical sequence when doing so, as if the viewer was moving in a circle around the object.

When using descriptive words such as adjectives, place them after the word they modify, so visitors know what the thing is before they are told what it looks like. For example, use "his fingers are long and thin" instead of "long, thin fingers." [Alonzo 2001]

Adapting Alonzo's Guidelines When Describing Charts and Graphs

Alonzo wrote his guidelines to help people describe works of visual art such as drawings, paintings, and sculptures. But you can adapt the guidelines to describe other types of visual material, such as the charts that are often important elements of Web content.

It's easy to make the mistake of thinking that all you need to do to "describe" a chart is to list the data on a separate page linked to the chart. There's even a tool (a very expensive one, in fact) called Pop-Chart that automates this process. But there's a world of difference between a list of numbers and, say, a pie chart or a bar graph—that's why Web designers use carefully constructed charts instead of simply listing a bunch of numbers. By the same logic, there's also a world of difference between a list of numbers and a *description* of the chart: the whole purpose of the chart is to help people *see* what the mere numbers really mean, and that's what you should aim for when describing the chart as well.

The following description of four pie charts was written by Glenda Sims of the Web office of the University of Texas at Austin for an accessibility workshop she copresented with John Slatin in December 2001. The text is a proposed description for a page maintained by the University's Office of Institutional Studies; the page includes several pie charts showing different aspects of the University's student body in fall 2000.

> Four pie charts depicting UT Student Characteristics for Fall 2000. The four pie charts represent ethnicity, gender, permanent home address and student classification.
>
> 1) Ethnicity Pie Chart—data are listed in descending order
>
> White: 62.7%
>
> Asian American: 12.5%
>
> IIispanic: 11.8%
>
> Foreign: 8.6%
>
> African American: 3.2%
>
> American Indian: 0.5%
>
> Unknown: 0.8%
>
> (Note: the non-white wedges are pulled out of the pie chart, forming a 37.3% wedge.)

People who design visual displays of quantitative information (to borrow the title from Edward Tufte's influential book [1983]) take very seriously the matter of deciding what type of chart to use. It's important, therefore, for verbal descriptions to include that information. Note, too, that the description indicates how the data are organized (in descending order), then concludes with a note about the pie chart itself and how it represents the size of the non-white minority segment of the University's student body.

SIGHT AND SOUND: EQUIVALENT ALTERNATIVES FOR AUDITORY ELEMENTS

We began this chapter with the prime directive, the fact that good design requires equivalent alternatives to visual and auditory elements of Web pages. We discuss audio in greater detail in Chapter 13 when we examine multimedia applications, but a few words are necessary here as well.

The Web is an intensely visual medium, and within the past few years it has become increasingly noisy as well. It's important to remember, however, not to depend on sound alone to deliver information. Millions of people who use the Web will not hear those sounds. This may be due to deafness or hearing impairments but may also result from lack of audio speakers (for example, many public computers in libraries and schools do not have speakers). As you incorporate audio elements, be sure to provide text alternatives or other visual equivalents and/or explanations of the information you're delivering.

As we discuss in Chapter 13, how you provide appropriate alternatives will depend on the kind of audio material you're using and the format in which that material is presented. A simple example is an online evaluation in which incorrect answers are greeted with a buzz and correct answers with a bell tone. If at the same time you provide a caption or other visual cue with the same information, you will have provided an acceptable equivalent alternative. For more substantive auditory material—such as a recorded news interview or a bit of oral history—both WCAG 1.0 and Section 508 require a complete, verbatim transcript of the audio material.

TURNING THE TELESCOPE AROUND: EQUIVALENT ALTERNATIVES FOR TEXT

Throughout this chapter (and for the most part throughout this book), we've been talking about creating equivalent *text* alternatives for nontextual material such as images, sounds, video and animation, scripts and applets, and so on. It is not particularly difficult, technically speaking, to include these text alternatives, which work across many platforms and browsing devices as well as many assistive technology devices. WCAG 1.0 and the Section 508 standards share this emphasis on text. But before we leave this topic, it's worth thinking for a moment about situations when text might *not* be the answer.

Reading is difficult for many people. In some cases, the difficulty is due to a learning disability or other cognitive impairment. In many other cases, the reading difficulty arises from the fact that the natural language of the text is not the native language of the person reading it, who may well be in a different country than the author. Among the people whose native language may be different than that in which the page is written are many deaf people, whose native language is the national sign language of their native country. (This is especially true for people born deaf; late-deafened people are more likely to be comfortable with text and less likely to be fluent signers.) In some cases, there may be nonliterate people using your pages.

Supplementing text with graphical and auditory equivalents to facilitate comprehension is only a Priority 3 item (Checkpoint 14.2) in WCAG 1.0, and it's not even mentioned in Section 508. But where maximum accessibility is concerned, it's important not to limit ourselves to thinking only in terms of *text* as the alternative to images and sounds. Meeting the needs of all our users may mean including visual and auditory material as equivalent alternatives for text.

This might mean different things in different places. For example, it might mean not replacing a graphical representation with text but instead providing both graphical and textual versions. In other cases, it might mean adding illustrations, appropriately captioned or transcribed audio explanations, or described animations of complex concepts and processes. This is yet another way in which it's important to remember that a commitment to accessibility doesn't mean giving up multimedia. On the contrary, you can create accessible multimedia and use it to provide accessibility!

10

Forms of Participation: Designing HTML Forms for Maximum Accessibility

INTERACTIVITY AND THE USE OF FORMS

Forms are a Web developer's most important tool for gathering information from users. E-commerce sites use forms to find out what people want to buy, where they want their purchases delivered, and how they're going to pay. Distance- and e-learning sites use forms for a variety of purposes. Students complete a form when they register or when they provide a profile to introduce themselves to other members of the class. Forms are at the heart of message boards, too. When a student contributes a message to a class discussion forum, she or he enters the text in a form. And when students take tests online, they usually use a form to record and submit their responses.

Forms are powerful tools. But they can pose significant accessibility barriers, especially for people who use screen readers, talking browsers, or refreshable Braille displays. In order for these assistive technology devices to work correctly, the form controls (text input fields, buttons, and so on) must be labeled in such a way that the assistive technology can associate the correct label with the form control.

HTML Elements and Attributes Addressed in This Chapter

Elements

`<form>`, `<fieldset>`, `<legend>`, `<caption>`, `<label>`, `<input>`, `<td>`, `<table>`, `<select>`, `<option>`

Attributes

`id, name, for, type, value, selected, checked`

Accessibility Checkpoints and Standards Addressed in This Chapter

Web Content Accessibility Guidelines 1.0 Checkpoints

9.3. For scripts, specify logical event handlers rather than device-dependent event handlers. [Priority 2]

10.2. Until user agents support explicit associations between labels and form controls, for all form controls with implicitly associated labels, ensure that the label is properly positioned. [Priority 2]

12.3. Divide large blocks of information into more manageable groups where natural and appropriate. [Priority 2]

12.4. Associate labels explicitly with their controls. [Priority 2]

Section 508 Standards, §1194.22

(**n**) When electronic forms are designed to be completed on-line, the form shall allow people using assistive technology to access the information, field elements, and functionality required for completion and submission of the form, including all directions and cues.

(**p**) When a timed response is required, the user shall be alerted and given sufficient time to indicate more time is required.

ACCESSIBILITY PROBLEMS AND HTML FORMS

If Web developers don't label their forms correctly, you might find yourself in a situation like the one shown in Figure 10–1.

No, you're not crazy! The fields aren't labeled, and neither are the radio buttons. Even the buttons where the Submit and Reset buttons usually appear are blank. How could you complete the form correctly? This is similar to the problem we encountered on the Smithsonian Institution site on our first visit back in September 2001: a pop-up window, removed in a later redesign, included a registration form with unlabeled input fields that the JAWS screen reader couldn't identify (see Chapter 7).

The point, of course, is that one of the most important things you can do to make your Web-based forms accessible to people with disabilities—especially people using screen readers, talking browsers,

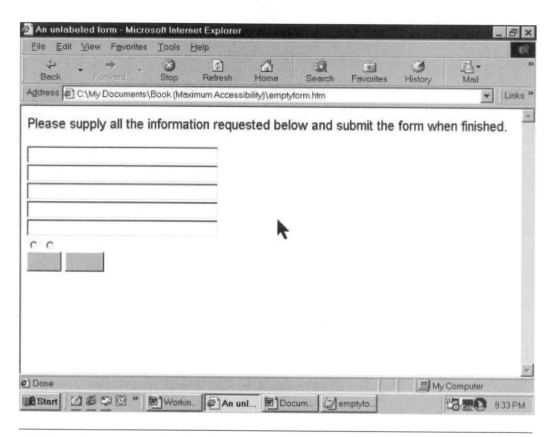

FIGURE 10–1 Screen shot of a form that has unlabeled input fields and buttons.

and screen magnifiers as well as refreshable Braille displays and text-only browsers—is to label each item on the form in such a way that assistive technology devices can identify and correctly report the labels. Without this, the person using a screen reader to work with the form will be in a bind like the one everyone would be in if they had to fill out the form shown in Figure 10–1.

Using the Keyboard to Interact with Forms

It's important to remember that people who use screen readers, talking browsers, and refreshable Braille displays to interact with forms on the Web typically don't use the mouse. Instead, they use the keyboard to navigate from field to field, to select options (for example, radio buttons, check boxes, or pull-down menus), and to submit the form. Of course, they usually can't see instructions and labels that appear beside or above the form fields and other elements on the form. And if the form isn't coded for accessibility, these users may not encounter the instructions and labels at all.

JAWS users, for example, have to **rely on** a special Forms Mode in order to interact with forms on the Web. To turn Forms Mode on, the user first listens for JAWS to indicate that it has found a field or other form element such as a radio button. When JAWS encounters an input field, for example, it speaks the label followed by the word "Edit." At this point, the user presses the enter key on the keyboard and JAWS says, "Forms Mode on." From this point, users typically tab through the remaining items on the form. When it encounters radio buttons or check boxes, JAWS says, for example, "Radio button checked," then reads the label for the radio button. To select a different option than the one currently selected, JAWS users can press the up or down arrow key on the keyboard. All goes smoothly—if all the items on the form are labeled in such a way that the assistive technology can identify them.

But there's more to it than simply labeling input fields and buttons. People who have limited use of their hands may also have difficulty completing online forms. For example, people with hand tremors resulting from cerebral palsy, Parkinson's disease, or other causes may find it difficult to select radio buttons that are too close together on the screen. Some quadriplegics and others who use on-screen representations of keyboards find it difficult to use forms whose controls aren't organized in a logical tab order or that require typing when they could use selection menus instead.

WORKING THROUGH AN EXAMPLE: THE AIR JUDGING FORM

In this chapter, we'll work through the process of converting into an online form the spreadsheet used to calculate the scores for participants in Knowbility's Accessibility Internet Rally. (For more information about AIR, see Chapter 4.) One reason for converting the spreadsheet to a form is to enable AIR judges, including judges who have disabilities, to do their scoring online. At the same time, however, we'll also make the logistics of judging this competition easier for everyone.

We'll concentrate on selecting the right types of elements for our form and on ensuring that those elements are accessible to people with disabilities. In other words, we won't be worrying here about making the form *look* good on the screen, and you shouldn't worry about it now, either—we'll talk about the form's visual appearance in Chapter 15 on Cascading Style Sheets.

The Old Form

The AIR judging form is the scoring instrument for a program produced each year in several cities to promote awareness of accessibility issues in Web design. The form has been developed over several years by a working group whose members include Jim Allan, Web master and Statewide Technical Specialist at the Texas School for the Blind and Visually Impaired and a member of the Web Accessibility Initiative; Phill Jenkins of IBM's Accessibility Center, also a member of the Web Accessibility Initiative; John Slatin of the University of Texas at Austin; and Jim Thatcher, an accessibility consultant formerly with IBM's Accessibility Center, inventor of the first screen reader for the graphical user interface, and a key player in developing the Section 508 accessibility standards.

Organization

The 2001 AIR form is a Microsoft Excel spreadsheet with several sections, as shown in Figure 10–2 and listed below.

- Site information (site name, URL, competition category, evaluator name, total score).
- Criteria for judging:
  - High-impact accessibility (6 items, 10 points each).
  - General accessibility (11 items, 5 points each).
  - Usability (12 items, 3 points each).
  - Appropriateness (up to 10 points).
  - Aesthetics (up to 10 points).
  - Bonus points (8 items, 1 point each).
  - Exemplary effort (1 item, up to 5 points).
  - Discretionary deductions (an arbitrary number of points deducted for major accessibility problems not captured above; requires the consensus of three judges).
- The scoring worksheet, which shows how to calculate the score for each section of judging criteria listed above.

The sections for the judging criteria on high-impact accessibility, general accessibility, usability, and appropriateness are formatted in four columns. Column A identifies where to input site information. The name of the item appears in column B along with the judging criteria for that item. Column C provides space for entering any points awarded for the item. Column D allows the evaluator to indicate

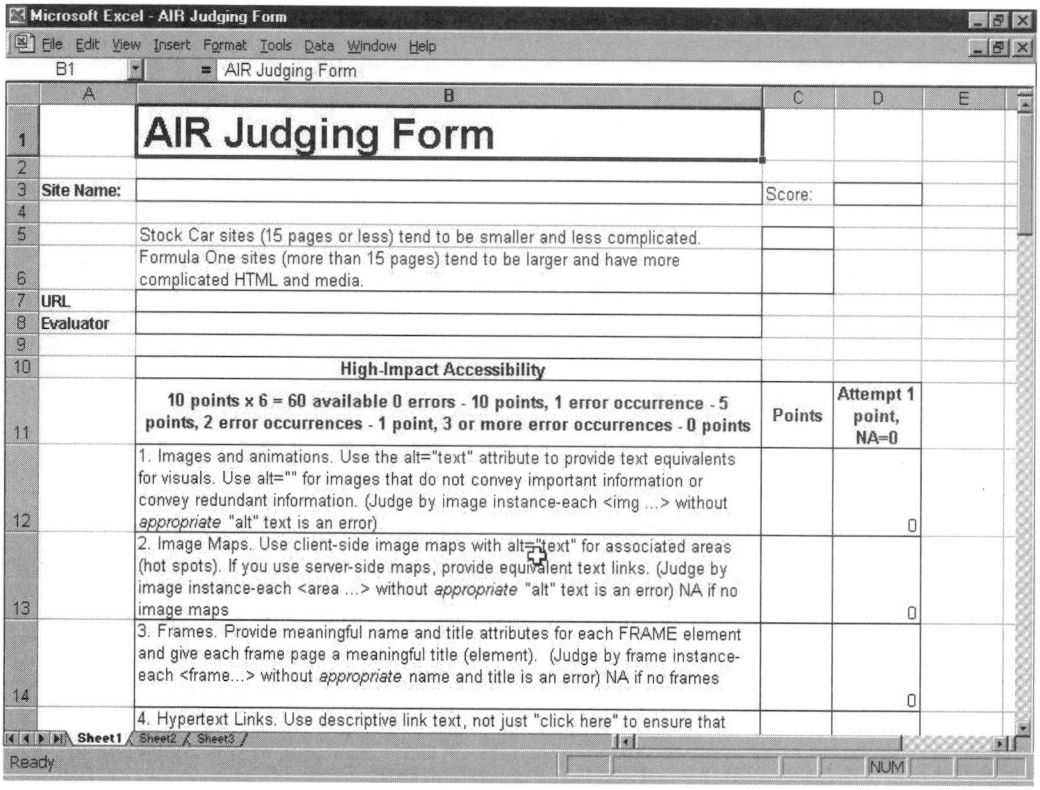
Microsoft Excel - AIR Judging Form

File Edit View Insert Format Tools Data Window Help

B1 = AIR Judging Form

	A	B	C	D	E
1		AIR Judging Form			
2					
3	Site Name:		Score:		
4					
5		Stock Car sites (15 pages or less) tend to be smaller and less complicated.			
6		Formula One sites (more than 15 pages) tend to be larger and have more complicated HTML and media.			
7	URL				
8	Evaluator				
9					
10		**High-Impact Accessibility**			
11		**10 points x 6 = 60 available 0 errors - 10 points, 1 error occurrence - 5 points, 2 error occurrences - 1 point, 3 or more error occurrences - 0 points**	**Points**	**Attempt 1 point, NA=0**	
12		1. Images and animations. Use the alt="text" attribute to provide text equivalents for visuals. Use alt="" for images that do not convey important information or convey redundant information. (Judge by image instance-each <img ...> without *appropriate* "alt" text is an error)		0	
13		2. Image Maps. Use client-side image maps with alt="text" for associated areas (hot spots). If you use server-side maps, provide equivalent text links. (Judge by image instance-each <area ...> without *appropriate* "alt" text is an error) NA if no image maps		0	
14		3. Frames. Provide meaningful name and title attributes for each FRAME element and give each frame page a meaningful title (element). (Judge by frame instance-each <frame...> without *appropriate* name and title is an error) NA if no frames		0	
		4. Hypertext Links. Use descriptive link text, not just "click here" to ensure that			

Sheet1 Sheet2 Sheet3

Ready NUM

FIGURE 10–2 The 2001 AIR judging form is an Excel spreadsheet. Visible in the screen shot are the site information section and the beginning of the High-Impact Accessibility section. Used with permission.

whether the site contains the feature in question or whether the item does not apply to the current site.

Scoring

The formula for calculating the final point total is fairly complicated. First of all, there is a different number of items in each category. Second, the items in each category are weighted differently. For each item in the high-impact and general accessibility categories, judges must award a fixed number of points based on the number of errors they find, with three or more errors resulting in a 0 score for the item. In the usability and bonus sections, however, even one error results in a 0 for the item.

For each of these categories, moreover, 1 point is awarded for each item attempted, whether or not the attempt was successful. Aesthetics and appropriateness are judged holistically and may be awarded up to 10 points each. Judges may also award up to 5 points for exemplary effort, for example, to acknowledge a particularly ingenious solution. A final option allows judges to deduct an arbitrary number of points for particularly egregious errors that cannot be factored into the scoring in any other way.

For example, suppose we have an educational site that contains several Java applets that illustrate dynamic processes of some sort. The applets are inaccessible, and the site does not provide equivalent alternatives either for their functionality or for the data they generate. However, in other respects the site is accessible (ALT text is associated with images, tables are correctly marked up, forms are labeled appropriately, and so on). The judges would award the site's developers 0 points for the scripts and applets item in the general accessibility category. In other words, the developers would lose 5 points. But say those applets constitute the core educational content of the site—the site exists primarily for the purpose of making the applets available to students in the class. Students with disabilities would then be denied access to learning opportunities that have been provided for classmates who do not have disabilities. Failure to make such critical content accessible should cost the developers more than 5 points. The judges would decide as a group how many points such a failure would cost.

Design Goals

So how do we want to improve the judging form? Let's start with what we don't want. We *don't* want simply to convert the existing spreadsheet to HTML—that would simply transfer the difficulties discussed above to another environment.

What we *do* want is to redesign the form in such a way that it:

- Provides better support for all judges, including those with disabilities who depend on assistive technology devices.
- Supports administration of the contest by facilitating improved data collection and reporting of results.
- Supports a judging process that provides useful feedback to contestants so they can use the form to guide later updates of their sites.

Let's explore these design goals further below.

Better Support for Judges

The desire to provide better support for judges leads to several action items.

- Reorder the way categories are listed on the form. For example, the list of 8 bonus items should follow the usability section. This would group together all categories where scoring is based on correct handling of specific elements. This kind of grouping of related items is consistent with WCAG Checkpoint 12.3 ("Divide large blocks of information into more manageable groups").

- Group all holistically scored items (appropriateness, aesthetics, exemplary effort, and discretionary deductions). This makes it easier to understand that these items are scored on a different basis from those in the previous categories, and it allows judges to "balance" the items against one another if they wish.
- For items where the number of points awarded is based on the number of errors encountered, allow judges to specify how many errors they've encountered and let the computer total the points. This frees judges from having to keep track of how many points the items in a given category are worth. This facilitates participation by judges with certain cognitive impairments and benefits all judges by reducing cognitive overhead.
- Make it easier for judges using screen readers, talking browsers, refreshable Braille displays, or screen magnifiers to enter scoring data without error.
- Allow judges to preview the results page at any point in the process; the preview should include a current score.
- Make it easier for judges to compare notes.
- Allow judges to jump directly to specific sections of the form (that is, make the form navigable).

Support for Contest Administration

Better support for contest administration can also improve the judging process. This adds more items to our list of enhancements.

- Create an online "cover sheet" for contestants to use when submitting their sites. Appropriate data from the cover sheet will be transferred automatically to the site information section of the judging form.

- Enable automatic updating of the scoreboard whenever a judge submits a completed form. This allows contest administrators and judges to see a running tally. The scoreboard will also show sites for which no score has yet been submitted and the names of judges and participants for each site. Judges and administrators will be able to go from the scoreboard to the individual scorecards and the sites themselves.

Support for a Judging Process That's More Useful to Contestants

Finally, putting the AIR judging form online will allow us to provide better, faster feedback to contest participants when the AIR program has ended. Bearing this goal in mind, we want to make sure certain features are present on the new judging form.

- Provide a field on the judging form for judges to use to explain to contest participants what makes specific features of the submitted sites especially effective or problematic.
- Add a feature so that each team can receive its scores, including judges' comments, via e-mail automatically generated at the end of the competition.

Implementing all these features would require far more than creating a single form, of course, and discussing them would take us far beyond the scope of this chapter. The rest of the chapter focuses on the judging form. However, it's important to keep in mind that users will rarely encounter a page that contains nothing but a form: the form is likely to be just one component of a larger site, and the page that contains it will probably contain other elements as well, including links to the rest of the site. With this in mind, it's also important to remember that forms usually imply some sort of social interaction, however minimal that interaction may be—they're almost always part of a larger process. The goal in designing a form is to provide a tool to facilitate that process.

The New Form

Grouping Related Items with the `<fieldset>` Element

WCAG 1.0 Checkpoint 12.3 calls for dividing large blocks of material into more manageable groups. That's information design. That's the hard part, and in the case of the AIR form, much of it has already been done. However, we want to rearrange and clarify the groupings on the existing form as we design the new one.

HTML 4.0 provides the `<fieldset>` and `<legend>` elements for this purpose. The `<fieldset>` element defines a group of related form controls. The `<legend>` element works like the `<caption>` element in a table, associating some onscreen text with the group to facilitate identification and navigation.

Figure 10–3 shows the organization of the form into three major groupings:

1. Site information.
2. Accessibility and usability.
3. Other considerations.

Within the accessibility and usability fieldset are four other fieldsets: high-impact accessibility, general accessibility, usability, and bonus items.

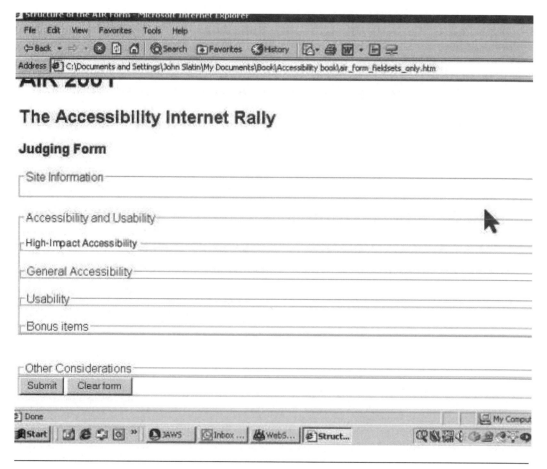

FIGURE 10–3 Screen shot showing how `<fieldset>` elements are used to structure the AIR judging form.

With this organizational issue resolved, we can move on to consider how to support easier and more accurate scoring.

Why Scoring Is Difficult on the Original AIR Judging Form

On the existing AIR form, judges mark one of two cells for each item in the high-impact accessibility, general accessibility, usability, and bonus items categories. In each case, the judges must determine what number to enter in the points field: 10 points if there are no errors, 5 points if one error, 1 point if two errors, or 0 points if three or more errors (under high-impact accessibility). The general accessibility category works the same way, but the numbers are different: 5 points if no errors, 3 points if one error, 1 point if two errors, or 0 points if three or more errors. Under usability, things *look* the same but aren't. Each item is worth 3 points, and there is no partial credit. The bonus items are worth 1 point each, again all or nothing. Items for which no attempt was made receive 0 points in the points field as well as 0 points in the applicability field.

This complexity creates a steep learning curve for new judges and causes some confusion even for experienced judges. For someone with short-term memory problems or a cognitive disability, it might well be impossible to keep track of this complex arrangement. For people with limited or no vision, the difficulty of remembering the point system is compounded by the need to keep track of their location in the spreadsheet itself.

The following questions are consistent across all these categories.

- Is the feature present or not?
- If present, is it used correctly in all instances or are there errors?
- If there are errors, how many?

We can use this consistency, rather than points, as the basis for handling scoring on the form. If the item is present, judges need only indicate how many errors they encountered (if any); otherwise, they can indicate that the item does not apply.

There are two design considerations here:

1. Selecting the most appropriate form controls.
2. Labeling items correctly, as required by Section 508 and WCAG 1.0.

Let's start with the need for correct labeling. For all practical purposes, Section 508, paragraph (n), requires labeling form controls: "When electronic forms are designed to be completed on-line, the form shall allow people using assistive technology to access the information, field elements, and functionality required for completion and submission of the form, including all directions and cues."

This Section 508 requirement is stronger than the similar WCAG 1.0 Checkpoints, which are rated only as Priority 2. Checkpoint 10.2 recommends that "Until user agents support explicit associations between labels and form controls, for all form controls with implicitly associated labels, ensure that the label is properly positioned. [Priority 2]." Checkpoint 12.4 urges developers to "Associate labels explicitly with their controls. [Priority 2]."

In other words, it may be possible to achieve level A conformance with WCAG 1.0 without fully addressing the accessibility of Web-based forms. Section 508 compliance, on the other hand, requires that forms be accessible. (In many other cases, however, satisfying WCAG's Priority 2 checkpoints benefits more users, though it's also more demanding for developers.)

Choosing the Form Controls: Radio Buttons

Radio buttons would seem to be ideal for this situation because they're designed to present mutually exclusive options. The judges need only select the appropriate button, and a script will assign the correct number of points. For example, the first high-impact accessibility item refers to images and animations (Figure 10–4). Five radio buttons are displayed in a table nested inside the cell at row 1, column 2 of a larger table used to lay out the form.

This looks like a plausible, even commonplace solution. The radio buttons allow judges to see all their scoring options at once; they can simply point, click, and move on to the next item.

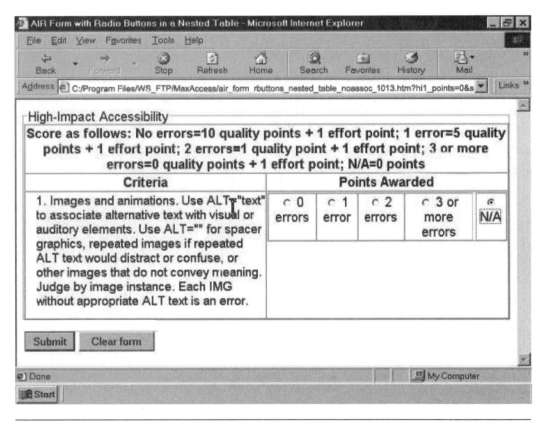

FIGURE 10–4 Screen shot of the first high-impact accessibility item on the AIR judging form. Radio buttons for scoring are displayed in a nested table immediately to the right of the text explaining how the item should be judged. The radio button for the last item (N/A for not applicable) is selected.

ACCESSIBILITY ISSUES WITH RADIO BUTTONS. But the situation may be somewhat different for people who have disabilities. For example, people using screen readers or talking browsers may find the radio button interface somewhat difficult to use. For them, the chief advantage of the radio buttons is gone: rather than *seeing* all the options at once, they'll be *listening* to the radio buttons *sequentially*. Similarly, someone with a hand tremor, limited hand–eye coordination, or low vision may have trouble pointing the mouse at the correct spot.

LABELING RADIO BUTTONS: THE `<label>` ELEMENT. The fact that people using screen readers and talking browsers hear the scoring options sequentially raises a host of new problems that have to do with labeling.

Visually, it's clear that this set of radio buttons is associated with the criteria for images and animations. But that implicit association will be lost for people using screen readers and talking browsers unless we take pains to label the buttons correctly.

The first step is to create an explicit, programmatic association between each radio button and its label, pairing the `<label for="inputid">` and `<input id="inputid">` elements and attributes, as shown below.

```
<input id="hi1a_points" name="hi1_points" type="radio"
  value="11">
<label for="hi1a_points">No errors</label>
```

Note that the `<input>` element's `id` attribute matches the `<label>` element's `for` attribute. Since the `id` attribute is designed as a unique identifier for HTML elements, this matchup forces screen readers and talking browsers to speak the words "No errors" and then report the status of the form control, like this: "No errors radio button not checked".

The <label> element may also be "wrapped around" the <input> element, as shown below.

```
<label for="hila_points"><input id="hila_points"
    name="hil_points"
    type="radio" value="11">No errors</label>
```

Under many circumstances, this is all that's needed. The site category item in the site information section of the AIR judging form is an example. The word "Category" is in column 1, and the radio buttons are in column 2, as shown in Figure 10–5.

Here is the source code for the Category radio buttons.

```
<td>Category:</td>
<td><input id="SC" name="site_category" type="radio"
    value="SC">Stock Car  
    <input id="FO" name="site_category" type="radio"
    value="FO">Formula One</td>
```

But it isn't always this easy.

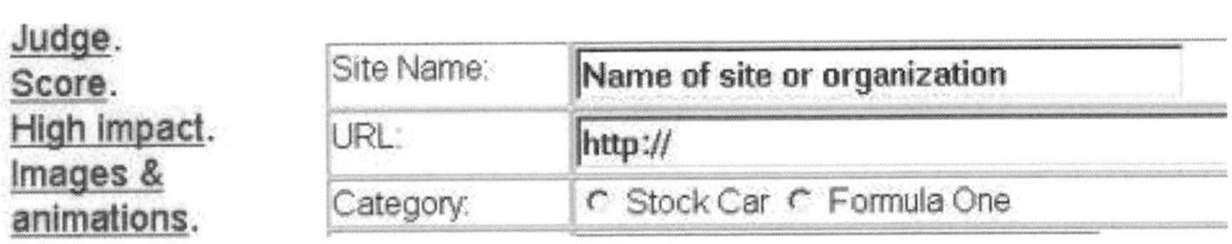

FIGURE 10–5 Site information section of the AIR judging form. Radio buttons for indicating the site's competition category appear at the bottom of the screen shot.

IMPLICIT ASSOCIATIONS FOR RADIO BUTTONS. Elsewhere on the AIR judging form, for example, it's actually necessary to associate the radio button with two pieces of text:

- The button label.
- The item being judged.

We've shown how to create an explicit association between each radio button and the text attached directly to it. But this is only part of the story: we also need an implicit association between the radio buttons as a group and the item that governs all of them.

On a multiple-choice test, for example, every question is associated with a list of possible answers. Likewise, on our judging form, each criterion is associated with a set of scoring options, like this:

1. Images and animations. Use ALT="text" to associate alternative text with visual or auditory elements. Use ALT="" for spacer graphics, repeated images if repeated ALT text would distract or confuse, or other images that do not convey meaning. Judge by image instance. Each IMG without appropriate ALT text is an error.

0 errors

1 error

2 errors

3 or more errors

N/A (not applicable)

Anyone who's ever taken a multiple-choice test or completed a questionnaire will recognize the association between the item on Images and animations and the scoring options. But assistive technology isn't necessarily smart enough to do that. On the judging form shown in Figure 10–4, the scoring options are represented by radio buttons, and we used the <label> element to create an explicit association between each radio button and the label beside it (for radio buttons, the label should be to the *right* of the button). But there is no way to create a similarly explicit association between the radio buttons *as a group* and the images and animations item. So assistive technology has to rely on positioning as a clue (this is the rationale for WCAG 1.0 Checkpoint 10.2). But positioning isn't always good enough. In the form shown in Figure 10–4, screen readers and talking browsers cannot recognize any implicit association between the radio buttons and the item to be scored—the text in row 1, column 1 of the outer table. Here's what we heard when we started tabbing through the form from the top of the page, using JAWS.

> 0 errors radio button not checked
>
> 1 error radio button not checked
>
> 2 errors radio button not checked
>
> 3 or more errors radio button not checked
>
> N slash A radio button checked

If JAWS users turn on Forms Mode by pressing the enter key, they'll hear the following:

> Forms Mode on
>
> N slash A radio button checked

If the same JAWS users now press the up arrow key on the keyboard, they'll hear:

> Three or more errors radio button checked

You get the idea: there's still no reference to the item (images and animations) and the judging criteria. The reason? Assistive technology can't recognize the relationship between the radio buttons and the images and animations item because we used a nested table to lay out the form; consequently, the images and animations item is in a *different* HTML table than the one that holds the radio buttons. To a screen reader, they might as well be on different planets. There's only one item to worry about in this example—not a major problem. But on the real form there are 38 items formatted this way! Judges relying on screen readers and talking browsers would quickly be lost.

Solving the Problem: Forcing an Implicit Association between Radio Buttons and Text

The screen shown in Figure 10–6 is very similar to the one in Figure 10–4. Now, however, there is a line of text above the five radio buttons. Beneath the radio buttons is another line of text, and beneath that is a small scrolling field where judges can enter their comments. What we're interested in here is the first line of text, the one above the radio buttons, which reads as follows: "Score for images and animations."

The text above the radio buttons is simply text, inserted as the content of a table cell that spans the five columns of radio buttons in the next row (`<td colspan="5">`). Because the text is now included in the same `<table>` element as the radio buttons, screen readers and talking browsers are able to recognize (or create) an implicit association between this text and the radio buttons. This changes what users hear when they tab through the form. The screen reader now goes directly to the default radio button (the one labeled N/A). First it speaks

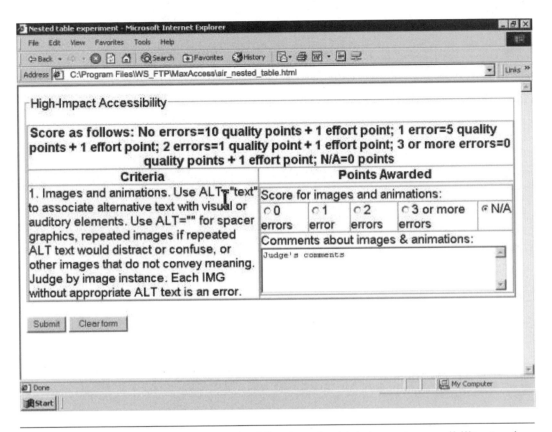

FIGURE 10–6 Screen shot of the revised first item for high-impact accessibility. Scoring options are presented as radio buttons in a nested table. A line of text above the radio buttons reads "Score for images and animations."

the implicitly associated text, then it identifies the radio button and its status:

> Score for images and animations
> N slash A radio button checked

The user then presses the up arrow key on the keyboard to move through the options. Each time, JAWS speaks the implicitly associated text before reporting the radio button and its status.

Choosing the Form Controls: Pull-Down Menus

The right-hand side of the table in Figure 10–6 is visually quite busy: a line of text followed by a line of five radio buttons (each with its own accompanying text), followed by a line of text, followed by a text area for judges' comments.

Figure 10–7 shows a different approach, substituting a pull-down menu (which JAWS calls a combo box) for the radio buttons in the previous example.

The screen shot in Figure 10–7 isn't quite as busy as the previous version. Where there had been a line of text above five radio buttons and their individual labels, there is now a single element, a pull-down menu. The default selection consists of the words "Award points for images & animations." To see all the options, the judge can pull down the menu, as shown in Figure 10–8.

Sighted users with good hand–eye coordination may find the radio buttons slightly faster: this is where the point-and-click method shows its value. However, for people using screen readers and talking browsers and others who don't use a mouse, the pull-down menu has some advantages. The keystrokes are exactly the same. The user would tab from item to item, then use the arrow keys to select radio buttons or menu options. But the pull-down menu has slightly less auditory clutter, and it's easier to be certain of having made the right selection.

LABELING `<select>` ELEMENTS: THE `<label>` ELEMENT. The technique for associating labels with pull-down menus is very similar to the technique for associating labels with radio buttons and text-input elements. Here's the syntax.

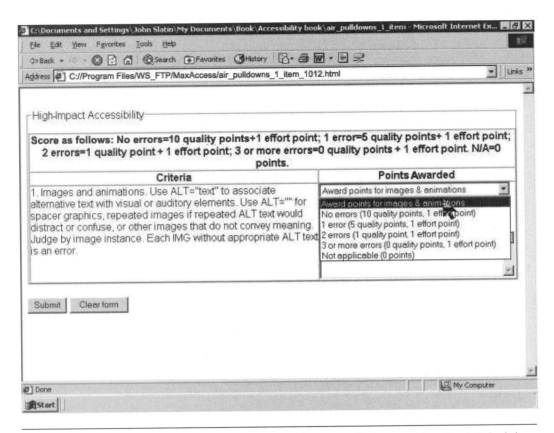

FIGURE 10–7 Pull-down menus as an alternative to radio buttons for the AIR judging form.

```
<label for="hi1_pts">Images &amp; animations.</label>
<select id="hi1_pts" name="hi1_pts" size="1">
<option selected value="">Award points for images &amp;
   animations</option>
<option value="11">No errors</option>
<option value="6">1 error </option>
<option value="2">2 errors </option>
<option value="1">3 or more errors </option>
<option value="0">Not applicable</option>
</select>
```

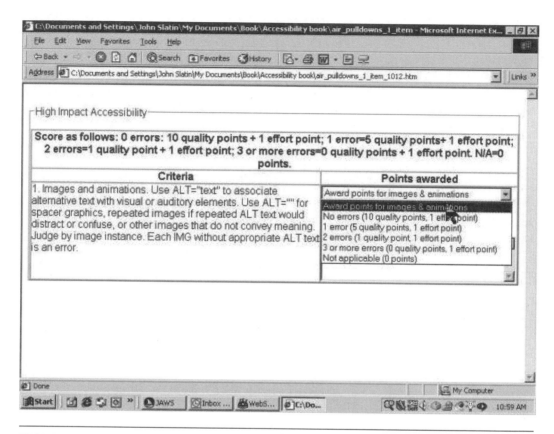

FIGURE 10–8   AIR judging form showing the options in the pull-down menu.

Again, note that the `<label>` element's `for` attribute matches the `<select>` element's `id` attribute. Now, when someone using a screen reader or talking browser tabs through the form, the contents of the `<label>` element will be spoken and the pull-down menu will automatically be selected. The default item in the menu will be spoken next.

A WORD OF WARNING: <select> MENUS AND JAVASCRIPT. Developers sometimes go for speed improvements in pull-down menus by using JavaScripts that are triggered by the onChange event handler the instant a user clicks on an item in the menu. This can have surprising effects for people using the keyboard who aren't aware that JavaScript is working behind the scenes. If you tab to a pull-down menu that has an onChange script and press the down arrow key, you'll automatically choose the first item on the menu, without necessarily knowing what that item is and without getting the chance to find out what else is available. Users can avoid falling into this trap by using Alt+Down-arrow to open the menu before starting to explore, but we've found that many people are unaware of this keystroke combination, and developers will get more predictable results by avoiding the onChange handler in this situation. (An analogous problem may occur when onChange handlers are associated with text-input elements. As noted earlier, JAWS users must press the enter key on the keyboard to turn Forms Mode on; however, doing so activates the onChange handler, sometimes submitting an empty form—and almost always leading to confusion.)

THE USES OF REDUNDANCY. We've added a bit of redundancy here as well: the default value is the instruction to award points for images and animations. This provides the necessary cues for people using older assistive technology devices that may not support the <label> element, while making it easier for everyone to recognize items that haven't been scored yet.

LABELING THE `<textarea>` ELEMENT. The same technique is used to label the `<textarea>` elements for judges' comments as well.

```
<label for="hi1_comments">Enter judge's comments about
    images &amp; animations:</label>
<textarea id ="hi1_comments" name="hi1_comments" cols="55"
    rows="4">Judge's comments here</textarea>
```

Again we've added redundant text to the `<textarea>` element it-self, to help people whose assistive technology devices may not sup-port the `<label>` element. (Note, however, that in some browsers judges may have to manually highlight and replace this default text. Many people—and not just people with disabilities—find this con-fusing, so it's a good idea to let test users tell you whether or not such placeholder or default text is useful.)

Making the Form Navigable

Now that we've worked out the organization of the form and the scoring method and labels for all items are working correctly, we can address the need to make the form itself navigable. In practice, judges don't work through the form item by item. Instead, they jump to dif-ferent items depending on the features of the Web site they're judg-ing. So they need to be able to move quickly from anyplace on the form to any other place.

The screen shot in Figure 10–9 shows the easy way out. We've added a column to the left side of the outer table. This is now column 1.

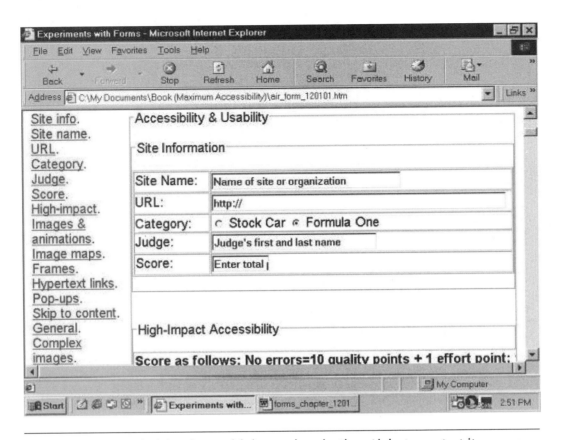

FIGURE 10–9 AIR judging form with internal navigation. Links to contest items are listed down the left side of the screen.

Column 1 provides a list of links to all the items on the judging form, in the order in which the items appear on the form.

We've also provided a simple contest navigation menu (see Figure 10–10) so judges can preview their scorecards before they submit the judging form and so they can check the scoreboard to see current standings as well as sites that remain to be judged.

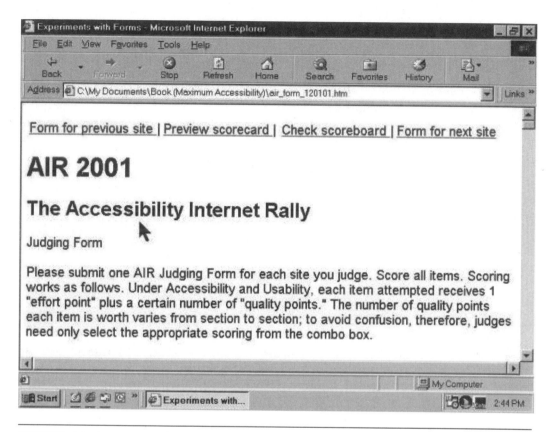

FIGURE 10–10 Screen shot showing the contest navigation menu at the top of the screen.

LOOKING AHEAD

In this chapter, we've worked through the process of redesigning the AIR judging form to provide better support for contest judges who have disabilities. We began by thinking through the features and the organization of the existing form and the challenges they posed—not just for people with disabilities but for everyone. We then restructured the form, using the `<fieldset>` element to define top-level logical structures. Then we looked at different ways to handle the scoring, deciding on pull-down menus using `<select>` and `<option>` elements in favor of radio buttons. Finally, we added navigation links to allow judges to jump quickly to any item on the form.

The result is a form that works well with screen readers and talking browsers, but it isn't much to look at. We'll address these visual issues in Chapter 15 on Cascading Style Sheets. But we have a number of other issues to take care of first. In the next chapter, we'll take up the challenge of designing accessible tables, using bus schedules like the ones we discussed in Chapter 5 as our examples.

11

Creating Accessible Tables

THE TROUBLE WITH TABLES

Basically, designers use two types of tables when creating Web sites.

1. *Layout tables* position items such as text and graphics on the page. For example, navigation bars are often laid out in a table.
2. *Data tables* use grids to organize information about relationships within the data set. For example, the bus schedules we tried to use in Chapter 5 are data tables.

Both uses of table structure are of great value to Web developers. Studies have shown, however, that tables can be variously troublesome to most users, even those without disabilities. Content organized in tables that contain accessibility barriers is content unavailable or meaningless to millions of users. With this in mind, we offer in this chapter a number of design techniques for creating trouble-free tables with maximum accessibility.

HTML Elements and Attributes Addressed in This Chapter

Elements

`<table>`, `<caption>`, `<thead>`, `<tbody>`, `<tr>`, `<th>`, `<td>`, `<abbr>`, `<acronym>`

Attributes

`id`, `headers`, `summary`

Accessibility Checkpoints and Standards Addressed in This Chapter

Web Content Accessibility Guidelines 1.0 Checkpoints

3.3. Use style sheets to control layout and presentation. [Priority 2]

5. Create tables that transform gracefully.

5.1. For data tables, identify row and column headers. [Priority 1]

5.2. For data tables that have two or more logical levels of row or column headers, use markup to associate data cells and header cells. [Priority 1]

5.3. Do not use tables for layout unless the table makes sense when linearized. Otherwise, if the table does not make sense, provide an alternative equivalent (which may be a linearized version). [Priority 2]

5.4. If a table is used for layout, do not use any structural markup for the purpose of visual formatting. [Priority 2]

5.5. Provide summaries for tables. [Priority 3]

5.6. Provide abbreviations for header labels. [Priority 3]

11.2. Avoid deprecated features of HTML. [Priority 2]

13. Provide clear navigation mechanisms.

13.4. Use navigation mechanisms in a consistent manner. [Priority 2]

Section 508 Standards, §1194.22

(**g**) Row and column headers shall be identified for data tables.

(**h**) Markup shall be used to associate data cells and header cells for data tables that have two or more logical levels of row or column headers.

WHAT IS A TABLE?

HTML tables consist of rows of cells organized into columns. In these cells, a Web developer may place numerical data, text, graphic images, or even other tables. In tables that present data (such as bus schedules), the cells often appear visually as a grid, though in some cases the designer may choose not to show the grid lines, instead using other techniques to make the items visually distinct.

As mentioned, it is also common for developers to use tables for page layout by placing certain blocks of text, navigation bars, or images in various cells to impart a particular look and feel to a Web page. This widespread practice emerged out of frustration. In the early days of the Web, designers with backgrounds in print media found HTML's almost total lack of support for precise and elegant page layout intolerable; they adapted the `<table>` element, introduced in HTML 2.0 in 1994, as a layout tool. Subsequently, the W3C developed a separate language, Cascading Style Sheets (CSS), to address designers' need for more precise control of presentation and layout. The checkpoints under WCAG 1.0 Guideline 3 ("Use structural markup and style sheets and do so correctly") are intended to encourage designers to respect the distinction between document content and structure on the one hand and presentation and layout on the other. In particular, a note following Checkpoint 5.3 urges designers to use the positioning features of CSS (instead of tables) to control page layout.

But even data tables are organized for the eye and not the ear, which is the source of some of the difficulties that people who depend on assistive technologies experience when using tabular information.

ACCESSIBILITY ISSUES FOR LAYOUT TABLES

Layout tables may create accessibility problems, especially for people using older browsers and/or older assistive technologies. For example, Web designers often use tables to lay out text in side-by-side columns. Older screen readers handled these columns poorly, reading horizontally across the table one line at a time instead of reading the contents of one cell followed by the contents of the next cell. The results were usually unintelligible or hilarious—or both. This problem has been largely resolved now, and contemporary screen readers usually "linearize" the text appropriately. That is, they read the contents of the cell at row 1, column 1 before moving on to row 1, column 2, and so on.

But linearization can create problems of its own, especially when nested tables are used—as we saw in Chapter 7 when we stumbled over the reading order of the text on the Metropolitan Museum's highlights pages. For example, suppose you've set up a table such that the contents of a `<td>` element at row 1, column 2 is another `<table>` element, which in turn has several rows and columns. Assistive technologies will read the contents of the cell at row 1, column 1; then, when they come to the `<table>` element embedded in the next cell, the assistive technology will read that *entire table*—including any additional tables that may be nested inside it—from left to right and top to bottom, before returning to the cell at row 1, column 3 of the *first* table. If you found the last couple of sentences confusing, just imagine what *listening* to a set of tables inside tables inside tables might be like!

In fact, the key to creating accessible tables, other than the markup you will learn in this chapter, is to think about the order in which the information will be aurally presented to the user. Remember that people using screen readers cannot use visual cues to figure out where to focus their attention. Rather, they must wait to make their choices as information is delivered in the order we've described. As we saw in Chapter 7, the WAVE accessibility checker (Figure 11–1) can be a very useful tool when you need help visualizing the order in which people using screen readers and talking browsers will hear the material on your pages. Authors can also use a browser called Opera to test reading order (and a number of other things as well). Opera can be configured to ignore tables; this forces it to "linearize" the contents and so reveals any problems with reading order.

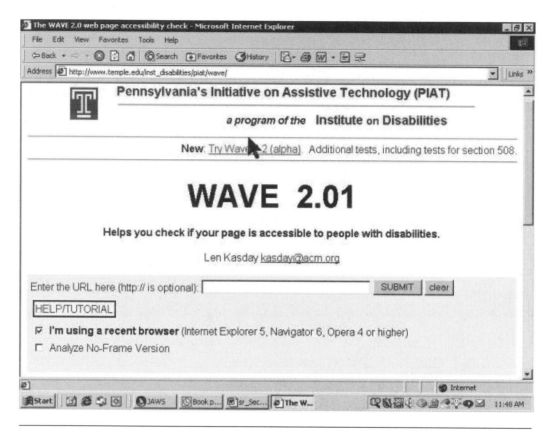

FIGURE 11–1 Screen shot of the WAVE, an accessibility evaluation tool that is helpful for understanding the order in which elements on a Web page will be read by screen readers and talking browsers. Accessed September 10, 2001, at *http://www.temple.edu/inst_disabilities/piat/wave/*. Used with permission.

ACCESSIBILITY ISSUES FOR DATA TABLES

Data tables also present accessibility challenges, and that's what we'll focus on in the rest of this chapter.

We consider data tables to be one of the most useful elements in a Web developer's tool kit, even though they were, at one time, the source of many common barriers encountered by Internet users with disabilities. Recent versions of HTML (especially HTML 4.0) have introduced elements and attributes that make basic table structure more accessible and therefore more versatile and useful for all users. In this chapter, we quickly review table markup and then examine accessibility features. We also refer to the bus schedule problems we experienced in Chapter 5. After reading this chapter, you should be able to solve those problems and create data tables that work for a great many more users.

So how do we combine table elements and attributes in such a way as to create a satisfying user experience for everyone, including those with disabilities?

DESIGN GOALS FOR ACCESSIBLE TABLES

Think back to our second user experience in Section 1—grappling with the bus schedule. Now that we have learned the capabilities of screen readers and talking browsers and the elements and attributes that make them most effective, let's write out some design goals we'd want to achieve if we were to design a transportation site.

- Create a single bus schedule that both sighted and visually impaired riders can use easily and effectively.
- Enable riders who use screen readers to locate route information quickly and easily.

These points may seem to go without saying. But that's the problem: when design goals go without saying, they all too often go without getting accomplished, too. Nobody means for this to happen. But it's all too easy to let unstated goals slide when deadline pressures get too intense or to forget to pass them on when new developers join the project in midstream.

And in any case, the first goal is apparently *not* all that obvious; in fact, quite a few designers seem to be convinced that it's better to create different versions to meet different needs, as both Capital Metro and the Santa Clara Valley Transportation Authority did at first (see Chapter 5 for details).

It may not seem intuitively obvious, either, that the best way to achieve that first goal, of designing a schedule that can be used with equal effectiveness by people with and without disabilities, is to concentrate on creating a schedule that people who are visually or cognitively impaired can use quickly and easily. This is the AccessFirst principle: if we make it our first priority to meet the needs of people with disabilities, we'll also do a better job when serving other users.

Coming at it from the other direction—that is, without taking the needs of people with disabilities explicitly into account in setting design goals—clearly does not work well, as we learned from the examples cited earlier. AccessFirst design serves the needs of all users, in large part because, in order to meet the needs of users who have disabilities, we have to be much clearer about all the elements, constraints, and opportunities involved in the design, clear about *structure* as well as content and presentation.

CREATING A MORE ACCESSIBLE BUS SCHEDULE

Let's begin to create a better bus schedule by listing the things we should consider when designing one that will work well for everyone.

- Route information is presented as a set of intersections that the bus passes through at specific times.
- Data cells show the time when the bus will reach a specific intersection.

- Displayed times may extend from 4:00 or 5:00 A.M. to midnight or later.
- Weekday schedules are often different from weekend schedules.
- Some routes do not run on Sundays and holidays, or Sunday and holiday schedules differ from weekday *and* Saturday schedules.
- Routes may be identified as northbound, southbound, eastbound, or westbound.
- Route numbers and names may change after buses cross specific points. (In Austin, for example, Town Lake divides north and south, while Congress Avenue is the line between east and west.)
- A visual map of the route may be helpful or even necessary for some passengers.

HTML Resources for Creating the Schedule

Table 11–1 lists the HTML resources we can draw upon as we devise a solution. The first column lists the elements we will use. Each attribute listed in the second column applies to the element shown directly above it. The third column contains a brief description of the function of the element or attribute.

Screen readers, talking browsers, refreshable Braille displays, and other user agents use these elements and attributes to render tabular information in a comprehensible form for people who either don't see the table at all or see only a small portion of it at a time. For example, screen readers and talking browsers supplement onscreen content by speaking the contents of the summary attribute and reporting the associations between data cells and column or row headers

TABLE 11–1 HTML Elements and Attributes Used to Design a More Accessible Bus Schedule

Element	Attribute	Function
`<table>`		Creates relationships between data elements by means of columns and rows.
	summary	Encapsulates the purpose and organization of the entire table. You might think of it as ALT text for a table since it is not displayed onscreen.
`<tr>`		Defines a row of data.
`<td>`		Defines a data cell.
	headers	Associates a data cell with a column or row header.
`<th>`		Identifies the contents of a data cell as a column or row heading.
	id	Assigns a unique identifier for each table cell.
`<caption>`		Provides clear visual and auditory identification of the table (the contents of the `<caption>` element appear on the screen).
`<thead>`		Defines a row (or rows) as the table head, causing it to appear at the top of every printed page and to allow associations with data cells.
`<tbody>`		Defines the body of the table, within which the `<td>` elements are defined and the data are placed.
`<tfoot>`		Defines a row as the table foot, causing it to appear at the foot of every printed page.
`<abbr>`		Indicates the abbreviation of a word, the expanded version of which should be pronounced by talking browsers. (Not specific to tables.)
`<acronym>`		Designates a word formed by combining a series of the first letters of a string of words. Once defined, the letters—rather than the word—are pronounced. (Not specific to tables.)

(those associations must be created with the id and headers attributes using the techniques we'll explain below). In the bus schedule we'll create, passengers who use screen readers and talking browsers will be able to read the schedule cell by cell across table rows or up and down columns to learn where and when to catch the bus. For layout tables, assistive technology devices can replace the visual display of information by reading ALT text and extended descriptions associated with images in the table—graphical navigation links, for example.

HTML Techniques for Accessible Tables

We'll now introduce several of the techniques that Web developers need to create accessible tables. We'll start by showing how to identify column and row headers using the <th> element. We'll use the <td> element to identify data cells and then explain how to associate data cells with the appropriate column and row headers. We'll illustrate these techniques by using information about intersections and times, building an accessible bus schedule as we go. (The names of the intersections are real, but the schedule is imaginary.)

Identifying Column Headers

The technique for identifying column headers is simple and straightforward. Use the <th> element as shown in the code sample below.

```
<table width="100%">
    <tr>
        <th>Sixth & Congress</th>
        <th>Eleventh & Congress</th>
        <th>Twelfth & Lavaca</th>
```

```
        <th>Fifteenth & Lavaca</th>
        <th>Martin Luther King & Lavaca</th>
        <th>Twenty-fourth & Guadalupe</th>
    </tr>
</table>
```

The example above is for the first row of a table with six columns. Each column shows the name of an intersection in Austin, Texas. Visually, the name will be displayed in boldface type and will be centered inside the cell, as shown in Figure 11–2. (This is the default

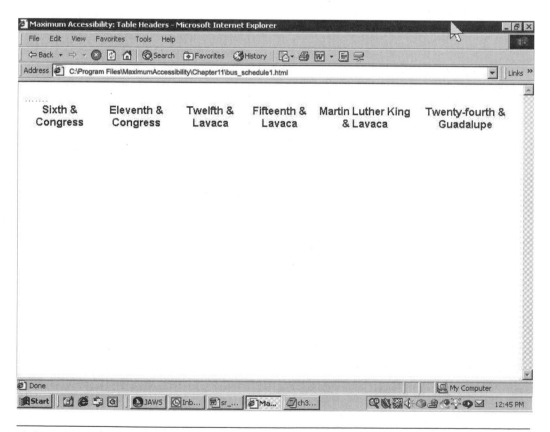

FIGURE 11–2 A row of intersections tagged as <th> elements. The names of the intersections are centered and boldfaced.

rendering for the <th> element. Developers can use CSS to override the default styling.)

But the point isn't simply that the <th> element is visually distinct from the remaining data cells. The <th> element is also *logically* different: use of the <th> element indicates that this cell has a specific place in the *structure* of the table and "exposes" that structure to assistive technologies as well as "mainstream" tools such as Microsoft Internet Explorer, Netscape Navigator, and other browsers.

Identifying Row Headers

You can use the same technique to identify the first cell in a row of data cells as a row header, as shown below.

```
<tr>
    <th>Row header</th>
    <td>Data cell</td>
    <td>Data cell</td>
    <td>Data cell</td>
</tr>
```

The first cell on this row will be formatted like those in the previous example—boldfaced and centered (Figure 11–3). The remaining cells will be formatted like the data cells in the table. Again, it's worth noting that use of the <th> element here enables assistive technologies to recognize the *structural* role of this cell as a row header and not just an "ordinary" data cell.

You can attach an id attribute to the row and column headers in order to associate them with specific data cells; we'll show you the technique in the section below on associating data cells with column headers.

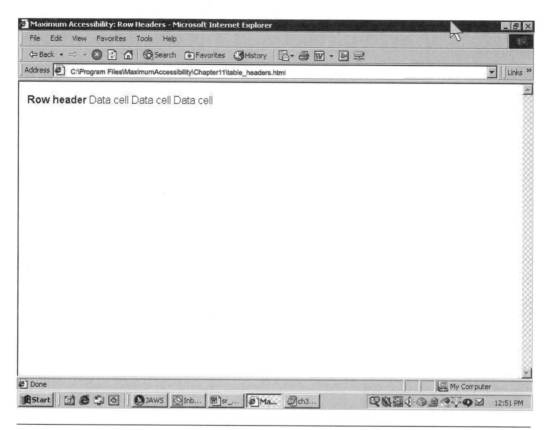

FIGURE 11–3 A table with one row. The first cell is identified as a row header and is centered and boldfaced.

Identifying Data Cells

First, though, let's add a row that shows what time the bus will reach each intersection; we'll include information about whether the time is before or after noon. We'll use the <td> element, with which you're probably familiar already. Here's the code for both rows.

```
<table width="100%" cellspacing="0" cellpadding="0">
    <tr>
        <th>Sixth & Congress</th>
        <th>Eleventh & Congress</th>
        <th>Twelfth & Lavaca</th>
```

```
      <th>Fifteenth & Lavaca</th>
      <th>Martin Luther King & Lavaca</th>
      <th>Twenty-fourth & Guadalupe</th>
   </tr>
   <tr>
      <td>10:33am</td>
      <td>10:36am</td>
      <td>10:42am</td>
      <td>10:45am</td>
      <td>10:50am</td>
      <td>10:55am</td>
   </tr>
</table>
```

Figure 11–4 shows how the table looks now. As in the previous example, the names of intersections are centered and boldfaced. In the second row, times are shown in regular font aligned to the left side of the cell—the default rendering for the <td> element.

Associating Data Cells with Column Headers

Many current-generation screen readers would be able to identify the appropriate column header for each data cell using only the markup shown above. But when the table has two or more logical levels, the WCAG 1.0 and Section 508 require that we use additional markup to create an explicit association between data cells and header cells. A table has two or more logical levels when, for example, it includes groups of rows or columns that contain related data. (The groundbreaking book by WAI cofounder Mike Paciello [2000], *Web Accessibility for People with Disabilities*, includes an excellent example of such a table: a spreadsheet listing travel expenses for multiple trips to multiple cities.) These groupings, created using attributes such as colspan

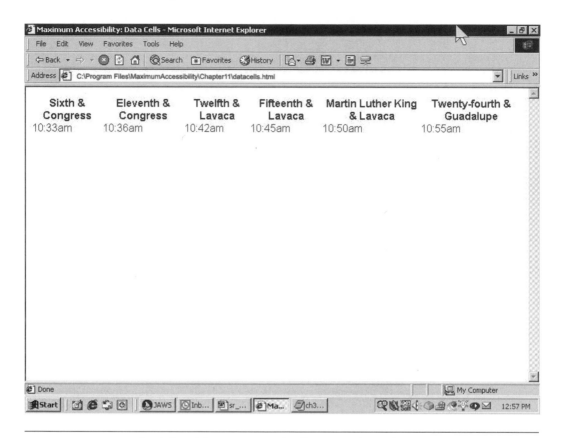

FIGURE 11–4 A schedule with two rows. The first row shows intersections tagged as `<th>` elements. The second row shows times tagged as `<td>` elements.

and `rowspan`, are rendered visually on the screen; but assistive technology can't recognize and report these aspects of the document's structure without additional markup. Providing this additional markup isn't hard to do at all: it's a matter of adding appropriate *attributes* to the `<th>` and `<td>` elements and making sure they're properly matched up. You can do it in two steps.

1. Assign an `id` attribute to each `<th>` element.

   ```
   <th id="intersection1">Sixth & Congress</th>
   ```

2. Assign a matching `headers` attribute to each `<td>` element.

```
<td headers="intersection1">10:33am</td>
```

Note that the `headers` attribute on the `<td>` element matches the `id` attribute on the `<th>` element. (The `label for` and `input id` pairings work the same way in forms. See Chapter 10 for details.) Assistive technology looks at the combination of `id` and `headers` attributes to determine which row and/or column heading(s) are associated with each data cell. In this case, a person using a screen reader should hear the name of the intersection, "Sixth and Congress," followed by the time, "10:33 A.M."

Let's put it all together to see what the code looks like.

```
<table width="100%">
  <tr>
     <th id="intersection1">Sixth & Congress</th>
     <th id="intersection2">Eleventh & Congress</th>
     <th id="intersection3">Twelfth & Lavaca</th>
     <th id="intersection4">Fifteenth & Lavaca</th>
     <th id="intersection5">Martin Luther King &
        Lavaca</th>
     <th id="intersection6">Twenty-fourth &
        Guadalupe</th>
  </tr>
  <tr>
    <td headers="intersection1">10:33am</td>
    <td headers="intersection2">10:36am</td>
    <td headers="intersection3">10:42am</td>
    <td headers="intersection4">10:45am</td>
    <td headers="intersection5">10:50am</td>
    <td headers="intersection6">10:55am</td>
  </tr>
</table>
```

This additional code won't affect the way the table *looks* at all; only people using assistive technologies like screen readers or talking browsers would notice the difference. The same applies for the `summary` attribute we'll add in the next section.

Identifying and Explaining the Table
with a `summary` Attribute

WCAG 1.0 Checkpoint 5.5 suggests providing a summary for the table itself. You can do this by using the `summary` attribute and the `<caption>` element (we'll explain below why it's a good idea to use both options). While this checkpoint is only a Priority 3 item (meaning that it is useful but not essential), carefully written summaries and captions can add significant value. Even with correct markup to associate data cells with headers, some people may need additional information to understand how the table is organized—and of course *everyone* needs to know what the table is supposed to show. As a designer, you can use the `summary` attribute to provide this information and explain how to navigate through the table, without having to account for the additional text as part of the visual design of the page (the `summary` attribute does not show on the page but is intended specifically for screen readers and talking browsers).

This is one key difference between the `summary` attribute, which is attached to the `<table>` element, and the `<caption>` element, which is an element like `<th>`, `<td>`, `<tr>`, and so forth (we'll discuss the `<caption>` element below). Like ALT text, the `summary` attribute is spoken by screen readers and talking browsers but doesn't appear on the screen, whereas the `<caption>` element is part of the onscreen text. This has implications for us as designers of a complete and satisfying user experience. So let's use the summary attribute to associate an explanation with the table. The source code looks like this.

```
<table width="100%" summary="The first line of this bus
   schedule lists selected intersections along the route,
   followed by the times when the bus stops at each
   intersection. To plan your trip, locate the intersection
   closest to where you want to get on the bus. Read down
   the column till you find the time closest to when you'd
   like to start your trip. Read across that row to find
   out when you'll reach the stop closest to your
   destination.">
```

As with the addition of the id and headers attributes discussed above, adding the summary attribute won't change the way your table appears on the screen.

Identifying the Table with a <caption> Element

To make sure that *everyone* who uses your site can identify the table, include a <caption> element within the table. You can think of the <caption> element as a title for the table. The <caption> element is different than the summary attribute: first of all, it's an *element* in its own right rather than an *attribute* (though it can only exist as part of a table, like <tr>, <td>, <th>, and so forth). Second, the <caption> element appears as onscreen text, and the summary attribute is read only by assistive technologies (this may change in future browser releases). The <caption> element shouldn't be identical to the contents of the summary attribute, since people using screen readers and talking browsers would then have to listen to the same text twice. Instead, you can use the <caption> element and the summary attribute in complementary ways. The <caption> element provides information that helps all users identify the table and its purpose; the summary attribute provides additional information for people who can't pick it up from the visual organization of the data in the table. So you can use the summary attribute and the <caption> element together to make the table and its purpose clearer for *all* your users.

Figure 11–5 shows the table from Figure 11–4 with a new <caption> element. Here's how the code looks.

```
<table width="100%" cellspacing="0" cellpadding="0"
summary="The first line of this bus schedule lists selected
   intersections along the route, followed by the times
   when the bus stops at each intersection. To plan your
   trip, locate the intersection closest to where you want
   to get on the bus. Read down the column till you find the
   time closest to when you'd like to start your trip. Read
   across that row to find out when you'll reach the stop
   closest to your destination.">
<caption>Schedule for Bus from Downtown</caption>
<tr>
   <th id="intersection1">Sixth & Congress</th>
   <th id="intersection2">Eleventh & Congress</th>
   <th id="intersection3">Twelfth & Lavaca</th>
   <th id="intersection4">Fifteenth & Lavaca</th>
   <th id="intersection5">Martin Luther King &
       Lavaca</th>
   <th id="intersection6">Twenty-fourth &
       Guadalupe</th></tr>
 <tr><td headers="intersection1">10:33am</td>
   <td headers="intersection2">10:36am</td>
   <td headers="intersection3">10:42am</td>
```

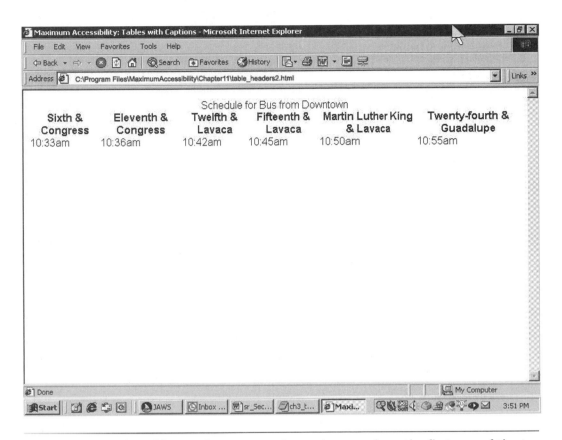

FIGURE 11–5 The table now has a `<caption>` element above the first row of the table. The caption reads, "Schedule for Bus from Downtown."

```
    <td headers="intersection4">10:45am</td>
    <td headers="intersection5">10:50am</td>
    <td headers="intersection6">10:55am</td>
 </tr></table>
```

Using the Schedule

Reading across the second row of the schedule, you stop at the time point 10:45 A.M. What intersection will the bus cross at this time? If you're a JAWS user, you can press Alt+Ctrl+NumKeypad5 to find out. Here's what you'll hear.

> Row 2 column 4
>
> 10:33am
>
> Fifteenth & Lavaca
>
> 10:45am

What is this? JAWS has actually gone farther than we did in coding the schedule. It has recognized the association between the time point and the intersection, in keeping with the way we matched the `id` and `headers` attributes. But it has also prefaced that information with two additional pieces of information: the row and column coordinates for the cell (row 2, column 4) and the first cell of the row. JAWS does this automatically, without any action on the user's part. This might be useful sometimes, but it can also interfere with efforts to orient users in other ways since there's no way for a person who can't see the screen to know that the number immediately following the row and column coordinates is *not* the data in the cell where his or her cursor is positioned. People with cognitive disabilities as well as limited or no vision might also find this extraneous auditory information confusing. So let's try a different technique.

Another Look at the Bus Schedule Using the Complex Table Model

The next example approaches the bus schedule in a different way, using additional features supported by HTML's Complex Table Model. This allows us to give riders the information we want to give them instead of whatever JAWS defaults to.

Using the <thead> Element

The code below uses a <thead> or table head element, which includes two rows (<tr>) of <th> elements. The first row spans all six columns and shows the direction in which the bus will travel. The second row contains the names of the intersections along the route. The <thead> element is then closed with the </thead> tag. Here is the code.

```
<thead>
   <tr>
      <th colspan="6" id="dir">Northbound</th>
   </tr>
   <tr>
      <th id="intersection1">Sixth & Congress</th>
      <th id="intersection2">Eleventh & Congress</th>
      <th id="intersection3">Twelfth & Lavaca</th>
      <th id="intersection4">Fifteenth & Lavaca</th>
      <th id="intersection5">Martin Luther King &
         Lavaca</th>
      <th id="intersection6">Twenty-fourth & Guadalupe</th>
   </tr>
</thead>
```

Using the <tbody> Element

Next comes a new table body element (<tbody>), which contains the data cells (<td>). Note that the contents of the headers attribute for each data cell now include two headers, the direction (dir) and the intersection.

```
<tbody>
   <tr>
      <td headers="dir intersection1">10:33am</td>
      <td headers="dir intersection2">10:36am</td>
      <td headers="dir intersection3">10:42am</td>
```

```
        <td headers="dir intersection4">10:45am</td>
        <td headers="dir intersection5">10:50am</td>
        <td headers="dir intersection6">10:55am</td>
    </tr>
</tbody>
```

On the screen, the cells in the <tbody> element look exactly as they did in the table shown in Figure 11–5.

Viewing the Improved Table

Incorporating these changes into our table gives us the following code.

```
<table width="100%" cellspacing="0" cellpadding="0"
summary="The first line of this bus schedule lists selected
    intersections along the route, followed by the times
    when the bus stops at each intersection. To plan your
    trip, locate the intersection closest to where you want
    to get on the bus. Read down the column till you find
    the time closest to when you'd like to start your trip.
    Read across that row to find out when you'll reach the
    stop closest to your destination.">
    <caption>Schedule for Bus from Downtown</caption>
<thead>
    <tr>
        <th colspan="6" id="dir">Northbound</th>
    </tr>
    <tr>
        <th id="intersection1">Sixth & Congress</th>
        <th id="intersection2">Eleventh & Congress</th>
        <th id="intersection3">Twelfth & Lavaca</th>
        <th id="intersection4">Fifteenth & Lavaca</th>
        <th id="intersection5">Martin Luther King &
            Lavaca</th>
        <th id="intersection6">Twenty-fourth & Guadalupe</th>
    </tr>
```

```
</thead>
<tbody>
   <tr>
     <td headers="dir intersection1">10:33am</td>
     <td headers="dir intersection2">10:36am</td>
     <td headers="dir intersection3">10:42am</td>
     <td headers="dir intersection4">10:45am</td>
     <td headers="dir intersection5">10:50am</td>
     <td headers="dir intersection6">10:55am</td>
   </tr>
</tbody>
</table>
```

Figure 11–6 shows how the new table looks. Note that there are now two header rows as well as a caption.

What's the Point?

The point is that screen readers and talking browsers can now tell their users what *direction* the bus is traveling as well as what intersection it will reach at the designated time. This may seem like a small thing—but for someone who can't scan visually up the column to check the name of the intersection and the direction of the route, or for a person with short-term memory limitations, it might be an enormous time-saver. You can apply this technique to far more complicated tables that represent several layers of relationships.

Using Additional WCAG Checkpoints to Enhance Accessibility and Usability

Well-designed Web pages that present accessible, well-designed tables almost always include other elements (navigation bars, graphics, text, and so on). Keeping accessibility in mind as you select and design

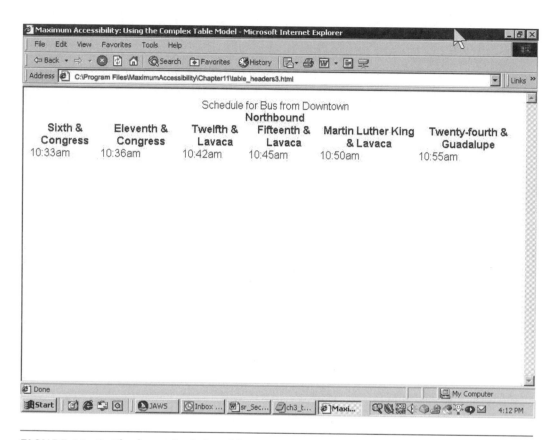

FIGURE 11–6 The bus schedule table created by using the Complex Table Model. The <thead> element includes two header rows. The <td> elements in the <tbody> element refer to header cells identifying both the intersection and the direction the bus is traveling.

those other elements will ensure that the effort you put into making your tables accessible won't be wasted. In the next few sections, we'll show you some additional WCAG checkpoints that can help you improve the accessibility and overall usability of pages that include tables like the bus schedule we've been discussing. First, though, let's talk a little about the relationship between WCAG 1.0 and the Section 508 Web accessibility standards, so you can see how they're similar and how they differ.

Where tables are concerned, there are no substantive differences between WCAG Checkpoints 5.1 and 5.2 and the Section 508 standards in paragraphs (g) and (h). Yet in the aggregate, WCAG 1.0 provides more *guidance* for Web designers—not only in what it says about tables but also in what it says about other issues on which Section 508 is more or less silent.

Frequently, also, WCAG 1.0 hints at aesthetic concerns that are deliberately excluded from the regulatory language of Section 508. For example, all of Guideline 5 applies to tables: "Create tables that transform gracefully." In other words, as an informative note in the Guidelines document explains, designers should "Ensure that tables have [the] necessary markup to be transformed by accessible browsers and other user agents."

Checkpoints 5.1 and 5.2 (which form the basis of the Section 508 standards) indicate two of the ways in which HTML can support graceful transformation—by identifying row and column headings, then creating an explicit programmatic association between data cells and specific headings by coupling id attributes attached to <th> elements with headers attributes for <td> elements. We have also seen the value of Checkpoint 5.5, which calls on us to use the summary attribute and/or the <caption> element. Let's look at how some other checkpoints might apply to table construction.

Other Applicable Checkpoints and Guidelines for Accessible Table Design

CHECKPOINT 5.6: USE <abbr> AND <acronym> ELEMENTS. Checkpoint 5.6 suggests using the abbreviation element (<abbr>) to help people using screen readers and talking browsers make sense of the terse abbreviations sometimes imposed on designers by the visual constraints of the screen. This is another Priority 3 item, but it would be very helpful for riders trying to determine which intersections the bus crosses. In fact, we have never seen bus schedules where the stops are written out in the manner of the example we have been using.

Unfortunately, as of this writing, screen readers and talking browsers do not yet support the automatic expansion of the <abbr> and <acronym> elements. (*Expansion,* in this context, means that the screen reader or talking browser speaks the full name instead of the abbreviation.) But that doesn't mean you have to give up on this point. Designers of the bus schedules on the Santa Clara Valley Transportation Authority site we discussed in Chapter 5 used a separate table of listings to identify intersections whose names are abbreviated in the schedule itself (see Figure 5–14). Such separate tables are a stopgap measure at best; they may be necessary, however, until assistive technology supports <abbr> and <acronym>.

GUIDELINE 12: PROVIDE CONTEXT AND ORIENTATION INFORMATION.

Web pages that display bus schedules and similar information are often dynamically generated. That is, the user's request to see the schedule for a particular route activates a script that retrieves the relevant data from a large database and displays it at predetermined places in a reusable template. Such dynamically generated pages often have generic titles ("Routes and Schedules," for example) rather than specific ones that clearly and accurately identify the material that is currently being displayed ("Schedule for Route 7 Duval," for instance). There is no guideline or standard that addresses precisely this problem: neither WCAG 1.0 nor Section 508 explicitly mandates providing informative titles for individual pages. In our view, however, accurate, meaningful titles for *all* pages on the site are essential context and orientation aids for users with and without disabilities: good titles help all of us maintain confidence that we have chosen the right links and found the pages we want. The Babylon Village schedule page discussed in Chapter 5, for example, is clearly titled, "Babylon Village Railroad Schedule" (see Figure 5–10).

GUIDELINE 13: PROVIDE CLEAR, CONSISTENT NAVIGATION. WCAG 1.0 Guideline 13, which has no real counterpart in the Section 508 Web standards, stipulates that designers should "Provide clear navigation mechanisms." An explanatory note in the Guidelines document adds that devices such as navigation bars, site maps, and orientation information are not only important for users who are blind or visually impaired but also helpful for all users. Consistency, the guideline editors add, is especially vital for people who have cognitive difficulties (Checkpoint 13.4).

The Whole Enchilada, One More Time

Finally, let's look at the whole table again, using the additional suggestions from the WCAG 1.0 checkpoints. The revised code appears below.

```
<!DOCTYPE HTML PUBLIC "-//W3C//DTD HTML 4.01
    Transitional//EN">
<html lang="EN-US">
<head>
    <meta http-equiv="Content-Type" content="text/html;
        charset=iso-8859-1">
    <title>Imaginary Bus Company Route 7 Bus
        Schedule</title>
</head>
```

```
<body>
    <p>The following bus schedule uses abbreviated street
        names. They are explained in the <a href="#legend">
        legend </a> below.</p>
    <table width="100%"
    summary="This bus schedule lists selected intersections
        along the route, followed by the times when the bus
        stops at each intersection. To plan your trip, locate
        the intersection closest to where you want to get on
        the bus. Read down the column till you find the time
        closest to when you'd like to start your trip. Read
        across that row to find out when you'll reach the
        stop closest to your destination.">
    <caption>Schedule for Bus from Downtown</caption>
    <thead>
        <tr><th colspan="9" id="dir">Northbound</th></tr>
        <tr><th id="intersection1">6th &amp;
            <abbr title="Congress
        Avenue">Con</abbr></th>
        <th id="intersection2">11th &amp;
            <abbr title="Congress
        Avenue">Con</abbr></th>
        <th id="intersection3">12th &amp;
            <abbr title="Lavaca
        Street">Lav</abbr></th>
        <th id="intersection4">15th &amp;
            <abbr title="Lavaca
        Street">Lav</abbr></th>
        <th id="intersection5">MLK &amp;
            <abbr title="Lavaca
        Street">Lav</abbr></th>
        <th id="intersection6">24th &amp;
            <abbr title="Guadalupe
        Street">Gua</abbr></th>
```

```
   <th id="intersection7">28th &amp;
      <abbr title="Guadalupe
   Street">Gua</abbr></th>
   <th id="intersection8">32nd &amp;
      <abbr title="Guadalupe Street">Gua</abbr></th>
   <th id="intersection9">32nd &amp;
      <abbr title="Rio
   Grande">Rio</abbr></th></tr>
</thead>
<tbody>
   <tr> <td headers="dir intersection1">10:33am</td>
   <td headers="dir intersection2">10:36am</td>
   <td headers="dir intersection3">10:42am</td>
   <td headers="dir intersection4">10:45am</td>
   <td headers="dir intersection5">10:50am</td>
   <td headers="dir intersection6">10:55am</td>
   <td headers="dir intersection7">11:03am</td>
   <td headers="dir intersection8">11:11am</td>
   <td headers="dir intersection9">11:17am</td></tr>
   <tr><td headers="dir intersection1">10:48am</td>
   <td headers="dir intersection2">10:51am</td>
   <td headers="dir intersection3">10:57am</td>
   <td headers="dir intersection4">11:00am</td>
   <td headers="dir intersection5">11:05am</td>
   <td headers="dir intersection6">11:10am</td>
   <td headers="dir intersection7">11:18am</td>
   <td headers="dir intersection8">11:26am</td>
   <td headers="dir intersection9">11:32am</td></tr>
   <tr><td headers="dir intersection1">11:03am</td>
   <td headers="dir intersection2">11:06am</td>
   <td headers="dir intersection3">11:12am</td>
   <td headers="dir intersection4">11:15am</td>
   <td headers="dir intersection5">11:20am</td>
   <td headers="dir intersection6">11:25am</td>
```

```
      <td headers="dir intersection7">11:33am</td>
      <td headers="dir intersection8">11:41am</td>
      <td headers="dir intersection9">11:47am</td></tr>
   </tbody>
   </table>
   <p></p>
   <table width="75%" summary="This table lists the
      abbreviated street names that are in the bus
      schedule, and gives the full street names. The
      abbreviations are listed in alphabetical order.">
   <caption><a name="legend">Legend of Abbreviations for
      Street Names</a></caption>
   <thead>
      <tr>
      <th id="T1">Abbreviated Street Name</th>
      <th id="T2"> Full Street Name</th></tr>
   </thead>
   <tbody>
      <tr><td headers="T1"> MLK</td>
      <td headers="T2"> Martin Luther King
         Boulevard</td></tr>
      <tr><td headers="T1"> Con</td>
      <td headers="T2"> Congress Avenue</td></tr>
      <tr><td headers="T1"> Gua</td>
      <td headers="T2"> Guadalupe Street</td></tr>
      <tr><td headers="T1"> Lav</td>
      <td headers="T2"> Lavaca Street</td></tr>
      <tr><td headers="T1"> Rio</td>
      <td headers="T2"> Rio Grande</td></tr>
   </tbody>
   </table>
</body>
</html>
```

The output of this code appears in Figure 11–7.

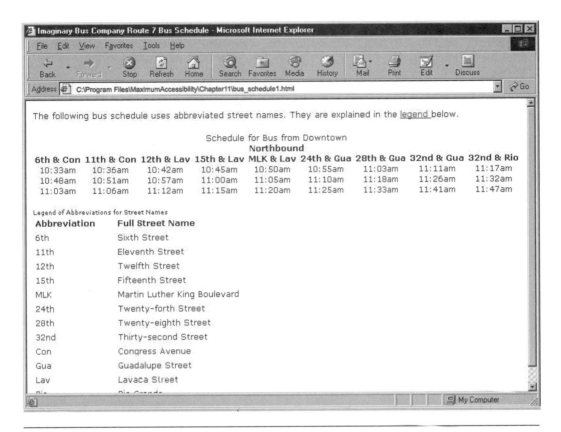

FIGURE 11–7 Screen shot of the imaginary bus schedule, including abbreviated intersection names and a table of abbreviations.

While this is clearly a rudimentary schedule, it does demonstrate the principles we have been discussing in this chapter. A couple of things are worth noting. First, the source code above contains only structural markup; presentation and layout could be taken care of with a style sheet (see Chapter 15 for discussion of Cascading Style Sheets). In addition, several of the accommodations we have made for people who use screen readers, talking browsers, or refreshable Braille displays do not show up on the screen at all. Both tables (the schedule and the list of abbreviations) include summary attributes that provide screen readers with information to help users access the schedule more effectively. The `<abbr>` element has been used; when assistive technologies support these elements, people using screen readers, talking browsers, and refreshable Braille displays will be able to read the full street names as well as the row and column headers— all without distracting sighted users.

To complete the design, we might consider using color differences to make it easier for sighted passengers to visually identify different areas of the schedule, such as morning and afternoon; a style sheet would be an excellent way to do this. We might supply route maps to allow riders with cognitive difficulties or low literacy skills to plan their travel more efficiently. And we might consider including anchor links to allow riders to go directly to relevant portions of the schedule (weekdays and weekends, for example) or to specific time points. In fact, the route maps could be effectively converted to client-side image maps, with links from each labeled stop to the timetable for that intersection; for passengers who cannot read maps or those who have trouble building a mental map of the route (including people new to the city or unfamiliar with the area they're going to), a narrative description of the route would be helpful as well (the Santa Clara Valley Transportation Authority makes such narrative descriptions available, as noted in Chapter 5).

Cost Saver

One more note: On many contemporary sites, things like bus schedules are generated automatically on demand by powerful scripts that retrieve up-to-the-minute information from a database and display it using a template created for that purpose. These scripts can automate the process of generating and matching `id` and `headers` attributes to create the necessary associations, saving developers countless hours of tedious repetition and avoiding countless tiny and nearly undetectable errors. The result is an enhanced user experience and better service for your customers and constituents.

LOOKING BEYOND HTML

This chapter and the previous two—on equivalent alternatives and forms, respectively—present accessibility solutions that can be achieved using HTML alone. In the next four chapters, we move on to consider several other technologies commonly used to create and deliver Web-based content. We start in Chapter 12 with Adobe Systems' powerful and immensely popular Portable Document Format (PDF), which has become very nearly the *de facto* standard for publishing certain types of information electronically (such as white papers, technical reports, and, until recently, government documents). Chapter 13 explains how to anticipate and avoid potential accessibility problems posed by multimedia materials—and how to use multimedia to enhance accessibility and reach a wider audience. In Chapter 14 we explore accessibility solutions for scripting and embedded applications such as multimedia players. Finally, in Chapter 15, we demonstrate how you can use Cascading Style Sheets to enhance accessibility while creating Web documents that are both easy to maintain and visually appealing.

12

Toward More
Accessible PDFs

PDF: SO NEAR AND YET SO FAR

Many people have asked us how accessibility standards apply to documents created in Adobe Acrobat's Portable Document Format (PDF). If you or your organization publish documents electronically, it's becoming increasingly likely that these activities are covered by either Section 508 or WCAG 1.0 or by an internal accessibility policy based on one or the other. To put it simply, the Section 508 federal accessibility standards and WCAG 1.0 both require that (1) electronic documents and (2) the software needed to read them must be accessible to people with disabilities. Even if these standards don't technically apply to you or your organization, we strongly recommend that you spend the few extra minutes necessary to publish accessible PDFs since by doing so you'll increase the reach of your work.

Until recently, the practice of using PDFs posed insurmountable barriers to computer users with visual impairments who use screen-reading software or refreshable Braille displays to read electronic documents. For these users, Acrobat's greatest strength—its ability to create documents that preserve the appearance of originals—was also its greatest limitation. Now, however, authors can easily create simple PDF documents that *can* be read, in many cases, by people using screen readers or refreshable Braille displays.

Note that all the following conditions must be true, however, in order for PDF documents to be accessible.

- The document was created using Acrobat 5 or later.
- The person reading the document has Acrobat Reader 5 or later.
- The user has a current-generation screen reader such as JAWS 4.x or Window-Eyes 4.x or later.

In other words, PDF still presents a major challenge to the principle that Web content created through new technologies must transform gracefully when rendered by assistive technologies. This chapter explores those challenges.

Acrobat is a complex tool, and PDF is a complex subject; we don't pretend to offer comprehensive coverage. We provide a brief overview of how to use Microsoft Word and Adobe Acrobat to create PDF documents that are accessible to people with disabilities, especially people with visual impairments who use screen readers or refreshable Braille displays. Much to our regret, the chapter also documents some flies in the ointment, that is, bugs in the software.

HTML Elements and Attributes
Addressed in This Chapter

Elements

`<table>, <img>`

Attributes

`id, headers, summary, alt`

Accessibility Checkpoints and Standards
Addressed in This Chapter

Web Content Accessibility Guidelines 1.0 Checkpoints

1.1. Provide a text equivalent for every non-text element. [Priority 1]

5.1. For data tables, identify row and column headers. [Priority 1]

6. Ensure that pages featuring new technologies transform gracefully.

Section 508 Standards, §1194.22

(**g**) Row and column headers shall be identified for data tables.

PROVIDING AN ACCESSIBLE PLUG-IN

Providing access to accessible software for reading PDF documents is straightforward. There are two ways to do it; we suggest offering both options on your Web site so your users can choose what's best for them.

1. Provide a link to the download page for the version of Acrobat Reader 5 that includes Search and Accessibility features; instructions are at *http://www.adobe.com/products/acrobat/ alternate.html.*

2. Provide a link to Adobe's online conversion tools for people who do not have or cannot install the Acrobat 5 Reader (for example, people with older equipment that may not support Acrobat 5 or people who aren't using their own computers and can't download software). These tools convert inaccessible PDFs created with older versions of Acrobat to either HTML or plain text, which screen readers are more likely to be able to read. (Readability may be affected by the complexity of the original document's layout.)

CREATING ACCESSIBLE PDF DOCUMENTS

You can satisfy the requirement for accessible documents—up to a point, at least—by using Acrobat 5 together with Microsoft Word 2000 to create "tagged PDF" files, which retain information about content, structure (chapters, sections, headings, tables, and so on), layout, and the order in which elements should be read aloud. (As explained in Chapters 7 and 9 and elsewhere, reading order is not always self-evident—for example, when text flows around an image, a text box, or a table.)

Installing Acrobat 5 adds a new Acrobat menu to Microsoft Office applications, including Word (Figure 12–1).

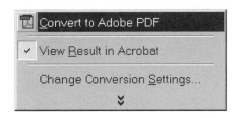

FIGURE 12–1 The Acrobat menu added to Microsoft Word 2000. Used with permission.

The Convert to Adobe PDF feature is the first option on the menu, but it's the last step in creating an accessible document. It takes structural and layout information from the Word document and integrates it into a new tagged PDF file. But it's not magic. It works well only if (1) the Word document contains the necessary structural information, and (2) the Acrobat Conversion Settings are correct. We'll talk about the Word document first, then look at the Conversion Settings.

Structuring the Word Document

Like accessible HTML documents, accessible PDF documents should have clearly defined structural elements; these not only help people using screen readers and Braille displays understand how the document is organized but also become tools that everyone can use for navigating the document. Accessible PDF documents should also provide equivalent alternatives for images and other nontext elements—again, just like HTML documents.

Structural Markup

As we note in Chapter 15 on Cascading Style Sheets, many people mark off sections in their documents by putting a section title on a line by itself and setting it in boldface type. Human readers can recognize this as structural information, but screen-reading software isn't smart enough to do that: it depends on markup. In an HTML document, for instance, a first-level heading is identified by surrounding a word or phrase with the <h1> and </h1> tags. Web authors insert the tags by hand or use authoring tools that generate the necessary code automatically.

The equivalent action in Word is to open the Format menu, select the Style. . . option, and then choose Heading 1, as shown in Figure 12–2.

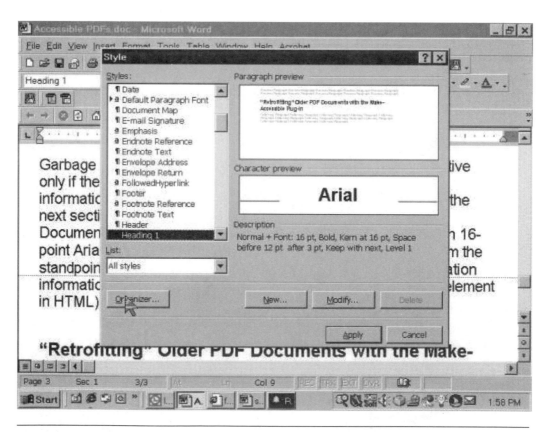

FIGURE 12–2   Screen shot of the Style dialog box in Microsoft Word 2000. Used with permission.

Alternative Text for Images

Acrobat 5 and later versions support ALT text for images and other nontext material in PDF documents. In order to be effective, text alternatives for images in PDF documents should have the same characteristics as ALT text for images that appear in HTML documents, so we'll repeat the criteria we listed in Chapter 9. ALT text should

- Be short: 150 characters or fewer, including spaces and punctuation.
- Make sense *out of context,* for example, when read aloud by itself or as an item in a list of links spoken by a screen reader or talking browser, or when rendered as Braille. (Examples of links presented in the JAWS Links List appear in Chapters 2, 5, and 8.)
- Make sense *in context,* for example, when read aloud as part of a larger page that contains other text.
- Contribute to the intelligibility of the page as an *auditory experience.*

Adding ALT text to an image in a Word document is easy. First, insert the image using the Insert → Picture option. Then use the Format Picture → Web option to add the ALT text. Acrobat will then include the ALT text in the tagged PDF document, and screen readers will speak it. Figure 12–3 shows the ALT text entered into the Format Picture dialog box.

Selecting the Acrobat Conversion Settings

Before converting your Word document to PDF, be sure the Conversion Settings are correct. According to Adobe's online booklet, "How to Create Accessible Adobe PDF Files" (*http://access.adobe.com/ booklet.html*), every time you want to convert a Word 2000 document

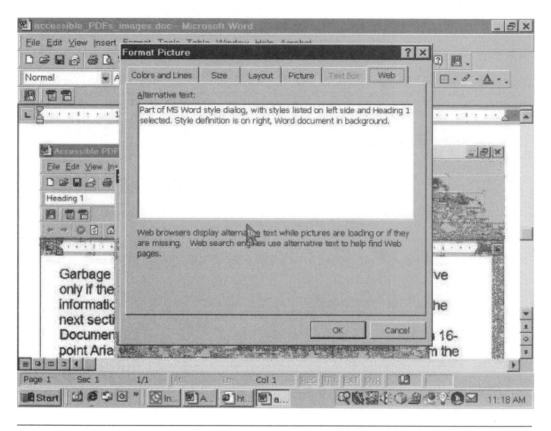

FIGURE 12–3 Screen shot of Word's Format Picture dialog box showing the ALT text for the image in Figure 12–2. Used with permission.

to tagged PDF, you should begin by selecting Change Conversion Settings. . . from the Acrobat menu. This opens the Conversion Settings dialog box.

From the Conversion Settings dialog box, follow the steps below.

1. Select the Office tab. The dialog box shown in Figure 12–4 will appear.
2. Make sure Embed Tags in PDF is turned *on* and Page Labels is turned *off* (these are the default settings).
3. Choose the Bookmarks tab.

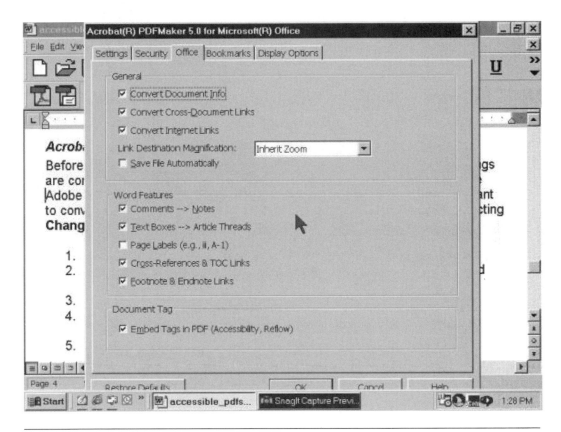

FIGURE 12–4 The Acrobat Conversion Settings dialog box, with the Office tab selected. Used with permission.

4. Select the Word styles for which you want to create Adobe PDF bookmarks (tags); by default, all the styles available in your Word document are selected. You can deselect the styles you haven't used in your document, or just select OK to accept the default settings.

5. If you want to control other aspects of your document's appearance, select the Display Options tab and change the settings as you like (Figure 12–5).

6. When you've chosen the options you want, select OK to close the Conversion Settings dialog box.

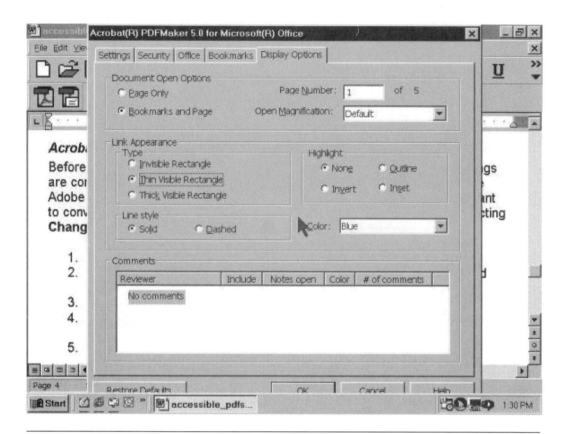

FIGURE 12–5 The Display Options tab in the Acrobat Conversion Settings dialog box. Links are set to appear in blue surrounded by a thin rectangle. Used with permission.

Converting the Word File to a PDF Document

When the Conversion Settings are correct, you're ready to convert the Word document to PDF. It's very simple, as outlined in the steps below.

1. Choose Acrobat → Convert to Adobe PDF on the Microsoft Office application menu bar, or select the Convert to Adobe PDF button on the application tool bar.
2. The tagged PDF file will open in Acrobat (if you selected the default option in the Conversion Settings dialog box).

3. Review and test the file for accessibility. Start by running Acrobat's new built-in Accessibility Checker. Correct any problems and retest the file; repeat as necessary. Ideally, an experienced user of screen readers or refreshable Braille displays will also perform a full accessibility review. If this isn't possible, download a demo version of JAWS or Window-Eyes and listen to the document yourself to catch problems with reading order or other unexpected behavior. Pay particular attention to places where text flows around graphics, tables, text boxes, and so forth since these can be quite tricky.

4. Name and save the file.

EXPERIMENTING WITH TABLES IN PDF

So far, so good. But it gets a bit trickier from here. According to Adobe, tagged PDF documents can support markup for data tables, including identification of row and column headers and association of data cells with those headers. (See Chapter 11 for details on how to mark up data tables in HTML using id and headers attributes on the <th> and <td> elements, respectively.) According to Adobe's online documentation, PDF now allows electronic publishers to

> . . . preserve markup in tables in an Adobe PDF file, including table rows, header cells and data cells. Acrobat 5.0 for Windows enables users to create tagged Adobe PDF files automatically from Microsoft Office 2000 for Windows applications. If the author defines table rows, header cells and data cells in the application, Acrobat 5.0 will automatically include that information in the PDF file. Users of Macintosh

or Windows versions can create or edit data table header information using the Acrobat tags palette. For more information, see the White Paper "Enhancing the Accessibility of the Web with Adobe Acrobat software."[1]

This makes it sound easy, but not so. Word 2000 does not have built-in mechanisms for HTML-style identification of column and row headers or for associating data cells with those headers. For example, we took the small table and pasted it into an otherwise empty Microsoft Word document, saved the file, and then converted it to PDF. The result appears in Figure 12–6.

The good news is that JAWS can read the items in the table and read them in the correct order. The bad news is that JAWS doesn't quite seem to recognize the table *as* a table. Actually, it's a little more ambiguous than that. Pressing Alt+Ctrl+NumKeypad5—the JAWS keystroke for querying the current data cell—yields the message "Row 0, Column 0" no matter what cell you're in. This would seem to indicate that JAWS recognizes the table but can't identify where the focus is. But pressing Alt+Ctrl+DownArrow—the keystroke for reading down the current column—returns an even more surprising result: "Not in a table," says JAWS, though clearly it *is* in a table.

We wondered whether this was a JAWS problem or an Acrobat problem, so we asked a friend to try reading the table with IBM Home Page Reader 3.0. He reported the same result: Home Page Reader read the words on the page in the correct order but did not recognize the presence of a table.

---

1. "Acrobat 5.0 and Section 508." Accessed February 10, 2002, at *http:// access.adobe.com/acr508_2.html.*

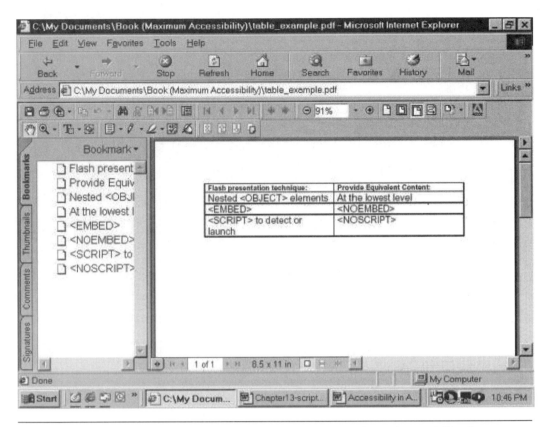

FIGURE 12–6 A tagged PDF document, created from a Microsoft Word file that contains only a small data table. The Acrobat Reader plug-in displays the PDF document in Internet Explorer 5.5. Used with permission.

Acrobat's Accessibility Checker

It should be possible to identify such problems and fix them: Acrobat 5 includes an Accessibility Checker licensed from SSB Technologies and based on SSB's InSight product. But the Accessibility Checker reports "no problems" in our new PDF document, even though the document contains nothing except our little table and there is clearly something wrong. The table doesn't meet the relevant WCAG 1.0 checkpoints or the Section 508 standard, and there's no reason the Accessibility Checker shouldn't be able to spot this.

Even when the Accessibility Checker does find problems, its reports are hardly useful. We ran the Accessibility Checker on a newsletter with a complicated layout and got a dialog box that offered the following report:

The checker found problems which may prevent the document from being fully accessible.

+ All of the text in this document lacks a language specification.

44 element(s) with no alternate text.

+ This document is unstructured; the reading order of the contents may be incorrect.

The report indicates that there are major problems, but it offers no information about how to find them in the document itself and no guidance about fixing them. With help like this. . . .

Acrobat's Tags Palette

Since we clearly couldn't count on the Accessibility Checker, we decided to try the Tags palette, which at first sight is both forbidding and unhelpful (Figure 12–7).

Sighted readers will quickly note that there's a small plus sign (+) just to the left of the phrase "Tags Root," indicating that the term can be expanded to reveal more levels. For some reason, however, the phrase "Tags Root" did not have focus (that is, it wasn't highlighted) when the Tags palette first appeared on the screen; it received focus only after we pressed Ctrl+Tab twice in succession. This took us first to the Fields view (which was completely empty) and then back to Tags view. At that point, JAWS reported the existence of the Tags Root and the option to expand it using the arrow keys. Pressing the right

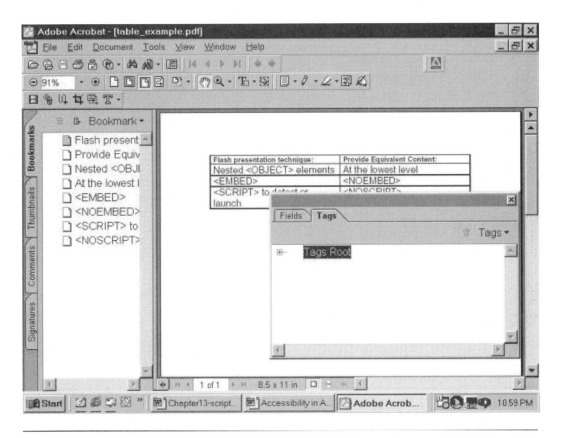

FIGURE 12–7 Acrobat 5's Tags palette opens in a small window inside the main document window. It partially overlaps the document's contents. The only thing visible in the Tags palette is the highlighted phrase "Tags Root." Used with permission.

arrow several times finally brought us to the contents of the first table row (<tr>) element (Figure 12–8), which is where the table headings (<th> elements) usually go.

This was helpful. It told us, first, that the document did indeed contain a <table> element. And we could also see that there were no column headers in the first table row as there should have been. To fix that, we brought up the applications menu and selected the Element Properties. . . option to open the dialog box shown in Figure 12–9.

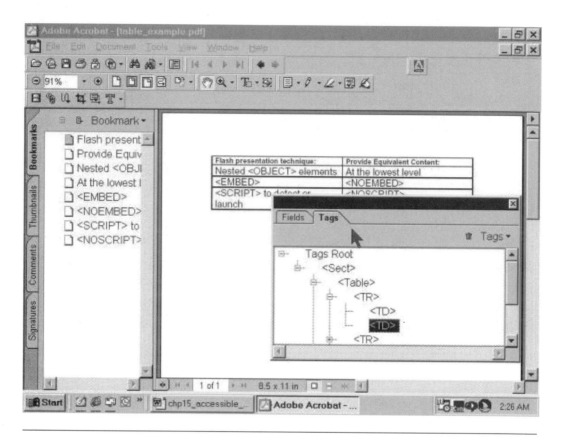

FIGURE 12–8 Acrobat's Tags palette in expanded view. The first table row contains two `<td>` elements instead of table headers. Used with permission.

We replaced the highlighted letters "TD" with "TH" for this element and the next one and, voilà, we had properly labeled the column headers (Figure 12–10).

We changed the tags in the first table row from `<td>` to `<th>`; we also changed the content of the cells by entering a new phrase in the field labeled "Actual text." However, the changes had no apparent effect. The content of the cells remained unchanged, and JAWS was again unable to report the table properly.

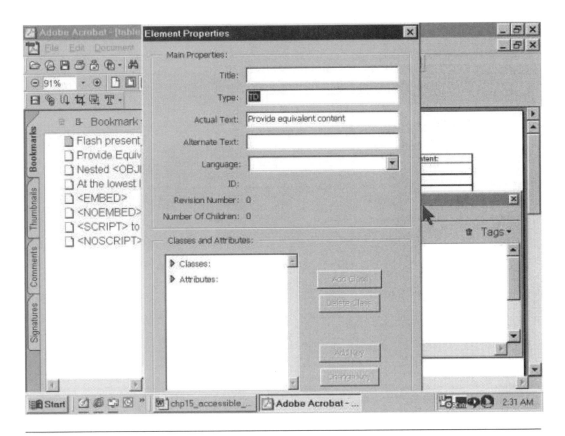

FIGURE 12–9 Acrobat's Element Properties dialog box is now overlaid on top of the Tags palette. The element name "TD" is highlighted. Used with permission.

We encountered other difficulties during this exercise as well. Not only did JAWS fail to report that "Tags Root" had focus when the Tags palette first appeared, but we were unable to return focus to other parts of the document without closing the Tags palette. The Tags palette itself has no Close, OK, Cancel, or Help buttons; the only way that someone using a screen reader can close it is by pressing Alt+F4. And, finally, if the user switches to another open application using Alt+Tab and then comes back to Acrobat the same way, the Tags palette will still

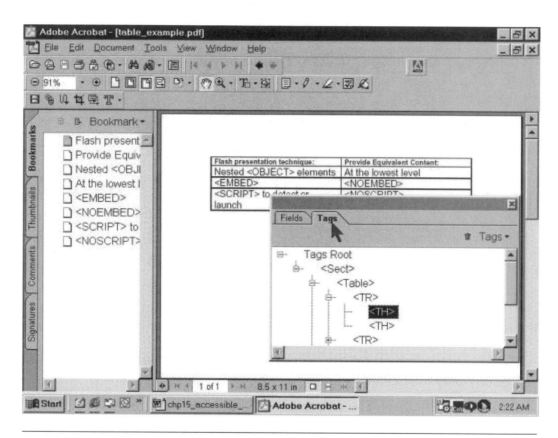

FIGURE 12–10 Another view of the Tags palette. The `<td>` elements shown in Figure 12–8 have now been replaced with `<th>` elements. Used with permission.

be visible on the screen—but the Tags palette will not have focus, and the only way to give it focus is apparently to click on it with the mouse. Catch 22 again.

Authors who are blind or who work exclusively at the keyboard will be seriously hindered by the problems with focus that we've described, though these problems will have less impact on those who are sighted and able to point and click. The problems with Acrobat's built-in repair tools are more serious since there appears to be no way to correct the table markup (unlike HTML, there is no "view source" option—or rather, the Tags palette is the equivalent mechanism).

BURDENS OF THE PAST: LEGACY PDFS AND THE CHALLENGE OF ACCESSIBILITY

Acrobat 5 also includes facilities for converting older PDF documents—those created with earlier versions of Acrobat, including image-only PDFs created from scanned documents—to more accessible forms. This involves using the Make Accessible plug-in included on the Acrobat installation CD. Given the difficulty of what should have been a simple, straightforward procedure—changing a couple of elements from data cells to table headers—and given the lack of information afforded by the Accessibility Checker, attempting to improve the accessibility of older PDF documents on any kind of scale is a daunting task, time-consuming and expensive.

Acrobat's built-in Accessibility Checker would be much more useful if it could point to specific locations that need attention, as Bobby and many other tools do when evaluating HTML documents; it would be helpful if it could indicate where there might be problems with reading order, as the WAVE does (see Chapter 7); and it would be even more valuable if it provided interactive tools for repairing the problems, in the style of A-Prompt. Then at least well-meaning individuals and organizations that were prepared to commit some time might know where to start.

The problem of retrofitting older PDF documents is huge, and for now the available solutions appear to be quite limited. The following examples provide some measure of the scale of the challenge. Like many federal, state, and local government entities, the Internal Revenue Service makes extensive use of PDF documents, including hundreds of tax forms. Forms created in PDF do not work with the current generation of screen readers, as Adobe acknowledges in its analysis of Acrobat and Section 508.[2] The Accessibility page on the IRS Web site contains a frank acknowledgment of the major effort that will be required to make all these forms accessible; for the time being, the IRS plans to provide the forms in plain ASCII text for conversion to speech or Braille.[3] And in Texas, where the state's Access Clause makes it illegal to spend state monies to purchase automated systems that are not accessible to people who are blind and visually impaired, the state has removed Acrobat from the approved list of commodity software that state agencies can buy through the state's Department of Information Resources.[4]

So, while we appreciate the fact that Adobe has made a genuine commitment to accessibility, the company clearly hasn't yet attained that goal. We are confident that as Adobe continues to work with the Web community and the W3C, a better solution will be available soon.

---

2. See *http://access.adobe.com/acr508.html.*
3. See *http://www.irs.gov/formspubs/display/0,,i1%3D50%26genericId% 3D78861,00.html#TopNavSkip* for details.
4. Personal communication from John King, an attorney in the Department of Information Resources.

13

Enhancing Accessibility through Multimedia

PUT *MULTI-* IN YOUR MEDIA!

Video, audio, and animation are important resources for many Web developers, especially those working on news, entertainment, and on-line learning. The ability to enrich a Web site with multimedia elements enables developers to provide the "equivalent alternatives" that we have emphasized throughout this book. These same elements, however, can pose formidable obstacles for people who are blind or visually impaired, people who are deaf or hard of hearing, or people with other challenges (such as cognitive impairments and learning disabilities) if they are not integrated into the site through accessible means.

If you are worried that making your Web sites more accessible for people with disabilities means giving up multimedia, you can relax. It's simply not true; in fact, the *opposite* may be closer to the truth. In some cases, the best way to enhance accessibility may be to use *more* media! Think about it for a minute—using more ways to deliver information means there are more ways for users to get to the information on your site. The key is to use these options as the alternatives they are and not to rely on a single sensory capability to receive important information. Used in the right way, multimedia is a critical resource for accessibility!

In this chapter, we talk about strategies and techniques for making multimedia accessible. We address the requirements for transcribing audio files and captioning the soundtrack in video presentations; we also explain how to add synchronized audio descriptions to video clips. We talk briefly about simple animations such as those created with animated GIF images, then move on to the thornier accessibility barriers posed by Flash movies created with Flash 5.0 and earlier versions, and we show you some workarounds. Let's dive in.

HTML Elements and Attributes
Addressed in This Chapter[1]

Elements

`<object>, <embed>, <noembed>`

Attributes

`param, name, value`

---

1. This chapter also contains references to elements and attributes of other markup languages, including Synchronized Multimedia Integration Language (SMIL), Extensible Markup Language (XML), and Synchronized Accessible Media Interchange (SAMI).

Accessibility Checkpoints and Standards Addressed in This Chapter

Web Content Accessibility Guidelines 1.0 Checkpoints

1.1. Provide a text equivalent for every non-text element. [Priority 1]

1.3. Until user agents can automatically read aloud the text equivalent of a visual track, provide an auditory description of the important information of the visual track of a multimedia presentation. [Priority 1]

1.4. For any time-based multimedia presentation (e.g., a movie or animation), synchronize equivalent alternatives (e.g., captions or auditory descriptions of the visual track) with the presentation. [Priority 1]

7.1. Until user agents allow users to control flickering, avoid causing the screen to flicker. [Priority 1]

8.1. Make programmatic elements such as scripts and applets directly accessible or compatible with assistive technologies. [Priority 1 if functionality is important and not presented elsewhere, otherwise Priority 2]

9.3. For scripts, specify logical event handlers rather than device-dependent event handlers. [Priority 2]

14.2. Supplement text with graphic or auditory presentations where they will facilitate comprehension of the page. [Priority 3]

Section 508 Standards, §1194.22

(b) Equivalent alternatives for any multimedia presentation shall be synchronized with the presentation.

(**j**) Pages shall be designed to avoid causing the screen to flicker with a frequency greater than 2 Hz and lower than 55 Hz.

(**m**) When a Web page requires that an applet, plug-in or other application be present on the client system to interpret page content, the page must provide a link to a plug-in or applet that complies with 1194.21(a) through (l) [Section 508 Software Accessibility Standards].

A REAL-WORLD EXAMPLE: THE ATSTAR PROJECT

In October 2000, the Austin Independent School District (AISD) was awarded a grant from the Texas Education Agency to develop a multimedia, Web-based, teacher-training curriculum to help classroom teachers and other campus-level educators learn about assistive technology (AT). The project was called Assistive Technology Strategies, Tools, Accommodations and Resources (ATSTAR) and was envisioned as a way to bring into the classroom the expertise needed to identify appropriate AT devices. Jan McSorley, the technology facilitator at Bedichek Middle School who designed the project, wanted to provide a practical solution to the challenges that teachers faced in trying to navigate the myriad AT devices available. She understood that, despite the fact that federal law requires schools to provide appropriate AT, it is impossible for classroom teachers to prescribe solutions of which they are entirely unaware. (For more about federal mandates for students with disabilities, see Chapter 3.) AISD, like the great majority of school districts in the United States, relies on a small cadre of AT specialists. In this district, where more than 12,000 children are eligible for AT assistance, there are only three AT specialists to assess and meet their needs. You don't have to do much math to realize that these numbers don't add up to reasonable accommodation.

McSorley and codirector Carye Abete designed ATSTAR to be a team-based, interactive learning experience through which teachers could first learn the process of making successful accommodation assessments and then work their way to finding the right AT solution for each individual student. They built a powerful coalition of national AT experts, students, parents, local educators, software developers, and disability advocates to develop a learning system that has the potential to change the way students with disabilities throughout the country receive services. Central to this mission is the development of the curriculum delivery mechanism. Videotaped scenarios illustrate a series of learning modules and lessons.

The ATSTAR screen pictured in Figure 13–1 displays a gold star with the acronym "AT" written across it. This star is embedded in interlocking puzzle pieces of various primary colors. The puzzle pieces represent the parts of the community that must work together in order to meet the AT needs of students with disabilities. Beneath the word "Welcome!," the page explains the ATSTAR mission and purpose.

The core group of educators who created ATSTAR was dedicated to creating a media-rich learning experience that would be fully accessible to learners with disabilities. (In this case, the learners are also teachers.) The group also wanted to demonstrate the rich possibilities of accessible multimedia. Throughout this chapter, we use examples from the ATSTAR development process to illustrate the value of multimedia for producing results that adhere to the principles of maximum accessibility.

FIGURE 13–1 The home page for ATSTAR (Assistive Technology Strategies, Tools, Accommodations and Resources). Accessed January 2, 2002, at *http://www.atstar.org*. Used with permission.

ATSTAR Accessibility Requirements

We served as consultants on the ATSTAR project and so helped to craft the accessibility specifications that were issued in the request for proposals (RFP) to do the project development work. The requirements document for the ATSTAR project included several pages of accessibility standards, including these from the ATSTAR RFP that relate to multimedia.

- Choose audio and video content with clear purpose.
- Accompany all video and audio content with captions and/or text-based scripts that provide equivalent information to visually impaired or hearing-impaired users.
- Text hyperlinks will be short phrases that are usable out of context (not "Link" or "Click here").
- Image maps will be accompanied by an alternative means of accessing the hot spots for mouseless, keyboard navigation. Examples might be `alt` tags and a logical tab order through the map or a link to a page with the hot spots rendered as text in alphabetical order, and so on.
- Choose scripts, applets, and plug-ins with accessibility in mind. If they pose significant accessibility barriers, use another method to convey information.
- Script multimedia elements for the highest level of accessibility. Use captions, transcripts, audio descriptions, and meaningful narration to ensure that content is accessible to all users.
- Test and verify all accessibility features.

These requirements seemed clear and straightforward when the ATSTAR development process began. What we found, however, was that, despite what seemed clear guidelines, the actual process of attaining maximum accessibility was much less clear. Evolving tools and techniques, confusion about definitions, and the fact that different members of the team had very different priorities caused conflicts that could have been avoided had we understood the following lesson, which we'll pass along so you don't have to learn it the hard way: *Creating an accessible multimedia product requires full commitment to accessibility—and a shared understanding among the team members of what it means—before a single line of code is written.*

MULTIMEDIA EXPANDS ACCESSIBILITY OPTIONS

In the context of Web design, we use the term *multimedia* to refer to audio and/or video content that is integrated with the static or animated text and graphic elements of a Web site. This is a fairly standard definition. Aiming for maximum accessibility, however, may also mean thinking about multimedia in a slightly different way than you're used to. It may mean broadening your definition of multimedia to include, for example, the synthetic speech that screen readers and talking browsers generate. It may mean combining media in new ways to meet the needs of a diverse user population. Accessibility isn't just about using text (either onscreen or off) as an "equivalent alternative" to graphics that are unintelligible to people who can't see them. Even though you may need to supplement a Flash movie by adding text to the `<object>` element that usually embeds the Flash on the page (we'll show you how later in the chapter), you may also be using that same Flash animation or other imagery to assist people who have reading difficulties.

We will demonstrate a few useful techniques for integrating multimedia. For example, closed captions—words moving on the screen in time to the rhythms of the soundtrack—help people who are deaf or hard of hearing as well as people who may be unfamiliar with the language spoken in the video. Written transcripts of audio files serve similar purposes when aural information is delivered on its own. Excellent results can also be achieved by adding a second audio track to a video clip—laying in short, narrative phrases in the little spaces where nothing's going on in the soundtrack. These synchronized audio descriptions—like ALT text on the fly, but spoken, not written—help people who can't see the screen or have trouble understanding what they see.

The ATSTAR team was well aware of the importance of clarity in determining when to use multimedia elements in the first place. Multimedia can be expensive; it can present accessibility barriers; and many people are simply annoyed by sound and moving images that do not seem to have a purpose. Kirk Walker of Knowbility's staff served as technical liaison between the ATSTAR educators and the contracted project developers. His task was the formidable one of balancing the accessibility goals of the ATSTAR team with the media design habits of the developers. The ATSTAR project has quite a bit of media-rich content. Why did the team members choose it?

The main goal of the ATSTAR team was to design a curriculum that would help teachers learn and practice specific steps in the process of identifying AT solutions for individual students (the ATSTAR process). Team members felt that the lessons would be more effective and more memorable if they included video that showed the dynamics of assessment teams at work as well as AT experts explaining key concepts.

Choosing Delivery Modes

If you are delivering your media-rich content entirely from the Web, you will need to make an early determination about whether to provide it in a streaming format, which will begin to play before the entire file is delivered, or as a downloadable file, which takes longer before it begins to play but can be of higher quality. Considerations of compatible client software—plug-ins and external viewers—can also become an issue, as we will see later in the chapter.

The content of the ATSTAR curriculum was, in fact, so heavily dependent on audio and video that the team members decided to avoid creating problems for school districts that might be "bandwidth impaired." Thus, the team produced a separate CD from which to deliver the multimedia elements and provide a seamless interface to the ATSTAR Web site.

In order for multimedia presentations to be accessible, users have to be able to control the content delivery. In fact, WCAG 1.0 Checkpoint 8.1 and Section 508 paragraph (m) require developers to provide access to accessible plug-ins and players (Section 508 seems to contain less wiggle room than WCAG on this point). This can be a difficult pill for multimedia designers and developers to swallow since *they* often like to be able to control exactly when and how their media will be displayed. But most users will, and users with disabilities often *must,* choose media players that allow them to exercise control over how they experience multimedia content. As we explore the options for creating accessible multimedia, we will discover the delicate balance between multimedia authoring techniques and the capabilities of the media plug-ins that play the content.

Letting Users Select the Content Delivery Mode

Figure 13–2 shows how ATSTAR provides users with several options for experiencing the contents of a lesson on its Web site.

The ATSTAR interface allows users to choose from three animated graphic links. One is for video only with no captions, one for

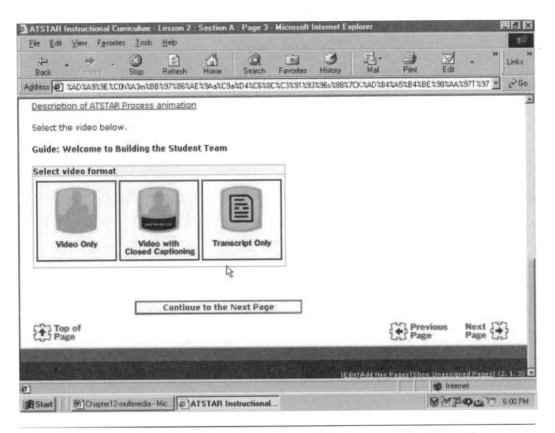

FIGURE 13–2 Screen shot of a page in Lesson 2 of the ATSTAR curriculum, where users choose the format in which they want a video clip to be displayed. Accessed via password on January 3, 2002, from the ATSTAR Web interface at *http://learning.atstar.org*. Used with permission.

video with closed captions, and one for the text transcript only. Why are there *three* versions of this material?

The W3C's User Agent Accessibility Guidelines 1.0,[2] published in February 2000, recommend that browsers and other devices that

---

2. See *http://www.w3.org/TR/UAAG10/*.

render Web-based content allow users to select from a full set of preferences. Synchronized Multimedia Integration Language (SMIL), which we'll explore further as we go on, is another W3C recommendation. SMIL includes *test attributes*, the means for developers to suggest how a presentation should vary according to user preferences. These test attributes will allow users to select for subtitles, overdubs, captions, content language, connection speed, screen depth, and screen size. Media players that support SMIL should allow users to set appropriate preferences for each test attribute. However, current-generation media players do not fully support those options. The ATSTAR interface design group, led by Alicia Ledezma, decided not to depend on player support for user preferences and instead provided a direct means for users to choose video with or without captions—or to read the transcript instead.

Providing Accessible Video

Now that we've talked about the factors underlying the way ATSTAR allows users to select their preferred mode for viewing video, let's look more closely at the issues the ATSTAR team had to address in creating accessible versions of the video materials. Here again we need to think in terms of "equivalent alternative" experiences. Maximum accessibility requires that we provide a way to include users who can't or won't see the video and others who can't or won't hear the soundtrack. In thinking about accessible video, we must consider how to create a multilayered experience that includes those who will not hear the content as well as those who will not see it.

Providing an equivalent alternative may involve one or more of the following three aids:

- Synchronized closed captioning.
- Synchronized audio description.
- Text transcripts.

ATSTAR uses closed captions and text transcripts, so let's start with captioning.

ACCESSIBLE VIDEO CONTENT REQUIRES CLOSED CAPTIONING

Video media elements typically rely on the user's ability to see and hear content in order to fully experience it. Users who do not hear or have turned off their speakers rely on a text caption track of the dialogue and other sounds that accompany the video. Besides making the soundtrack accessible to some 20 million Americans who are deaf or hard of hearing, these closed captions are useful for people with cognitive disabilities; captions are also helpful to individuals who are learning the language spoken in the video. WCAG 1.0 Checkpoint 1.4 and Section 508 paragraph (b) specify that the captions must be synchronized with the delivery of the video and audio presentation.

You've probably seen closed captioning many times—for example, on televisions located in crowded or noisy public spaces such as hotel and airport lobbies, bars, restaurants, and so forth. All U.S. televisions manufactured since 1992 can display closed captions, so if you've never really thought about how they work, we recommend that you try this experiment at home. Turn on the closed captions on your television set. Turn off the sound. Watch the news or several of your favorite shows using only the captions. Spend enough time doing this so that the novelty and initial frustration wear off, and note how different types of elements and events are represented in the caption—dialog, music, background noises, other sound effects.

Guidelines for Closed Captioning

Closed captioning has been around since the 1970s, and as a result there are excellent resources you can consult for information about how to handle the many different possibilities that might come up in the video material you'll need to caption. Closed captioning was pioneered by the Caption Center at WGBH, the Boston, Massachusetts PBS affiliate that has also pioneered descriptive video. The Caption Center publishes an excellent guide called "How It Works," which offers some useful tips on captioning style. Some of the details pertain specifically to television, and you'll need to adapt the tips for presentation on the Web or other media. The Caption Center guidelines address a wide variety of topics. We mention just a few here and refer you to the guidelines for additional information.[3]

---

3. All material in this section is based on information presented in "How It Works," a guide to closed captioning produced by WGBH in Boston, MA. Accessed January 21, 2002, at *http://main.wgbh.org/wgbh/pages/captioncenter/ccstyles.html*. Quotations used with permission.

In the early days of captioning, captions often represented heavily edited versions of what was actually said in the dialog. According to the Caption Center:

> The rationale for this was that this type of editing would make it easier for the deaf and hard-of-hearing audience to understand the program. Experience has shown, however, that much of the caption-viewing audience prefers to have a verbatim or near-verbatim rendering of the audio; therefore, any editing that occurs nowadays is usually for reading speed only. Strive for a reading speed that allows the viewer enough time to read the captions yet still keep an eye on the program video. Once you reach a decision on caption reading speed, use that speed consistently in your work.

There are occasions when limited reading time makes it necessary to edit—viewers couldn't possibly keep up with verbatim captions that change at the speed of rapid-fire dialog. When this happens, the Caption Center advises, "try to maintain precisely the original meaning and flavor of the language as well as the personality of the speaker." When captioning "classic" movies, literary works, or the speech of important personalities, it's best to avoid editing if at all possible.

It's sometimes possible to place captions on the screen to indicate who is speaking at a given point (this is one reason why, as we discuss below, captioning formats for the Web include features that let you control the visual presentation of the captions). This technique doesn't always work, though, so it may be necessary to include the speaker's name or other identifier in square brackets. The experts at the Caption Center advise:

> When considering the placement of captions, keep in mind what action is occurring in a given scene. If only one person talks throughout a scene, captions are generally placed at bottom center. If there are multiple characters in a scene, caption placement on or near individual speakers is used to indicate who is saying what.

As we've noted, both WCAG 1.0 and Section 508 require that captions be synchronized with the soundtrack. SMIL and other media languages control the timing of caption changes to synchronize them to the video elements. The Caption Center's guidelines help us understand why this is so important:

> To convey pacing appropriate to humor, suspense and drama, as well as to indicate who is speaking, captions may be timed to appear and disappear precisely when the words are spoken. The text may be timed to change with shot changes for readability and aesthetic purposes. In applying timing conventions, consider that logical caption division should not be sacrificed for exactitude in timing. Readability should always be the first priority.

The guidelines also cover sound effects. It may not be possible (or desirable) to provide a caption for every sound, no matter how insignificant it may be; but all sounds that contribute to understanding should be represented in the captions. Since these are not actually spoken, references to sound effects should be distinguished typographically from the dialog. The Caption Center uses italics in parentheses to identify such effects, including such things as indicating when a speaker is whispering, shouting, and so on.

To indicate that music is playing or that someone is singing, place a graphic of a musical note at the beginning and end of the caption. Captions for songs, advertising jingles, and so on should be verbatim. Include song titles when possible; if they're not part of the dialogue, make sure they're typographically different than the lyrics or spoken dialog.

For numbers, the Caption Center suggests following widely used conventions. For example, spell out numbers from one to ten, and use numerals for larger numbers (21, for instance, or 252,971). This convention holds unless a large number is the only text in the caption; then the number should be spelled out (for example, two million two hundred fifty thousand).

Spelling and punctuation should be consistent and again should follow widely used conventions. The Caption Center recommends equipping yourself with good reference materials such as *The Chicago Manual of Style* as well as a dictionary, a thesaurus, and an encyclopedia.

When Captioning Is Not Enough: Providing Signed Interpretation

It's important to realize, however, that captioning is not a universal solvent for making audio material accessible to people who cannot hear it. Captions work well for "late-deafened" individuals such as the many senior citizens who suffer hearing loss as they age. Such individuals have spent most of their lives as hearing people, and for them, spoken and written language are the most natural means of communication. But that's not true for everyone. Linguist Leland McCleary of the University of Sao Paolo explains:

> Only a very few of those individuals who are born deaf or who become deaf at an early age achieve fluency in the spoken language of their community, and only then with great effort. For the deaf, the only route to full language mastery is through a sign language; but access to sign language is not always guaranteed, since the majority of those born deaf are born into hearing families. [McCleary 2001]

For millions of deaf persons in the United States, the native language is American Sign Language (ASL); millions of other deaf individuals around the world use the signed languages of their native countries. Sign is the first language for these individuals, just as English is the first language for most people in the United States. This has important consequences. As the European author of "Guidelines for Signed Books" wrote, "Deaf people have their own language and their own culture. It is difficult for a French producer to make a typically English production. It is as difficult for a hearing producer to make a Deaf production" [Pyfers 1999]. Many people for whom Sign is the first language and the natural medium of expression find written language difficult, especially when it appears and disappears quickly, as synchronized captions do. This is not a trivial issue: to quote the "Guidelines" again, "Deaf adults need video for information on Deaf issues and Deaf culture, but also for easy access to information, education, politics, culture, etc. of the larger, hearing community" [Pyfers 1999]. To ensure maximum accessibility for the deaf audience, you may create a Sign version in addition to the caption track. Applications that automatically convert text or speech to Sign are starting to come onto the market, but there is no substitute for experienced and fluent signers and interpreters. Signed interpretation services are also available through commercial providers.

Captioning on the Web

On the Web, a typical video element consists of a video file, which usually contains the video imagery and the accompanying audio. The dominant browser-based video players—RealNetworks' RealPlayer (now RealOne), Apple's QuickTime player, and Microsoft's Windows Media Player—allow for the inclusion of other tracks, such as text captions, additional audio narration, and graphics. Each of these technologies uses a proprietary video and text file format and synchronization method. In addition to these proprietary methods of synchronization, most of these players include some level of support for SMIL. Developed by the W3C, SMIL enables Web developers to divide multimedia content into separate files and streams (audio, video, text, and images) and send them to a user's computer individually, greatly reducing the size of the multimedia file. Separate files and streams are synchronized to display together as if they are a single multimedia stream. The ability to separate out the static text and images and the resulting reduction in file size minimize the time it takes to transfer the files over the Internet. SMIL is based on the Extensible Markup Language (XML). Rather than defining the actual formats used to represent multimedia data, it defines the commands that specify whether the various multimedia components should be played together or in sequence. SMIL version 2.0, published in February 2001, is similar in simplicity to HTML and can be written using a simple text editor. SMIL forms the basis for many of the captioning solutions we examine in this chapter and includes the ability for the user to turn captions on or off.

The primary benefit to using SMIL for synchronization is that it allows the author to program switch conditions to provide captions, images, or alternative language formats. A player that fully supports SMIL displays tracks according to how the user configures the player settings. If QuickTime 5 worked in this way, there would have been no need for the ATSTAR team to supply separate versions of the same media or for the user to make a choice each time video material is presented, as in Figure 13–2. In addition to providing a way to synchronize media elements and provide conditions for their display, SMIL also allows the author to configure the space in which these elements are displayed.

In an ideal world, all of the third-party plug-in developers would fully implement the W3C recommendations that affect their products. However, this rarely happens, and it takes some time when it does. The W3C has recently introduced some changes in the process for developing guidelines: a draft cannot be published as a formal Recommendation until at least two implementations of each checkpoint have been located. These changes are designed to reduce the lag time between publication of W3C recommendations and the availability of applications that support them. Even so, the Web author who is concerned about accessibility should understand the differences between the product choices available and what measures must be taken to deliver an accessible presentation. Although SMIL may still be considered an emerging method until the user agents fully accommodate it, we stress its importance here because in the long run, a growing compliance with a standards-based mechanism for delivering multimedia will benefit everyone involved in the process. The code mechanism for presenting multimedia would be consistent across browsers, players, and operating systems, thereby easing the burden on Web authors. The user experience would be more consistent and controllable, and upgrades to tools and methods would be based on a wider range of user and author experiences.

Before we describe the major differences between the popular media players available today, let's explore a little further the caption component of the multimedia presentation. As we mentioned above, the caption element of a video or audio segment is presented to the user as a text equivalent of the dialog synchronized with the multimedia event. To produce this caption track, we must first transcribe the media event into a script, identify the speakers for each segment, and place a timecode on each segment to synchronize it with the media. Transcribing the media is a manual process and can be quite demanding if the soundtrack is complex; fortunately, you can use professional captioning services if you decide to outsource this part of the work. After you have the transcription of the media, you can generate the caption file with a text editor by adding the timecodes and other necessary formatting codes in the format appropriate to the media player you are using. Each of the media players has a proprietary markup for their caption files, though all of them start with ASCII text (as does HTML, of course). The most difficult task in converting transcript files to caption files is the timecode stamping for synchronization. Fortunately there are applications available to assist with this process. In the next section, we introduce a free tool that supports all three of the major media players.

MAGpie: The Media Access Generator from NCAM

MAGpie is the acronym for the Media Access Generator developed by the National Center for Accessible Media (NCAM) at WGBH, the PBS affiliate in Boston, Massachusetts, that has pioneered many important accessibility advances for broadcast and Internet media, including closed captioning and descriptive video. You can download MAGpie for free from the NCAM site at *http://ncam.wgbh.org/ Webaccess/MAGpie/*.

You can use MAGpie 1.0 to add captions to three multimedia formats: Apple's QuickTime, the W3C's SMIL (via RealOne's RealText), and Microsoft's Synchronized Accessible Media Interchange (SAMI) format for Windows Media Player. MAGpie 1.0 can also integrate audio descriptions into SMIL presentations. A beta version of MAGpie was released in fall 2001. The final release will include these additional features:

- Java-based application for Windows and Mac OS X.
- Improved editing behavior.
- XML output.
- Output support for Web-embedded media (RealText, SAMI, SMIL, and QT text).
- Full audio description support, including audio recording and playback.

- Karaoke-style highlighting.
- Improved support for media types—all types supported by Windows Media Player, QuickTime, and RealOne.

With MAGpie, you can easily add caption lines, speaker identification, and time stamps to accompany a video or audio segment. MAGpie 1.0 uses Windows Media Player to display video and audio tracks of resources to be captioned.

When you create a project and identify the media element you wish to caption, MAGpie creates a new caption stream and opens the media resource in Windows Media Player. MAGpie controls Windows Media Player and includes functionality to play, pause, stop, and jump forward or backward. The most important feature, however, is the ability to "grab" the timecode with the press of a function key (F9). Then, as the media segment plays, MAGpie captures and inserts the appropriate segment of caption text. MAGpie allows you to edit the caption text and the timecodes, delete and add events, and split or combine events. When you're finished, you can export the project in SAMI format, QuickText format, or SMIL, which will produce a RealText (.rt) file and SMIL code to synchronize it with.

Figure 13–3 shows a screen shot of our example ATSTAR video being edited with MAGpie 1.0 and Windows Media Player. This illustration shows the MAGpie application on the left and the video playing in Windows Media Player on the right. The MAGpie window is in table format with header information at the top and several rows of caption entries indicating the timecode, the speaker, and the caption text. The initial row has only a timecode of 00:00:00 and no text to initiate the file.

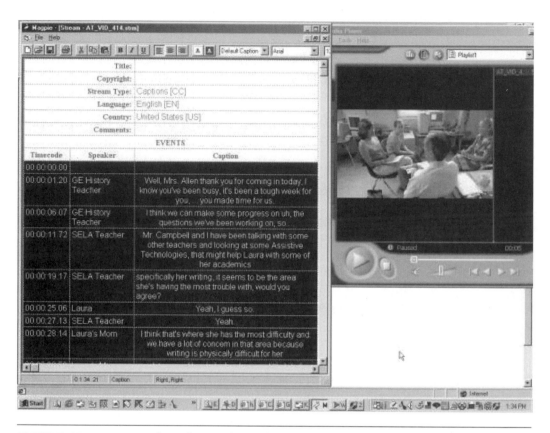

FIGURE 13–3 Screen shot of MAGpie editing session with Windows Media Player. Used with permission.

MAGpie is an indispensable tool for timecoding complex caption data.

Comparing the Popular Media Players

RealPlayer

At the time of this writing, RealOne offers the most support for SMIL among the major video players. At this time, RealOne is the newest player by RealNetworks. RealOne is available only for Windows at this point, so we will center our discussion on RealPlayer 8, which is available for both Windows and Macintosh. RealPlayer uses a caption format known as RealText to display and synchronize text captions. RealText markup contains the following elements and attributes.

- `<window bgcolor="#RRGGBB" wordwrap="true | false" duration="hh:mm:ss.ss">` sets the window characteristics for displaying the captions.
  - `bgcolor` sets the background color of the caption window. RRGGBB represents the red, green, and blue color reference in hex format.
  - `wordwrap` determines whether text should be wrapped to window size if a line of text is too wide for the window.
  - `duration` sets the length of time the text presentation will last in hours, minutes, and seconds.
- `<font size="size" face="font-family" color="#RRGGBB">` sets font characteristics.
  - `size` values can be –2, –1, +0, +1, +2, +3, or +4.
  - `face` sets the font face used to render the captions. Values are font families like Arial and Helvetica (the default is Times New Roman).
  - `color` sets the font color. RRGGBB represents the red, green, and blue color reference in hex format.
- `<time begin="hh:mm:ss.ss"/>` sets the start time for a caption in hours, minutes, and seconds.
- `<center>` centers a caption in a presentation window.
- `<br>` creates a line break.

Using these elements, the author can control the background and font color, font size and face, and time stamp for each caption line; she or he can also center the caption in the space. We suggest following the guidelines published by the Caption Center at WGBH when deciding what to include in your captions and how to format them. (See the Guidelines for Closed Captioning section earlier in this chapter for selections from the Caption Center guidelines.)

Below is an example of RealText markup and the description of the code function from one of the ATSTAR videos.

```
<window bgcolor="000000" wordwrap="true"
    duration="00:05:29.08">
<font size="1" face="Arial" color="#FFFFFF">
<center>
<time begin="00:00:00.00"/>
<clear/>
<time begin="00:00:01.20"/><clear/>
</center>GE History Teacher<br>
<center>Well, Mrs. Allen thank you for coming in today, I
    know you've been busy, it's been a tough week for you,
    ... you made time for us.<br>
<time begin="00:00:06.07"/><clear/>
</center>GE History Teacher<br>
<center>I think we can make some progress on the questions
    we've been working on, so...<br>
. . .
<time begin="00:05:29.08"/><clear/> 
</center>
</font>
</window>
```

RealPlayer's user preferences include Accessibility Settings that allow users to elect to show captions. RealPlayer uses the SMIL `<switch>`

element to determine whether or not to display the RealText file, depending on how the user has set this preference. Figure 13–4 shows the RealPlayer Accessibility Settings dialog box with the Show Captions radio button selected.

QuickTime

The QuickTime player allows caption tracks as well as other media tracks to be synchronized with the video. QuickTime 5 does support SMIL but does not yet support the SMIL switch to activate the captioning according to the user settings. Therefore, to give the user a choice of captioned or noncaptioned video using QuickTime, you

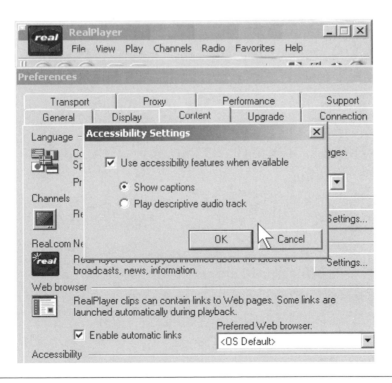

FIGURE 13–4 Screen shot of the RealPlayer Accessibility Settings dialog box. Used with permission.

must create two separate movies to be played and provide links to each for the user, as in the ATSTAR example above.

To create captioned video using QuickTime, you must create a caption file using QuickText with time stamps that synchronize with the video dialog or action. QuickTime Pro allows you to then "compile" the QuickTime movie including a video file (.mov), a QuickText caption file (.txt.mov), and graphic files for background images with a synchronization file. When the user activates the video, it is the synchronization file that runs. (If you choose, you can use MAGpie to add the new tracks and create the synchronization file.)

QuickText markup contains the following elements.

- {QText} starts the QuickText document.
- {font: font-family} sets the current font family.
- {justify: left, center or right} sets the alignment of text.
- {backcolor: red, blue, green} specifies the color of text based on red, blue, and green values (0–255 for each color).
- {timescale: number} sets the time scale used for determining synchronization cues.
- {width: pixels} specifies the width of the window used by the QuickTime player to render the text.
- {height: pixels} specifies the height of the window used by the QuickTime player to render the text.
- [hh:mm:ss.ss] text element sets the synchronization time for rendering the next QuickText element.

You can also control font family, text justification, and background color for the caption space. You can adjust the timescale as well. A time stamp synchronizes the rendering of the caption.

Important note: You must create a space for the captioning to be rendered by using a graphic spacer that is played throughout the duration of a video rendered in QuickTime; otherwise, the caption text will be overlaid on the video itself and may become illegible.

Figure 13–5 shows a video frame from the ATSTAR curriculum with captioning as rendered by the QuickTime player. The ATSTAR video frame pictures a large green puzzle piece, a video frame in the top center, and caption text below the video frame all within the green graphic. The QuickTime control slider rests on the bottom edge. Each of these components is a separate element of the QuickTime media

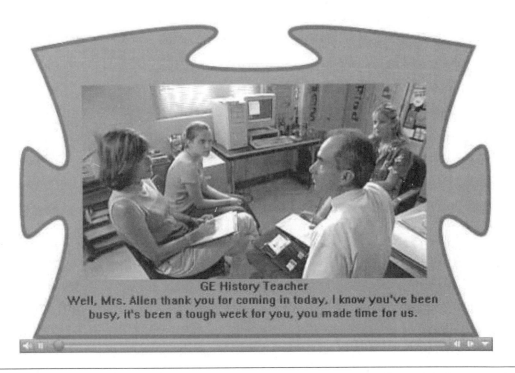

FIGURE 13–5 ATSTAR video frame showing captioning rendered by QuickTime. Used with permission.

group. The media group also includes a green graphic the size of the caption block (not distinguishable from the background image) and a synchronization file. When ATSTAR users choose to view video without captions, another synchronization file activates a visually similar frame that references this same movie and background images but not the caption file. Thus, offering viewers a choice between video with and without captions does not require duplicating the actual video files themselves.

A portion of the QuickText caption file for this ATSTAR video appears below.

```
{QTtext}{font:Arial}{justify:center}{size:12}
{backcolor:0,0,0}
{timescale:100}{width:400}{height:0}
[00:00:00.00]
[00:00:01.20]
{justify:left}GE History Teacher
    {justify:center}Well, Mrs. Allen thank you for coming
    in today, I know you've been busy, it's been a tough
    week for you, ... you made time for us.
[00:00:06.07]
{justify:left}GE History Teacher
{justify:center}I think we can make some progress on uh,
    the questions we've been working on, so...
    . . .
[00:05:29.07]
[00:05:29.08]
```

There are many steps to creating this group of elements in Quick-Time, including the following.

- Creating the QuickText file.
- Importing and configuring this file in QuickTime Pro.

- Creating a text track.
- Adding the text track to the video track.
- Positioning the text track in the video frame.
- Saving the result as a separate file, with the appropriate suffix.

QuickTime does allow the inclusion of various media elements, but the methods are somewhat cumbersome.

Windows Media Player

Windows Media Player does not support SMIL at this time, and the Microsoft SAMI caption format can be used only for captions and not for the other media elements that QuickTime and RealOne allow. That said, some people find Windows Media Player easier to use. Windows Media Player does allow users to choose whether to view captions, so you need to create only one version of the video module. However, you must create different versions for disk-based and Web-based presentations. For disk-based resources, you create a caption file (.smi) with the same name as the video file but with a .asf extension. The caption files play automatically if the user preferences are set to display them. For Web-based presentations, you must bind the caption file to the media file with a .asx file; Windows Media Player will then run the .asx file. The captions are displayed in a separate, fixed window, so you do not have to worry about background color or interference with the video.

SAMI markup is styled after HTML, and you can use Cascading Style Sheets for text styling. Below is a list of the elements of SAMI markup.

- <sami> indicates the file is a SAMI-based caption file.
- <head> defines the head block, which contains title and styling information.

- `<title>` is used for informational purposes; it is optional.
- `<style>` defines styles for caption elements; uses CSS conventions.
- `<body>` contains the synchronization cues.
- `<sync start=milliseconds>` sets the time synchronization cue for a text element, in milliseconds.
- `<p class=style ref>` text specifies the text element(s) for the current synchronization element.

The code below presents an example of a SAMI file for the same ATSTAR video we discussed previously.

```
<sami>
<head>
    <copyright="">
    <title></title>
    <style type="text/css">
    <!--
        p {
            font-size:12pt;
            font-family: Arial;
            font-weight: normal;
            color: #FFFFFF;
            background-color: #000000;
            text-align: center;
        }
        .ENUSCC { Name: English;
            lang: EN-US-CC; }
        #Source {
            font-size:12pt;
            font-family: Arial;
            font-weight: normal;
            color: #FFFFFF;
            background-color: #000000;
```

```
            text-align: left;
            margin-bottom: -12pt;
        }
    -->
    </style>
</head>
<body>
<sync start=0>
    <p class=ENUSCC ID=Source> </p>
    <p class=ENUSCC></p>
</sync>
<sync start=1200>
    <p class=ENUSCC id=Source>GE History Teacher</p>
    <p class=ENUSCC><table align=center>
    Well, Mrs. Allen thank you for coming in today, I know
        you've been busy, it's been a tough week for you,
        ... you made time for us.
    </table></p>
</sync>
<sync start=6070>
    <p class=ENUSCC id=Source>GE History Teacher</p>
    <p class=ENUSCC><table align=center>
    I think we can make some progress on uh, the questions
        we've been working on, so...
    </table></p>
. . .
<sync start=329080>
    <p class=ENUSCC> </p>
</sync>
</body>
</sami>
```

Windows Media metafile extensions are used to identify the format of the file that a metafile references. Windows Media metafiles with .wax, .wvx, or .asx extensions reference files with .wma (Windows

Media Audio), .wmv (Windows Media Video), and .asf (Windows Media file) extensions, respectively. All metafiles, regardless of the file name extension used, have the <ASX> element tag at the beginning of the file with the version attribute specified. The ASX code below gives an example of how the video file and caption file are bound together for Web-based presentation. The code is similar to XML, and at this writing it is better supported by Microsoft Internet Explorer than by Netscape Navigator or other user agents.

```
<ASX version = "3.0">
<title>SAMI Captioning Demo</title>
<entry> <title>Student Scenario</title>
<author>ATSTAR</author> <copyright>2001</copyright>
<ref href = "at_vid_414.asf" />
</entry>
<entry>
<ref href="at_vid_414.smi" />
</entry>
</ASX>
```

More about SMIL Attributes

There are excellent tutorials that will help you learn more about how to use SMIL to effectively and accessibly include multimedia elements in your work. Like HTML, SMIL includes useful attributes that will support the accessibility of your pages. We list a few of them below; you'll notice some familiar terms, along with some we haven't encountered before.

- alt: When used as an attribute of a media object, alt specifies a brief text message about the function of that object. Media players may render alternative text in place of or in addition to media content, for instance when images or sound are turned off or not supported.

- longdesc: As in HTML, the longdesc attribute links to a more complete description of media content. Authors should provide long descriptions of complex content, such as charts and graphs or works of art. The longdesc attribute is also useful to designate a text transcript of audio and video information.

- title: This one can be used as an attribute of most SMIL elements to provide advisory information about the nature of the element. The SMIL specification explains how to use the title attribute for a given element type. For example, for links, use it to describe the target of the link.

- author: Use this attribute to specify text metadata about document elements. Metadata generally promote accessibility by providing more context and orientation.

- abstract: Optional metadata about document elements, the abstract attribute, like the author attribute, increase context and orientation information for the user. We encourage you to use these attributes to provide more equivalent user experiences in your multimedia presentations. Text metadata provide a number of access options since they may be rendered in a variety of ways—on the screen, as speech, or on a refreshable Braille display.

The overview of captioning considerations and options presented here is only an introduction. Multimedia applications are changing rapidly as the trend toward greater accessibility increases. We encourage you to stay abreast of changes and provide the highest degree of user choice in your multimedia presentations. Among other emerging practices is the field of audio description.

ENHANCE USER EXPERIENCE WITH AUDIO DESCRIPTION

Synchronized audio description—a spoken description of the activities presented through video—is another essential element in making video accessible, in this case for people who are unable to see the video, whether because they are blind or for some other reason. The audio description is recorded on a separate track, which is usually inserted into natural pauses in the soundtrack. It describes key visual elements of the presentation. The audio description may include information that describes the scene, the characters, their body language, and any other visual elements that may be important to understanding the video but are not available from the soundtrack alone. Like captions, audio descriptions must be synchronized with the video stream they describe.

Like closed captioning and other accessibility techniques, audio description existed before the Web was born. But it's not all *that* old, either. Audio description of live theater events began in 1981 with the pioneering work of Margaret and Cody Pfanstiehl of the Metropolitan Washington Ear, along with Arena Stage in Washington, DC. Now audio description can be found in several other states as well as the District of Columbia. In 1987, the Boston PBS affiliate, WGBH, which had pioneered closed captioning in the early 1970s, launched its Descriptive Video Service (DVS). In 1989, Congress for the first time appropriated funds for described television, as authorized by the Education of the Handicapped Act. By 1997, WGBH had established a policy that all national programming would be described.[4] The Na-

---

4. "DVS Milestones." Accessed January 19, 2002, at *http://main.wgbh.org/wgbh/ access/dvs/dvsmilestones.html.*

tional Academy of Television Arts and Sciences awarded Margaret Pfanstiehl an Emmy for "leadership and persistence" in pioneering accessible TV for people who are visually impaired, and the DVS has received many national and international awards as well.

Why Describe?

Why bother describing video content? After all, it seems logical to assume that the 6.5 million people in the U.S. who are blind or severely visually impaired don't watch much video. But that's not so. In 1997, the American Foundation for the Blind (AFB) published "Who's Watching? A Profile of the Blind and Visually Impaired Audience for Television and Video" [Packer and Kirchner 1997]. The study found that 99 percent of blind and visually impaired respondents owned television sets, and 83 percent owned VCRs; these figures are virtually the same as those for the general population. The study also found that more blind and visually impaired people were cable subscribers. Respondents watched a mean of 24 hours of television per week. In these and most other respects, the AFB researchers found, the statistics about people who are blind and visually impaired were very similar to those for the U.S. population as a whole. The AFB report also indicates that 96 percent of persons with no usable vision state that description is very important to their enjoyment of television or videos. More than 75 percent of all respondents claim that the benefits of description include enhancing the overall viewing experience as well as the learning and social experiences of television and video [Packer and Kirchner 1997].

Audio description doesn't just make TV and video more fun for people who have trouble seeing. Audio description, like other accessibility techniques we have presented, has wider benefits as well. An earlier study conducted by the AFB with support from the National

Science Foundation concluded that "description has positive impacts in psychological, social, and cognitive domains on blind and severely visually impaired individuals."[5]

Differences between Audio Descriptions and Closed Captions

There are some important differences between audio descriptions and closed captions. First, of course, they serve different needs. Closed captions help people who can't hear the soundtrack or may have difficulty understanding it. Audio descriptions help people who can't see the visual material or have trouble understanding it. This means that making your video material accessible isn't a matter of choosing between closed captioning and audio description: WCAG 1.0 and Section 508 require both techniques.

That brings us to a second difference. As the Caption Center guidelines discussed earlier make clear, closed captions are verbatim or nearly verbatim transcripts of *exactly* what's spoken in the video soundtrack (including interruptions) and by whom. Captions should also include notations for other significant sound elements: music, laughter, applause, gunshots, cars backfiring, the murmur of voices in the background in a cocktail party scene, and so on. Audio descriptions, on the other hand, can't possibly include everything going on in the scene. Audio descriptions usually last only a couple of seconds— they have to fit into the pauses in dialog and other spaces where they

---

5. "DVS Milestones." Accessed January 19, 2002, at *http://main.wgbh.org/wgbh/ access/dvs/dvsmilestones.html.*

won't interfere with the actual soundtrack. SMIL version 2.0, published in February 2001, contains features that let developers "expand" those pauses, "freezing" the action and dropping in longer descriptions; but these features aren't yet well supported and we won't address them here. Under the current circumstances, the describer has to *select* what to describe.

A number of organizations offer training in audio description. VSA Arts of Texas (formerly Austin Access Arts), for example, conducts workshops at conferences throughout Texas and across the Southwest and offers an excellent series of videotapes and accompanying workbooks for those who want to learn the techniques of describing a wide variety of performances and other events. As of this writing (June 2002), however, there are no standards for audio description comparable to the WCAG. That may change very soon: the first conference of a new organization, Audio Description International, was held in March 2002. The agenda included consideration of the questions involved in developing official international standards for audio description, as well as training and certification programs. The proceedings from the conference are available online at *http://www.adinternational.org/conference/2002/*.

Deciding What to Describe

In the meantime, though, you have decisions to make about those video clips you plan to include on your site. How do you decide what to describe? It helps to keep in mind that audio description is aimed at people who can hear the soundtrack but can't see what's happening on the screen. So you should focus on describing *only critical details that can't be deduced from the soundtrack*.

Note, too, that we keep using words related to *description*. This isn't an accident: an audio description should be as neutral as possible with respect to what it describes. Instead of expressing your own value judgments or ideas about why things are happening on the screen, your job as describer is to present the scene in such a way that people who can't see it can form their own conclusions about what's going on, just as people who can see the video will draw their own conclusions.

Joe Clark published a proposed list of five principles (he calls them "techniques," but they're not) for audio description in advance of his presentation at the first Audio Description International conference in March 2002. Although these are somewhat controversial—they are considerably less detailed, for example, than those published by the United Kingdom's Independent Television Council in the year 2000[6]—they may be useful for people just getting started, so we offer them here.

1. Describe what you observe.
2. Describers and narrators serve the audience and the production, not themselves.
3. If time limits force you to be selective, first describe what is essential to know, such as actions and details that would confuse or mislead the audience if omitted.

---

6. The Independent Television Council's "Guidance on Standards for Audio Description" is available in Microsoft Word format at *http://www.itc.org.uk/divisions/eng_div/subtitle/Audio_Description.doc*. This document includes a good deal of information that is quite specific to British television.

4. Whenever possible, describe actions and details that add to the understanding of personal appearance, setting, atmosphere, and *mise-en-scène* [loosely translated, the *mise-en-scène* is the setting, or the placement of people and objects in the scene, as on a movie set].

5. Since it is more important to make a production understandable than to preserve every detail of the original soundtrack, it is permissible to describe over dialog and other audio when necessary. [Clark 2001]

Now that we have at least a basic understanding of audio description, let's move on to an example of audio description in action.

An Example of Audio Description: The TX2K Video

In 2001, the Institute for Technology and Learning (ITAL) commissioned a short video about an educational Web project called *TX2K: The Texas 2000 Living Museum*.[7] The K–12 students who participate in the TX2K project research and create multimedia "exhibits" about the past, present, and future of each of their own communities. Students publish their completed exhibits in the TX2K museum gallery for viewing by their peers and anyone else who might be interested (Figure 13–6).

The two-and-a-half-minute video was designed for inclusion on a CD-ROM that would be distributed to schools across Texas. The CD provided a comprehensive overview of the project. It explained

---

7. The TX2K video was produced by Linda Litowski and Henry Miller of L&M Pro Video in Austin, Texas.

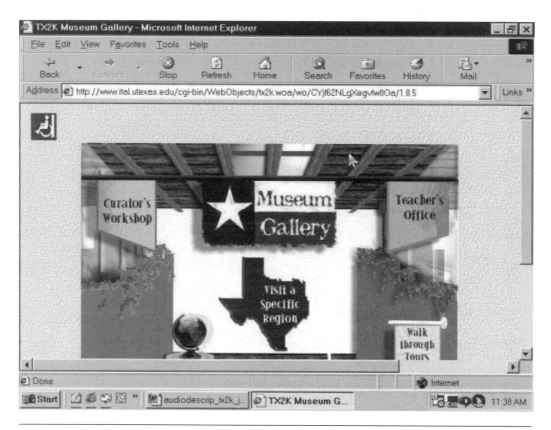

FIGURE 13–6 Screen shot of the TX2K Gallery, where student exhibits may be viewed. In the center of this virtual room's "rear wall," the words "Museum Gallery" are superimposed on an image of the Texas flag above the Texas map. Accessed January 19, 2002, at *http://www.ital.utexas.edu*. Used with permission.

the activities and resources included in TX2K, outlined the state curriculum requirements addressed by the project, and described the accessibility features that had earned TX2K first place for Extraordinary Web Design in a national competition sponsored by Project EASI (Equal Access to Software and Information). The video itself was intended as an introduction to the CD. It was also meant to demonstrate accessible video. Both closed captions and audio descriptions are available. (Since we covered closed captioning extensively in our discussion of the ATSTAR video, we concentrate on audio description here.)

The Video

Scenes showing intensely engaged children and teachers in classrooms and computer labs were intercut with screen shots from the TX2K site and "talking head" shots of educators explaining why they liked the project. One outdoor scene was shot at an abandoned rural cemetery where children were researching a yellow-fever epidemic that devastated the area shortly after the Civil War.

The Descriptions

In the soundtrack for most of the classroom scenes, the voice of a teacher is heard above the buzz of children's voices and background music. In one such scene, a teacher, pointing to a spot on the Web page that a fourth-grader had found, tells the child about an important figure in Texas history who is named on the page. When the scene opens, though, the soundtrack contains only background music: there is no way for someone who cannot see the screen to tell what is on the screen. This is where the describer comes in, with a quick remark to set the scene: "Boys and girls in a computer classroom." At another point, the camera cuts away to a screen shot; the audio describer notes simply, "TX2K login screen." Still later, the scene shifts to the abandoned cemetery where two children are looking at an old tombstone. The soundtrack offers only background music, and again the audio description kicks in to tell us where we are and what's happening. "In an historic cemetery, a girl kneels to trace the letters on an old tombstone," the describer says. "Another girl uses a digital camera to photograph another tombstone."

The Describer

The describer was Connie McMillan, an experienced volunteer trained in audio description by VSA Arts of Texas. McMillan accompanied ITAL staff to the L&M studio on a rainy February day. The group of us watched the video several times and discussed the essential points the video was meant to convey and the emotional charge we wanted to create. Then we went through the video again, this time pausing the video where descriptions were needed; McMillan tried out different variations until everyone was satisfied. This actually turned out to be the next-to-last version: producer Linda Litowski had transcribed it, and when she read back the individual segments, we found ourselves making some slight changes along the way. Then McMillan read each item while Emmy Award–winning soundman Henry Miller captured her voice.

If the process we've described seems cumbersome, consider this: the best way to reduce the time needed for creating effective audio descriptions is to incorporate them into the scripting process for the video. Review the shot list and the captions to determine where descriptions are necessary; then write a description script and record someone reading the descriptions. Then, at the appropriate point in the production process, synchronize the captions and audio descriptions with the main video element, using MAGpie or another tool designed for the purpose. This works best, of course, when you have full control over the video script; but it can also be adapted when it's necessary to produce descriptions after the fact, when you're "repairing" older video that lacks captions and descriptions.

The SMIL File

As with the ATSTAR video discussed earlier, the SMIL file handles the synchronization of the video, closed captions, and audio descriptions. The code below gives an example.

```
<smil>
<head>
<meta name="title" content="The Texas 2000 Living Museum"/>
   <layout system-captions="on">
<root-layout background-color="black" height="315"
   width="357"/>
<region id="videoregion" background-color="black" top="5"
   left="5" height="240" width="352"/>
<region id="textregion" background-color="#000000"
   top="255"
   left="5" height="60" width="352"/>
</layout>
</head>
<body>
<par>
<!-- VIDEO -->
<video src="open_mv.mpg" system-captions="off"/>
<video src="open_mv.mpg" region="videoregion"
   system-captions="on"/>
<!-- CAPTIONS -->
<switch>
   <textstream src="open_cc.avi" region="textregion"
      system-language="en" system-overdub-or-caption
         ="caption"
      system-captions="on" title="TX2K Museum Captions"
         alt="TX2K
      Museum Captions"/>
<!-- AUDIO DESCRIPTION -->
   <audio src="open_ad5.mpg" system-language="en"
      system-captions="on"/>
```

```
</switch>
</par>
</body></smil>
```

The SMIL file is organized very much like an HTML file (note, however, that since SMIL is actually an XML application, it follows XML conventions, which require both element and attribute names to be written in lowercase letters). The SMIL file begins by opening a `<smil>` element and ends by closing it (`</smil>`). The document includes `<head>` and `<body>` elements, just as HTML documents do. Like many HTML documents, the `<head>` element includes a `<meta>` element, which contains information about the document itself. The unfamiliar element is called `<layout>`. With this element, the code above defines two "regions," one for the video itself and one for the captions.

The `<body>` element includes a `<par>` element. Nested inside the `<par>` element are the elements to be played in parallel—that is, the video stream, the caption track, and the audio description track.

The first element is the video stream. This `<video>` element has two attributes: `src`, identifying the actual filename, and `system-captions`, telling the player whether to turn the closed captions on or off.

Following the `<video>` element is another element, `<switch>`; this element includes the `<textstream>` element that identifies the captions and the `<audio>` element for the audio description file. Each of these elements has `src` and `system-captions` attributes. The `<textstream>` element also has a `region` attribute, which tells the player to display the captions in the text region defined in the `<layout>` element. It also has a `title` attribute (this is optional, but can be helpful for search engines and other purposes) and the `alt` attribute required for nontext elements.

When to Use Audio Description

Some videos may not require audio description. For example, if you're in the fortunate position of creating or commissioning the video specifically for your current project, it may be possible to script it in such a way that it doesn't need to be described. The ATSTAR project includes a video enactment of the process of assessing the AT needs of a student who has been having trouble performing a specific classroom task. In the video, teachers and counselors meet to discuss the situation and try to find a solution.

Is an audio description necessary? Not in this case, because the "action" is almost entirely dialog-based. The video was purposely scripted so that the characters announce themselves and set the scene in their dialog. Audio descriptions would be redundant here because ATSTAR users who do not see the action will receive all the essential information from the soundtrack while closed captions deliver the content to users who do not hear the dialog. A transcript of the exchange provides text that can be accessed by people using Braille displays and others who don't have video players installed.

In most cases, though, you'll be working with existing video material, and you'll have to determine whether it requires description or not. The decision depends on the information being conveyed. For example, if the video content is more action-oriented, such as a car race or a sporting event, or if the meaning of the scene depends partly on the features of the setting where it takes place, then the soundtrack alone will not convey enough information to provide an equivalent alternative to what is shown on the screen. Or perhaps a dynamic graph is being generated while members of a group discuss employment trends. In this case, audio description is absolutely essential, and a complete text transcript would include both the captions *and* the audio description.

USING TRANSCRIPTS AS EQUIVALENT ALTERNATIVES

A caption is basically a transcript that has been synchronized to the video presentation. Transcripts provide a text version of the audio portion—the dialog and other sounds—of the video presentation. To provide the greatest user independence, transcripts of the audio track and any audio descriptions should be provided in addition to the captioned video files. A transcript is usually but not necessarily provided as a link to a separate page and will be accessed when audio and video are turned off or not supported. A transcript can be linked from the main page by means of a `longdesc` attribute or a text link. Remember that the text link has to be meaningful both in and out of context. For example, "Assistive technology team dialog" is meaningful in a list of links. "Transcript" is not.

It bears repeating that in order to be accessible—that is, to provide equivalent alternatives to audio content—audio files *must* have an associated text transcript. This holds for the audio track of a video, an audio description when present, or an audio file without video. An example shows why this is important.

We are deeply concerned with accessibility in online learning applications and recently surveyed online course offerings that purported to provide tools to create accessible e-learning platforms. This is a critically important field since transportation can be a major barrier to education access for people with disabilities. Course delivery to the student's home computer can tremendously increase options and opportunities. Imagine our surprise, then, when an audio file containing a very informative, lively lecture on accessible e-learning tools was delivered—but with no transcript! The disclaimer simply said, "We regret that no text transcript is available at this time." We can only suppose that the instructors expected us to do as they said, not as they did. We believe that the instructors had no business including the materials until they made them accessible to everyone. To do less not only sent the wrong message but also undermined their credibility as experts on the subject of accessible e-learning.

ALTERNATIVES FOR STAND-ALONE AND OTHER AUDIO

The WCAG 1.0 checkpoints and Section 508 federal mandates that require a text equivalent for every nontext element apply not just to graphic elements but also to audio material—including audio material that's not part of a video. We have already seen how the audio portion of a video display can be made accessible to users who will not hear the sounds. These may be users with hearing impairments but are just as likely to include those who are accessing the Web by means of a public computer station, such as those provided in libraries, schools, and many community recreation centers. Millions of people use public access technology; although some of these facilities may provide headphones for private listening, a developer who is aiming for maximum accessibility will not depend on sound alone to convey important information.

If information is provided as voice narration in a stand-alone audio file, then a text transcript is the most straightforward accessibility solution. Crafting alternatives for musical content requires a bit more thought, however. What is the purpose of the music? Is it simply decorative, akin to elevator music for the site? If so, a simple ALT text attached to the .wav file or other sound element (alt="background music", for example) should suffice, although you must also provide the means for users to choose to hear the music—or not, as we mentioned in our earlier discussion about giving users control over media playback.

Now, if the purpose is to set a tone or mood in which the rest of the content is placed, a longer description of the type of music, its speed, and its other qualities would be appropriate. Such a description will help nonlistening visitors to have an experience more equivalent to the one you intend. Similarly, in cases where sounds other than music contribute to the general experience, description is required.

But where music or other sound is truly integral to the presentation, it is worth giving careful thought to the notion of "equivalence." Author M. D. Coverley submitted a complex multimedia work for publication in the journal *Currents in Electronic Literacy.* The journal requires authors to follow WCAG. In the passage below, Coverley explains how she thought through the issue of music as she reworked her *Mirror of Annihilated Simple Souls,* originally done in Flash:

> . . . [T]he first job was to survey the image, motion, and sound elements and determine how to replace each of them with a representation in a different medium. The sound was the easiest, so I began with that. But here, immediately, . . . aesthetic considerations arose. The MIDI sequence . . . is a 16th century air from the Court of Henry the 8th. While it was a simple enough matter to provide an explanation of the

harpsichord-like sound and the articulated, antique notes, it was less clear that the "text" was in any way an "equivalent." Unless the reader could, in fact, imagine a dark-light melody from five hundred years ago, then the effect [of the combined sounds, images, and text] became much less resonant. I began to see, in a way that had not been evident to me previously, that multimedia writing depends on a carefully constructed oscillation between the visual, the aural, and the textual. . . . It wasn't so critical that a reader could actually hear the sound in and of itself, yet the sound acted in concert with other sensory signifiers. The problem I faced in making the sound accessible to the hearing impaired was that the images and text relied upon the sound for completion.

Technical problems arose, as well. Screen readers, for example, are aural devices, and the reader needs to be able to hear the text read aloud. The music, one media element that visually impaired readers could access and enjoy, interfered with the [screen] reader—so [visually impaired] readers benefit from an easy way to stop the sound. Currently, each of the browsers handles the loading of MIDI files differently, and the creation of a JavaScript that allows manipulation of the sound will not work cross-browser. The solution was to turn the sound down—and even that strategy tended to relegate the sound more to the background, muting the sense of oscillation between aural and visual. . . .[8]

---

8. From M. D. Coverley, "The White Wall: Reframing the Mirror," *Currents in Electronic Literacy* Fall 2001 (5). Accessed June 28, 2002. Current link is *http://currents.curl.utexas.edu/archives/fall01/fall01/coverley.html*.

Alternative Audio Examples

Let's try a couple of simpler examples. The first is a short and simple audio clip that demonstrates the song of the golden-cheeked warbler. Figure 13–7 shows the page. Here's the code below.

```
<html><head><title>warblerpage</title></head>
<body>
    <table border=0 width="85%">
    <tr><td>
    . . .
    <tr>
```

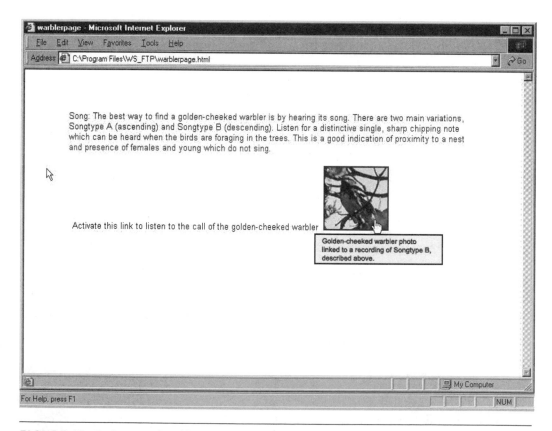

FIGURE 13–7   Screen shot illustrating how the code for the birdsong will render on the page.

```
<td>Activate this link to listen to the call of the
   golden-cheeked warbler. </font><a href="warbler.wav">
   <img SRC="warbler.jpg" ALT="Golden-cheeked warbler
   photo linked to a recording of Songtype B, described
   above"></a>
</tr>
</table>
</body>
</html>
```

The code creates a graphic link from the picture of the bird to a sound file of the bird's song. As the image for the sound file is accessed, the ALT message appears briefly on the screen and is made available to assistive devices. In this case, the ALT text describes the picture and suggests how the file sounds when it plays. All the information is easily delivered to those who are not seeing the page, as well as those who are not hearing it.

But suppose we want to include more information. In addition to a recording of the warbler's call, we want to include a longer voiceover describing the bird's habitat. In this case, we will also need a link to an HTML file that contains a complete text transcript of the habitat description. Theoretically, this can be done either through a direct link on the screen or by supplementing the ALT text for the warbler.jpg image with a longdesc attribute containing the name of the transcript file. Because the longdesc attribute has not been well supported until quite recently (as we noted in Chapter 9), we include both options in the next example.

```
<html><head><title>warblernarrativepage</title></head>
<body>
   <table border=0 width="85%">
   <tr><td>
   . . .
```

```
<tr>
<td>Activate this link to listen to the call of the
   golden-cheeked warbler and a description of its
   habitat.
   <a href="warblernarration.wav"><img src="warbler.jpg"
   alt="Warbler photo activates audio narration"
   longdesc="warblernarration.html"></a></td>
</tr>
<tr>
<td>Not using audio? Read the
   <a href="warblernarration.html">
   full text of the warbler narration</a></td>
</tr>
</table>
</body>
</html>
```

Figure 13–8 shows how the code above will render.

The alt tag describes the image and the fact that it links to an audio file. The longdesc attribute is also associated with the image, indicating the availability of a text transcript of the audio file. In addition, the alternative is explicitly offered by means of the sentence "Not using audio?" with a link to the text transcript. Note that this can be accomplished as well by associating a d-link with the longdesc attribute. This practice is not widely accepted, however. In part, the lack of acceptance may come from the fact that, as the longdesc attribute becomes fully supported by browsers and assistive devices, the d-link will no longer be necessary. Finally, the purpose is simply to use the best tools to ensure that important content is available to everyone. As your commitment to making accessible multimedia grows, we believe you will find a related growth in your creative thinking about the associated challenges. How, for example, can you

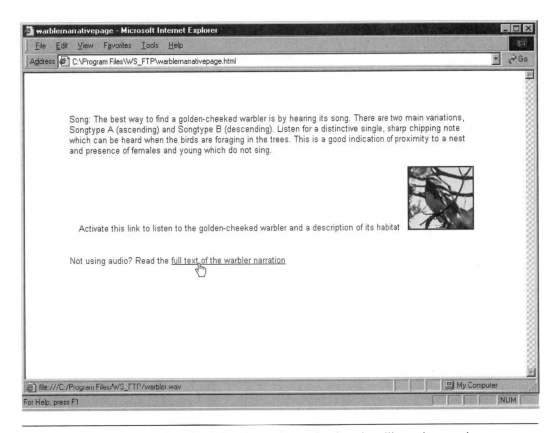

FIGURE 13–8 Screen shot depicting how the revised code will render on the page.

create an accessible experience for something as visual as animation? Let's find out.

MEETING THE ACCESSIBILITY CHALLENGES OF ANIMATION

Like audio and video, animation is an extremely powerful design resource. Well-conceived, well-executed animations can entertain and inform. They can bring abstract material to life (that's what the term *animation* means, actually!) and help us understand complex processes that are difficult for most of us to observe firsthand. They can help us understand how things change over time or under certain conditions, and so on.

But animations pose major accessibility challenges, too—not to mention the fact that they can create major headaches even for people who don't have disabilities. So, as you would with any other design element, think hard about what you're animating and why animation is the right thing to do. We've all seen too many animations that are more flash than substance (pun intended); make sure yours isn't one of them.

In the following sections, we offer some suggestions about how to anticipate and solve accessibility problems if you do decide to go with animation. We begin by considering the real health risks posed by some moving content and then examine the use of animated GIFs, Flash animation, and other issues.

Blinking, Flashing, and Seizures

As we examine the types of animated content you may wish to include in your Web sites, we can begin by visiting a site that permits free download of animated graphic images. The site shown in Figure 13–9 contains a dizzying array of flashing, moving animations, not one of which has ALT text of any sort. On this page, users can select from a series of horizontal bars that zip across the page. To make that choice, visitors use a mouse pointer that trails fairy dust behind it as it moves across the screen. Yikes! The first choice on the page is a series of multicolored circles that flash in different colors.

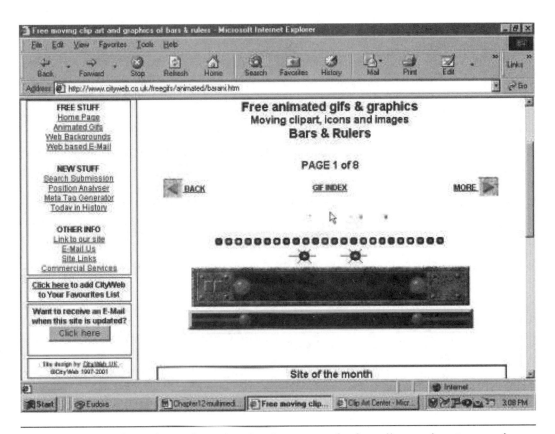

FIGURE 13–9   The Animated Bars and Rulers page of a free clip art site. Accessed January 9, 2002, at *http://www.cityweb.co.uk/freegifs/animated/barani.htm*. Used with permission.

Most Web users find this sort of blinking, flashing "stuff" annoying at best. But for some users it's much worse than that. You may recall hearing about a television animation in December 1997 that sent more than 700 Japanese children to the hospital with seizures. Without going into too much of the neurology, the fact is that images flickering at certain frequencies can trigger an epilepsy-like response. In the Japanese animation, the lead animated character's red eyes flashed rhythmically for 5 seconds.

Does this mean that animation should be excluded from your Web development tool kit? By no means. In fact, the National Epilepsy Awareness Web site has an animated GIF on every page. (We will look in more detail at animated GIFs in the next section.) Figure 13–10 shows a page that provides links to animations of brain activity during a seizure. The site displays an elegant profile of a grey-haired woman and a picture of a human brain on a swirled purple background. The screen was captured as the pointer highlights a dark

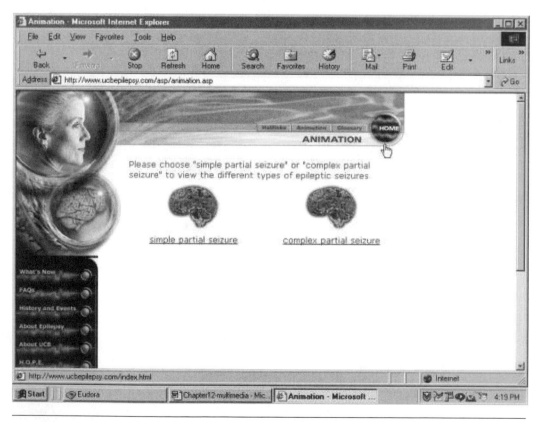

FIGURE 13–10 A page from the site of the National Epilepsy Awareness campaign. Accessed January 9, 2002, at *http://www.ucbepilepsy.com/asp/animation.asp*. Used with permission.

purple sphere with three waves, each being traversed by a moving point of light. ALT text tells us that this image is a link to the home page of the site.

Certain flicker rates have been specifically associated with inducing seizures. This is why Section 508 paragraph (j) is so specific: it forbids blinking and flickering between 2 and 55 Hz (or cycles per second), and WCAG 1.0 makes this a Priority 1 checkpoint (7.1). The United States uses NTSC video signals at 60 Hz. That's faster than Europe and Japan, which both use a 50 Hz cycle. A strobe light at 10–15 Hz can induce seizures in people with a certain genetic makeup. While this is not a common occurrence, it is essential to keep flicker rates in mind if you build animation into your multimedia materials. Give users the ability to pause, resume, and stop playback of your animations. This in turn means using plug-ins that allow users to access these controls. (See Chapter 14 for further discussion of accessible uses of scripts, applets, and plug-ins.) If possible, avoid creating strobe-like effects with rapid alternation between dark and light images. If you must use such effects, alert users that these effects are employed, and let the *user* control when—and whether—to view the animation.

Animated GIFs

As we saw on the National Epilepsy Awareness page, the GIF image format allows a single file to contain multiple images or frames. The file displays the frames one after another, as a loop, creating the effect of a short animation. Animated GIFs are popular on the Web since they are widely supported by most browsers and don't require special programming skills. We assume that you know how to create animated GIFs, so we focus instead on how to use them for maximum accessibility. But if you don't know how to create animated GIFs, many of them are available to download for free from sites such as the one shown in Figure 13–9.

Text Alternatives for Animated GIFs

Sites that provide free downloads of animated GIFs do not, however, customarily provide text alternatives to the animations. You must use the alt attribute to do so. Because images in GIF animations are dynamic, you need to provide a full description of what is occurring. The login page for ITAL's Texas 2000 Living Museum (TX2K), for example, includes an animated GIF, shown in a "suspended" view in Figure 13–11.

The ALT text for the TX2K animated GIF provides a simple description of what the animation does. It reads as follows: "Animated curtains unveiling the TX2K logo." Depending on the complexity of the animation, you may use simple ALT text, the longdesc attribute, a text link, or a combination of these to convey the meaning of the animated image.

Animation through JavaScript

Many developers create animation effects with scripts written in JavaScript. Because JavaScript is interpreted by the user's browser (as opposed to the Web server), JavaScripts are client-side scripts. We'll discuss JavaScript more fully in Chapter 14 when we explore how to create accessible content using scripts, applets, and plug-ins. For now, it is sufficient to remember that scripted animations also require

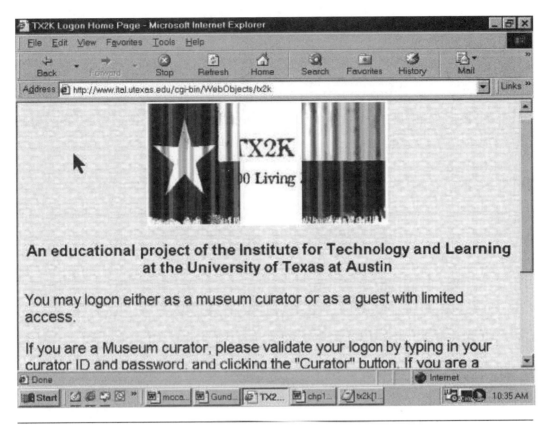

FIGURE 13–11 Screen shot of the TX2K login page. Accessed March 27, 2002, at *http:// www.ital.utexas.edu/cgi-bin/WebObjects/tx2k*. Used with permission.

equivalent content by means of the <noscript> element, whose content will be rendered if scripts are not supported.

Flash Animation

Macromedia's Flash is among the most popular tools in the Web developer's repertoire. Flash content requires a plug-in and works in any browser that supports Java. It is quite popular—and, until very recently, quite inaccessible to blind or visually impaired users. In Flash animations, the content is displayed as an `<object>` element; in versions up to and including 5.0, there is no built-in way to provide an equivalent alternative without extensive programming skills. (Flash plug-ins up to and including version 5.0 create their own accessibility challenges, which we'll discuss in Chapter 14; here we focus on authoring issues.) Macromedia is aware of the industry trend toward greater accessibility, and the company has entered into partnership with the National Center for Accessible Media. Flash MX, the new version of Flash released on March 15, 2002, includes a number of accessibility enhancements, as does the Flash 6.0 player released on the same date. Flash MX is written to conform with Microsoft's Active Accessibility (MSAA), the Application Programming Interface designed to help Windows applications interoperate with AT devices. As a result, versions 4.2 and higher of the Window-Eyes screen reader can report Flash content, including reading the text in Flash movies. (JAWS does not support MSAA in the same way, so there is as yet no JAWS support for Flash.)

Developers now have the opportunity to beta test a tool that employs MAGpie to further improve the accessibility of Flash 5 or MX when played on a Flash 6 player. Jason Smith from the American Academy for the Advancement of Science has created an extension for adding captions to Flash using MAGpie's XML data file. The tool is available for beta testing along with MAGpie and will soon be downloadable from the Macromedia Extension site.

Macromedia acknowledges that there is still considerable room for improvement. We had the good fortune to see the new Flash player and Window-Eyes in action at the 2002 South by Southwest Interactive festival in March 2002 in Austin, Texas, and we want to acknowledge here that Macromedia has made a significant move in the right direction. We look forward to continued improvements!

Many thousands of copies of the older, inaccessible versions of Flash are still in use as of this writing, however, and it's still too soon for all the strengths and limitations of the new version to reveal themselves. In the meantime, we have to look for useful workarounds that allow us to use Flash and at the same time make sure that no one is left out of the total experience of our sites.

One Solution to Flash Access Barriers

The ATSTAR project chose to use Flash animation. The designers knew that the teachers taking the course would be doing so between classes, in the middle of a workday, or in short breaks, with the possibility of distractions. The designers wanted to include stimulating visual and audio cues at the beginning of lessons and to emphasize certain points to help busy teachers stay alert to important messages. Figure 13–12 shows an example.

In Lesson 2 of the ATSTAR curriculum, learners are introduced to the first step of the ATSTAR process: Building the Student Team. The wheel spins, showing how the six parts of the process come together to create the whole. Then a particular puzzle piece, the one corresponding to the current lesson, flies out of the puzzle, and words about the learning goals are dynamically generated on the graphic element. Further down on the page is a text link that reads "Description of ATSTAR process animation." Activating that link takes us to the page shown in Figure 13–13.

This page describes the ATSTAR process chart. It consists of the static ATSTAR logo and a headline, "ATSTAR Assessment Process:

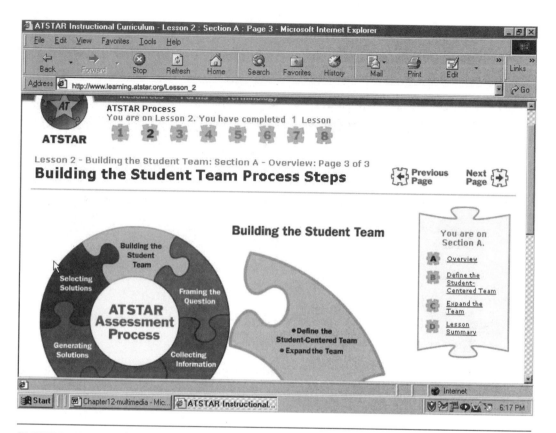

FIGURE 13–12 The introductory page to Lesson 2 of the ATSTAR curriculum. Accessed January 2, 2002, at *http://learning.atstar.org/Lesson_2*. Used with permission.

Step 1—Building the Student Team," which is similar to the one on the animated page. Users who have chosen to follow the description link can now read the explanation of what the Flash animation demonstrates:

> The ATSTAR Process graphic consists of a Flash (tm) animation that presents a wheel shaped chart consisting of six puzzle pieces. These interlocking puzzle pieces describe the six steps

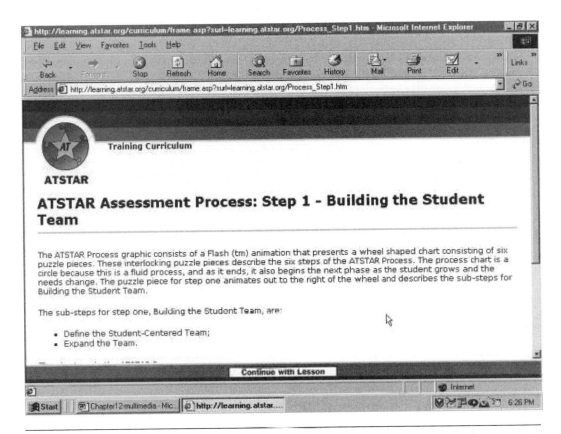

FIGURE 13–13 Description of a Flash graphic from ATSTAR Lesson 2. Accessed January 2, 2002, at *http://learning.atstar.org/curriculum/frame.asp?surl=learning.atstar.org/Process_Step1.htm*. Used with permission.

of the ATSTAR Process. The process chart is a circle because this is a fluid process, and as it ends, it also begins the next phase as the student grows and the needs change. The puzzle piece for step one animates out to the right of the wheel and describes the sub-steps for Building the Student Team.

The page goes on to describe the other graphic elements of the animated process chart, then provides a link to "Continue with Lesson."

Other Solutions

The strategy described above is only one way to work around the accessibility problems that Flash poses. There are other, more elegant solutions. It is quite possible, for example, to integrate the text description of the ATSTAR process wheel on the same page where the flowchart appears. In that way, the description would be immediately available to *all* users without requiring them to follow the link, and our experience suggests that this would help many people—not just people with disabilities—understand the animation more fully. Using that solution in this case, however, would have violated the ATSTAR goal of minimizing the need for scrolling, which serves a different accessibility purpose (scrolling can be confusing for people using screen magnification software and tiring for those with limited hand mobility).

A third solution would be to integrate a JPEG or GIF version of the ATSTAR process wheel into the <object> element itself, coupled with the text description. The static image would be visible only to users who don't have Flash installed. This would not require any additional programming by the developers—the <object> element is set up such that the browser renders whatever it's capable of rendering. The browser displays the Flash movie if Flash is installed but displays the alternative provided (text, GIF, JPEG, and so on) if Flash is not available on the user's machine. An animated GIF depicting a simplified version of the process wheel could then be provided as the alternative. The simplified GIF animation would therefore be displayed—with appropriate text from the alt and longdesc attributes—for users who don't have Flash. Unfortunately, this last approach won't help people using computers on which Flash 5 (or an earlier version) is installed—in school computer labs, for example, or public libraries. In such cases, the best approach is probably the one we described first: include an extended text description *in addition to* the Flash animation.

Adding ALT Text to Embedded Objects

Here's an illustration of what we mean. It is common for many sites to include a Flash movie that plays beneath the central image on the screen. The movie may consist of text, including links to other parts of a large site. The following code sample shows how to include alternative text within the `<object>` element. (Our thanks to Jim Allan for this solution.)

```
<object classid=clsid:D27CDB6E-AE6D-11cf-96B8-444553540000
    codeBase=http://active.macromedia.com/flash2/cabs/
    swflash.
    cab#version=4,0,0,0
    height=48 id=ma_scroller width=212><param name="movie"
    value="http://www.maxaccess.com/ma_scroller.swf">
<param name="menu" value="false"><param name="quality"
    value="autolow"><param name="salign" value="LT">
<param name="bgcolor" value="#445436">
    <p><ul><li>
<a href="http://www.maxaccess.com/accessibleFLASHdemo1/">
    About Us </a></li><li>
<a href="http://www.maxaccess.com/accessibleFLASHdemo2">
    News </a></li><li>
<a href="http://www.maxaccess.com/accessibleFLASHdemo3">
    Shop Online </a></li><li>
<a href="http://www.maxaccess.com/accessibleFLASHdemo4">
    Contact Us </a></li></ul></p>
<noembed><img SRC="http://www.maxaccess.com/media_images/
    ma_scroller.gif" width=212 height=47 order=0>
</noembed></object>
```

The code creates a list of links centered on the screen at the location where the Flash movie will play if Flash is installed. The links are displayed *only* if Flash is *not* installed on the user's computer. The same technique could also be used to display a static image, such as a GIF or JPEG, in place of a dynamic or static image done in Flash. This works because the browser "looks at" the content of the `<object>` element and renders the first thing it's capable of rendering; since it can't display Flash movies without Flash, the browser will keep looking until it finds the HTML text or some other element it knows how to render.

(The Macromedia Flash Accessibility site offers a downloadable extension, called the Accessibility HTML Publish Template, that is supposed to accomplish something very similar to what we've shown above.)

Adding Accessibility Features to Flash Movies

The techniques we've just shown you work only for users who don't have the Flash player installed on their computers. But it's also important to take steps to make Flash movies themselves more accessible to people who *do* have the Flash player. After all, where accessibility requirements are concerned, Flash movies are no different from any other kind of video or animation, and the same requirements apply. WCAG Checkpoint 1.4 puts it very clearly: "For *any* time-based multimedia presentation (e.g., a movie *or animation*), synchronize equivalent alternatives (e.g., captions or auditory descriptions of the visual track) with the presentation. [Priority 1]" (emphasis added).

You can do a number of things to fulfill these requirements. None of those options is fully satisfactory, perhaps, but they may be better than nothing. Let's start by talking about adding limited keyboard accessibility to pages that include Flash movies and then go on to discuss adding closed captions and audio descriptions.

ADDING LIMITED KEYBOARD ACCESSIBILITY. Flash presents some very real challenges to people who navigate the Web exclusively via the keyboard, including people who are blind and people who use a wide variety of alternative input devices that "map" onto the keyboard (that is, devices that translate user actions into keystrokes, so that the application behaves as if the user had pressed those keys). But within limits, there *are* things you can do to add some keyboard accessibility to Flash presentations. Basically, you have to follow two steps.

1. In HTML, add an `accesskey` attribute to the `<object>` element that contains the Flash movie. For example, if your source document includes the code `<object accesskey="z">`, then users can press Alt+z to jump directly to the Flash movie.
2. Add keyboard equivalents to the Flash movie itself, using the techniques described on Macromedia's Flash Accessibility site (*http://www.macromedia.com/macromedia/accessibility/*). At a minimum, you should include keyboard equivalents for starting, pausing, and stopping the movie. (For a demonstration of these techniques, visit the WebSavvy site at *http://www.Websavvy-access.org.*)

This approach has serious limitations, unfortunately, so adding these keyboard equivalents doesn't automatically solve all your accessibility problems. For one thing, the `accesskey` attribute works in Microsoft Internet Explorer 4.0 and higher, but for Netscape Navigator, it works only in version 6.2 or later. And in Internet Explorer, users who use the keyboard to get into the Flash movie and to start, pause, or stop it *can't* use the keyboard to get back out of the movie to the rest of the page!

(It appears, however, that the JAWS Links List is still available. Thus a JAWS user who found him- or herself seemingly stuck in a Flash movie *could* press Ins+F7 to bring up the Links List, then select the "Skip to main content" link to jump back up to the top of the page. Of course, the user would have to know that this technique was available—and there would have to *be* a "Skip to main content" link on the page. And, even supposing both of these conditions hold, the user would have to be willing to listen to the page again, from the top, in order to get to the material that follows the Flash movie. This user is unlikely to be a very happy camper. . . .)

ADDING CLOSED CAPTIONS FOR FLASH. Like the video presentations discussed earlier in this chapter, many Flash movies include high-quality audio as well as graphics and animations. You can use Flash's audio facilities to include audio descriptions of the objects and events taking place on the screen, as well as other audio material. If you prefer, you may add a second track for the audio description, using SMIL. You can also include closed captions for all audio material that is part of your Flash movie.

A group called WebSavvy—part of the Adaptive Technology Resource Center at the University of Toronto, a leading accessibility research group—has created an impressive demonstration of closed captions for the soundtrack of a Flash movie. Like the captions for the ATSTAR video we discussed earlier in this chapter, the captions are included in a RealText file. An SMIL file coordinates the Flash movie, the captions, and an audio track. The WebSavvy site provides instructions for viewing the SMIL source as well as a link to the RealText file that contains the captions. The end result is displayed in RealPlayer. (See *http://www.Websavvy-access.org/resources/real_demo.shtml.*)

ADDING AUDIO DESCRIPTIONS. Earlier in this chapter, we explained how we added an audio description track to a video presentation about ITAL's TX2K project. You can use those same techniques, with appropriate modifications for a different media type (*animation* instead of *video*), to synchronize an audio description with a Flash animation.

The RealPlayer G2 Production Guide provides detailed information about how to include Flash movies in an SMIL presentation that will be displayed using RealPlayer 7 or higher. (See *http://docs.real.com/ docs/smil/prodguideupdateg2_7.pdf.*)

GO FORTH AND MULTI!

The bottom line? Multimedia is a wonderful asset that can significantly enhance the accessibility of your site and create a richer experience for all your users. Use video. Use audio. You can even use Flash—it's an extraordinary tool—but be aware that in doing so you incur major challenges where accessibility is concerned. Think carefully about how to meet those challenges—and when you find a way to do it, share your discovery!

14

Accessible Use of Scripts, Applets, and Plug-ins

PLUG AND PLAY? NOT YET

In the previous chapter, we discovered ways in which multimedia *content* can be rendered most accessibly. This chapter explores in greater detail the tools that create and render that content. Scripts, applets, and plug-ins are some of the most powerful tools available to Web authors who wish to add a high level of interactivity and variety to the content they offer on their Web pages. Use of sophisticated interactive tools can greatly increase the functionality of Web pages but too often results in content that is inaccessible. It need not be so. As the need for universal access has become more widely understood and accepted, cooperative efforts have emerged for the purpose of creating cross-browser accessibility solutions and alternatives for the use of plug-ins, applets, and scripts. IBM, Sun Microsystems, and the National Center for Accessible Media are among the leaders whose work in publicizing and implementing W3C recommendations and

Section 508 federal standards for accessible emerging technologies we explore in this chapter.

To ensure that Web pages that employ scripts, applets, and plug-ins can deliver content that is accessible to everyone, Web authors must be aware of accessibility principles and fully integrate those principles into programming and development. This chapter applies general accessibility principles to the process of interactive Web page development, regardless of the script, applet, or plug-in chosen for the task. We ask you once again to think always in terms of delivering content that is separate from presentation (see Chapter 15 for further discussion of this point). Important information exchange can thus be made accessible for all users, not just those with graphical browsers attached to fast networks.

HTML Elements and Attributes Addressed in This Chapter

Elements

`<script>`, `<object>`, `<noscript>`, `<noframes>`, `<applet>`

Attributes

`type`, `src`, `language`, `defer`

Accessibility Checkpoints and Standards Addressed in This Chapter

Web Content Accessibility Guidelines 1.0 Checkpoints

6. Ensure that pages featuring new technologies transform gracefully.

6.3. Ensure that pages are usable when scripts, applets, or other programmatic objects are turned off or not supported. If this is not possible, provide equivalent information on an alternative accessible page. [Priority 1]

6.4. For scripts and applets, ensure that event handlers are input device-independent. [Priority 2]

8.1. Make programmatic elements such as scripts and applets directly accessible or compatible with assistive technologies. [Priority 1 if functionality is important and not presented elsewhere, otherwise Priority 2]

9.3. For scripts, specify logical event handlers rather than device-dependent event handlers. [Priority 2]

12.1. Title each frame to facilitate frame identification and navigation. [Priority 1]

Section 508 Standards, §1194.22

(**i**) Frames shall be titled with text that facilitates frame identification and navigation.

(**l**) When pages utilize scripting languages to display content, or to create interface elements, the information provided by the script shall be identified with functional text that can be read by assistive technology.

(**m**) When a Web page requires that an applet, plug-in or other application be present on the client system to interpret page content, the page must provide a link to a plug-in or applet that complies with §1194.21 (a) through (l).

SCRIPTS

Server-side scripts, such as Common Gateway Interface (CGI), are run on the Web server and triggered by a request from the browser. Client-side scripts, such as JavaScript, create programs that may accompany an HTML document or be embedded directly in it. Client-side scripts often run on the user machine when the document loads. A script may also run at other times, such as when a user selects a link. HTML support for scripts is independent of the scripting language, which allows Web authors to extend HTML documents in highly active and interactive ways.

For example, scripts may be evaluated as a document loads to dynamically modify the contents of a document. Scripts may accompany a form to process input as it is entered. A scripted program may dynamically fill out parts of a form based on the values of other fields and ensure that fields are mutually consistent. Scripts may be triggered by events that affect the document, such as loading, unloading, element focus, or mouse movement. Scripts may be linked to form controls to produce graphical user interface elements. All of these can create accessibility barriers—but it doesn't *have* to be that way!

Let's begin by considering the `<script>` element and some of the common attributes you might find in the code samples included in this chapter. The `type` attribute specifies the scripting language of the element's contents as a content type (for example, `"text/javascript"`). You should specify the `type` attribute for each instance of a `<script>` element within a document. Using the attribute overrides the default scripting language. Authors must supply a value for this attribute since there is no default value. Note that while it is still common to find the language attribute used, it has been deprecated. The language attribute specifies the scripting language for the <script> element. Its value is an identifier for the language, but because the identifiers are not standard, this attribute has been deprecated in favor of type. The defer attribute can be set as a Boolean indicator that the script is not going to generate any document content. For example, if it is set, the defer attribute will defer the document.write command in JavaScript, allowing the user agent to continue parsing and rendering.

Now let's look at some of the common uses for scripts and how to make them most accessible.

Scripting Rollovers for Accessibility

One of the most popular JavaScript functions is to animate a graphic link when the mouse rolls over that area of the screen—a mouseover event. This mouseover technique is often used to provide feedback about user actions, for example, by changing the color of a link when the mouse moves across it. It's also used to provide additional information: when the mouse pointer moves across the image, the image seems to be replaced by text, which disappears when the user moves the mouse again. (This text isn't really text, however—it's actually an *image* of text, which means that many people can read it but screen readers can't, and it may be difficult for some people to read, too, since the text is often displayed in a very small font.)

Rollovers provide feedback about user actions on the Knowbility Web site shown in Figure 14–1. The Knowbility site uses a vertical navigation scheme with an orange background and graphic tags indicating the interest areas to which the user may link. As the mouse

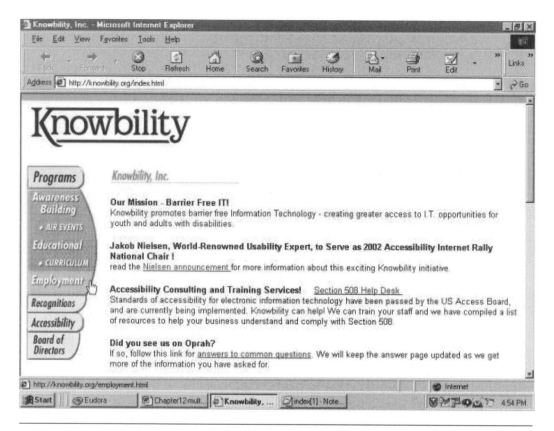

FIGURE 14–1 Screen shot of the Knowbility home page, which demonstrates the use of mouseovers coded in JavaScript to create animated color changes that aid users when navigating the site. Accessed January 10, 2002, at *http://www.knowbility.org*. Used with permission.

travels across the navigation bar, the background of the potentially activated link changes from orange to yellow.

To ensure maximum accessibility for an event of this type, you must provide two things: keyboard navigation and a text alternative. First, the link itself must be accessible by means other than the mouse—in other words, through keyboard navigation. As we've seen throughout this book, a button or any other part of the interface that can be reached only by clicking or dragging the mouse is inaccessible for users of screen readers or those with motor impairments who use the keyboard to navigate the screen. (Many other alternative input devices convert their signals to keystrokes, so making an application keyboard accessible is a good way to make it accessible to people using other input devices as well.)

In technical terms, the scripts triggered by a user event such as a mouse click or keystroke are known as *event handlers*. Some event handlers work by clicking or moving the mouse; examples are the mouseover and mouseout events commonly used in scripting rollover buttons. These are known as *device-dependent* event handlers because they require a specific device in order to work. Since people with disabilities use such a wide variety of devices, these device-dependent event handlers can cause many accessibility problems. Fortunately, substitutes can often accomplish the same thing in a device-*independent* way—that is, they make no assumptions about the kind of device used. Using device-independent event handlers is a Priority 2 item in WCAG 1.0. (Checkpoint 9.3 reads, "For scripts, specify logical event handlers rather than device-dependent event handlers. [Priority 2]")

Here is the source code for a rollover event on the Knowbility site.

```
<script language="JavaScript">
<!--function MM_swapImgRestore() { //v3.0
var i,x,a=document.MM_sr; for(i=0;a&&i<a.length&&(x=a[i])
   &&x.oSrc;i++) x.src=x.oSrc;}
function MM_swapImage() { //v3.0
   var i,j=0,x,a=MM_swapImage.arguments;
      document.MM_sr=new Array;
   for(i=0;i<(a.length-2);i+=3)}
</script>
```

```
<a href="employment.html"
onMouseOut="MM_swapImgRestore()"
onBlur="MM_swapImgRestore()
    " onMouseOver="MM_swapImage
    ('employment_bt','',
    'images/employment_bt_f2.gif',1)"
  onFocus="MM_swapImage('employment_bt
    ','','images/employment_bt_f2.gif',1)">
    <img name="employment_bt" src="images/
        employment_bt.gif"
    width="109" height="34" border="0"
        alt="Employment"></a>
```

The script above includes both device-dependent event handlers (onMouseOver, onMouseOut and logical ones (onBlur, onFocus). The redundancy is necessary because onFocus and onBlur are not truly device-independent. As a result, navigating the page with either the mouse or the tab key will move us consecutively from one graphical link to the next. Landing on the link triggers the event handler, which replaces the orange image with an otherwise identical yellow one; the ALT text announces the link destination. In this case, the change in background color is achieved through swapping images. As we'll explain below, this effect could be achieved just as effectively by using Cascading Style Sheets (CSS).

This brings us to the second aspect of making rollover buttons accessible: ALT text. We do not know of any way to associate ALT text with the "swap image," that is, with the image that replaces the image that "receives" the user event. It's crucial, therefore, that the ALT text for that initial image be both meaningful and self-sufficient, since people using screen readers, talking browsers, refreshable Braille displays, or text-only displays will not hear the images of text so frequently associated with rollovers. This is why Kara Pernice Coyne and Jakob Nielsen recommend against using rollovers to convey "any information" in their 2001 report, *Beyond ALT Text*. Note that the ALT text in the code above corresponds exactly to the named link.

JavaScript is great stuff, and Web authors have shown great imagination in using these capabilities to create highly functional and useful Web-based information. But some user agents cannot handle scripts: the text-only browser, Lynx, is one example, and screen readers such as JAWS and Window-Eyes often have difficulty with scripted pages. Support for scripts is sometimes disabled in public-access computer facilities and school computer labs—and in some households. This is why WCAG 1.0 Checkpoint 6.3 requires that pages work when scripting is turned off—or, when that isn't possible, that developers provide an equivalent alternative.

Alternatives to Scripts

The <noscript> element was developed as a way to provide content in an alternative manner. If the user agent supports scripts, then the scripted events that accompany the HTML document will run (assuming that the scripting is correct, of course!). If scripts are turned off or not supported by the browser, however, then the <noscript> element (if present) determines how content should be presented. In the absence of the <noscript> element, results may be unpredictable: the browser will search for the next valid HTML element or other statement it is capable of processing. On the Knowbility page shown in Figure 14–1, if scripts are turned off or not supported, the functions are delivered through HTML elements that do not require scripts (Figure 14–2).

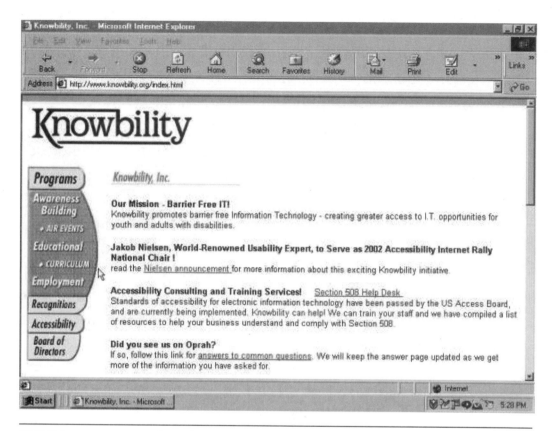

FIGURE 14–2 Screen shot of the Knowbility home page with scripts turned off. Accessed January 11, 2002, at *http://www.knowbility.org*. Used with permission.

When scripts are turned off, navigating the Knowbility home page with the mouse or the tab key no longer results in the same color change behind activated links that occurred when scripts were enabled. However, the links still work: we get meaningful ALT text, and all functions are delivered via HTML. Since the browser ignores the JavaScript instructions it cannot recognize when scripts are turned off, it simply continues until it finds HTML code it can render. In this case, the browser starts with the anchor tag, skips the now useless JavaScript statements, then locates the image element and its alt attribute. In other words, the browser behaves as if the source code actually contained only the following code. In fact, this is the actual source code from the page, and we have simply removed the Java-Script statements.

```
<a href="employment.html">
<img name="employment_bt"
   src="images/employment_bt.gif"
   width="109" height="34" border="0"
   alt="Employment"></a>
```

Look, Ma, No Scripts! (And No Images, Either)

There's a way to produce an identical visual effect without using either graphics or scripting. This method involves creating text links, then using the CSS background-color property to set the background color for the link and to change it with a CSS "pseudoselector" called :hover when the mouse moves across the link text. The style sheet might look something like the following one, which uses the :hover pseudoselector instead of JavaScript to change the background color and size of a link when the mouse passes over it.

```
a{background-color:orange;
color:black;
font-family:arial,helvetica,sans-serif;
font-size:100%}
:hover{
background-color:yellow;
color:black;
border:thin,ridge,outset;
font-family:arial,helvetica,sans-serif;
font-size:125%}
```

This simple style sheet does two things. First, it "styles" the `<anchor>` element (`<a>`), the essential element for hyperlinks. As a result, link text will be displayed in Arial or another available sans serif font, using the browser's default font size; the text will be black against an orange background. The effect of the `:hover` pseudoselector will be (1) to change the background color to yellow and (2) to enlarge the font by 25 percent whenever the mouse "hovers" over the link. Like the JavaScript rollover, these stylistic changes make it easier for users to tell when the mouse has entered a clickable area. Because there are no images to load, there is no need to write ALT text (and no possibility of forgetting to do it!), and the page will load faster as well. (For more information about using CSS to support maximum accessibility, please see Chapter 15.)

Using the `<noscript>` Element

A user's ability to identify and use links on the Knowbility site is not affected by the presence or absence of JavaScript support. But where JavaScript is essential for functionality, it's necessary to provide access to equivalent functionality or to the information generated by that functionality, as WCAG 1.0 and Section 508 require. In that case, you should follow the JavaScript with an opening `<noscript>` tag and then enter the alternative content. You must close the `<noscript>` element with an end tag (`</noscript>`) when you have delivered the alternative content. It is important to note that the alternative content may include graphics files and links; in fact, it is this capability that gives the `<noscript>` element its power.

Imagine that we have a Web page that enables a user to get information about what garden plants to grow at what time of the year, depending on geographical location. Various functions are enabled as the user enters and evaluates information, creating a dynamic experience. For maximum accessibility, the <noscript> alternative would include a description of these functions and perhaps a graphic image for browsers that do not support JavaScript. Here's an example of code that uses the <noscript> element to provide equivalent alternative content on our gardening site.

```
<noscript> <IMG src="garden.gif" alt="garden of blooming
    flowers and shrubs">
  You are visiting the Interactive Gardener, a dynamic
    instruction site that provides information for
    planting various garden plants. Visitors using
    JavaScript-enabled browsers can answer questions about
    their location, soil type, and plant preferences for
    customized information about garden plants best suited
    to their interests. For our other visitors, we provide
    more general information about planting seasons in
    various parts of the US on our <a href="http://
    www.usgardenersalternative.com">
    alternative gardening information </a> site.
</noscript>
```

This is an acceptable alternative, but the alternative information provided is not *strictly* "equivalent," since it does not have the same dynamic nature as the site that uses JavaScript. An even more useful alternative would be to have a server-side script collect the same information by means of a form and return the results to the user. The time lag would be greater, but the full function could be delivered by alternative means.

The Olympics Committee Leaves Out Millions—Again!

One thing that is *not* acceptable is simply to tell visitors they are out of luck if they don't use JavaScript, as was recently done, to much notoriety, on the Web site of the 2002 Salt Lake Olympic Winter Games, found at *http://www.saltlake 2002.com*. We need to make a side observation here about our use of screen shots of the actual Web sites of real organizations. Throughout this book, we used many real-world examples to illustrate the barriers encountered by millions of users with disabilities every day. As we contacted businesses, agencies, and institutions to seek permission to reprint illustrations of their sites, we were generally met with cooperation and interest. Several of them, including Austin's Capital Metro, actually changed their sites to be more accessible. The folks in charge of the Olympics seem to feel that if they simply ignore the problem of accessibility, it will go away. After several exchanges and our inclusion of edits requested by them, the people in charge of granting permission to reprint images of the 2002 Olympic Winter Games site simply stopped responding to us. As a result, we will describe what we found on the site without the benefit of illustrations.

In February 2002, the home page of the 2002 Olympic Winter Games contained a horizontal purple header with the Winter Olympics logo and the words "Salt Lake 2002—Official Site of the 2002 Olympic Winter Games." The ALT text, however, simply said "Salt Lake 2002." An ad promoting a contest appeared at the top of the page. The only ALT text provided said, "Click here." This was worse than useless—it was actually misleading since it created the impression that the user had to follow the link in order to "enter" the Olympics site.

Navigation links were presented by means of a segmented gold bar that ran horizontally beneath the logo space. The link categories were the following:

- Sports.
- Schedules.
- Athletes.
- Spectator Info.
- Shopping.
- Games Programs.
- Tickets.

Each segment opened into a cascading menu of nested links activated through JavaScript. For example, the Spectator Info category pulled down a menu with links to FAQs, specific information about accommodations, tickets, weather, and other useful facts for visitors. Within each pull-down menu, nested subcategories provided greater detail about each item. Such cascading menus are problematic for people using screen readers; Coyne and Nielsen [2001b] have reported that cascading menus also posed problems for test participants who used screen magnifiers and may cause problems for others with low vision who use high-contrast settings in their browsers or operating systems (for example, in the Windows Accessibility Options control panel).

You might have assumed that the Salt Lake Olympic Committee would have learned from the outcry over the inaccessibility of the site for the 2000 Olympics in Sydney, Australia. As we mentioned in Chapter 3, a complaint to the Australian Human Rights and Equal Opportunity Commission by Bruce Maguire in 1999, 15 months before the games began, resulted in a damage award of $20,000 (Australian) to

Maguire. The judgment also forced the Sydney Organizing Committee for the Olympic Games (SOCOG) to hire IBM, which had built the site in the first place, to retrofit it for accessibility at a cost SOCOG estimated at $2.2 million (Australian). The Equal Opportunity Commission rejected SOCOG's outlandish cost estimates and ordered that the changes be implemented. Clearly, though, the torch of accessibility awareness was not passed along to the 2002 Salt Lake committee. The problem this time was not a complete absence of ALT text (although the ALT text on the 2002 Olympic Winter Games site was often a meaningless "Click Here"). The most astounding aspect of the 2002 Winter Olympics site was that a user with JavaScript turned off or not supported was redirected to a page that was completely blank except for the message "This site requires javascript [sic] enabled on your browser."

To make matters worse, the JAWS screen reader was unable to report this message—users who couldn't see the message were simply left hanging, with no idea why their screens had gone suddenly silent.

When we explored the 2002 Olympic Winter Games site to discover reasons for such heavy reliance on JavaScript, we found frames throughout that were written by means of the JavaScript `document.write` command. This gives developers the flexibility to generate a different number of frames on different pages. JAWS reported that there were four frames on the home page, for example, six on the Sports page, two on the page about the Olympic Torch Relay (which opened without warning in a new browser window titled, interestingly enough, "2002 Chevrolet.com"), and seven frames on the page for the Paralympics (formerly the Special Olympics). But there were no `<noscript>` element alternatives for users whose browsers don't support JavaScript—and there weren't any `<noframes>` element options, either, for people whose browsers don't support frames. Nor did the existing frames have names that would be meaningful to users, as WCAG 1.0 Checkpoint 12.1 and Section 508 paragraph (i) require. The main page for the Paralympics site, for example, had three frames, called "Top," "Middle," and "Bottom." We found no reason why the developers couldn't have written their scripts to generate meaningful names for these frames.

Of course, that wouldn't remove the barriers for people whose browsers don't support JavaScript. Activating the Sports link (one of the top-level links on the home page menu bar) took us to a new page that listed the submenu items as graphic links. These were not highly interactive pages. There was no increase in functionality offered by the reliance on scripting, no whiz-bang application that could have been offered in only this way. We must infer that simple thoughtlessness about the accessibility of their pages led the developers of the 2002 Olympic Winter Games site to create the unnecessary barriers we encountered there. The `<noscript>` element could have easily been used to include a link to HTML pages that delivered the same content to nonscript-enabled browsers. The JavaScripted pull-down menus provided link choices on that one page that were also available as graphic links on subsequent pages. The additional functionality offered was merely the ability to skip a link step—hardly worth locking significant numbers of people out of the ability to navigate the site at all. Simple HTML links within a `<noscript>` element could have made all this information available to users who cannot or do not use JavaScript.

Perhaps the developers of the 2002 Olympic Winter Games site were operating on the assumption that current versions of the most popular screen-reading software do support JavaScript. This is a correct assumption. It by no means follows, however, that because the software is available everyone owns it. Many individuals, schools, and organizations that provide services to people with disabilities are still using older software. There are also many others who deliberately choose to work with scripting disabled, for a variety of reasons. While there are those among our colleagues who insist that not supporting JavaScript is equivalent to hanging on to your rotary phone—too outdated to justify—we do not agree. We believe that technology is not yet sufficiently disseminated throughout society to allow us to deny access to information to those who are lagging behind current technology applications. The bottom line is that, with or without ALT text, users of screen readers or other assistive technologies that do not support JavaScript were denied access to any information whatsoever about the 2002 Olympic Winter Games on the "Official Site." Even information about the Paralympics schedule, the competition for athletes with disabilities, was completely inaccessible to anyone whose browser was not JavaScript-enabled!

We can only conclude that the Olympics site was designed without input, testing, or feedback from users with disabilities. Indeed, the designers must not have even tested the site on a Mac. WebReference.com's Andy King [2002] described the numerous JavaScript errors that interrupted his visit to the Olympics site from his Mac. Thinking to avoid the pesky, repetitive error messages, he turned off the scripting—and was locked out of the site entirely! This is an extreme example but not an uncommon one. The lesson to take away from Salt Lake City is that, in designing for maximum accessibility, the developer must ensure that the functionality and, most important, the content of the page does not depend solely on scripts.

APPLETS

Applets are small programs, generally written in the Java programming language, delivered as Web content and carried out by the user agent. Applets depend on other programs to convert the Java program code into usable instructions for the user device. Originally developed by Sun Microsystems as a multiplatform, platform-independent, object-oriented programming language, Java allows versatility limited only by the imagination of the programmer. Many Java applets are freely available for download from the Web to perform a variety of functions, from simple tasks such as special visual effects to more complex functions such as weather simulations, site search engines, online games, and mathematical and financial calculations. As applets were introduced to the Web via Sun's HotJava browser, they excited the industry but posed serious accessibility barriers.

Most assistive technologies are not written to support the Java platform, so Java environments, including applets for the Web, were completely inaccessible to most assistive technologies for several years after Java was launched publicly in 1996. The Trace Research and Development Center, in Madison, Wisconsin, fostered cooperative, industry-wide research to address the accessibility problems created by Java applets. In 1998, Sun introduced the Java Access Bridge, a technology targeted at developers of assistive technologies, to enable designers to create products that can work with Windows and Java applications. The Java2 platform introduced the Java Accessibility API, which has the goal of creating the appropriate hooks to allow assistive technology devices to interact with Java applications.

Welcome progress, indeed, but the actual application of the technology is still in its infancy and requires very specific conditions in order for assistive technologies to accurately render the dynamic information usually contained within Java applets. Sun and IBM are to be commended for their excellent work on the Java Accessibility API. In March 2001, the American Foundation of the Blind cited the achievements of Sun's Accessibility Team and presented Sun with the 2001 Access Award for building accessibility into the Java platform.

As with many new technologies, however, while the promise is great, the reality is that we must still incorporate inclusive design strategies to ensure that our use of applets delivers important information and functionality to all users. Version compatibility between the Java Access Bridge and the Java RunTime Environment has been an issue. Browser considerations, installers, and keyboard control continue to affect the ultimate accessibility of Java applets for users with disabilities. Alternatives are therefore still needed; in many cases, fortunately, those alternatives are not difficult to provide.

ALT Text for Java Applets

The first accessibility goal is to ensure that the user of a text-based browser or assistive technology device is made aware that the applet exists on the page. In addition, the purpose of the applet must be communicated. These two goals may be accomplished simply by following the "prime directive" of accessibility—to provide equivalent alternatives for all nontext elements on the page. The `<applet>` tag should include an explanatory `alt` attribute (and may even contain a graphic image) to give all users more information about the missing content.

Suppose we have a Java applet that creates a scrolling ticker tape on a Web site. Its code might look something like this.

```
<applet code="TickerTape.class" width=460 height=160
    param name=appletParameter1 value=value alt="An applet
    of a scrolling ticker tape with information about cur-
    rent stock prices. A static listing is updated daily at
    http://staticpage.com."> </applet>
```

A browser that doesn't render the `<applet>` tag will ignore the `<applet>` and `<param>` tags, instead interpreting any HTML code between the `<applet>` and `</applet>` tags. (The alternative HTML code should appear after the last `<param>` element and before the tag that closes the `<applet>` element.) This is one method for providing equivalent alternatives to content that might be generated by an applet. For example, if the applet demonstrates the steps involved in a process, the alternative HTML code might provide a sequence of static images representing those steps, along with appropriate ALT text and extended descriptions. This technique is similar to the one we recommended in Chapter 13 for using the `<object>` element to display alternative content when Flash or other necessary plug-ins are not available on the client computer.

Note that the `<applet>` element is "deprecated" in HTML 4.0, and the W3C encourages developers to use the `<object>` element as the way to embed Java applets on their pages. However, browser support for the `<object>` element is still inconsistent, so you'll need to make sure that your target browsers support what you're trying to do. When using the `<object>` element for applets, you must of course still provide equivalent alternatives as described.

Providing truly equivalent alternatives for applets that perform more complex tasks such as simulations or dynamic visualizations of large data sets is a nontrivial challenge for which there are no ready-made solutions. The best advice we can offer at this time is to consider other alternatives from the outset. Consult the Section 508 accessibility standards for software as well as those for Web accessibility; refer, also, to documentation for Microsoft's Active Accessibility API and to materials about Java accessibility produced by IBM and Sun Microsystems. The National Center for Accessible Media provides excellent references to these and other materials about accessible software design in its guide, "Making Educational Software Accessible," available at *http://ncam.wgbh.org/cdrom/guideline/*. (This guide is well worth reading even if you are not producing educational applications.) The U.S. Access Board has also provided a detailed guide to the Section 508 software standards; the guide is available at *http://www.access-board.gov/sec508/guide/1194.21.htm*.

Finally, allow yourself to consider the possibility that Java may not be the right language at this time. As the Access Board's guide cited above puts it, "In some cases it is possible that a particular programming language may not possess the features necessary to fulfill these requirements. In those instances, another language for creating the program would most likely have to be considered for the product to meet the standards" [U.S. Access Board 2001]. As we saw in the example from the 2002 Winter Olympic Games, full functionality can often be delivered in a more accessible fashion.

PLUG-INS

Plug-ins resemble applets in the sense that both are software applications that run within the browser. But applets remain separate from the browser; they can be run only from within the page where the `<applet>` or `<object>` element invokes them because they require the browser to run the code. Plug-ins can render material such as video clips, 3D animations, and audio files within the browser. In some cases, though, the plug-in acts as a stand-alone application, spawning a new window on the screen and displaying the content in that window. Web authors may have a choice between these two methods; the choice should always be made in favor of greater accessibility, and with sufficient planning, this need not mean sacrificing visual elegance. It is important as well to remember to inform the user that a new window will open to play the media content, just as you would inform him or her of new windows opened for any other reason.

Plug-ins also resemble applets in that they need to be understood from at least two different perspectives.

1. As Web content, plug-ins are governed by WCAG 1.0, to which we've referred so often throughout this book, and by Section 508's Web accessibility standards (§1194, Chapter 22). Relevant portions of these documents are listed at the beginning of this chapter.
2. Plug-ins also *render* Web content. That is, they are user agents, and as such they fall within the purview of the WAI's User Agent Accessibility Guidelines 1.0 (UAAG) and the U.S. Access Board's Software Applications and Operating Systems (§1194, Chapter 21).

Although we will not examine it in great detail, a brief look at UAAG 1.0 will help you understand industry trends in support of accessible plug-ins.

The User Agent Accessibility Guidelines

WCAG 1.0 is just one part of the WAI's comprehensive strategy for achieving Web accessibility. The first step was to integrate better support for accessibility into HTML itself; this effort resulted in the transition from HTML 3.2 to HTML 4.0 (published in December 1997). Next came WCAG 1.0, published as a formal W3C recommendation in May 1999. As we've seen, WCAG provides advice about how to take advantage of the accessibility features in HTML to create more accessible Web content. WCAG 1.0 was followed in February 2000 by the Authoring Tool Accessibility Guidelines 1.0 (ATAG), which explain how authoring tools such as Macromedia Dreamweaver, Microsoft Frontpage, IBM Home Page Builder, and similar tools should make it easier for Web authors—including Web authors with disabilities—to *produce* content that conforms to WCAG. Finally, UAAG 1.0 offers recommendations for *rendering* accessible content in an accessible manner via Web browsers, media players, and other user agents.

The 12 guidelines listed below are taken from the most recent draft of the UAAG, which was published as a W3C Candidate Recommendation on September 12, 2001. Publication of a Candidate Recommendation launches the period in the W3C process during which interested parties can exchange implementation experiences of the specification requirements; at least two implementations of each requirement must be found (or created) before the recommendation can move on to final approval by the W3C membership. A Candidate Recommendation for UAAG is close to final form as of this writing, in June 2002, so we offer the following list of guidelines as the best currently available information.

1. Support input and output device-independence.
2. Ensure user access to all content.

3. Allow configuration not to render some content that may reduce accessibility.

4. Ensure user control of rendering.

5. Ensure user control of user interface behavior.

6. Implement interoperable application programming interfaces.

7. Observe operating environment conventions.

8. Implement specifications that benefit accessibility.

9. Provide navigation mechanisms.

10. Orient the user.

11. Allow configuration and customization.

12. Provide accessible user agent documentation and help.[1]

Detailed examination of the UAAG—and especially of the individual checkpoints that bring each of the guidelines to life—is beyond the scope of this book, and indeed it will likely be some time until user agents that implement these recommendations become widely available. Interested readers may wish to see the W3C's "User Agent Implementation Report" at *http://www.w3.org/WAI/UA/implementation/report-cr2.html* to learn more.

The Section 508 Software Applications and Operating Systems Standards

Until now, we have been referring to Chapter 22 of the Section 508 accessibility standards. When discussing the accessibility of plug-ins, however, it is more relevant to refer to Chapter 21. We list these

---

1. From the Candidate Recommendation of the UAAG published September 12, 2001, at *http://www.w3.org/TR/UAAG10/*.

provisions below for your information and note that we expect it to be some time before we see a generation of plug-ins that fully meet the standard defined in Section 508, §1194.21.

(**a**) When software is designed to run on a system that has a keyboard, product functions shall be executable from a keyboard where the function itself or the result of performing a function can be discerned textually.

(**b**) Applications shall not disrupt or disable activated features of other products that are identified as accessibility features, where those features are developed and documented according to industry standards. Applications also shall not disrupt or disable activated features of any operating system that are identified as accessibility features where the application programming interface for those accessibility features has been documented by the manufacturer of the operating system and is available to the product developer.

(**c**) A well-defined on-screen indication of the current focus shall be provided that moves among interactive interface elements as the input focus changes. The focus shall be programmatically exposed so that assistive technology can track focus and focus changes.

(**d**) Sufficient information about a user interface element including the identity, operation, and state of the element shall be available to assistive technology. When an image represents a program element, the information conveyed by the image must also be available in text.

(**e**) When bitmap images are used to identify controls, status indicators, or other programmatic elements, the meaning assigned to those images shall be consistent throughout an application's performance.

(**f**) Textual information shall be provided through operating system functions for displaying text. The minimum information that shall be made available is text content, text input caret location, and text attributes.

(**g**) Applications shall not override user-selected contrast and color selections and other individual display attributes.

(**h**) When animation is displayed, the information shall be displayable in at least one non-animated presentation mode at the option of the user.

(**i**) Color coding shall not be used as the only means of conveying information, indicating an action, prompting a response, or distinguishing a visual element.

(**j**) When a product permits a user to adjust color and contrast settings, a variety of color selections capable of producing a range of contrast levels shall be provided.

(**k**) Software shall not use flashing or blinking text, objects, or other elements having a flash or blink frequency greater than 2 Hz and lower than 55 Hz.

(**l**) When electronic forms are used, the form shall allow people using assistive technology to access the information, field elements, and functionality required for completion and submission of the form, including all directions and cues.[2]

---

2. From the Section 508 standard published December 2000 at *http://www.section508.gov/index.cfm?FuseAction=Content&ID=12#Web*.

We won't be discussing these standards in detail. However, UAAG and Section 508, §1194.21, offer a useful angle from which to consider the accessibility of media players and other plug-ins such as Adobe Acrobat Reader. In Chapter 13, we demonstrated techniques that make multimedia content more accessible to users with disabilities. Now let's explore the accessibility of the plug-ins themselves.

MEDIA PLAYERS

The most popular media players—Apple's QuickTime, RealNetworks' RealPlayer and RealOne, and Microsoft's Windows Media Player—are available both as stand-alone desktop applications and as browser plug-ins. These media players address accessibility in different ways and have different strengths and weaknesses; there are even differences between stand-alone and plug-in versions made by the same vendor. So we can't just tell you to use certain plug-ins and stay away from other ones. Instead, we'll try to provide some guidelines and principles you can use when you need to decide what's best for a particular application. In addition to the following discussion, we summarize our comments in Table 14–1.

Of course, a central component of an accessible media player is its ability to display alternative content, such as captions and audio description tracks. Equally important is the degree of device independence that a player provides when enabling user control. Simply said, can the media player support captioning and synchronous audio tracks as we discussed in Chapter 13? Can the user control the player or plug-in using only the keyboard or assistive technology tools? Is the desired behavior consistent across platforms and browsers? The following sections detail what we found.

TABLE 14–1 Support for Various Accessibility Features Offered by Popular Media Players

Player	Platform	Keyboard Access	User Preferences	Screen Reader Access	Synchronization Method
RealOne, stand-alone	Windows	Full menu	Captions and/or audio descriptions	None—must provide transcript	SMIL/RealText
RealOne, embedded	Windows	None	Captions and/or audio descriptions	None—must provide transcript	SMIL/RealText
RealPlayer 8, stand-alone	Windows, Mac, various UNIX	Full menu (some controls not available—volume)	Captions or audio descriptions	None—must provide transcript	SMIL/RealText
RealPlayer 8, embedded	Windows, Mac, various UNIX	None	Captions or audio descriptions	None—must provide transcript	SMIL/RealText
QuickTime 5, stand-alone	Windows, Macintosh	Partial menu	None—must provide separate file	None—must provide transcript	Separate file/ partial SMIL
QuickTime 5, embedded	Windows, Macintosh	Full menu	None—must provide separate file	None—must provide transcript	Separate file/ partial SMIL

Table continued on next page.

TABLE 14–1 *Continued*

Microsoft Windows Media Player XP, stand-alone	Windows	Full menu	Captions	None—must provide transcript	ASX/SAMI
Microsoft Windows Media Player XP, embedded	Windows	Partial menu	Captions	None—must provide transcript	ASX/SAMI
Microsoft Windows Media Player 7.1, stand-alone	Windows, Macintosh (most functionality), Solaris	Full menu	Captions	None—must provide transcript	ASX/SAMI
Microsoft Windows Media Player 7.1, embedded	Windows, Macintosh (most functionality), Solaris	None—if implemented in separate window	Captions	None—must provide transcript	ASX/SAMI
Flash 5	Windows, Macintosh	Can tab in but not out	None—author dependent	None—must provide transcript	Programmatic
Flash MX/Flash 6.0	Windows	Can tab in but not out	None—author dependent	MSAA compliant (Window-Eyes)	Programmatic

Abbreviations: ASX, Advanced Streaming Format XML Redirector; MSAA, Microsoft Active Accessibility; SAMI, Synchronized Accessible Media Interchange; SMIL, Synchronized Multimedia Integration Language.

Caution: Captions Are Not Text Alternatives

The Real players, QuickTime, and Windows Media Player all support closed captions—testimony to the success of the technique in broadcast television. It is very important to note, however, that the caption track displayed on the screen is *not* available to assistive technology devices *as text*. It is, in fact, more like an image file. This means that screen readers cannot read the caption track. At first glance, this may not seem important since someone using a screen reader will hear the audio track. Some users of the Internet have hearing as well as visual impairments, however, as Helen Keller did many years ago. People who are deaf-blind or have low vision as well as little or no hearing often employ refreshable Braille displays; some users who are blind prefer refreshable Braille devices as well. Like people who prefer synthetic speech (or who don't read Braille well enough to keep up with the refreshable display), these individuals generally use screen readers like JAWS and Window-Eyes, which are capable of converting on-screen text into both Braille and synthetic speech. Since deaf-blind users and others with visual and hearing impairments can neither see nor hear the captions, it is important to provide an additional text transcript for all video and audio elements, as the ATSTAR curriculum described in Chapter 13 does. Unlike the caption track, the transcript *can* be rendered as Braille.

Media player technology is one of the most rapidly changing elements of the Web. With the advent of recommendations and standards like UAAG and increased support for SMIL, we can expect that multimedia accessibility will continue to improve. Product descriptions and techniques presented in this chapter are likely to have evolved somewhat even by the time you read this chapter. However, the principles that we urge you to bear in mind when selecting media applications remain the same:

- Device-independence.
- Predictability of function (across browsers, operating systems, assistive technologies, and player versions).
- Integrated support for caption text, audio descriptions, and synchronization.
- User ability to control the interface and presentation.

Consider these principles as we examine the functions of the various media players and the Flash plug-in.

RealNetworks' RealOne

RealOne is the latest version of RealNetworks' media player. The Real players are available for Microsoft Internet Explorer and Netscape Navigator on Windows and Macintosh operating systems, as well as several flavors of UNIX. The stand-alone version of RealOne offers increased accessibility and increased user control of the way content is presented. The menu now includes options that allow users to increase and decrease volume and to display closed captions and audio descriptions simultaneously (previous versions forced a choice between them). The application menus are accessible by many assistive technology tools. In addition, RealOne includes many keyboard shortcuts to control the player; these are listed in the application's Help pages.

We get a very different picture, however, when we look at the plug-in version of RealOne. The plug-in version of RealOne remains completely inaccessible to keyboard or other assistive technology devices, which means that users will be unable to control the presentation of multimedia materials with anything other than a mouse. Therefore, RealOne or RealPlayer 8 should be considered only if a stand-alone application is absolutely required. This means that these players should not be embedded into Web pages when presenting Real media files.

As we saw in Chapter 13, RealOne does accommodate equivalent alternatives for multimedia content, including both closed captions and audio descriptions, as well as ALT text for graphics and other types of media files. As previously noted, the RealOne player uses SMIL code to synchronize captions and audio descriptions with the video stream. RealOne's support for the SMIL caption switch gives it a clear advantage if disk space is an important consideration. You can provide one version of the multimedia material, including both captions and audio descriptions. Users can then decide whether to view the captions or listen to the descriptions, or both, or neither.

The sample code below illustrates how SMIL is used to establish a presentation layout, define regions for each media element including the RealText caption track and the video stream, and synchronize them with the <par> element. Note that the caption track is preceded by an SMIL <switch> element. The player responds to the caption track if the user preferences for accessibility are set to "show captions."

```
<smil>
<head>
   <meta name="title" content="SMIL Wrapper"/>
   <layout>
      <root-layout background-color="black"
         height="315"
         width="325"/>
      <region id="videoregion"
         background-color="black"
```

```
                top="5"
                left="5"
                height="240"
                width="320"/>
         <region id="textregion"
             background-color="black"
             top="255"
             left="5"
             height="60"
             width="320"/>
      </layout>
 </head>
 <body>
    <par>
    <!-- VIDEO -->
       <video src="video.mpg" region="videoregion"/>
    <!-- CAPTIONS -->
       <switch>
          <textstream src="video.rt"
              region="textregion"
              system-language="en"
              system-captions="on"
              title="english captions"
              alt="english captions"/>
       </switch>
    </par>
 </body>
 </smil>
```

Apple's QuickTime

The QuickTime player is available for the Windows and Macintosh platforms and most of the popular browsers. QuickTime 5 is the most recent version of this media player at the time of this writing.

Apple has been working to improve QuickTime's accessibility, and both the stand-alone and plug-in versions of QuickTime 5 give people with disabilities more control than previous versions did. Keyboard equivalents for most menu functions are available in the stand-alone version, and the plug-in version has a clear advantage over Real-One in this respect. The QuickTime browser plug-in has useful keyboard shortcuts, as shown in Table 14–2.

QuickTime 5 also supports the presentation of video with synchronized captions and audio descriptions, as we demonstrated in Chapter 13. It is worth reiterating here, however, that QuickTime 5 does not support the SMIL caption switch. This means that if you want to offer your users a choice between versions with and without captions and with and without audio descriptions, you'll have to provide a separate link to each version. RealOne has the advantage here since it allows users to toggle captions and audio descriptions on and off and can provide just one file that includes both options. So you (or your client) will need to decide how important it is to embed the player in the Web document instead of running the player as a stand-alone application.

TABLE 14–2 Keyboard Controls for the QuickTime Browser Plug-in

Keystroke	Function
Space bar	Start or stop the movie (toggle)
Up arrow	Increase volume
Down arrow	Decrease volume
Right arrow	Step movie forward
Left arrow	Step movie backward

Apple makes very specific recommendations on how to implement the player in the Web page. Apple's QuickTime developer site states:

> The <EMBED> tag allows media file types other than those directly supported by the browser to be handled with an external application or plugin. In this case, the external application is QuickTime Player and the plugin is the QuickTime Plugin.
>
> With the release of Internet Explorer 5.5 SP2 and later, you must use an <OBJECT> tag in addition to the <EMBED> tag for your Web pages to be compatible with both Netscape and Internet Explorer on Mac and Windows systems. . . .[3]

An example of how to accessibly embed the QuickTime player on a Web page is illustrated in the ATSTAR video caption example in Chapter 13. The code for that implementation appears below.

```
<div align="center"><p>
<object title="QuickTime Movie" classid= "clsid:02BF25D5-
    8C17-4B23 BC80-D3488ABDDC6B" width="420" height="368"
    codebase="http://www.apple.com/qtactivex/
    qtplugin.cab" name="vid">
<param name="src" value="file:/// D:/content/
    AT_CON_319_SHOW.mov">
<param name="AUTOPLAY" value="false">
```

---

3. From "Embedding QuickTime for Web Delivery." Accessed March 29, 2002, at *http://developer.apple.com/quicktime/quicktimeintro/tools/embed.html.*

```
<param name="CONTROLLER" value="true">
<param name="enablejavascript" value="true">
<embed width="420" height="368" controller="true"
    src="file:///D:/content/AT_CON_319_SHOW.mov"
    bgcolor="FFFFFF" border="0" pluginspage="http://
    www.apple.com/quicktime/download/index.html"
    loop="FALSE" autoplay="FALSE"
    enablejavascript="true"   name="vid">
</embed>QuickTime movie</object>
</div><br>
<a tabindex="5" href="javascript:setqfoc()"
    hreflang="en"><IMG
    src="/images/spacer.gif" width="10" height="10"
    alt="Activate QuickTime keyboard controls."
      border="0"></a><br>
</p></div>
```

This code example includes redundant mechanisms for integrating the QuickTime player within the Web page. This is necessary in order to make the player compatible with both Internet Explorer 5.5 and later and with Netscape. A sequence of <param> elements within the <object> element provides details on the location of the source file (the movie to be shown), as well as whether to display the controller (yes), to run the movie automatically (no), and whether to enable JavaScript (yes). The <object> tag also contains code to download the plug-in if it is not installed via an ActiveX install component.

Within the <object> element, the <embed> tag contains parameters for all the same functions in a format Netscape can use. Note that the <embed> element is not valid HTML (it will be flagged as an error by the W3C's HTML Validation Service), but it must be used in order to ensure compatibility with Netscape (which has supported the `<embed>` tag since Navigator 2.0 in 1995). In this case, if the plug-in is not available, Netscape is directed to Apple's download page. Following the tag that closes the `<embed>` element is HTML text that will be displayed if the user chooses not to install QuickTime.

There is also a JavaScript that allows users to regain keyboard control of the QuickTime plug-in if they accidentally tab to (or click on) a part of the page outside the area defined by the `<object>` element. (Technically, when this happens, the QuickTime player "loses focus," so the user will be unable to start or stop the movie or control the volume from the keyboard.)

The JavaScript that "returns focus" to the QuickTime plug-in is referenced by a link attached to a transparent image that isn't visible on the page (its only purpose is to anchor this link). Someone using a screen reader could listen for the ALT text—"Activate QuickTime keyboard controls"—and understand what to do. However, the link target (that is, what the `href` attribute points to) is `javascript:setqfoc()`. WCAG 1.0 warns against this technique in the explanation that follows Checkpoint 6.3: "For example, ensure that links that trigger scripts work when scripts are turned off or not supported (e.g., do not use "javascript:" as the link target)."

Fortunately, the code shown above includes statements that turn JavaScript on if it isn't already enabled in the browser. As a result, even users who normally disable scripting will be able to regain keyboard control over the QuickTime plug-in—unless, of course, they're using a browser like Lynx, which doesn't support JavaScript under any circumstances. (Lynx does not support JavaScript, but it *does* allow users to display multimedia and other content using the stand-alone version of the relevant plug-in.)

Microsoft's Windows Media Player

There are several versions of Windows Media Player in release at the time of this writing: 7.1 for most Windows and Mac operating systems, plus separate versions for Windows XP, Mac OS X, and Solaris as well as other versions for consumer devices.

The latest versions of Windows Media Player do offer considerable accessible user control by providing keyboard equivalents for most menu options, including turning captions on and off. The Windows Media Player plug-in is partially accessible in Internet Explorer 6 under Windows XP, but earlier releases are not accessible when the player is embedded in a Web page.

The typical implementation of a SAMI caption file in Microsoft Windows Media Player is to create an ASX metafile that binds the media file and the SAMI text file in an XML-based code format. Users then link directly to this metafile from the Web page. The ASX metafile ensures that older browsers (or those not made by Microsoft) will launch the stand-alone version of Windows Media Player and deliver content to it, rather than downloading the material and trying to open it within the Web page. Here's an example of the code for an ASX metafile that displays multimedia content in Windows Media Player.

```
<asx version="3.0">
<title>External Caption Test</title>
<entry> <title>Caption Test</title>
<author>Webmaster A</author>
<copyright>2002</copyright>
<ref href="SAMI_test.wmv"/>
</entry>
<entry>
<ref href="SAMI_Demo.smi"/>
```

```
</entry>
</asx>
```

The Macintosh version of Microsoft's Media Player does not support specifying the SAMI file in an ASX multipart reference. This means that Macintosh browsers need a different way to invoke the SAMI file, as shown here:

```
http://server/filename.asf?sami=http://server/
   samifile.smi.
```

Microsoft's Windows Media Player for Mac provides syntax for embedding the media player on the Microsoft Developer Network Web site. But there is still a huge installed base of browsers that predate Internet Explorer 6, and we do not recommend embedding the player unless (as with QuickTime) you're willing and able to provide links to media that will run in the stand-alone player as well.

Perhaps the most important drawback of the Windows Media Player is that it does not support audio description in either the stand-alone or the plug-in version. It does enable captioning through Microsoft's SAMI language, which we explored in Chapter 13. Lack of support for a separate audio description is a very serious limitation. If your video files require audio descriptions (see Chapter 13 for discussion of when descriptions are necessary), you can't use the Windows Media Player unless you're willing to provide the same media in either RealOne (RealPlayer) or QuickTime format as well.

Macromedia's Flash

So far, our encounters with Flash have mostly been problematic. Either a user experience was interrupted with a series of alert boxes asking us to install the Flash plug-in, or we were trying to construct usable workarounds to barriers imposed by Flash content. Macromedia released a new version of the Flash Player (version 6.0) in March 2002. Flash 6.0 represents a significant improvement over all previous versions of the Flash player where accessibility is concerned. But as of this writing, the new version works with only one screen reader—Window-Eyes—and only with the latest version of that program (4.2, just released). JAWS and Home Page Reader do not yet support Flash 6.0. It can be said that Macromedia made a good faith effort in designing to the MSAA standard. In this view, part of the burden of compatibility must fall as well on the makers of JAWS to design software to a common industry standard. Even so, many users still have older versions of Flash on their computers, and it will be some time before developers can be reasonably confident that most users have Flash 6.0 or later. In the meantime, then, it's important to be aware of the accessibility barriers that people with disabilities will encounter when using older versions of the Flash player and to provide alternatives for those instances.

Central to the accessibility barriers that we encounter when we consider the Flash plug-in as Web *content* is the question of focus. As we've explained previously, an interface element "has the focus" when the next thing the program does will be triggered by the user's interacting with that element. For example, the Submit button on a form "gets focus" when a user tabs to it after filling out the form: if the Submit button has focus, pressing the return key will submit the form. With Flash, it is possible for users to tab *into* the `<object>` element that contains the Flash movie and, *if* the developer has taken pains to support tabbing within the Flash movie—a very big *if*—then it will be possible to tab within the Flash movie.

It may even be possible—though again, only if the developer has taken considerable care—to interact via the keyboard with some elements of the Flash movie. But it is *not* possible to tab *out* of the Flash movie, nor is there any other keystroke or combination of keystrokes that will allow you to get out of that particular briar patch once you've strayed into it. This is due to a bug in Internet Explorer that also affects software other than the Flash plug-in. Nevertheless, the only way out is to click the mouse somewhere outside the borders of the movie, which of course requires (1) that you have a mouse and are able to use it, (2) that you can see enough to find another location on the page, and (3) that there is a location on the page that lies outside the Flash movie.

Suppose that the home page of a corporate Web site consists entirely of a Flash movie that acts as a kind of splash screen. The company logo rotates slowly, then comes to rest above the company name. Users can control the movie via the application menu for the Flash plug-in. The options on this menu (Play, Pause, Rewind, and so on) are accessible via the keyboard. The catch, though, is that there's no way to bring that application menu up via the keyboard! Newer keyboards designed expressly for Windows include an application menu key on the right side of the bottom row. Pressing the application menu key, however, brings up the application menu for Internet Explorer, not for Flash. Similarly, pressing Shift-F10 (a standard Windows command) gives the focus to Internet Explorer's main menu bar rather than the Flash menu. So the only way to bring up the Flash menu is to right-click on the screen (that is, click the right mouse button). But even if you're able to do this (there is no right mouse button on the Macintosh mouse), the only thing you can do on this page is to play the movie, or pause it, or rewind it—JAWS does not recognize the text on the screen that identifies the company, nor does JAWS recognize any links that may be encoded in the Flash object.

Flash movies may include graphics, text, video, animation, and sound as well as links, all wrapped into one envelope and dropped onto the Web page. People who do not have Flash installed and people with certain disabilities—especially visual disabilities—often find the envelope empty. Prior to the release of the Flash MX authoring tool and the Flash 6.0 player, there were no readily available ways of making these elements accessible to screen readers and other assistive technology devices. In other words, earlier versions of Flash failed the accessibility test, both as Web content and as user agents designed to render Web content.

This is why it's worth noting again that the situation we've just described is changing. If the user has Flash 6.0 and Window-Eyes 4.2 instead of JAWS or an older version of Flash, Window-Eyes would speak the text on the page and identify any links or buttons. Flash has been extremely useful for people with learning disabilities like dyslexia, who can benefit tremendously from compelling multimedia. Now people with other disabilities—and everyone else—stand to gain a great deal as Macromedia works to integrate fuller support for accessibility into future releases of Flash and other products.

Meanwhile, since there's still a huge installed base of older Flash players and authoring tools and the content produced by those tools, developers striving for maximum accessibility must include accessibility features not available through the Flash player itself. As we saw in the previous chapter, the workarounds for providing accessible alternative HTML content for Flash movies are not difficult, but they may have uneven or unpredictable results. It is no more acceptable to insist that "You must have Flash to use this site" than it is to require support for JavaScript (as the 2002 Winter Olympic Games site does). The burden is on the developer to include equivalent content. As our discussion of the 2002 Winter Olympic Games site suggests, it is always necessary to ensure the availability of redundant navigation mechanisms that do not require Flash. Table 14–3 provides a reminder of some of the methods we discussed in Chapter 13. The table suggests ways to provide equivalent content. We suggest that you use these techniques in a nested manner starting at the top of the table. If each time you use one of the Flash attributes in the first column you include equivalent alternatives by means of the corresponding tag or method from the second column, you will improve the accessibility of your Flash content.

Macromedia has begun to make good on its public commitment to accessibility. In the meantime, if you do use Flash in your work, visit the Macromedia Accessibility site at *http://www.macromedia.com/ macromedia/accessibility/features/flash/* and download the Flash Accessibility Developers Kit. The kit contains source files in four categories—audio, text equivalents, keyboard access, and tabbing—and an Accessibility HTML Template for publishing Flash movies on the Web. These are new and relatively untested. Before you publish, test

TABLE 14–3 Techniques for Maximum Flash Accessibility

Flash Presentation Technique	Provide Equivalent Content
Nested `<object>` elements	At the lowest level
`<embed>`	`<noembed>`
`<script>` to detect or launch	`<noscript>`

for accessibility using assistive technology devices and users with disabilities.

Adobe's Acrobat Reader

Adobe Systems has also put some money where its mouth is. The current version of Adobe's Acrobat Reader, version 5.0.5, offers significantly improved support for accessibility both as a stand-alone application and as a browser plug-in. Support for accessibility in Acrobat 5.0.5 extends both to the application itself and to the content it renders.

The first indication of the improved support for accessibility in Acrobat Reader 5.0.5 is that user interface elements that can be accessed through menus and dialog boxes can now also be accessed via the keyboard. According to Adobe's documentation, Acrobat Reader 5.0.5 meets many other requirements of the Section 508 Software Applications and Operating Systems standards as well. Adobe's accessibility site, *http://access.adobe.com*, presents point-for-point tables showing how Acrobat Reader meets (or does not meet) the Section 508 standards for both software and Web content.

Adobe explains that this has been accomplished by rewriting the application to conform with Microsoft's Active Accessibility (MSAA), an API specifically designed to facilitate behind-the-scenes communication between Windows applications and assistive technology devices. (The devices, of course, must also be programmed to take advantage of MSAA; this is true for GW Micro's Window-Eyes as well as Freedom Scientific's JAWS.)

There is at least one exception, however. Oddly, it affects another important accessibility feature required by both the UAAG and the

Section 508 Software Applications and Operating Systems standards. Acrobat Reader allows users to choose their own color schemes (using either the Windows system colors or a custom scheme; see Figure 14–3). This meets the UAAG requirements to ensure user control of rendering and to provide configuration and customization options; it also satisfies Section 508's requirements to respect users' prior color choices as well as allowing high-contrast color schemes within the application. But the JAWS screen reader does not recognize the buttons for setting

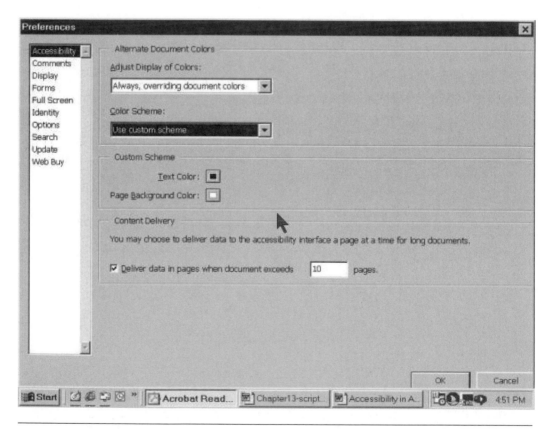

FIGURE 14–3 Screen shot of the Accessibility settings dialog in Acrobat Reader 5.0.5. Selected options include "Use custom scheme" for color and "Always, overriding document colors." Buttons for selecting background and text colors are visible on the screen but not recognized by JAWS. Used with permission.

text and background colors, a (presumably accidental) violation of the Section 508 requirement that information about user interface elements must be available to assistive technology devices. This might seem a trivial point since you might reasonably assume that people who are blind simply don't worry about screen colors and therefore wouldn't miss these buttons. But some people with low vision use screen magnifiers together with screen readers, and it's important that these users receive consistent information from *all* the assistive technology devices they might use.

But while it's true that the bug we've just reported may cause real problems for some users, it's equally true that such problems aren't on the same plane as the accessibility problems we've discussed with respect to Flash 5.0 and earlier versions.

PDF documents may contain some multimedia materials, including QuickTime movies and stand-alone audio (.wav) files. Adobe Acrobat 5.0 does not provide direct support for captioning or describing audio or video—that is, you can't use Acrobat to add captions or descriptions to existing video or audio files—but it *will* display QuickTime movies that include captions and audio descriptions. Authors can also include transcripts of stand-alone audio files, either as part of the document itself or as links from the document to other PDF or HTML documents. (Kara Pernice Coyne and Jakob Nielsen's *Beyond ALT Text,* published as a PDF document in 2001, includes audio transcripts in the main document, then provides links to the .wav files for those who want to hear them.)

Acrobat Reader 5.0.5 is a significant advance toward improved accessibility of PDF documents when used in conjunction with the recently developed tagged content, and Adobe deserves credit for that. Let's hope the company keeps moving in this promising direction.

USE THE RIGHT TOOL FOR THE JOB

This has been an intricate look at a wide array of applications. And, as we mentioned, this is probably the most rapidly changing area of Web development. The take-away message once more is to use the right tool for the job. Think deliberately about your choices. Don't use sophisticated applications simply because you have them; use them only if they improve your ability to convey your message. Don't lock millions out simply because they can't or don't choose the same tools you do. Take the time to think about the multiplicity of ways you can communicate with your audience, and include as many of those modes as needed to reach the largest number of people.

An unfortunate side effect as many people first learn of the need for accessibility is the perception that creativity must be "limited" by accessibility constraints. The Human Factors International listserv has a chat feature on which a recent anonymous poster lamented the fact that ". . . many times in designing a site for accessibility we need to water things down so much that the interface design will suffer for people who prefer visual learning with GUI's."[4] Our experience suggests that the belief that accessibility "water[s] things down" is most often the result of a lack of real understanding and practical application. Developers who are just learning about accessibility tend to think there is no way to create accessible content without sacrificing visual elegance or impact. We believe that as they gain experience in accessible design, the world begins to open up again for these devel-

---

4. Anonymous post submitted on June 16, 2002, at *http://www.humanfactors.com/ downloads/askericanswers.asp.*

opers and that most will come to understand that accessibility means using all the multiple modes of the Web to best advantage.

Our sincere hope is that the information you have gained from this and other chapters has given you this wider perspective. Armed with an understanding of the many options available and supported by the increased commitment to accessibility from makers of innovative software, you have an unprecedented opportunity to communicate. Stay in touch.

15

Supporting Accessibility with Cascading Style Sheets

STYLIN' FOR MAXIMUM ACCESSIBILITY

In this chapter, we'll explore yet another powerful tool in the repertoire of accessible design: Cascading Style Sheets (CSS). CSS is a language, like HTML, and is likewise under the auspices of the W3C. Used in tandem with HTML (or XML), CSS gives Web designers powerful tools for controlling the presentation of documents on the Web. The CSS2 specification introduced in 1998 (approximately a year and a half after CSS1 was published) includes the potential, as yet unrealized, for controlling the way documents are rendered in Braille, print, or synthetic speech. The CSS3 specification, currently in Working Draft, will give developers even more flexibility and control. But browser support for CSS has been slow in coming, and it may be some time before designers can fully exploit the power of CSS.

So far CSS has been used almost exclusively to control *visual* presentation, and that's what we'll focus on in this chapter. We'll show

how font selection, size, and spacing work together with color and contrast to produce documents that are more readable for everyone as well as being usable by people with disabilities. As a running example throughout much of the chapter, we'll again work with the AIR judging form whose content and structure we discussed at length in Chapter 10. Now we'll show you how to manage its appearance by applying styles to it.

HTML Elements and Attributes Addressed in This Chapter

Because CSS can be associated with *all* HTML elements, we do not list specific elements here.

Accessibility Checkpoints and Standards Addressed in This Chapter

Web Content Accessibility Guidelines 1.0 Checkpoints

2. Don't rely on color alone.

2.1. Ensure that all information conveyed with color is also available without color, for example from context or markup. [Priority 1]

2.2. Ensure that foreground and background color combinations provide sufficient contrast when viewed by someone having color deficits or when viewed on a black-and-white screen. [Priority 2 for images, Priority 3 for text]

3. Use markup and style sheets and do so properly.

3.3. Use style sheets to control layout and presentation. [Priority 2]

3.4. Use relative rather than absolute units in markup language attribute values and style sheet property values. [Priority 2]

6.1. Organize documents so they may be read without style sheets. For example, when an HTML document is rendered without associated style sheets, it must still be possible to read the document. [Priority 1]

Section 508 Standards, §1194.22

(c) Web pages shall be designed so that all information conveyed with color is also available without color, for example from context or markup.

(d) Documents shall be organized so they are readable without requiring an associated style sheet.

BENEATH THE VISUAL ASPECTS OF THE WEB

Up to this point we've concentrated heavily on designing to meet the needs of people who use screen readers and talking browsers—people who don't see the screen and who use the keyboard, not the mouse or some other pointing device, to interact with the Web and other applications. This is important because many other kinds of assistive technologies, including voice recognition systems, switches, and other alternative input devices, are "mapped" to the keyboard. That is, the user's actions are "translated" into keystrokes and then carried out.

But of course the Web is an intensely visual environment, and most people—including most people with disabilities—interact with it visually. In this chapter, we'll talk about some of the visual aspects of accessible design. We'll pay special attention to the needs of people with low vision and people with cognitive disabilities such as dyslexia, Attention Deficit Disorder (ADD), and Traumatic Brain Injury (TBI). These disabilities are often called "invisible" because they can be difficult for even trained observers to detect, but they may have a significant impact on the way individuals use computers in general and the Web in particular.

You may be wondering what it means to be encouraged on the one hand to "use style sheets to control presentation and layout" (WCAG 1.0 Checkpoint 3.3) at the same time that you're *required,* on the other hand, to ensure that "documents . . . are readable without requiring an associated style sheet" (Section 508, paragraph (d); also WCAG 1.0 Checkpoint 6.1).

Once you understand the idea of separating content and structure from presentation and layout, however, you'll recognize that these requirements aren't as contradictory as they may seem at first glance.

Content and Structure versus Presentation and Layout

The separation of content and structure from layout and presentation is an important concept that applies to all aspects of Web authoring.

Here's how WCAG 1.0 defines structure and content as well as presentation and layout:

> The content of a document refers to what it says to the user through natural language, images, sounds, movies, animations, etc. The structure of a document is how it is organized logically (e.g., by chapter, with an introduction and table of contents, etc.). An element (e.g., P, STRONG, BLOCKQUOTE in HTML) that specifies document structure is called a structural element. The presentation of a document is how the document is rendered (e.g., as print, as a two-dimensional

graphical presentation, as [a] text-only presentation, as synthesized speech, as Braille, etc.) An element that specifies document presentation (e.g., B, FONT, CENTER) is called a presentation element. Consider a document header, for example. The content of the header is what the header says (e.g., "Sailboats"). In HTML, the header is a structural element marked up with, for example, an H2 element. Finally, the presentation of the header might be a bold block text in the margin, a centered line of text, a title spoken with a certain voice style (like an aural font), etc.

This means that the HTML document should include only the document *content*—words, sentences, paragraphs, images, sounds, scripts, applets, and so on—and the markup that describes their *logical* or *structural* functions and relationships.

Content consists of both block-level and inline elements. *Block-level elements* usually begin on a new line in the document. Some examples of commonly used block-level elements include

- Headers (<h1>, <h2>, <h3> ... <h6>).
- Divisions (<div> elements).
- Paragraphs (<p> elements).
- Ordered and unordered lists (<ol> and <ul>, respectively) and the items that belong to them (<li> elements).
- Forms (<form> elements) and the elements they contain (<input> elements, <select> elements, and so on).
- Data tables (<table> elements and their constituents, such as header cells (<th> elements) and data cells (<td> elements)).

These are all examples of *structural* elements.

Inline elements such as strong or emphasized text (`<strong>` and `<em>`, respectively) occur inside block-level elements. Text that has been tagged as `<strong>` is usually **boldfaced,** while words and phrases tagged with the `<em>` element are usually *italicized.* The visual effect is identical to the effect produced by the bold (`<b>`) and italic (`<i>`) tags. The difference is that **bold** and *italic* are purely presentational elements—and purely visual ones at that—whereas `<strong>` and `<em>` indicate the logical or rhetorical force of the word or phrase they embrace.

Using markup to provide information about the structural and logical dimensions of your document is important because in each of these cases, the browser (Microsoft Internet Explorer, Netscape Navigator, Opera) or other user agent determines how each element will be rendered (displayed, printed, and so on)—that is, unless the author overrides the built-in rendering instructions with a style sheet. Individual users may also override both the default renderings *and* the style sheets associated with the Web pages they're reading by telling their browsers to ignore author-defined fonts, colors, and style sheets in favor of a style sheet that the *user* specifies.

If you are prepared to accept the default rendering, you don't need to do anything at all once you've created the content and tagged its structural and logical components with the appropriate HTML elements. But if you were prepared to accept the defaults, you probably wouldn't have read this far. So let's talk about how using style sheets can help you. There are definite advantages both for Web design in general and for accessibility in particular.

THE ADVANTAGES OF USING STYLE SHEETS

In general, enforcing the separation of content and structure from presentation and layout results in Web documents that load faster and are easier to maintain and update. Source documents that contain only content and structural markup are easier for people (like Web developers) to read and understand than documents that include lots of complex formatting instructions. Therefore, those documents are easier and less expensive to update when necessary—even if the person responsible for updating the site is not the person who designed and built it.

Content can be changed independently of formatting because presentation and layout are handled in CSS. This means you can leverage the skills of graphic designers and typographers on your team by allowing them to focus on the visual design while writers and communication specialists work on textual content. And you can change presentation and layout on hundreds or even thousands of pages at once simply by changing the external style sheet to which those pages are linked.

Style sheets have similar benefits even for single documents. For example, suppose you repeatedly use the same element such as a <blockquote> or a horizontal rule (<hr>) at different times on a page. If you want to change the way these elements look but don't use style sheets, you'll have to specify the appearance of the element each time you use it; with a style sheet, you only have to do it once. Obviously, this can be a huge time-saver.

Working with style sheets also has important benefits for accessibility. First, you can offer users a choice of styles without having to modify the source document. And you can easily verify that the source document works effectively with assistive technologies before applying any styles at all. Finally, using markup and style sheets together, and doing so correctly (WCAG 1.0 Guideline 3), makes it possible to avoid design and coding practices that may create unintended barriers to accessibility. (We'll show you some examples later in this chapter.)

A DIFFERENT APPROACH TO DESIGN

Designing for maximum accessibility often means approaching your projects in a different way than many other designers. For example, many Web designers tend to start with an image in mind—once they have a rough idea of the site's subject and purpose, they start working to develop the right "look and feel." In fact, customers may come to a designer with little more than a sense that they want a site that *looks* a certain way—something contemporary, say, something that shows the world that they're smart, hip, competent, cutting-edge. . . .

But good design is accessible design. We saw over and over again in our user experience chapters that when design begins with look and feel, it usually ends as bad design, meaning that it's inaccessible—it leaves people with disabilities out in the cold, along with people using cell phones and PDAs or others who can't (or don't want to) spend a lot of time working through a site to find what they need.

Shortcut Techniques to Avoid

Designers who make look and feel their first priority often use one of the following techniques as a shortcut.

1. Using HTML structural elements for visual effect.
2. Using HTML presentation elements to "simulate" structural elements.

These techniques are mirror images of each other. They may be shortcuts for designers, but they can create accessibility barriers, as we explain in the next two sections.

Using HTML Structural Elements to Achieve Visual Effects

In the days before CSS was introduced, one of the only ways designers could achieve certain visual effects was to use HTML markup that was intended for other things. Frequent candidates included headings (especially <h2> and <h3>), used to change font sizes and styles; lists (especially definition lists, <dl>), used to create a format in which every other line is indented, as in some poems; and block quotations (<blockquote>), used to indent text. There are still plenty of examples around.

The home page for Yale University's Collection of Musical Instruments, for instance, uses the <h6> element to format the page heading and the navigation links on the left side of the page, while the <h4> element is used to format the address of the collection (Figure 15–1).

In other words, at least two different header elements are used on this page, but they convey no structural information. They're even somewhat misleading visually: the <h6> element assigned to the text links on the left side of the screen appears to use a larger font than the <h4> element used for the collection's address, even though <h4> is *logically* higher than <h6>. The better approach would have been to use the CSS font-size property to create the desired typographic effect.

Avoid Using HTML Presentation Elements to Simulate Structure

Another fairly widespread design practice is basically the mirror image of the one we just discussed. Designers sometimes use <font>, <b>, and other presentation elements such as <center> and attributes like align to do the work that would be better done by structural

FIGURE 15–1   Screen shot of the home page for Yale University's important collection of historic musical instruments. The home page uses HTML headings for visual effects and not to indicate logical relationships. Accessed December 3, 2001, at *http:// www.yale.edu/musicalinstruments/*. Used with permission.

markup. For example, these presentation tags are used to format subheadings within a page instead of the HTML elements that would define those sections as structural components. In fact, certain presentation tags such as <font> have actually been deprecated in the HTML 4 and XHTML standards. In addition, the font properties defined in CSS1 and CSS2 provide much greater flexibility and control of text presentation.

How These Shortcut Techniques Create Accessibility Barriers

Why does it matter whether or not you use structural elements and use them correctly, as long as you get the look and feel you're after?

It matters because clearly structured Web documents are easier for everyone to understand—especially for people with visual impairments or cognitive disabilities. An outline of the document can guide attention to key sections of the page for people with cognitive impairments, some of whom have trouble distinguishing signal from noise—critical from noncritical information. People who are blind or who have low vision can benefit as well. The current generation of screen readers and talking browsers uses these structural elements to help blind and visually impaired users navigate the Web. For example, IBM's Home Page Reader (version 3.0) and JAWS (beginning with version 4.01) both allow users to jump from one heading to another. If those headings aren't there, the user loses important clues about the way the document is organized. But it's just as bad if the headings are there and they're being used only for visual effect. In either case, someone using a screen reader or talking browser gets misleading information about the document's structure. Users of handheld and WebTV devices also benefit from proper HTML markup since these devices rely on correct structure for very specialized presentation.

Using HTML Headings Correctly

The W3C's site offers a good example of how to use headings (Figure 15–2). There are 18 headings on the page. JAWS 4.01 displays them in a scrolling list, much like the Links List discussed earlier.

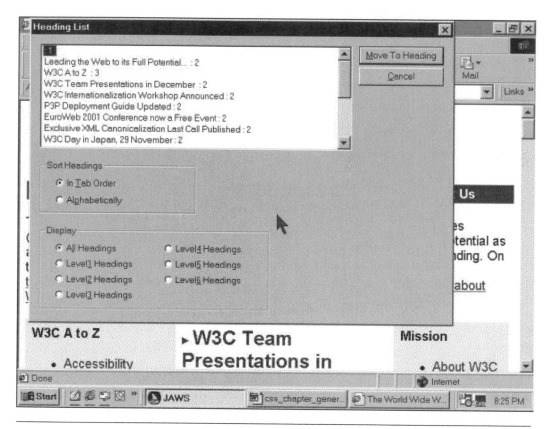

FIGURE 15–2 Screen shot of the W3C home page with the JAWS Heading List superimposed. Accessed December 3, 2001, at *http://www.w3.org*. Used with permission.

Beyond Headings

It's not just about headings, of course. Paying careful attention to HTML structure makes it possible to use CSS for a variety of tasks, as on the Texas School for the Blind and Visually Impaired (TSBVI) Web site (Figure 15–3).

At the very top of the screen are four links, including three text links and a Skip to Main Content link attached to a small image of the Texas map above a horizontal line. In the center of the screen are the

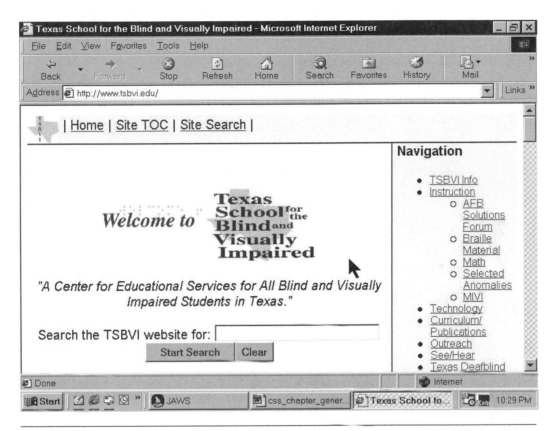

FIGURE 15–3 Partial screen shot of the home page for the Texas School for the Blind and Visually Impaired. Accessed December 3, 2001, at *http://www.tsbvi.edu*. Used with permission.

words "Welcome to Texas School for the Blind and Visually Impaired"; the school name is superimposed on a larger version of the same Texas map used for the Skip to Main Content link. Below this logo is a search field. To the right is a navigation menu with 15 links in a bulleted list.

Visually, the welcome message dominates the screen. But if we simply let JAWS read down the page in Say-all mode, we first hear the links at the top of the screen, then the navigation menu on the right, and then the welcome message.

All of this formatting and layout is handled by style sheets, including both an external style sheet referenced via a `<link>` element in the document's `<head>` element, as well as a number of style definitions that are embedded in the document itself. The external style sheet governs many pages on the large TSBVI site; the embedded style declarations are local to the current page and aren't needed elsewhere on the site. (This is a good example of how "cascading" works. Suppose you have a document that contains a `<style>` element and a link to an external style sheet. Now suppose that both the `<style>` element and the external style sheet include instructions for formatting the `<h2>` element. Which instructions will the browser follow? The local ones—that is, the `<style>` element in the document will trump the external style sheet.)

Color and contrast are also important aspects of visual presentation that can contribute to accessibility. But color and contrast can also create unintended accessibility barriers. We'll address the use of color and contrast below, in relation to the AIR judging form.

METHODS OF ASSOCIATING STYLE SHEETS WITH DOCUMENTS

There are several ways to associate styles with Web documents. We'll quickly mention the three methods that are most commonly used, and then the rest of the chapter will focus on the first of these methods.

1. External style sheets.
2. Embedded style sheets.
3. Inline style attributes.

External Style Sheets

An external style sheet is a separate text file that can be associated with one or more HTML documents. A single style sheet can be associated with thousands of HTML documents. This makes the external style sheet an extremely powerful tool, and it's the method we'll focus on in the rest of this chapter.

For example, here is the style sheet we associated with the AIR judging form we created in Chapter 10. This style sheet will be discussed throughout this chapter.

```
body{
font-family:arial,verdana,sans-serif;
font-size:1em;
font-weight:normal;
font-style:normal;
line-height:1.25em;
color:black;
background-color:white
}
fieldset{
padding-top:1em;
padding-left:1em;
padding-right:1em;
border:groove
}
legend{
font-family:arial,verdana,sans-serif;
font-size:1.4em;
font-weight:bold;
font-style:italic;
color:yellow;
background-color:black;
border:outset}
```

```
.item{
font-family:arial,verdana,sans-serif;
font-size:1.2em;
font-weight:bold;
font-style:normal;
color:black;
background-color:silver}
.menu{
font-family:arial,verdana,sans-serif;
font-size:1em;
font-weight:normal;
font-style:normal;
color:black;
background-color:white;
text-indent:-5%;
margin-left:5%;
margin-top:0 em;
margin-bottom:0 em
}
```

To associate an external style sheet with an HTML document, include a <link> element like the one below in the <head> element of your HTML document.

```
<html>
<head>
<title>My Stylish Page</title>
<link rel="stylesheet" href="mystyle.css" type="text/css">
</head>
. . .
</html>
```

Embedded Style Sheets

In some cases, it's appropriate to *embed* a style sheet within a specific document—for example, when the document has specific presentation and layout that are different from other pages on the same site. If a document includes both a <link> element that points to an external style sheet and an embedded style sheet, the embedded style sheet "wins": that is, if both style sheets apply formatting to the same elements (such as a table), the browser will render the table according to the embedded style sheet. As we pointed out earlier, this is what the term *Cascading Style Sheets* means.

For example, we could create an embedded style sheet to override the style for the <legend> element as we defined it above. The embedded style sheet might look like this.

```
<style type="text/css">
<!--
legend{
font-family:arial,verdana,sans-serif;
font-size:1.25 em;
font-style:italic;
font-weight:bold;
color:white;
background-color:maroon;
border:outset
}
-->
</style>
```

Note that the embedded style sheet is actually a <style> element with all style definitions enclosed between the <style> and </style>

tags. (The `<style>` element must be contained within the document's `<head>` element.) Note, also, that the contents of the `<style>` element are shown as an HTML *comment*, marked by `<!--` at the beginning of the comment and `-->` at the end. This forces older browsers that do not support embedded style sheets to ignore the style declarations instead of trying to render them—and failing.

Inline Style Attributes

This third method may be used in conjunction with the techniques described above; it's appropriate when you want to format a single element or `<span>` within a larger element. In the same way that the embedded style sheet overrides the external one, an inline `style` attribute overrides style declarations in external and embedded style sheets.

Inline style differs from external and embedded styles in several important respects. First of all, an inline style is an attribute rather than an element or a separate document, as shown in the code below.

```
<p style="font-family:takoma; font-style:italic; font-
    weight:bold"> The text of this paragraph is formatted
    in Takoma bold italic.</p>
```

In order for this inline style to take effect, the document's `<head>` element has to include a *style declaration,* such as the `<meta>` tag in the example below.

```
<html>
<head>
<title>Style Sheets</title>
```

```
<meta http-equiv="content-style-type" content="text/css">
. . .
</head>
. . .
</html>
```

The inline `style` attribute should be used sparingly—for example, when a single element in a document needs to be formatted in a special way.

As John Pozadzides and Liam Quinn [1999] of the Web Design Group point out, if you rely too much on inline styles you forfeit many of the benefits of using style sheets in the first place. For example, the source code for your main document gets cluttered up with presentation instructions, becoming harder to maintain and upgrade the more style attributes occur within the document. And instead of being able to change the appearance of dozens or thousands of pages by modifying a single external style sheet, you now have to locate every instance of the `style` attribute in every document where you want the change to take effect. This can be even more burdensome if you are serving up dynamic Web pages and the content is stored in a database or otherwise not easily modifiable.

USING STYLE SHEETS TO ENHANCE ACCESSIBILITY FOR PEOPLE WITH LOW VISION OR COGNITIVE DISABILITIES

In this chapter, we use CSS to address some of the problems that people with cognitive disabilities or low vision might encounter when using the AIR judging form. Before we discuss the design, however, let's take a look at the terms *low vision* and *cognitive disabilities.*

Low Vision

The term *low vision* covers a very broad range of conditions. The number of people who have partial or limited vision far exceeds the number of people who have no useful vision at all. There is a substantially higher incidence of low vision among people over 50 than in the general population, resulting from such conditions as macular degeneration, glaucoma, and diabetic retinopathy, which often worsen with age. According to Jupiter Research, people over 50 represent a larger number of users (23,000,000 by the end of 2000) than kids, teens, or college students.[1] And people over 65 form the fastest-growing group in the population as a whole. So designers can expect more and more people with limited vision to visit Web sites.

People with low or limited vision tend to benefit from larger, simpler, open fonts such as Arial, Verdana, Geneva, and other sans-serif typefaces (this book, for example, uses 14-point Minion). They also benefit from clearly contrasting colors. Some users set their browser or system preferences to use large font sizes; some rely on screen magnification software such as AI Squared's ZoomText or Freedom Scientific's Magic. Others use both techniques. As we noted earlier, sophisticated users can even specify their own style sheet to override the designers' styles to modify background and font color,

---

1. Cited in "Jupiter Research—Digital Divides," accessed December 1, 2001, at *http://www.agelight.org/news/6-15jupiter.htm.*

font size, and other properties to meet the users' particular needs. But many people with limited vision—especially elderly users—don't think of themselves as having disabilities or don't realize they can customize the software they use (or both).

Cognitive Disabilities

The term *cognitive disabilities* also covers a huge range of conditions. Many of these conditions are difficult to quantify or even to detect, and for that reason they are sometimes called *hidden* or *invisible* disabilities. But whether you can see them or not, they are very real.

People who have cognitive disabilities—such as those associated with ADD or caused by TBI—may view the screen at a standard resolution (such as 800 × 600). But they, too, may find "busy" pages and complicated layouts difficult or even impossible to use. Like people with limited vision, people with ADD or TBI may have trouble distinguishing foreground images and text from background material. Or, faced with a large number of options, they may have difficulty recognizing the choice most appropriate to their needs at the moment.

Some people with cognitive impairments use assistive technology that guides their attention by masking many of the elements on the screen or highlighting the element that currently has the focus. People with reading disabilities such as dyslexia may use assistive technology that combines masking techniques and screen-reading software for simultaneous visual and auditory input. But such technologies are beyond the financial reach of many individuals—and many cognitive disabilities go unrecognized and undiagnosed.

Style Sheets and Conflicting Needs

The AIR judging form might present problems for both groups. The items on the AIR judging form we explored in Chapter 10 may be too densely packed for a judge with ADD or TBI to negotiate successfully. Similarly, someone with limited vision may have trouble recognizing where one section or item ends and the next one begins.

There is some evidence to suggest that design solutions that satisfy the needs of users with low vision may cause problems for users with cognitive difficulties, and vice versa. This doesn't mean that you, as a Web designer, should just throw up your hands! This is the very kind of dilemma that style sheets are designed to resolve. We'll try to find a solution that works for everyone; if we can't, we may be able to use CSS to let users themselves choose the alternative that works best for them.

STYLING THE AIR JUDGING FORM

Let's take another look at the AIR judging form we developed in Chapter 10. Now, however, we'll focus on the visual presentation of the form. Instead of using structural elements to achieve presentation effects or using presentation elements to create the appearance of structure, we'll use CSS to *bring out the structure* of the form. This is what we meant when we said earlier that there isn't a real contradiction between the WCAG 1.0's recommendation to use style sheets to control presentation and layout and the Section 508 requirement to organize documents in such a way that they can be read without style sheets.

Reviewing the AIR Judging Form

We discussed the AIR judging form in detail in Chapter 10. Here we'll just remind you that the form contains a number of different sections, with a different number of items in each one—and a different scoring system. We used `<fieldset>` and `<legend>` elements to define the various sections, and we decided to use pull-down menus (`<select>` and `<option>` elements) so that judges wouldn't have to remember how many points to assign in a given instance.

In other words, we used HTML markup to indicate the logical *structure* of the judging form. We paid little or no attention to presentation and layout issues such as fonts, highlighting, and so on. Not surprisingly, the resulting form wasn't much to look at—but it might be *too* much for some prospective judges.

Determining the Design Goals and Strategy for the New Form

The overall task for users of the judging form is to participate in judging the Accessibility Internet Rally. This requires successfully completing a judging form for each assigned site. Specifically, judges must be able to

- Locate scoring items quickly and easily.
- Recognize the salient points in each item, such as item name, criteria, scoring options, and comment areas.
- Select the appropriate scoring option for each item judged.
- Enter required and optional information.

We want to make it easier for judges with low vision and/or cognitive disabilities to locate the various parts of the form as well as the individual items and to make it easier for *all* judges to find what they need.

Defining what users need to be able to do makes it easier to list our design goals below.

- Make it easy for people, including people with low vision and people with cognitive disabilities, to identify the separate sections of the long, complex judging form.
- Help people using the form to identify and locate individual items within the sections of the form.
- Help users recognize and locate the form controls used for scoring.
- Make the form visually attractive.

In short, we want to use CSS to bring out the structural elements of the AIR judging form so all the judges can more easily identify them. The style sheet will make the form easier to scan for:

- Major sections such as General Accessibility or Usability.
- Individual scoring items.
- Navigation links.

We also want to make individual items more readable.

Using Font Selection and Spacing to Improve Legibility

We can accomplish many of the goals listed above by choosing a readable font and using spacing to improve legibility.

Font Selection

According to Dr. Aries Arditi [1997b] of Lighthouse International, people with low vision find open, sans-serif fonts such as Arial more readable than closed, serif fonts like Times New Roman. A combination of upper- and lowercase lettering is also more readable than ALL CAPS.

We'll use the `font-family` property to indicate a range of acceptable fonts. The line of code below gives an example of how to use this property.

```
font-family:arial,verdana,sans-serif;
```

This statement takes into account the wide range of fonts installed on computers that access the Internet. Instead of insisting on a single font, this code tells the browser to use the Arial font if it's available on the user's system. If Arial isn't installed, the browser will look for another sans-serif font called Verdana. If *that's* also not available, the browser will use whatever sans-serif font it can find.

Arditi writes that people designing print documents should choose 16- or even 18-point fonts to ensure that their work is legible to people with limited vision. Those readers might find the same font sizes useful on the Web as well. But here's one of many places where Web design techniques differ from the techniques that work for print. Instead of specifying the `font-size` property in terms of points or pixels, Web designers should use the *relative units* of measure supported by CSS, such as `em`, percent (%), or the verbal descriptors `largest`, `larger`, `medium`, `smaller`, or `smallest`. These are called *relative measures* because the font size shown on the screen is relative to each individual user's default font settings.

For example, if the default font is 16-point Arial, then each of the following three lines of CSS code would display text in that font.

```
font-size:1em;
font-size:100%;
font-size:medium;
```

All three of the statements above do the same thing: set the size of the display font to match the user's default settings. One advantage of doing it this way is that it allows individual users to change their font sizes as they choose. For example, they can use the View → Text option in Internet Explorer to adjust the font size, as shown in Figure 15–4.

If you've used a relative measure to set the `font-size` property, your design won't "break" when a user decides to enlarge or shrink the font size to suit his or her needs or taste. In fact, your design will be preserved since all the font sizes will change relative to the user's newly declared base size. By contrast, if you use an absolute measure (`font-size:12pt;` for example) there's no telling what might happen!

For the improved AIR form whose style sheet is listed at the beginning of this chapter, we used relative measures to set font sizes for text in the `<body>` and `<legend>` elements. We also defined a `.item`

FIGURE 15–4 Screen shot of the Text submenu of Internet Explorer 5.5, showing five options ranging from Largest to Smallest. The current selection, Medium, is identified by a small bullet to the left of the selection.

selector so we can associate a style with the name of each item to be scored. For the <body> element, we set the size to 1 em, matching the user's default font size. Text assigned to the .item class is slightly larger (1.2 em), and the <legend> element is larger still, at 1.4 em.

Spacing

Spacing is another important tool for improving legibility. Readers with limited vision often have difficulty locating the beginning of new lines as they read down the page. Arditi [1997b] of Lighthouse International explains that setting what typographers call *leading* (which essentially determines the vertical space between lines) to 25–30 percent above the font size helps these readers track the text more effectively. (In this book, for example, the leading has been set to approximately 28.5 percent above the font size.) With this in mind, we set the line-height property for text in the AIR form's <body> element to 1.25 em, thus adding an additional 25 percent to the space between lines.

```
body{
font-family:arial,verdana,sans-serif;
font-size:1em;
font-weight:normal;
font-style:normal;
line-height:1.25em;
color:black;
background-color:white
}
```

In addition to opening up the space between lines of text, the style sheet we showed you at the beginning of this chapter also pads the space around `<fieldset>` elements to make them stand out more clearly as well.

```
fieldset{
padding-top:1em;
padding-left:1em;
padding-right:1em;
border:groove
}
```

We also defined the border of each `<fieldset>` element, using the groove style included as part of CSS.

Finally, we needed to make sure that judges using the navigation links to jump from item to item on the form would be able to distinguish items that wrapped around to the next line. For this purpose, our style sheet defined a `.menu` selector that uses both the `text-indent` and `margin-left` properties as well as `margin-top` and `margin-bottom`. This way the menu items that wrap to the next line are indented on the second line. We adjusted the margin properties to limit the space between each line so that the menu length is manageable.

```
.menu{
font-family:arial,verdana,sans-serif;
font-size:1em;
font-weight:normal;
font-style:normal;
color:black;
background-color:white;
text-indent:-5%;
margin-left:5%;
margin-top:0em;
margin-bottom:0em
}
```

This code coordinates the `text-indent` and `margin-left` properties to create hanging indents in the AIR form's navigation menu.

Using Color and Contrast to Enhance Legibility

To supplement our use of font selection, font sizes, and spacing, we've also used color and contrast to make it easier for judges to locate different elements on the AIR form. Like our use of fonts and spacing, our use of color is designed to bring out the structural elements we defined through HTML markup.

Overview of Color and Contrast Issues

Color is an incredibly important design tool. It's used for so many things: indicating the status of a visited link, defining blocks of related material, highlighting important information, guiding users to an appropriate action, and so forth. But here, too, it's important to avoid creating unintended accessibility barriers. The Section 508 standards and WCAG 1.0 agree that it's important to ensure that information presented with color is also available in the absence of color and that color contrasts are strong enough for users to distinguish between foreground and background.

Here's an example of how inadvertent barriers can be created when color is the only indicator of important information. In the multiple-choice test shown below, high school–aged students preparing for England's national A-Level examinations are instructed to select a red button to mark the correct answer (Figure 15–5).

Approximately 10 percent of males are unable to perceive red or green. It's quite possible, therefore, that some students would have serious difficulty with this practice test. It could be argued that there's

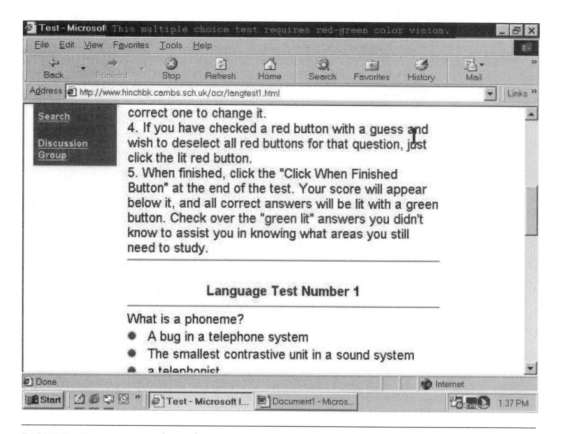

FIGURE 15–5 Screen shot of a multiple-choice test that requires students to see and differentiate the colors red and green to mark their answers. Accessed December 8, 2001, at *http://www.hinchbk.cambs.sch.uk/ocr/langtest1.html*. Used with permission.

no real problem in this case, since there's only one button next to each choice. But step 5 of the instructions says that when students receive feedback on the test, incorrect answers will be identified by a "green lit" button. In other words, students will need to be able to tell the difference between red and green in order to see which questions they answered correctly—precisely the colors that 10 percent of male students can't distinguish! If the red buttons were form elements such as an `<input>` element of `type="image"` or `type="radio"` they could be associated with `<label>` elements using the techniques described in Chapter 10. However, these buttons are actually graphical links; they have no ALT text, and all of them have the same name, which JAWS reports as "ocr/mctest." So a student with red-green color deficiency would find this practice test extremely frustrating, if not downright impossible to work with.

There's nothing wrong with using color. But when you do, make sure that color isn't the only way your users will be able to identify important information. For example, feedback to students taking the practice test shown above could simply group correct and incorrect responses under headings marked up as <h2> or <h3> elements (depending on the logical structure of the page). The designers could still display a green button beside each incorrect response if they choose. In fact that might be a good idea, since the heading text and the presence of the buttons would reinforce each other.

Most people with limited vision—whatever the cause—have difficulty with at least some color distinctions. According to Arditi [1997a], people with partial sight and inherited or acquired color deficiencies are likely to experience diminished perceptual capability across all three dimensions of color: hue, lightness, and saturation. Arditi notes that lightness is the most important perceptual attribute in terms of making color contrast effective but adds that the most effective page designs are those where colors "differ dramatically" across all three dimensions.

An Experiment in Yellow and Black

Personal experience suggests, and Arditi's research confirms, that many people with low vision find yellow text on a black background readable and relatively easy on the eyes. So we started by trying to apply this principle to the presentation of the entire AIR form (Figure 15–6).

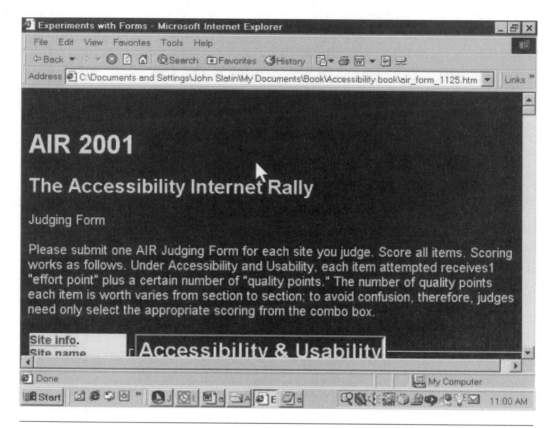

FIGURE 15–6 Screen shot of the AIR judging form with yellow text on a black background. The navigation links on the lower-left side of the screen are black on a yellow background.

The result was disastrous. While this presentation might work for judges with low vision, it had a startling effect when we showed it to someone with TBI. The reaction was instantaneous and sharply negative. The subject told us a few days later that she had continued to experience "aftereffects" for some three hours after she viewed this screen—even though she had only looked at it briefly.

Even after we changed the style sheet to display white text on a blue background, this informant explained that for her the multiple colors used to differentiate various sections of the form were simply additional information that she *had* to take into account. She reported that the "background" colors never receded into the background but remained in her consciousness and demanded attention each time she looked at the screen. The effect was to siphon off energy that she would rather have used to read the items on the form and to make the decisions that judging requires.

Back to the Drawing Board

Next we tried a more selective approach, one that would highlight specific features of the page instead of the entire form. This was more successful: the same individual indicated that the presentation of the form as shown in Figures 15–7 and 15–8 *would* work for her, provided that we change the yellow-on-black of the `<legend>` elements to a less shocking color combination.

To ease identification of the major sections of the AIR judging form, we used our style sheet to add text and background colors to the `<legend>` elements. Together with the enlarged font size (1.4 em) and an outset border, this makes the `<legend>` elements stand out from the page. But since yellow text on black still caused problems for our subject, we used a different high-contrast combination to reduce the interference.

You may be wondering why we didn't use graphics instead of styled text—another technique that's often used in cases like this. There's a three-part answer to this.

1. The page would have been more complicated because we would have then needed to size and position the image and assign ALT text to say exactly the same thing as the word(s) represented in the graphic.

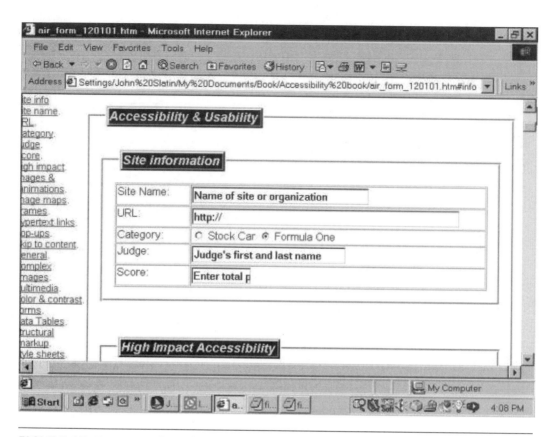

FIGURE 15–7 Screen shot of the AIR judging form, which shows the `<legend>` elements set off in yellow text on a black background. The `<fieldset>` elements are padded so that their nesting is visible.

2. The page would "break" if a user changed the font sizes: the text would change but the graphic wouldn't, and the results might be pretty ugly.

3. Finally, with CSS it's far easier to experiment with different color combinations: we can change the `color` and `background-color` properties in the style sheet, then refresh the page and test the results much faster than if we had to edit the image.

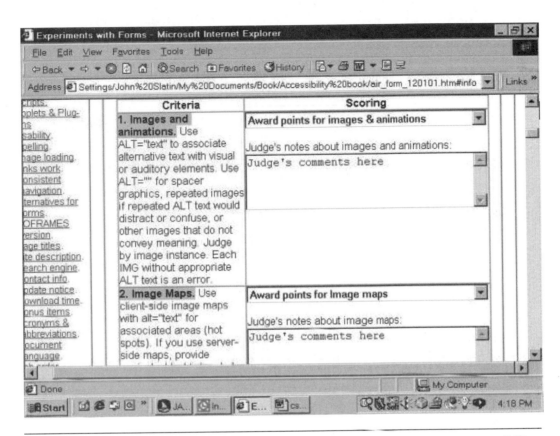

FIGURE 15–8 Screen shot showing the first two items in the High Impact Accessibility section of the AIR judging form. The terms *Images and animations* and *Image Maps* are highlighted to indicate where each item begins.

After we made the color change discussed above, the CSS code for the <legend> elements looked like this.

```
legend{
font-family:arial,verdana,sans-serif;
font-size:1.4em;
font-weight:bold;
font-style:italic;
color:white;
```

```
background-color:blue;
border:outset}
```

It's worth noting that a very similar technique can also be used to simulate buttons for navigation or interaction; unlike images used as buttons, the style of these "text-buttons" can even be modified or overridden by users who prefer to apply their own style sheets.

We also used text and background colors to help judges locate where each scoring item begins. To do this, we added a .item selector to our style sheet, as shown in the listing earlier in this chapter. This allows us to treat a piece of text (a <span> element) as if it were a true HTML element, so we can associate a style with it.

Here's the CSS code we used for the .item selector.

```
.item{
font-family:arial,verdana,sans-serif;
font-size:1.2em;
font-weight:bold;
font-style:normal;
color:black;
background-color:silver}
```

The phrases we wanted to highlight are part of the <label> element for the pull-down menus from which judges will select the scoring option they need. We didn't want to apply the style to the entire label—that would defeat the purpose of highlighting the beginning of each scoring item! So we used the <span> element, which was introduced into HTML specifically to allow designers to mark off a portion of a larger element—that is, to define a *span* of material that will be styled differently from the material that surrounds it. Then we used the `class` attribute to assign the `.item` style to the `<span>` element, as shown in the listings below and in Figure 15–8.

```
<label for="hi1_pts"><span class="item">Images and
     animations
   </span> . . . </label>
```

Throughout this discussion of the AIR judging form, we've used CSS to *highlight* the structure of the document, thereby making it easier for users to identify and navigate the components of the judging form. In our next example, a Web site for a class at the University of Texas, we'll take a different tack: we'll *exploit* the separation of content and structure from presentation and layout to create a design that's effective for users who are blind as well as those who are sighted.

CSS POSITIONING, READING ORDER, AND NAVIGATION LINKS

The `<div>` element is similar to the `<span>` element in that the only reason it exists is to allow designers to associate styles with chunks of material. But the chunks that the `<div>` element works with are generally bigger. The `<div>` element is a block-level element, meaning that it can encompass a variety of other elements, including paragraphs, tables, lists, other `<div>` elements, and so on. By contrast, the `<span>` element is an inline element, meaning that it always ropes off a "span" *inside* another element—part of a paragraph, part of a table row, part of a label, and so on.

The `<div>` element is also an important tool for using CSS to position elements on the screen—to take them out of the document's normal "flow" and put them where you want them. In fact, you can use CSS positioning to accomplish many of the layout tasks often handled with tables. This brings us back to the problem of reading order, which surfaced when we visited the Metropolitan Museum site in Chapter 7.

As with layout tables, when you use CSS positioning you have to bear in mind that the order in which elements *appear* on the screen may not match the order in which people using screen readers and talking browsers will *hear* them. But with CSS, this can actually be a plus: with CSS, reading order isn't necessarily bound to the display order. Screen readers and talking browsers base their reading order on the order in which they encounter elements in the *source document*. This means that you can sequence elements in the source document so that they'll play well on screen readers and talking browsers, then use CSS to create the *visual* arrangement that works best as well. Two for the price of one!

That's what we've done in our next example. Here we'll show you a technique that could straighten out the problem with reading order we described in Chapter 7 while simultaneously enabling people who use screen readers and talking browsers to hear the main content of the page first, instead of plodding through all the navigation links before getting the information they want. Figure 15–9 shows a mock-up page for a class taught at the University of Texas in fall 2002. Visually, the page is divided into two areas. There is a navigation bar on the left side of the screen, with several links starting about a third of the way down the screen. The main body of the page shows the course title, a table of information about where and when to find the class and the

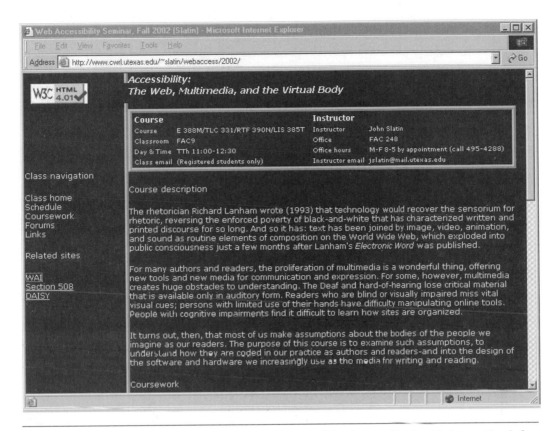

FIGURE 15–9 Screen shot of a page using CSS positioning to display links on the left side of the screen.

instructor, and a paragraph headed "Course description." The navigation bar and the body of the page are separated by a thick white vertical line that runs the length of the screen.

Visually, there is nothing remarkable about this page at all. And that is precisely our point! Most Web users expect to find a navigation bar on the left side of the screen, like the one on this page. But for people who use screen readers, talking browsers, and refreshable Braille displays, it can be extremely inconvenient to hear all those navigation links before they get to the "meat" of the page. This is why

Section 508 requires a way to bypass those links. The Skip Navigation or Skip to Main Content link is a clunky workaround, as we noted earlier. So here is another solution: we've used CSS positioning and HTML structural markup to make both groups of users happy at the same time. The links are displayed on the left in the conventional way, but screen readers and talking browsers will speak them *after* reading the rest of the page.

We can thank CSS positioning and HTML's block-level elements for this. The page has two main divisions (<div> elements). The first one holds the material in the main content area. The second major <div> element contains the navigation links.

Placing the <div> elements in this order in the source code ensures that screen readers and talking browsers will read the main content area first. CSS positioning allows us to create the kind of visual layout that experienced Web users have come to expect, with the navigation links on the left. Here's the CSS code for the style sheet used to position the navigation links to the left of the main content while screen readers and talking browsers read the main content first.

```
body{
position:relative;
top:0;
left:0;
font-family:verdana,arial,sans-serif;
font-weight:normal;
font-size:1em;
background-color:black;
color:white}

.main{
position:absolute;
```

```
top: 0;
left:20%;
border-left:thick white ridge
}

h1{
font-family:verdana,arial,sans-serif;
font-size:1.4em;
font-weight:bold;
font-style:italic;
line-height:1.25em;
color:white
}

h2{
font-family:verdana,arial,sans-serif;
font-size:1.25em;
font-weight:normal;
text-decoration:none;
color:white
}

.navlinks{
position:absolute;
top:30%;
left:0;
width:20%;
}

a{
font-family:verdana,arial,sans-serif;
font-size:1.2em;
font-weight:normal;
color:white;
line-height:1.2em;
}
```

The style sheet listed above adapts an idea from a CSS tutorial by Stephanos Piperoglou [2000]. Piperoglou explains that setting an element's `position` property to `relative` (the other choices are `absolute`, `fixed`, and `static`) has an interesting effect when the `position` property of any element that's contained inside the first element is set to `absolute`. What happens is that the "child" element's position is now defined as absolute *in relation to* its "parent" element (that is, the element that contains it). In other words, setting the `position` property of the `<body>` element to `relative` allows us to manipulate the positions of the `main` and `navlinks` `<div>` elements in relation to the `<body>` element.

ONCE MORE, WITH FEELING: GOOD DESIGN IS ACCESSIBLE DESIGN

CSS is a powerful addition to the repertoire for accessible Web design. We've shown the benefits of distinguishing content and structure from presentation and layout and shown how styles can be used to enhance accessibility by highlighting important structural elements of the document. We've discussed font selection and spacing as well as color and contrast. We've explained that you can use CSS positioning to replace layout tables, making navigation schemes more accessible and sites easier to maintain. We've also shown how important it is to include individuals with different disabilities in user testing—that's the best way to be sure you're aware of any unintended consequences that your design decisions may have. Especially when there's a chance that specific effects created to serve one group of users may pose problems for others, user testing is the *only* way to tell whether you've devised a viable solution. It's also important to test your CSS with several browsers since there are still significant inconsistencies in the way different browsers render some styles. And since there's no way to be absolutely certain that a design meets the needs of every single user, keep in mind that another benefit of using CSS is that individual users can override your style sheets and replace them with style sheets tailored specifically for them.

We've reached the end of this book, but the journey toward maximum accessibility is just beginning. The Web is what it is—a remarkable, enormous, fast-growing, constantly changing phenomenon—because so many thousands, even millions, of talented people like you have poured their creativity and energy into inventing and reinventing it many times over the past decade. As a result, the Web has helped to bring about amazing transformations in business, education, and government as well as many other aspects of society. But it's not over yet: we invite you to join us in reinventing the Web yet again, this time as a resource that's fully accessible anywhere, anytime, to anyone—and everyone. And of course we invite you to join us on the Web at *http://www.maximumaccessibility.com*, where we'll keep you up to date on new trends and developments—and where you can tell us about your success on the road to accessibility.

A

Resources and Tools
for Accessible Design[1]

INFORMATION RESOURCES

1. Web Accessibility Initiative (WAI), at *http://www.w3.org/wai*. A major activity of the World Wide Web Consortium, the WAI is a broad collaboration among industry, academic research, and members of the disability community to define standards and techniques for maximizing the accessibility of Web-based materials for all users.

2. WAI Web Content Accessibility Guidelines (including checklist and techniques documents), at *http://www.w3.org/tr/wcag10.* These Guidelines are the closest thing to a universally accepted standard for accessible Web content (though this

---

1. Developed by John Slatin and Jim Allan to accompany a presentation at the Government Technology Conference in Austin, Texas, on February 15, 2002. Copyright © 2002 John M. Slatin and Jim Allan. Used with permission.

525

position may be challenged by the U.S. government's Section 508 standards; see below). (Note: the WAI site also includes useful information about use of color, etc.)

3. Section 508 Final Standards, at *http://www.section508.gov/index.cfm?FuseAction=Content&ID=12#Web.* These standards became effective on June 21, 2001, and govern IT accessibility for all federal agencies and entities operating federal contracts. These standards are expected to have significant impact in the private and nonprofit sectors as well as in government.

4. IBM Web Accessibility Checklist and Tutorial, at *http://www-3.ibm.com/able/accessweb.html.* The most recent version of IBM's accessibility checklist is closely aligned with Section 508 federal standards. Each checkpoint includes a link to a short, clear tutorial about basic design and testing techniques.

5. Information Technology Technical Assistance Training Center (ITTATC) Web Accessibility Course, at *http://www.ittatc.org/training/webcourse/index.cfm#AboutAuthor.* This course was developed by Jim Thatcher, a member of the panel that developed the accessibility standards for Section 508. Thatcher developed the first screen reader for computers using a graphical user interface.

6. "Web Accessibility for Section 508," at *http://www.jimthatcher.com/webcourse1.htm.* The online accessibility course described in the previous entry, on the site of the person who wrote it. Thatcher's site (*http://www.jimthatcher.com*) includes other valuable information, including a comparison chart with side-by-side views of Section 508 requirements and related WCAG Checkpoints.

7. Knowbility online accessibility course, at *http://www. knowbility.org/curriculum*. An overview of accessibility issues, tools, and techniques for designing accessible Web sites.

8. WebABLE Solutions, at *http://www.webABLE.com*. Site maintained by Mike Paciello, founder of the Web Accessibility Initiative. Good design and usability information plus links to hundreds of other resources, including the WAI site.

9. HTML Writer's Guild Web site, at *http://www.hwg.org*, and the Guild's AWARE Center (Accessible Web Authoring Resources and Education), at *http://www.awarecenter.org/*. Site was last updated in April 2001, but authoring resources are still useful.

10. International Center for Disability Resources on the Internet, Section 508 Resource Page, at *http://www.icdri.org/ section_508_resource_page.htm*. Substantial listing of government, industry, and academic resources related to federal accessibility standards as defined by Section 508 of the Rehabilitation Act.

11. Trace Research and Development Center at the University of Wisconsin–Madison, at *http://www.trace.wisc.edu*. Probably the leading center for research on information technology and people with disabilities.

12. Texas School for the Blind and Visually Impaired Web site, at *http://www.tsbvi.edu*. This site, maintained by Jim Allan, Webmaster and Statewide Technical Specialist, provides a wealth of information on a broad range of accessibility topics. Allan is a member of the WAI Interest Group.

13. Adaptive Technology Resource Center, University of Toronto, at *http://www.utoronto.ca/atrc/*. Wide-ranging research and

development program related to adaptive technologies for persons with disabilities, including excellent work on Web and software accessibility. See also the Special Needs Opportunity Window (SNOW) project site, at *http://snow.utoronto.ca/ index.html.*

14. *Making Educational Software Accessible*, at *http:// ncam.wgbh.org/cdrom/guideline/.* The National Center for Accessible Media's excellent, detailed guidelines for CD-ROM– based multimedia. The guidelines aim at education but are much more broadly applicable. Site includes downloadable prototypes and information about accessibility issues related to specific development platforms.

15. National Center for Accessible Media (NCAM), at *http:// ncam.wgbh.org/.* NCAM has pioneered such important developments as closed captioning and descriptive video service and continues to conduct innovative research on ways to make video and other media both interactive and accessible. Free download of NCAM's MAGpie software for captioning and describing video.

16. Lighthouse International, at *http://www.lighthouse.org.* This organization has created guides to improved legibility through font selection and sizing and effective use of color and contrast. "Simple Steps to More Readable Type through Universal Graphic Design" is available at *http://www.lighthouse.org/ bigtype/universal_graphic_design.htm.* "Making Text Legible: Designing for People with Partial Sight" is available at *http:// www.lighthouse.org/print_leg.htm.*

17. "Safe Web Colours for Colour-Deficient Vision," at *http:// more.btexact.com/ces/colours/.* Guidelines for selecting Web

colors that work for people who have difficulty seeing certain colors. Excellent illustrations. By Christine Rigdon of British Telecom.

18. WebAim: Web Accessibility in Mind, at *http://www.webaim.org/*. The Section 508 checklist with success/failure criteria is especially helpful—*http://www.webaim.org/standards/508/checklist*.

19. Microsoft's Enable site, at *http://www.microsoft.com/enable*. Substantial site providing information about and access to many Microsoft tools for accessible design, plus links to many other resources including information about Microsoft's Active Accessibility (MSAA) Application Programming Interface (API) for Windows.

20. UseIt!, at *http://www.useit.com*. Web site maintained by Jakob Nielsen, a leading usability expert who has written some useful pointers about accessible design.

21. AccessFirst site of the Institute for Technology and Learning (ITAL), at *http://www.ital.utexas.edu/accessfirst/*. Information about the AccessFirst Design & Usability Studio and other AccessFirst design projects.

22. Accessibility guidelines and standards for Texas state agencies, at *http://www.dir.state.tx.us/standards/srrpub11-accessibility.htm*. A guide to state policy and legislation concerning the accessibility of Web- and other technology-based information resources.

23. WebSavvy, at *http://www.websavvy-access.org*. Useful tutorials and other information on accessible design, including Flash, from the University of Toronto.

VALIDATION AND REPAIR TOOLS

1. Bobby, the automated accessibility checker, at *http://www.cast.org/bobby*. Comes in two versions—one on the Web, one stand-alone (Java-based) application. Stand-alone version can check a whole Web site; the online version checks one page at a time and has trouble with dynamically generated pages. Be aware that no automated tool can possibly detect all accessibility problems. Humans are necessary!

2. A-Prompt, at *http://aprompt.snow.utoronto.ca/*. An evaluation and repair tool developed jointly by Toronto's Adaptive Technology Resource Center and Wisconsin's Trace Research and Development Center (see above).

3. W3C's HTML Validation Service, at *http://validator.w3.org/*.

4. HTML-Kit, at *http://www.chami.com/html-kit*. This powerful Web-authoring tool performs several useful and important functions, including HTML validation and conversion to XHTML. It also cleans up extraneous HTML code generated when Microsoft Office documents are saved as Web pages.

5. The WAVE, at *http://www.temple.edu/inst_disabilities/piat/wave/*. Developed at Temple University (Philadelphia) by the late Len Kasday, the WAVE is especially useful in helping sighted developers *see* ALT text and recognize the order in which items on their pages will be read by screen readers and talking browsers.

6. Microsoft Powerpoint WWW Accessibility Wizard, at *http://www.rehab.uiuc.edu/ppt/index.html*. Developed by the Division of Education-Rehabilitation Services at the University of Illinois–Urbana-Champaign. This tool steps PowerPoint au-

thors through the process of converting PowerPoint presentations into accessible Web-based presentations.

7. WAI Evaluation and Repair Tools Working Group list of free and commercial evaluation and repair tools, at *http://www.w3.org/WAI/ER/existingtools.html*. The list is frequently updated.

8. UsableNet's LIFT suite of software authoring tool extensions, at *http://usablenet.com*. Designed to allow authors to continue to use the design tools they prefer by providing additional functionality that prompts for compliance with guidelines and standards chosen by the author.

AUTHORING TOOLS REPORTED TO PROVIDE SOME SUPPORT FOR CREATING ACCESSIBLE CONTENT

1. IBM Home Page Builder configurable accessibility checker, at *http://www-3.ibm.com/software/webservers/hpbuilder/win/*. Much of its extensive functionality is accessible from the keyboard.

2. Macromedia Dreamweaver extensions for checking compliance with Section 508 and with general usability guidelines, at *http://www.macromedia.com/macromedia/accessibility/*. The Dreamweaver MX product, released as this book was going to press, provides substantially more support for authoring accessible content, as well as improved accessibility for authors who have disabilities.

3. Information about accessibility features for Adobe products, at *http://access.adobe.com*. Includes instructions on using Acrobat 5 and Microsoft Word 2000 to create accessible PDF documents.

TOOLS FOR CAPTIONING
AND DESCRIPTIVE VIDEO

1. MAGpie (Media Access Generator), at *http://ncam.wgbh.org*.
    Produced by the National Center for Accessible Media
    (NCAM) at WGBH (PBS) in Boston, MA. Tool for producing
    closed captions, descriptive video, etc., and outputting files in
    multiple formats including QuickTime, RealPlayer, SMIL, and
    SAMI. Version 2.0 is currently in beta testing.

2. Apple QuickTime Pro (widely available), at *http://
    www.apple.com/quicktime/products/*. Supports multiple
    tracks for video, audio, closed captioning, description, etc.
    Limitation of current version is that captions, etc., are all
    part of one QuickTime file and therefore not read by screen
    readers such as JAWS and Window-Eyes. Reportedly this will
    be solved in the next version, which will also provide better
    support for SMIL (see Chapter 14).

3. Synchronized Multimedia Integration Language (SMIL), at
    http://www.w3.org/AudioVideo/. A W3C specification for coor-
    dinating synchronized display of multiple media tracks such as
    video, audio, captions, descriptions, etc. SMIL is an XML ap-
    plication. RealPlayer 8 Basic can play SMIL documents, allow-
    ing users to toggle audio descriptions and captions on and off.

B

Why Is Accessibility on the Internet Important?[1]

- Would you construct a building for your organization that was not accessible for someone using a wheelchair?
- Would your company have a promotional event at a club that excluded certain people from attending?
- Would you produce a brochure with a color scheme that rendered it unreadable to those with color vision impairments?
- Would you want to build a Web site that some potential clients, customers, staff, press representatives, or others would not be able to access?

---

1. Reprinted from Knowbility's site at *http://www.knowbility.org/curriculum/intro.html*. Copyright © 2002 Knowbility, Inc. Used with permission. For copyright and reproduction policy, visit *http://www.knowbility.org/curriculum/credits.html*.

Most everyone would reply to the questions above with a resounding "no." And yet, people with disabilities are often locked out of Web sites because their needs are not considered as the sites are designed.

More than 55 million Americans have some type of disability. You might want to consider YOURSELF "temporarily abled." U.S. Census data indicate that one in every five Americans has a disability. As our society grows proportionally older, the need for disability access will increase along with these numbers. The U.S. federal government and many other governments around the world maintain standards of accessibility for government Web sites and software vendors who contract with them.

Internet User Scenarios to Consider

- A sight-impaired person may use a Web browser that reads content on a Web page aloud, and this software is often "confused" by image maps, frames, JavaScripts, and other Web design elements.
- A deaf person requires a text version of audio information in order to be able to access the site information.
- Some people perceive certain colors differently and may not be able to see light-colored type on colored backgrounds.
- Someone with limited hand movement may not be able to hold down more than one key on their keyboard at once. Well-designed Web menus will provide alternative navigation methods.

Designing your Web site to be accessible to people using assistive technologies and others with disabilities is very simple and costs very little if it is done as you build your Web site. Making accommodations on your Web site for the greatest number of users increases the availability and usefulness of those materials. If systems are flexible enough to meet the needs and preferences of the broadest range of users of computers and telecommunications equipment, regardless of age or disability, your potential audience is immediately increased by millions of users.

C

Linearized Tables

This appendix presents linearized versions of four tables included in the main text.

Table C–1 provides the name of the museum, its URL, and some brief, noncomprehensive comments about the barriers we encountered on each site. All sites were accessed on June 8, 2002, except for the Smithsonian site, accessed February 16, 2002.

TABLE C–1 Accessibility Barriers on Selected Museum Web Sites

---

Museum: Chicago Museum of Science & Industry

URL: *http://www.msichicago.org*

Comments: Graphical links have no meaningful information, for example, "link graphic button." Text links have redundant titles, making them difficult to sort and therefore to use by users with screen readers.

Museum: Houston Museum of Natural Science

URL: *http://www.hmns.org/*

Comments: No alternatives are provided for graphic information—including important navigation links.

TABLE C–1 *Continued*

Museum: Musée du Louvre

URL: *http://www.louvre.fr/*

Comments: Frames names provide no orientation information. Graphic image links appear without meaningful ALT texts.

Museum: Museum of Fine Arts Boston

URL: *http://www.mfa.org/*

Comments: Splash screen with untagged image automatically redirects to front page with pop-up window containing untagged images. Online collection database search is usable but returns unintelligible links that are database records.

Museum: National Museum of Australia

URL: *http://www.nma.gov.au/*

Comments: ALT text could be more meaningful, and there is an inaccessible calendar of events, but by and large, a fairly usable site.

Museum: Smithsonian Institution

URL: *http://www.si.edu/*

Comments: Mislabeled forms, use of inaccessible Java elements, pop-up windows, lack of ALT text on image maps, and misleading page titles.

Museum: The Guggenheim (Bilbao, Spain)

URL: *http://www.guggenheim-bilbao.es/*

Comments: Pop-up windows are unannounced, graphic links with no ALT text.

Museum: The Menil Collection

URL: *http://www.menil.org/collections.html*

Comments: Unlabeled graphic links, unannounced auto-refresh to a home page that contains links labeled Button 6, Button 8, Button 7, Button 3, Button 4—not in numerical order!

TABLE C–1 *Continued*

Museum: Whitney Museum of American Art

URL: *http://www.whitney.org/*

Comments: Site has insufficient user control options (font size is specified in style sheets) and inconsistent use of `alt` tags for graphics.

The following abbreviations are used in Table C–2: ASX, Advanced Streaming Format XML Redirector; MSAA, Microsoft Active Accessibility; SAMI, Synchronized Accessible Media Interchange; SMIL, Synchronized Multimedia Integration Language.

TABLE C–2 Support for Various Accessibility Features Offered by Popular Media Players

Player: RealOne, stand-alone

Platform: Windows

Keyboard Access: Full menu

User Preferences: Captions and/or audio descriptions

Screen Reader Access: None—must provide transcript

Synchronization Method: SMIL/RealText

Player: RealOne, embedded

Platform: Windows

Keyboard Access: None

User Preferences: Captions and/or audio descriptions

Screen Reader Access: None—must provide transcript

Synchronization Method: SMIL/RealText

TABLE C–2 *Continued*

Player: RealPlayer 8, stand-alone

Platform: Windows, Mac, various UNIX

Keyboard Access: Full menu (some controls not available—volume)

User Preferences: Captions or audio descriptions

Screen Reader Access: None—must provide transcript

Synchronization Method: SMIL/RealText

Player: RealPlayer 8, embedded

Platform: Windows, Mac, various UNIX

Keyboard Access: None

User Preferences: Captions or audio descriptions

Screen Reader Access: None—must provide transcript

Synchronization Method: SMIL/RealText

Player: QuickTime 5, stand-alone

Platform: Windows, Macintosh

Keyboard Access: Partial menu

User Preferences: None—must provide separate file

Screen Reader Access: None—must provide transcript

Synchronization Method: Separate file/partial SMIL

Player: QuickTime 5, embedded

Platform: Windows, Macintosh

Keyboard Access: Full menu

User Preferences: None—must provide separate file

Screen Reader Access: None—must provide transcript

Synchronization Method: Separate file/partial SMIL

TABLE C–2 *Continued*

Player: Microsoft Windows Media Player XP, stand-alone

Platform: Windows

Keyboard Access: Full menu

User Preferences: Captions

Screen Reader Access: None—must provide transcript

Synchronization Method: ASX/SAMI

Player: Microsoft Windows Media Player XP, embedded

Platform: Windows

Keyboard Access: Partial menu

User Preferences: Captions

Screen Reader Access: None—must provide transcript

Synchronization Method: ASX/SAMI

Player: Microsoft Windows Media Player 7.1, stand-alone

Platform: Windows, Macintosh (most functionality), Solaris

Keyboard Access: Full menu

User Preferences: Captions

Screen Reader Access: None—must provide transcript

Synchronization Method: ASX/SAMI

Player: Microsoft Windows Media Player 7.1, embedded

Platform: Windows, Macintosh (most functionality), Solaris

Keyboard Access: None—if implemented in separate window

User Preferences: Captions

Screen Reader Access: None—must provide transcript

Synchronization Method: ASX/SAMI

TABLE C–2 *Continued*

Player: Flash 5

Platform: Windows, Macintosh

Keyboard Access: Can tab in but not out

User Preferences: None—author dependent

Screen Reader Access: None—must provide transcript

Synchronization Method: Programmatic

Player: Flash MX/Flash 6.0

Platform: Windows

Keyboard Access: Can tab in but not out

User Preferences: None—author dependent

Screen Reader Access: MSAA compliant (Window-Eyes)

Synchronization Method: Programmatic

Table C–3 lists useful keyboard shortcuts for the QuickTime browser plug-in.

TABLE C–3 Keyboard Controls for the QuickTime Browser Plug-in

Keystroke: Space bar

Function: Start or stop the movie (toggle)

Keystroke: Up arrow

Function: Increase volume

Keystroke: Down arrow

Function: Decrease volume

TABLE C–3 *Continued*

Keystroke: Right arrow

Function: Step movie forward

Keystroke: Left arrow

Function: Step movie backward

Table C–4 suggests ways to provide equivalent content. We suggest that you use these techniques in a nested manner starting at the top of the table. If each time you use one of the Flash attributes in the first column you include equivalent alternatives by means of the corresponding tag or method from the second column, you will improve the accessibility of your Flash content.

TABLE C–4 Techniques for Maximum Flash Accessibility

Flash Presentation Technique: Nested <object> elements

Provide Equivalent Content: At the lowest level

Flash Presentation Technique: <embed>

Provide Equivalent Content: <noembed>

Flash Presentation Technique: <script> to detect or launch

Provide Equivalent Content: <noscript>

Bibliography

Adobe Systems. 2002. "Acrobat 5.0 and Section 508." Accessed February 10, 2002, at *http://access.adobe.com/acr508_2.html*.

Alonzo, Adam. 2001. "A Picture Is Worth 300 Words: Writing Visual Descriptions for an Art Museum Web Site." Presented at the 16th Conference on Technology and Persons with Disabilities held by California State University, Northridge. Accessed August 6, 2001, at *http://www.csun.edu/cod/conf2001/proceedings/0031alonzo.html*.

American Association of Museums. 2001. "Technical Information Service Resource List." Accessed August 5, 2001, at *http://www.aam-us.org/infocenter/info12.htm*.

Apple Computer, Inc. 2000. "Embedding QuickTime for Web Delivery." Accessed March 29, 2002, at *http://developer.apple.com/quicktime/quicktimeintro/tools/embed.html*.

Arditi, Aries. 1997a. "Effective Color Contrast: Designing for People with Partial Sight and Color Deficiencies." Lighthouse International. Accessed July 4, 2002, at *http://www.lighthouse.org/color_contrast.htm.*

———. 1997b. "Making Text Legible: Designing for People with Partial Sight." Lighthouse International. Accessed July 4, 2002, at *http://www.lighthouse.org/print_leg.htm.*

Australian Human Rights and Equal Opportunity Commission (HREOC). 1999. "World Wide Web Access: Disability Discrimination Act Advisory Notes." Accessed May 17, 2002, at *http://www.hreoc.gov.au/disability_rights/standards/www_3/www_3.html.*

Bias, Randolph G., and Deborah J. Mayhew, eds. 1994. *Cost-Justifying Usability.* Boston, MA: Academic Press.

Bley, Mary Frances. 2001. "RL30500: Appropriations Overview for FY 2001." National Council for Science and the Environment. Accessed April 6, 2002, at *http://cnie.org/NLE/CRSreports/legislative/leg-36.cfm.*

Bureau of the Census. 1997. "Americans with Disabilities." Accessed May 1, 2002, at *http://www.census.gov/prod/2001pubs/p70-73.pdf.*

Bosson, Edward. 2002. "A Pause That Ponders." E-mail communication on January 4 to Email Alert Group at *relaytx@puc.state.tx.us.*

Caldwell, James L. 1998. "Employers, Employment and People with Disabilities." Speech to the Central Texas Business Leadership Network, Austin, Texas, January 23.

Chisholm, Wendy, Gregg Vanderheiden, and Ian Jacobs, eds. 1999. "Web Content Accessibility Guidelines 1.0." Accessed July 8, 2002, at *http://www.w3.org/tr/wcag10/*.

Clark, Joe. 2000. "Flash Access: Unclear on the Concept." Accessed April 6, 2002, at *http://www.alistapart.com/stories/unclear/*.

———. 2001. "Standard Techniques for Audio Description." Accessed January 19, 2002, at *http://www.joeclark.org/ad-principles.html*.

Clewley, Robin. 2001. "I Have a (Digital) Dream." *Wired Magazine* online. Accessed May 28, 2002, at *http://www.wired.com/news/politics/0,1283,43349,00.html*.

Community Action Network. 2001. "Report" [based on preliminary U.S. census data]. Austin, TX: Community Action Network.

Coverley, M. D. "The White Wall: Reframing the Mirror." *Currents in Electronic Literacy*, Fall 2001 (5). Accessed July 30, 2002, at *http://currents.cwrl.utexas.edu/archive/fall01/fall01/coverly.html*.

Cox, Beth. 2001. "Accommodating Visually Impaired Shoppers." *E-Commerce News* December 6. Accessed June 3, 2002, at *http://www.internetnews.com/ec-news/article.php/4_935161*.

Coyne, Kara Pernice, and Jakob Nielsen. 2001a. "Beyond Accessibility: Treating Users with Disabilities as People." *Alertbox* November 11. Accessed May 26, 2002, at *http://www.useit.com/alertbox/20011111.html*.

———. 2001b. *Beyond ALT Text: Making the Web Easy to Use for Users with Disabilities*. Fremont, CA: Nielsen-Norman Group.

Desai, M., L. Pratt, H. Lintzner, and K. Robinson. 2001. *Trends in Health Among Older Americans. Aging Trends, No. 2.* Hyattsville, MD: National Center for Health Statistics.

Donahue, George M., Susan Weinschenk, and Julie Nowicki. 1999. "Usability Is Good Business." Accessed June 9, 2002, at *http://www.weinschenk.com/knowledge/usability.pdf.*

Federal Acquisition Rules. 2001. *Federal Register* April 25:20894.

General Services Administration. 2001. "Section 508—The Road to Accessibility." Accessed April 5, 2002, at *http://www.section508.gov.*

Gingold, Diane. 2001. "Managing a Diverse Corporate Culture." *Fortune Magazine Online.* Accessed May 27, 2002, at *http://www.fortune.com/sitelets/sections/fortune/corp/2001_06diversity.html.*

Goldstein, Lauren. 2000. "Newest of the New." *Time Magazine, European Edition* 186(18):10.

Guidelines for Signed Books. Undated. Accessed March 28, 2002, at *http://www.sign-lang.uni-hamburg.de/signingbooks/SBRC/Grid/d71/guide00.htm.*

Gunderson, Jon, and Ian Jacobs. 2001. "User Agent Implementation Report." Accessed July 5, 2002, at *http://www.w3.org/WAI/UA/implementation/report-cr2.html.*

Houston Museum of Natural Science. 2001. "News." *Satrosphere* 16(3). Online newsletter of the Houston Museum of Natural Science. Accessed August 5, 2001, at *http://www.satrosphere.net/friends/maga16_3.htm.*

Independent Television Council. 1999. "Guidance on Standards for Audio Description." Accessed July 8, 2002, at *http://www.itc.org.uk/ itc_publications/codes_guidance/audio_description/index.asp.*

"Internet Archive." 2001. Accessed February 23, 2002, at *http:// www.archive.org/index.html.*

Jenkins, P. 2001. "Creating Accessible HTML Structures: Forms, Frames, and Tables." Accessed on May 21, 2001, at *http:// www-3.ibm.com/able/Webcourse/.*

Jupiter Research. 2000. "Digital Divides." Accessed April 6, 2002, at *http://www.agelight.org/news/6-15jupiter.htm.*

Kaiser, Shirley. 2002. "Brainstorms and Raves." Online. Accessed February 4, 2002, at *http://www.brainstormsandraves.com/ 2002_01_13_archive.shtml.*

Karat, C.-M. 1994. "Business Case Approach to Cost Justification." In *Cost-Justifying Usability*, R. G. Bias and D. J. Mayhew, eds. Boston, MA: Academic Press, pp. 45–70.

King, Andy. 2002. "2002 Olympics—Site Review—Webreference Update." Accessed February 4, 2002, at *http://www.Webreference. com/new/020117.html.*

Knowbility. 2001. "Dr. Jakob Nielsen Joins Knowbility to Increase Awareness of Web Access for Users with Disabilities." Press release, November 2. Accessed May 28, 2002, at *http:// knowbility.org/airchair.html.*

LaPlante, Mitchell, and Dawn Carlson. 1996. *Disability in the United States: Prevalence and Causes.* Washington, DC: U.S. Department of Education, National Institute on Disability and Rehabilitation Research.

Mackenzie, Kieran. 2000. "Usability vs. Interactivity on the Web." Accessed June 9, 2002, at *http://www.virtual-fx.net/articles/ usability.htm.*

Majewski, Jan. Undated. "Guidelines for Accessible Exhibition Design." Accessed April 6, 2002, at *http://www.si.edu/opa/ accessibility/exdesign/start.htm.*

Maurer, Marc. 2000. "President's Report to the National Federation for the Blind." Speech delivered June 5, 2000. *The Braille Monitor* August/September:4. Also available online at *http://www.nfb.org/ bm/bm00/bm0008/bm000803.htm.*

————. 2001. "AOL Progress Report." *The Braille Monitor* February. Accessed May 17, 2002, at *http://www.nfb.org/bm/bm01/bm0102/ bm010203.htm.*

McCleary, Leland. 2001. "Technologies of Language and the Embodied History of the Deaf." *Currents in Electronic Literacy* Spring (4). Accessed March 28, 2002, at *http://www.cwrl.utexas.edu/currents/ spr01/mccleary.html.*

McNabb, Brenda. 1999. "Museums on the Internet and Their Public." University of Saskatchewan, Department of Art and Art History. Accessed April 6, 2002, at *http://www.usask.ca/art/digital_culture/ mcnabb/museums3.html.*

McNeil, John M. 2001. *Americans with Disabilities: Household Economic Studies.* Washington, DC: U.S. Bureau of the Census.

Metropolitan Museum of Art. 2001. "The Collection." Accessed April 6, 2002, at *http://www.metmuseum.org/collection/index.asp.*

National Center for Accessible Media. 2001. "Making Educational Software Accessible." Accessed July 5, 2002, at *http://ncam.wgbh.org/cdrom/guideline/.*

National Museum of American History. Undated. "Virtual Exhibitions." Accessed April 5, 2002, at *http://americanhistory.si.edu/disabilityrights/.*

Office of Disability Employment. 2001. "New Freedom Initiative: Disability Direct: Information on Disabilities." Accessed April 5, 2002, at *http://www.disability.gov/category/17/.*

Nielsen, Jakob. 2000. *Designing Web Usability: The Practice of Simplicity.* Indianapolis, IN: New Riders.

Noonan, Tim. 1999. "Accessible E-Commerce in Australia: A Discussion Paper about the Effects of Electronic Commerce Developments on People with Disabilities." Blind Citizens Australia. Accessed April 6, 2002, at *http://www.bca.org.au/ecrep.htm.*

"Olympic Website and IBM Dragged Kicking and Screaming into Accessibility." Undated. *Ten-20 Magazine.* Accessed April 5, 2002, at *http://www.ten-20.com/2olympicwebsite.html.*

Paciello, Michael. 2000. *Web Accessibility for People with Disabilities.* Lawrence, KS: CMP Publications.

Packer, Jaclyn, and Corinne Kirchner. 1997. "Who's Watching? A Profile of the Blind and Visually Impaired Audience for Television and Video." American Foundation for the Blind. Accessed January 19, 2002, at *http://www.afb.org/info_document_view. asp?documentid=1232#c1.*

Piperoglou, Stephanos. 2000. "Tutorial 18: CSS Positioning, Part 1—HTML with Style." Accessed December 26, 2001, at *http://www.Webreference.com/html/tutorial18/.*

Pozadzides, John, and Liam Quinn. 1999. "Linking Style Sheets to HTML." Accessed December 13, 2001, at *http://www.htmlhelp.com/reference/css/style-html.html.*

Pyfers, Liesbeth. 1999. "Guidelines for Signed Books." Intersign: Sign Linguistics and Data Exchange Project of the European Science Foundation. Accessed March 28, 2002, at *http://www.sign-lang.uni-hamburg.de/signingbooks/SBRC/Grid/d71/guide01.htm.*

Reams, Bernard, Peter J. McGovern, and Jon S. Schultz, eds. 1992. *Disability Law in the United States.* Buffalo, NY: William S. Hein.

"Rehabilitation Act of 1973." 1973. Accessed April 5, 2002, at *http://www.dot.gov/ost/docr/regulations/library/REHABACT.HTM.*

Shockey, Bonnie A. 2000. "From the President's Desk." *Allison-Antrim Museum Newsletter* 3(4). Accessed April 6, 2002, at *http://www.greencastlemuseum.org/2000July.htm.*

Singer, Nancy. 2000. U.S. Small Business Administration press release issued November 1. Accessed May 27, 2002, at *http://www.sba.gov/news/archive00/00-97.html.*

Slatin, John M. 2000. "The Art of ALT: Toward a More Accessible Web." *Computers and Composition: An International Journal* 18(1–2):73–82.

———. 2001. "Equivalent Alternatives? Electronic Poetry and Readers with Disabilities." *Currents in Electronic Literacy* Fall (5). Accessed January 13, 2002, at *http://www.cwrl.utexas.edu/currents/fall01/slatin/slatin.html*.

———. 2002. "The Imagination Gap: Making Web-Based Instructional Resources Accessible to Students and Colleagues with Disabilities." *Currents in Electronic Literacy* Spring (6). Accessed June 8, 2002, at *http://www.cwrl.utexas.edu/currents/spring02/slatin.html*.

Smithsonian Institution. 2001. "Info Center: About the Smithsonian." Accessed April 6, 2002, at *http://www.si.edu/portal/t2-infocenter-aboutsi.htm*.

Souza, R., H. Manning, H. Goldman, and J. Tong. 2000. *The Best of Retail Site Design*. TechStrategy Report. Accessed July 8, 2002, at *http://powerrankings.forrester.com/ER/Research/Report/Summary/0,1338,10003,FF.html*.

Spool, Jared M., Tara Scannon, Carolyn Snyder, and Terri DeAngelo. 1997. *Web Site Usability: A Designer's Guide*. Boston, MA: User Interface Engineering.

Streten, Katie. 2000. "Towards a Visitor-Centered Web Experience." Keynote address at Museums and the Web 2000, April 16–18, 2000, Minneapolis, MN. Accessed April 6, 2002, at *http://www.archimuse.com/mw2000/papers/streten/streten.html*.

"Telecommunications Act, Section 255, Subpart A, Section 1193.1." 1998. *Federal Register* February 3. Accessed May 20, 2002, at *http://www.access-board.gov/telecomm/html/telfinal.htm.*

Thatcher, Jim. 2001a. "Accessible Navigation." Accessed April 6, 2002, at *http://www.jimthatcher.com/webcourse4.htm.*

———. 2001b. "Web Accessibility for Section 508." Accessed May 24, 2002, at *http://www.jimthatcher.com/webcourse1.htm.*

The Treasury Board Secretariat of Canada. *Government of Canada Internet Guide.* Accessed in March 2002 at *http://www.cio-dpi.gc.ca/ig-gi/.*

Tufte, Edward R. 1983. *The Visual Display of Quantitative Information.* Cheshire, CN: Graphics Press.

United Nations. 2000. "The United Nations and Persons with Disabilities: The First 50 Years."Accessed May 2, 2002, at *http://www.un.org/esa/socdev/enable/dis50y00.htm.*

U.S. Access Board. 2000. "Section 508 of the Rehabilitation Act: Electronic and Information Technology Accessibility Standards." Accessed May 8, 2002, at *http://www.section508.gov/index.cfm?FuseAction=Content&ID=14.* Also available at *http://www.access-board.gov/sec508/508standards.htm#PART%201194.*

———. 2001. "Guide to the Section 508 Standards for Electronic and Information Technology." Accessed July 5, 2002, at *http://www.access-board.gov/sec508/guide/1194.21.htm.*

U.S. Department of Commerce. 1995–2000. *Falling through the Net.* [Four studies of trends in computer and Internet access and use in

U.S. homes from 1984 through 2000.] Accessed May 28, 2002, at *http://www.ntia.doc.gov/ntiahome/digitaldivide/*.

———. 2000. "The United States International Travel Industry: Key Facts about Inbound Tourism." Accessed April 6, 2002, at *http://tinet.ita.doc.gov/analysis/keyfacts99.html*.

U.S. Department of Health and Human Services. 2002. "Delivering on the Promise: Preliminary Report." Accessed May 28, 2002, at *http://www.hhs.gov/newfreedom/prelim/backdrop.html*.

U.S. House of Representatives. 2000. "Applicability of the Americans with Disabilities Act (ADA) to Private Internet Sites: Hearing Before the Subcommittee on the Constitution of the Committee on the Judiciary." Accessed April 5, 2002, at *http://commdocs.house.gov/committees/judiciary/hju65010.000/hju65010_0f.htm*.

WGBH. 2002. "DVS Milestones." Accessed April 6, 2002, at *http://main.wgbh.org/wgbh/access/dvs/dvsmilestones.html*.

WGBH Caption Center. "Suggested Styles and Conventions for Closed Captioning." Accessed April 6, 2002, at *http://main.wgbh.org/wgbh/pages/captioncenter/ccstyles.html*.

Wong, Stephanie. 1999. "Estimated $4.35 Billion in E-commerce Sales at Risk Each Year." Accessed July 25, 2001, at *http://www.zonaresearch.com/info/press/99-jun30.htm*.

World Wide Web Consortium. 2002. "Policies Relating to Web Accessibility." Accessed from July 2001 through March 2002 at *http://www.w3.org/WAI/Policy/*.

Yee, Roger. 2001. "More Than a Half-Billion Served." Accessed August 5, 2001, at *http://www.contractmagazine.com/projects/halfbillion.html*. Cached version available at *http://www.google.com* on April 6, 2002.

Credits

Figures 2–1, 2–2, 2–3, 8–5, 8–6, 8–7, 8–8, 8–9, 8–10, 8–11, 8–12, 8–13, 8–14, 8–15	Courtesy of Amazon.com, Inc.
Figure 4–1	Courtesy of City of San Jose, California.
Figures 5–11, 5–12, 5–13, 5–14	Courtesy of Santa Clara Valley Transportation Authority (VTA).
Figure 5–15	Courtesy of Tri–Met.
Figure 6–3	Copyright © 2002 World Wide Web Consortium, (Massachusetts Institute of Technology, Institut National de Recherche en Informatique et en Automatique, Keio University). All Rights Reserved. *http://www.w3.org/Consortium/Legal/*
Figure 6–5	Bobby is a product of CAST, Peabody, Massachusetts.
Figures 7–5, 7–6, 7–7, 7–8, 7–9, 7–10, 7–11, 7–12, 7–13	Copyright © 2000–2002 The Metropolitan Museum of Art. All rights reserved.
Figures 8–3, 8–4,	Copyright © NPR® 2001. This material is used with the permission of NPR, Inc. Any unauthorized duplication is strictly prohibited.
Figure 9–1	Copyright © 1996–2002 The Institute for Technology and Learning. All rights reserved.
Figure 10–2	Accessibility Internet Rally (AIR) is a registered trademark of Knowbility. Used with permission.
Figure 11–1	Kasday, L (2001). The WAVE 2.01. Institute on Disabilities, Temple University, *http://www.temple.edu/inst_disabilities/piat/wave/*

Figures 12–1, 12–2, 12–3, 12–4, 12–5, 12–6, 12–7, 12–8, 12–9, 12–10, 14–3	Copyright © 2001 Adobe Systems Incorporated. All rights reserved. Adobe, Acrobat and Acrobat Reader is/are either [a] registered trademark[s] of Adobe Systems Incorporated in the United States and/or other countries.
Figures 13–1, 13–2, 13–5, 13–12, 13–13	The ATSTAR Project was funded by a grant from the Texas Education Agency. Used with permission.
Figure 13–4	Copyright © 1995–2000 RealNetworks, Inc. All rights reserved. RealNetworks, Real.com, RealAudio, RealVideo, RealSystem, RealPlayer, RealJukebox and RealMedia are trademarks or registered trademarks of RealNetworks, Inc.
Figures 13–6, 13–11	Copyright 1997–2002 The Institute for Technology and Learning. All rights reserved.
Figures 14–1, 14–2,	Knowbility, Inc. Used with permission. For copyright and reproduction policy, visit *http://www.knowbility.org/curriculum/credits.html*
Figure 15–1	Copyright © 2001 Yale University. Copyrights and credits are at *http://www.yale.edu/musicalinstruments/copyright.html*
Figure 15–2	Copyright © 2001 World Wide Web Consortium, (Massachusetts Institute of Technology, Institut National de Recherche en Informatique et en Automatique, Keio University). All Rights Reserved. *http://www.w3.org/Consortium/Legal/*
Figure 15–3	Courtesy of Texas School for the Blind and Visually Impaired.
Figure 15–5	Courtesy of Duncan Grey.

Index

informIT

www.informit.com

YOUR GUIDE TO IT REFERENCE

Articles

Keep your edge with thousands of free articles, in-depth features, interviews, and IT reference recommendations – all written by experts you know and trust.

Online Books

Answers in an instant from **InformIT Online Book's** 600+ fully searchable on line books. For a limited time, you can get your first 14 days **free**.

Safari
TECH BOOKS ONLINE

Catalog

Review online sample chapters, author biographies and customer rankings and choose exactly the right book from a selection of over 5,000 titles.

Wouldn't it be great

if the world's leading technical publishers joined forces to deliver their best tech books in a common digital reference platform?

They have. Introducing
InformIT Online Books
powered by Safari.

■ Specific answers to specific questions.

formIT Online Books' powerful search engine gives you relevance-
nked results in a matter of seconds.

■ Immediate results.

/ith InformIT Online Books, you can select the book you want
nd view the chapter or section you need immediately.

■ Cut, paste and annotate.

aste code to save time and eliminate typographical errors.
Aake notes on the material you find useful and choose whether
r not to share them with your work group.

■ Customized for your enterprise.

ustomize a library for you, your department or your entire
rganization. You only pay for what you need.

Get your first 14 days FREE!

or a limited time, InformIT Online Books is offering its
nembers a 10 book subscription risk-free for 14 days. Visit
http://www.informit.com/onlinebooks for details.

Register
Your Book

at www.awprofessional.com/register

You may be eligible to receive:

- Advance notice of forthcoming editions of the book
- Related book recommendations
- Chapter excerpts and supplements of forthcoming titles
- Information about special contests and promotions throughout the year
- Notices and reminders about author appearances, tradeshows, and online chats with special guests

Contact us

If you are interested in writing a book or reviewing manuscripts prior to publication, please write to us at:

Editorial Department
Addison-Wesley Professional
75 Arlington Street, Suite 300
Boston, MA 02116 USA
Email: AWPro@aw.com

Addison-Wesley

Visit us on the Web: http://www.awprofessional.com